Examining Comprehensive
School Reform

Also of interest from the Urban Institute Press:

Beyond "Bilingual" Education: New Immigrants and Public School Policies in California, by Alec Ian Gershberg, Anne Danenberg, and Patricia Sánchez

Black Males Left Behind, edited by Ronald B. Mincy

Reconnecting Disadvantaged Young Men, by Peter Edelman, Harry J. Holzer, and Paul Offner

Examining Comprehensive
School Reform

Edited by
Daniel K. Aladjem and
Kathryn M. Borman

THE URBAN INSTITUTE PRESS
Washington, D.C.

THE URBAN INSTITUTE PRESS
2100 M Street, N.W.
Washington, D.C. 20037

Library of Congress Cataloging-in-Publication Data

Examining comprehensive school reform / edited by Daniel K. Aladjem and Kathryn M. Borman.
       p. cm.
  Includes bibliographical references and index.
  ISBN 0-87766-733-0 (pbk. : alk. paper)
  1. School improvement programs—United States.   2. Education—Standards—United States.   I. Aladjem, Daniel K.   II. Borman, Kathryn M.
    LB2822.82.E915 2006
    371.200973—dc22

Printed in the United States of America

10 09 08 07 06   1 2 3 4 5

THE URBAN INSTITUTE is a nonprofit, nonpartisan policy research and educational organization established in Washington, D.C., in 1968. Its staff investigates the social, economic, and governance problems confronting the nation and evaluates the public and private means to alleviate them. The Institute disseminates its research findings through publications, its web site, the media, seminars, and forums.

Through work that ranges from broad conceptual studies to administrative and technical assistance, Institute researchers contribute to the stock of knowledge available to guide decisionmaking in the public interest.

Conclusions or opinions expressed in Institute publications are those of the authors and do not necessarily reflect the views of officers or trustees of the Institute, advisory groups, or any organizations that provide financial support to the Institute.

CONTENTS

1

AN INTRODUCTION TO COMPREHENSIVE SCHOOL REFORM

Daniel K. Aladjem and Kathryn M. Borman

Urban school reformers for decades have focused on ways to improve educational outcomes for underserved and disadvantaged students. School reform has involved multiple actors at multiple levels. Local school- and district-based reformers have been assisted by a strikingly large number of federal and state policies that have evolved over the past 40 years. These policies have shifted from targeting individual students for additional assistance through Title I and other similar programs to developing and institutionalizing universal high standards governing teaching and learning for all students, emphasizing schools as the most effective sites for change. Many now assert that systemic reform strategies involving national, state, and local policies are required for long-term change (Borman and Associates 2005).

Over the past 15 years, comprehensive school reform (CSR) has emerged as a key instantiation of the "whole-school" approach to reform (Borman et al. 2004). CSR generally involves school-level adoption and implementation of externally developed, research-based school reform models and approaches. While no exact count exists, data suggest that CSR has been tried in thousands of schools nationwide.

While CSR implementation strategies, funding streams, and other structures and processes may have changed since the first models were designed in the late 1980s,[1] three characteristics distinguish CSR from others.

First, model developers provide initial training or orientation to help school-level educators understand the model's organizing framework and goals.

Second, each model has a blueprint or set of specifications that vary from being more or less "prescriptive." For example, Success for All is a highly scripted model endorsed by many educators working with the least prepared students (Borman et al. 2003). In contrast, the Modern Red SchoolHouse instructional modules, at least in their earliest manifestations, were developed as site-specific curricula by teachers at participating schools.

Third, each model developer (and his or her organization) is highly sensitive to market forces, modifying, enlarging, and expanding its target audiences—state departments of education, districts, or schools—as market forces change.

The goals of the federal CSR program are to support the implementation of comprehensive school reform, especially in high-poverty Title I schools, and to improve efforts that enable all children, particularly low-achieving students in low-performing schools, to meet challenging academic standards. Schools that receive federal CSR funds must adopt approaches that address components outlined in the No Child Left Behind Act (NCLB). For all intents and purposes, this set of components can serve as a de facto definition of CSR.

- CSR is based on scientific research and has been replicated in diverse schools;
- CSR integrates instruction, assessment, classroom management, and professional development into a schoolwide reform plan;
- CSR prioritizes professional development for teachers and staff;
- CSR sets measurable goals for student performance;
- CSR is supported by school faculty, administrators, and other staff;
- CSR in turn, supports school faculty, administrators, and other staff;
- CSR involves parents and the community;
- CSR is assisted by an established comprehensive school reform entity;
- CSR is regularly evaluated on implementation, as well as on students' outcomes; and
- CSR coordinates federal, state, local, and private resources to help support and sustain reform.

In chapter 4, "The Influence of States and Districts on Comprehensive School Reform," Naida Tushnet and Donna M. Harris address these components in some detail, applying them to their research. Their analysis makes clear that CSR must accommodate NCLB to remain a viable alternative in reforming school practices.

CHALLENGES AND OPPORTUNITIES FOR COMPREHENSIVE SCHOOL REFORM

A number of challenges confront schools and school districts using CSR models in whole-school reform, such as finding financial support for implementation. However, No Child Left Behind and, most recently, other federal policies aimed at high school reform demand increasingly higher levels of student performance as well as increasingly challenging curricula. As a result, avenues of opportunity remain open for those undertaking CSR implementation, since CSR is holistic and in line with rigorous standards. In this section, we attempt to look ahead in our analysis of the possibilities and constraints now affecting CSR adoption.

First, it has become increasingly clear to those undertaking school reform that contextual factors in the state, district, school, and classroom matter greatly (Rowan, Barnes, and Camburn 2004). In addition to the characteristics of the CSR model itself (e.g., more or less prescriptive; more or less reliant upon teachers' and principals' leadership, etc.), context arguably most affects how reform will be implemented and sustained over time. In fact, Borman and her colleagues with the National Longitudinal Evaluation of Comprehensive School Reform argue that aligning national, state, district, and school policies constitutes one of the "necessary conditions" in determining CSR outcomes (Borman et al. 2004).

Second, at this writing, how states will assist so-called low-performing schools under NCLB remains unclear. In a recent report, Laguarda (2003) argues that under NCLB's accountability provisions, states are increasingly under pressure to provide "meaningful assistance" to struggling schools. In the nine states included in Laguarda's intensive study of state-sponsored assistance to low-performing schools,[2] virtually all relied upon Title I funds to support assistance efforts. Following the discontinuation of support through CSR Demonstration legislation and the Obey-Porter bill, CSR implementation has largely relied on funds from Title I sources. Whether a systemic approach to assisting low-performing schools will emerge remains unclear. Currently, most states providing assistance rely upon teams of local state or district staff, as well as field consultants charged with addressing failing schools' needs. Rather than using specific CSR packages or models, these reformers are likely to use sets of "best practices" that address the state's approach to reading and language arts, mathematics, and most recently, science. Taken together, the effects of NCLB and the end of explicit CSR funding suggest that CSR faces an uncertain future in the early years of the 21st century.

STUDIES OF COMPREHENSIVE SCHOOL REFORM

Most of the chapters in this volume draw upon research on the impact and outcomes of CSR models. The one exception is chapter 2, "The Development of Comprehensive School Reform Models," by Sally Kilgore, who draws upon her experience managing and guiding the CSR model Modern Red SchoolHouse. Kilgore explores CSR from the outset of its development and notes that CSR has been characterized by ambitious goals and by contrasting and conflicting views of how to realize them. Chapter 2 also examines the history and development of the CSR movement, tracing it from its inception in the early 1990s to the present.

Four of the chapters (3, "Comprehensive School Reform and State Accountability Systems," 6, "Mandates and Support of Comprehensive School Reform" 7, "Comprehensive School Reform vs. No Child Left Behind," and 12, "Comprehensive School Reform Models vs. Instructional Practices") are based on research conducted under the auspices of the National Longitudinal Evaluation of Comprehensive School Reform (NLECSR). The NLECSR is a quantitative and qualitative study of behavior, decisions, and processes, as well as outcomes, employing a quasi-experimental design with matched treatment and comparison schools. Having begun in the fall of 2000, NLECSR concluded in the spring of 2006.

A major purpose of the NLECSR was to determine the effects of CSR models on student achievement in more than 650 elementary and middle schools (grades 3 through 8), identifying the most effective components of CSR models as well as describing the situations and populations for which specific CSR models are most effective. We also are noting the contextual supports that contribute to a CSR model's effectiveness. The 650 participating schools are located in 21 districts, primarily urban, across 16 states. NLECSR involves longitudinal surveys of district administrators (64), principals (650), and teachers (about 5,000) over the course of three years, as well as the collection of student record data (achievement and enrollment) for those districts, schools, and classes.

To complement national survey data, NLCSR researchers also conducted qualitative research in 34 "high-performing" and "high-potential" CSR schools, located in five districts. These qualitative case studies are contributing to an understanding of both the implementation and the effects of the CSR models' key components and overall effectiveness. NLECSR researchers observed classes to evaluate instruction; interviewed teachers and administrators about instruction, implementation, and their experiences with the CSR effort; and collected extant documents about reform, student achievement, and school demographics from each school.

Three research questions, focusing on outcomes and implementation, drive the NLECSR.

- How effective are specific externally developed, research-based CSR models in improving the achievement of all students?
- How are model characteristics related to the success of model implementation and to improvement in teaching and learning, in what settings, and with what students?
- What supporting conditions and strategies are necessary to effectively implement and sustain CSR models in schools and school districts?

To enhance a thorough understanding of CSR effects and to do so in the context of rigorous research, sponsors, including the U.S. Department of Education and the Bill & Melinda Gates Foundation, funded multiple studies beginning in 2000. In September 2000, the Department of Education awarded grants to six groups of researchers. Among those, in addition to American Institutes for Research and the University of South Florida, were the Success for All Foundation (SFAF), and Policy Studies Associates (PSA). The following year (2001), the Department of Education contracted with WestED to conduct an evaluation of CSR schools that received federal funding. SFAF is conducting a mixed-methods randomized experiment of Success for All under Geoffrey Borman's leadership; in chapter 9, "School-Level Factors in Comprehensive School Reform," he and his coauthors draw upon results from year two of this ongoing study. PSA's research, also quasi-experimental and mixed methods, looks more directly at the district's role in supporting CSR. Brenda J. Turnbull shows in chapter 5, "Comprehensive School Reform as a District Strategy," how district support for CSR diminished over observed years of implementation. As accountability concerns increased, CSR schools were pressured to abandon their models or combine them with other district-sanctioned approaches to curriculum and instruction. Many CSR schools also changed leadership, often due to district policies. Nonetheless, despite limited and dwindling district support, many schools continued to use CSR principles or practices as a strategy for school improvement.

Bringing an educational reform effort to scale and sustaining it past the period of funding remain challenging issues. Chapter 10, "Partnerships in Middle Grades Comprehensive School Reform," emphasizes that sharing resources, expertise, and responsibility adds value to the work that individual schools, districts, and educational organizations could accomplish on their own. Drawing upon data from three different studies, including a qualitative study funded by the W. K. Kellogg Foundation, H. Dickson Corbett, Cheri Fancsali, Pritha Gopalan, Alexandra Weinbaum, and Bruce L. Wilson suggest that educational partnerships can positively influence scale-up and sustainability as initiatives mature.

Roughly contemporaneous with the Department of Education's efforts, the Bill & Melinda Gates Foundation launched its own school reform initiative. Though not explicitly defined as a CSR effort, many of the programs funded by the Gates Foundation are CSR models. In early 2001, the foundation contracted with the American Institutes for Research and SRI International to conduct a large-scale, quasi-experimental, mixed-methods study of its efforts. In chapter 11, "Comprehensive School Reform in High Schools," Don Dailey, Becky Smerdon, and Barbara Means demonstrate the foundation's effectiveness in creating innovative schools by remaining open and flexible in their approach to supporting high school reforms.

Our Approach

The studies reported in this volume take a number of different methodological approaches to studying CSR. Both the researchers (who are in most cases the authors of the chapters) and the editors approached our work informed by a range of social science disciplines including sociology, political science, and policy analysis. However, underneath it all, the work represented here is fundamentally policy analytic research and evaluation.

Cuban (2001) has described the primary targets of CSR as the roughly one-third of schools whose students historically have performed poorly. These schools face particularly intractable problems of high staff turnover, inexperienced principals and teachers, limited resources, and racial strife, as well as fragmented curricula and low-quality instruction. We can identify three problems as being of central interest and importance to the analyses in this volume. The myriad other problems can all be defined as subsets of these three.

First, low-performing schools in urban settings often suffer from a lack of coherence among the instructional and related activities undertaken by school personnel. This lack of coherence includes, for example, fragmentation of the curriculum and the school day, poorly related or incompatible instructional strategies, inconsistent behavioral expectations, and a lack of shared values. These problems at the school and classroom levels collectively result in low expectations for students and generally low academic performance and achievement.

The second problem facing these schools is the lack of information, knowledge, and skills needed for effective reform. Principals, teachers, and school staff have tremendous information, knowledge, and skills but lack the time and resources to exploit them, and especially to gain new information, knowledge, and skills to undertake the radical transformations required by CSR. In the best-case scenario, most school professionals will have a year of graduate education plus a few additional courses. This formal education will likely have focused on daily instructional tasks. It is highly unlikely that school professionals will have much training in organizational theory, management, or strategic change.

Last, there are strong disincentives to enter and remain in professional careers in schools, and for those who do remain, there are precious few incentives to develop advanced pedagogical skills, let alone the skill to undertake a complex organizational transformation.

The U.S. Department of Education, New American Schools, CSR model developers, and others posit that CSR offers a solution to this problem (although they might define it somewhat differently). The overriding question for the studies presented in this volume and for others committed to CSR is whether this confidence in CSR is well founded. On its face, CSR seems promising, and research on some selected models is promising (Borman et al. 2003; Herman et al. 1999). CSR explicitly addresses the first two prongs of the problem by offering ways to foster program coherence in schools and by providing external technical assistance that should solve the information problems facing school professionals. CSR should address the third prong as well, but changing the incentives accorded principals and teachers is beyond the control of any single school. The extent to which CSR model staff work with state, district, and school staff will determine, in part, the extent to which CSR can successfully change the incentive system.[3]

The range of activity related to comprehensive school reform is impressive. Thousands of schools have implemented CSR programs over the past decade, using either self-developed models or externally developed models. This breadth of activity has spawned an almost equally wide variety of research into CSR. Despite the popularity of many CSR schools and models, and despite the research base on which these models rest, Herman and her colleagues' (1999) literature review demonstrated that the research on different CSR models' effects on student outcomes is relatively weak. Indeed, of the 24 models reviewed, only 3 had strong evidence of positive effects on student achievement. Similarly, Borman and his colleagues' recent review (2003) of studies on 29 widely implemented CSR models found that research evidence on CSR's effectiveness is somewhat inconsistent, with only 3 models showing strong evidence of improving student performance (a different 3, however, than those identified by Herman).

Our Purpose

While policymakers, practitioners, and researchers have paid much attention to CSR for over a decade, the debate on CSR has only recently begun to accelerate. A number of long-term studies are concluding as this volume is being prepared. Most will produce a number of journal publications in the next one to two years, drawing more attention to the debate and providing a clearer picture of CSR's implementation and impact. Journal articles, however, cannot pull together varied points of view and multiple sources of data to address the full system of influences around a reform like CSR. As schools and districts face increasing pressure to improve student achievement under NCLB, several important issues for CSR arise:

- What support is necessary from external model providers?
- What are the responsibilities of external model providers?
- How does CSR intersect with state accountability systems?
- How can states build coherent systems, or must CSR necessarily conflict with state accountability regimes?
- How might the imperatives of accountability divert stakeholders' attention?
- What support is necessary from local school districts?
- What conditions are necessary to implement and sustain reform?
- What factors produce positive student outcomes?

These issues are addressed in the chapters that follow.

The policy question that drives CSR and other school reform research is how best to improve America's schools, especially for those that schools have not traditionally served well—impoverished urban children. Our intent is not only to build knowledge for knowledge's sake, but to engineer a better society, characterized by schools that nurture the talents of all children.

NOTES

1. See chapter 2 in this volume.
2. The states included in Laguarda's study are Arkansas, California, Florida, Indiana, Nevada, North Carolina, Vermont, West Virginia, and Wyoming.
3. One might argue that CSR need not address each of these aspects of the problem. If CSR is to be truly comprehensive, however, it seems not unreasonable to hold CSR models to a standard that requires addressing the full problem, not just two-thirds of it.

REFERENCES

Borman, G. D., G. M. Hewes, L. T. Overman, and S. Brown. 2003. "Comprehensive School Reform and Achievement: A Meta-Analysis." *Review of Educational Research* 73(2): 125–230.

Borman, K. M., and Associates. 2005. *Meaningful Urban Education Reform: Confronting the Learning Crisis in Mathematics and Science.* Albany: SUNY Press.

Borman, K. M., K. Carter, D. K. Aladjem, and K. C. Le Floch. 2004. "Challenges for the Future of Comprehensive School Reform." In *Putting the Pieces Together: Lessons from Comprehensive School Reform Research,* edited by C. T. Cross (109–50). Washington, DC: George Washington University Press.

Cuban, L. 2001. "Improving Urban Schools in the 21st Century: Dos and Don'ts, or Advice to True Believers and Skeptics of Whole School Reform." Paper presented at the OERI Symposium on Comprehensive School Reform Research and Evaluation, Denver, July 18–20.

Herman, R., D. Aladjem, P. McMahon, A. O'Malley, S. Quinones, and D. Woodruff. 1999. *An Educator's Guide to Schoolwide Reform.* Washington, DC: American Institutes for Research.

Laguarda, K. 2003. "State-Sponsored Technical Assistance to Low-Performing Schools: Strategies from Nine States." Paper presented at the annual meeting of the American Educational Research Association, Chicago, April 23.

Rowan, B., C. Barnes, and E. Camburn. 2004. "Benefiting from Comprehensive School Reform: A Review of Research on CSR Implementation." In *Putting the Pieces Together: Lessons from Comprehensive School Reform Research,* edited by C. T. Cross (1–52). Washington, DC: George Washington University Press.

2

THE DEVELOPMENT OF COMPREHENSIVE SCHOOL REFORM MODELS

Sally B. Kilgore

It was 1991 when the nation's secretary of education, Lamar Alexander, gave the clarion call for "a new generation of schools" for the 21st century. The 10th anniversary of the release of *A Nation at Risk* (National Commission on Excellence in Education 1983) had approached amid meager evidence of improved student learning but clear evidence of growing international competition in industry. To respond to the conclusions from *A Nation at Risk*, states had focused on strengthening academic graduation requirements (Ravitch 2000; Sebring 1987; Wilson and Rossman 1993). High school dropout rates, however, remained stable (if hard to quantify) and the proportion of entering college freshmen in need of remedial courses in mathematics or reading remained stable and costly. The National Assessment of Education Progress did show a significant improvement in achievement for 17-year-olds between 1980 and 1988, but alas, scores actually dropped significantly for 9- and 13-year-old students (National Center for Education Statistics 2000).

With their sights on the 21st century, state governors committed themselves to ambitious goals for the nation's schools and students—once and for all, youth would enter the labor market or college prepared and ready for responsible citizenship. Governors committed that, by the year 2000, all children would enter school ready to learn; high school graduation rates would reach at least 90 percent; students would leave grades 4, 8, and 12 demonstrating proficiency; American high school students would be first in the world in mathematics and science achievement; and every school would be free of drugs and violence with a disciplined environment conducive to learning. Adopted by the George H. W. Bush administration in the early 1990s and known as AMERICA 2000, this commitment continued with an expanded set of goals through the Clinton administration as GOALS 2000.

THE CALL FOR A NEW GENERATION OF SCHOOLS

Central to those ambitious goals in 1991, so the thinking went, was the need to design a new generation of schools for the 21st century—ones that radically improved the learning outcomes for all students. Secretary Alexander went to corporate leaders with the request: help us design "break the mold" schools, ones that can provide *all* children with a world-class education. Corporate leaders obligingly established the New American Schools Development Corporation (NASDC) as a nonprofit organization with a five-year life span, during which it would oversee the development of a number of new designs for America's public schools. In soliciting proposals to design these schools, the creators articulated a number of expectations (New American Schools Development Corporation 1991). In brief: the change in school life must be comprehensive, performance must be benchmarked against world-class academic standards,[1] and designs must be capable of going to scale.

Change in School Life Must Be Comprehensive

Just as the automotive industry's historical focus on changing fenders or headlights gave consumers little advantage in fuel efficiency, reliability, or safety, student outcomes would not radically change with a new class schedule, a new textbook, or even more academic coursework, said NASDC leaders. NASDC asked that designs incorporate "all facets of the school's life (including instruction, curriculum, and school climate) in pursuit of high levels of student achievement" (New American

Schools Development Corporation 1991). The research reports on Title I schools (Birman 1987) suggested that high-poverty schools, at least, had become places with numerous, and often contradictory, programs, initiatives, and policies that led to inchoate school experiences for students.

The concept of comprehensive school reform was not without precedent. Programs such as Success for All and the Coalition of Essential Schools sought a more holistic view of school improvement, focused largely on changing classroom instruction and staffing. Accelerated Schools and Comer's School Development Program also constituted comprehensive initiatives, but with greater emphasis on school culture and community and family relations than on curriculum. NASDC's effort, then, was unique in two respects: (1) "break the mold" schools were expected to change *both* classroom and school practices in ways that supported high academic performance for all schools, and (2) teams were expected to develop explicit strategies for scaling up in a large number of schools.

Performance Must Be Benchmarked against World-Class Academic Standards

Research evidence was and is fairly convincing on one claim: What is taught sets the boundaries for what is learned, especially for children from families with weak literacy skills (Coleman, Hoffer, and Kilgore 1982; Dreeben and Gamoran 1986; Garet and DeLany 1988; Schmidt 1983).

On the other hand, consensus on the usefulness of "world-class" academic benchmarks (soon to become "academic standards") was absent. At least three positions had emerged in the early 1990s. Advocates of uniform academic standards, including most prominently Al Shanker, president of the American Federation of Teachers, and Chester Finn, a policy analyst and former official in the Reagan administration, grounded their position on equity—and subsequently (at the National Education Summit in 2000) on the transparency needed if accountability for outcomes was to be fair. Ted Sizer (1992), supported the need for academic standards but argued, consistent with the traditions of liberal arts colleges and elite private schools, that each school's faculty should construct their own academic standards. Finally, many practitioners and some policy analysts were quite circumspect about world-class benchmarks for *all* students. Some argued, legitimately, that not even other nations held such ambitions.

Implicitly, NASDC leaned toward school-specific standards, since design applicants were expected to articulate how they would establish world-class standards, short-term benchmarks, and ultimate goals for success. Applicants were to articulate what they would measure and establish benchmarks against which to assess progress, using "a variety of assessment techniques" (New American Schools Development Corporation 1991).

Designs Must Be Capable of Going to Scale

The original request for proposals made clear that designs were to be adaptable for many communities, not be prescriptive "cookie cutter" models. Moreover, the designers had to explicitly address how they would proceed in the face of existing federal, state, and local regulations. Not inclined to leave any stone unturned, NASDC also encouraged applicants to "consider the teaching implications of the changes they propose, and to address issues related to teacher preparation and training" (New American Schools Development Corporation 1991). While researchers generally agreed on the need to unravel the complexities of the regulatory environment, not much thinking, much less research, had considered the relative advantage of prescriptive approaches versus more adaptable designs in scaling up a new generation of schools.

Scaling up, (that is, vastly expanding the number of partner schools) was to begin in the fourth year of the NASDC effort, after a year of developing materials and designing implementation strategies and two years of piloting them in existing schools. This was one of the first efforts in American education to design a plan for "going to scale" nationally.

Eleven of the more than 600 proposed designs were selected to take up the challenge.[2] The visionaries were incubated in a variety of institutional settings—a cutting-edge technology firm, school districts, think tanks, a research university, an outdoor adventure–based program, a firm devoted to academically challenging curriculum materials, and a college that integrated real-world experiences into its curriculum.

Subsequent sections of this chapter recount the evolution of the NASDC designs, using my experience as the founding director and then–president and CEO of the Modern Red SchoolHouse (MRSH) as a primary source for illustrating the choices made by design teams. That said, I have tried to attend to the varying strategies adopted by teams at each stage. I put this history into three major phases of development: (1) starting the initiative's design and piloting phase, (2) going to scale, and (3) federal expansion. In the final section, I reflect upon the lessons learned from this national effort to provide comprehensive improvement strategies to the nation's public schools.

GETTING STARTED

Two teams imploded within the initiative's first two years—the only two, in fact, incubated within school districts. In one instance, a teacher's union protested collaboration with the corporate-sponsored NASDC. In the other, parents perceived the promised curriculum as dangerous and possibly satanic; with this and the untimely loss of the team leader, development was doomed (Mickelson and Wadsworth 1996; Mirel 1994).

NASDC did not appear especially stable either (Glennan 1998). At the end of the first year, efforts to secure special funding for summer institutes for pilot sites had been unsuccessful. Interactions between NASDC and the design teams had other points of strain, best explained by the yawning gap between the culture of schools and that of industry. RAND served as the broker and mediator between these two worlds. NASDC leadership changed three times within as many years. Only the immense respect accorded board chairman David Kearns, former CEO of Xerox, by NASDC's fellow corporate leaders held the effort together during this early period.

Design Development

In the early stages of the effort, NASDC set the framework for the developer's comprehensive approach—standards, curriculum, technology, parent and community involvement, and school governance. Three designers chose to develop standards and assessments; others chose or adapted existing standards such as the International Baccalaureate.

In addressing their curricula, nearly all of the original design models sought to provide an approach for *instructional design*—how teachers organize the content of instruction. Driven by the same research base on learning, developers were more alike than different in their assumptions about what constituted good teaching, but the designs' organizing principles were different. Expeditions became the organizing principle for Expeditionary Learning Schools Outward Bound (ELS). While not all expeditions involved leaving the school grounds, they did involve constructing an active, interdisciplinary journey of discovery. Co-nect organized instruction around students using technology in project-based learning. The Audrey Cohen model expected educators to organize instruction around a larger purpose—serving the social good. ATLAS took an intellectual approach, encouraging teachers to reflect upon research and their own practice. Initially, Roots & Wings (an expansion of Success for All) was the only design that aspired to a prescribed set of texts and instructional materials relied upon by all their schools to deliver instruction. With a strong background in serving urban Title I schools, where high mobility rates for both teachers and students were common and failure in reading fairly pervasive, Roots & Wings saw a need for explicit and detailed instructional materials.

First and foremost, MRSH was driven by the fundamental principle of organizing meaningful instruction around academic standards. Consistent with the later work of Wiggins and McTighe (1998), Modern Red SchoolHouse supported the development of interdisciplinary, standards-driven instruction, beginning with the end in mind (i.e., a culminating assessment that demonstrated mastery of standards). Second was building an organizational infrastructure that fostered a collegial environment among educators and a participatory management system that gave teachers some influence on and responsibility for the quality of education.

While the designs' points for initiating change differed, all were consistent with sociological theories of change. Some, such as MRSH, ATLAS, and ELS, began by building a professional and trusting culture among educators in the school. Others started with educators aligning content across grades and classes, from which a collegial culture might emerge. Co-nect began by introducing classroom technology that could reshape the student-teacher relationship as well as the ways students acquired knowledge and demonstrated proficiency. The Urban Learning Center first established the centrality of their K–12 school in the larger community, with health clinics, social work services, adult education classes, and preschool services all housed within the school campus. Roots & Wings chose to focus on structure, specifying class size, staffing, and grouping.

In attempting to specify a process for transforming schools, designers took into account preceding reform efforts. Developers saw that innovation in school practice did not spread naturally from a few innovators within a school to all teachers, as was the strategy in Ted Sizer's Coalition of Essential Schools. Certainly, the imposition of a reform initiative from district offices had a checkered history of success and McLaughlin's (1987) insightful analysis of change led developers to uniformly insist that teachers consent, or preferably desire, to work with a new design.

Designs also differed in the unit of change: school, pathway, district, or state. While most designs framed the unit of change at the school level, ATLAS used the *pathway*, the series of schools a student would take from kindergarten through high school. The National Alliance for Restructuring Education (NARE)—subsequently renamed America's Choice—considered an entire state or district as the unit of change.

Throughout the design phase, MRSH convened national study groups comprised of representatives from each of its partnering districts, and in the first year gathered national experts to examine standards and assessment, curriculum and instruction, technology, parent and community involvement, organization and finance, and professional development. The work of the standards and assessment study group was surely the most volatile, but also the most productive. Debates about specificity, balance (building on history vs. innovating), and rigor riveted the group and anticipated the subsequent experiences in many state efforts 6 to 10 years later.

Perhaps the most critical decision in MRSH's evolution was to establish a national advisory board that included superintendents from six partner districts as well as the design team experts in each core area. Regular meetings afforded superintendents a better understanding of the design as it evolved, and the national team acquired an early assessment of the feasibility of specific design elements.

Conterminous with the articulation of the various design elements were decisions about the pilot phase. What type and level of investment in pilot schools' infrastructure was needed, what would be the strategy for supporting schools in the transformation, and what were the criteria for selecting pilot sites? In part, these decisions were driven by the vision for schools. Given that the feasibility of MRSH's design was predicated on a sophisticated instructional management system with an open architecture that would allow teachers to develop and revise instructional programs, heavy investment in technology was required for each school. Other design team members chose to minimize their investments for sound reasons: they wanted participating schools clearly motivated by the design, not the potential financial benefits accompanying the choice.

Piloting the Designs

Pilot districts were motivated to join the enterprise for different, but often strategic, reasons. National recognition drew some district leaders to the effort and others anticipated adding resources to their schools (usually computers). Principals were also strategic players in this pilot phase; it was usually left to the teachers to apply the hard-nosed assessment—how is this going to improve life in my classroom?

As the pilots began in the early 1990s, states were just beginning to develop academic standards. Those that existed were usually vague, and strategies for establishing accountability were experimental. Vermont had just encountered problems in reliably evaluating student writing. Kentucky and Maryland were moving swiftly to install performance-based school assessments, but no one, including the test developers, quite knew what standards either state was using to develop them. District policies were leaning toward site-based management, which accorded principals considerable discretion in expending funds and hiring staff, and in some instances, required some level of participative management with teachers or parents.

Initially the design teams' relations with their sponsor had some rough edges. But, in the second year of piloting former IBM executive John Anderson joined NASDC, marking the beginning of open and healthy exchanges among participants. The RAND evaluation team, conducting annual visits to most pilot sites, made independent assessments of programs against the benchmarks each design had established and often surfaced or confirmed concerns at pilot sites (Bodilly 2001). That said, the opportunities for design teams to learn from each other remained limited to late-night chats after meetings convened by NASDC. Both NASDC staff and the team leaders surely felt that the other failed to understand their circumstances, or the needs of their respective clients. NASDC needed results; teams needed time.

In the piloting phase, each team was in charge of managing its own relations with district and state officials. Given the presumed controversial nature of the MRSH design, I welcomed the quarterly meetings held by a state teachers' association; invited were design team staff and representatives from teacher associations in partnering districts. We collaborated with district offices to increase the number of professional development days in the school calendar and to increase the time available for departmental meetings.

MRSH and most other designers assigned a full-time facilitator to each school. The facilitators were not only deeply immersed in the design, but also provided the design team with continuous feedback about the barriers to implementation. One of NASDC's guiding principles was that schools' operating costs should be no greater after implementation than before. Teams varied in how they sought to honor that requirement and at the same time have on-site facilitators. Some teams required that school staff be assigned to the role; MRSH chose to provide financial support for a full-time site coordinator in each district. To honor NASDC's expectation that no additional operational costs would be incurred, the MRSH dictum was that facilitators should be working themselves out of a job within three years by building the school staff's capacity to manage the work independently.[3]

Models usually relied on mixed methods for helping school staff become familiar with their designs and develop their own site-specific plans. A few designs, such as NARE, relied exclusively on turnkey training using either district staff or site coordinators to provide support, guidance, or training. Given my concern with schoolwide adoption, MRSH's summer workshops included all teachers in on-site seminars and coaching. Where multiple schools were located in one district, teachers or principals implementing the same model often met to share specific implementation strategies or to raise issues that required the attention of district officials or design teams.

Design leaders quickly learned, even in the pilot phase, that no one—not anyone—had the power to give schools substantial control over their own policies and practices. A superintendent could declare it, associations could agree to support it, but in the end, control was found in the small silos of district and state bureaucracies. But, teachers and building administrators were so acclimated to barriers that problems seldom surfaced. For example, one MRSH school leadership team proposed to solve vandalism problems by rescheduling their maintenance staff to allow some coverage of their building during evening hours. That was quickly overruled by the district's director of facilities. In a town with four schools, two years of negotiation with bus drivers was necessary before the elementary school "late bus" would transport students who needed additional academic support rather than those living closest to the driver's residence.

Creating "break the mold" schools in existing institutions—schools with existing norms, cliques, and expectations, districts with legal and contractual constraints, and states with laws on budgeting and teaching—was going to be quite different from building such processes, technologies, and relationships from scratch.

GOING TO SCALE

Design team leaders, NASDC leaders, and RAND advisors met for a multiday retreat in Armonk, New York, to achieve consensus (or more likely, buy-in) on what scale-up would look like. From NASDC's perspective, one thing was nonnegotiable: teams in the same districts would scale up together. Solid reasoning supported this approach. Education leaders had already established that they could create a few highly successful schools in any district. The challenge was whether all schools in a district—or at least a critical mass—could be brought to scale. *That's* what needed to be proved: high quality is scaleable.

Chief among the design teams' concerns was the issue of school autonomy. The pilot phase had demonstrated the complexity of negotiating changes in practice, even with well-intentioned, committed administrators. "Break the mold" designs were inevitably going to require some latitude in staffing, leadership, and curriculum content. Of equal importance to the teams was the amount of professional development time available for each school. Most teams estimated that they would need 12 to 18 days per year, for three years—a significant portion of which should be in the summer.

Given that implementation was going to be a considerable burden to staff at any given school, NASDC and the design teams agreed that teachers must be the critical decisionmakers on which design their school would use. The standard was set high: 80 percent of the teachers had to vote to adopt a design. (Someone asked if the designs were ever intended to work in high schools, since high school teachers, like most university faculty, never had 80 percent agreement on anything.)

In this scale-up phase, NASDC assumed the role of broker, identifying districts receptive to having at least 30 percent of their schools adopt a design. NASDC insisted that districts allow their schools to look at the entire menu of offerings, not just the designs district officials thought were a "best fit." NASDC also arranged for schools to become acquainted with the designs, while districts set up procedures for schools to partner with various design teams. NASDC provided each district with $250,000 to support implementation and required a memorandum of understanding endorsed not just by the superintendent, but also by the district's business community, teacher associations, school board, and parent-teacher organizations. Conversations with the superintendent became largely NASDC's responsibility. Over the course of three years, NASDC signed agreements with seven major jurisdictions. During this same period, NASDC shortened its corporate name to New American Schools (NAS) and the remainder of this narrative will refer to them as such.

Choosing to go to scale in large urban districts gave all designs a reasonable opportunity to find partner schools and manage their support for schools efficiently. Selecting large urban districts for scale-up, however, maximized the level of complexity within which schools and teams operated (Bodilly 2001). And while state regulations and systems of accountability were changing for all school districts, large urban systems were by far the most vulnerable in the emerging chaos. State standards were under development; assessments were changing (and usually not aligned with the standards), and students' performance increasingly had consequences for the school and district. While the urgency for change was palpable, the time horizons had shrunk noticeably from the pilot phase.

The First Step

The first "design fair" was held in Memphis in 1996. Design team leaders and practitioners from pilot schools held one-hour sessions for interested educators and community leaders to learn about the various designs. At the end of the day, teachers met with their principal to decide which design they would adopt. The faint feeling of sorority rush filled the air as some educators struggled to choose among designs.

As has been noted elsewhere, the compressed time for deciding upon a design led to misperceptions and incongruity (Bodilly 2001). Having strictly adhered to teachers' preferences in adopting a design, Superintendent Gerry House offered easy transfers to teachers who were uncomfortable with their school's selection.

Selection decisions were followed by a competitive application in which each interested school completed a written proposal for their potential partnership. Schools varied considerably in how they developed the applications. At one extreme, a dedicated librarian retired to her office and wrote the entire proposal. At another, teachers collaborated in developing the application, but created a document compromised by the predictable incoherence of multiple voices and vision.

A total of 18 schools in Memphis were initially selected to begin implementing a comprehensive school reform (CSR) design. Hoping to speed the adoption process, NAS offered additional incentives in the second year to help Memphis increase the number of schools that could become partners with CSR designs. While the number of schools increased to 30, district funding of the initial cohort was dropped. Instead, the initial cohort of schools was expected to use their own discretionary Title I funds. Yet a number of those schools (middle and high schools mostly) lacked access to Title I or any other discretionary funds.

The Second Step

Few superintendents have demonstrated greater support for comprehensive school reform than Diana Lam in San Antonio in the late 1990s. But, it is also true that few organizational leaders have attempted so many remedies and mandates at one time (Berends, Chun, et al. 2002).

Diana Lam was on a mission of great urgency, and rightly so. San Antonio had a poor track record on students' state assessment scores. She was determined to liberate the system from mediocrity and give all children the opportunity to become high achievers. Lam had served as a district superintendent in the Northeast and in the Midwest and as a developer of one of the comprehensive school reform designs sponsored by NAS. With experience and vision, then, she arrived in San Antonio fully charged.

To give credence and steam to her commitment to improving instruction, Lam reorganized the central office to provide schools with four instructional stewards. The stewards were responsible, as their title implied, for improving instruction in the schools assigned them—a responsibility that distinguished them from typical area superintendents whose responsibilities may include facilities, bus schedules, and the like. Each steward was assigned to work with a design team involving schools both in and outside his or her assigned area. All schools received an instructional guide—a senior teacher available full-time to serve as an instructional coach for teachers.

The school year had been altered to have four short breaks rather than the traditional summer break of three months—a practice consistent with the research on low-income children's needs, and one that gave design teams sensible opportunities to work with teachers and administrators.

In 1995, several schools chose to adopt the comprehensive design with which Lam was acquainted. In the fall of 1996, Lam welcomed another design—one that focused on developing a standards-driven school and classrooms. Lam convened a meeting for schools needing substantial gains in achievement, offering her full support to those choosing to implement the design. Five elementary schools achieved the necessary support from teachers to begin implementation in the spring of 1997.

During the 1997–1998 academic year, NAS reached an agreement with the appropriate parties to establish San Antonio Independent School District as a New American Schools district. At the same time, Lam adopted a literacy program and mathematics textbook series. The literacy program trained teachers in effective practices and instructional strategies, but lacked a textbook series. The mathematics series, considered one of the most sophisticated programs in the country, came with textbooks, manipulatives, teacher materials, and training. Schools pursuing the implementation of a CSR design initially were given some "relief" from the district's myriad of professional development requirements. The notion was to stagger their adoption of the various curriculum programs.

Within a year, district academic standards were under development, as were revisions of the state standards. Surprise visits to schools to assess how closely the reading and mathematics programs were being followed intimidated teachers. Principals at implementing sites were moved to other schools to address more pressing problems. In short, teachers' lives in San Antonio's public schools transformed in painful ways as they stood in a vortex of expectations that showed no signs of abating.

Some design teams did seek to build congruence between the district initiatives and their work. For instance, MRSH sought unsuccessfully to help our partner schools make a successful transition from MRSH standards to the district's (and soon-to-be, state's) newly developed standards. A longitudinal survey of 26 teachers in NAS schools found that strong support for the NAS designs dropped from 54 percent to 25 percent between 1997 and 1998 (Berends, Chun, et al. 2002). With that small sample, one can posit considerable variation across schools and designs, but the evidence is consistent with what design teams heard.

The "going got tough" politically when Lam decided to require a historically prestigious high school to join the comprehensive school reform initiative. The school was to be divided into four smaller high schools adopting four different designs. And, current teachers would be required to reapply for teaching positions at one of these four schools. Within the year, teachers organized to support new school board members. Just months after their successful election, Diana Lam's contract was bought out. In another few months, the highly successful mathematics program was abandoned, as were the design team initiatives.[4]

To suggest that the design teams, or even the mathematics program, just evaporated from the schools would be a gross distortion. Some elements of one or more designs were instituted as practices throughout the system. Teachers likely had a better grasp of mathematical concepts as a consequence of their experience with the text series. That said, San Antonio's teachers likely became more reluctant to buy into any new visions for education.

Design team work in Miami-Dade illustrates the peculiar challenges that can occur in any large urban district, regardless of the type of reform effort. Stability in leadership appeared "best in class." Both the superintendent and president of the teachers' association had had a long tenure. Sign-off on the memorandum of understanding with NAS went smoothly, the now-traditional design fair was held, and work began a few months later. Again, each team was assigned a contact person within the central office.

Within months of the agreement, though, a federal court issued a decision on school board membership in Miami-Dade. School board members would no longer be elected "at-large" but rather regionally, to better represent the increasingly diverse population. The superintendent, unwilling to engage in the arduous task of developing a working relationship with a new set of board members, resigned. Subsequently, central office staff positions appeared to shift almost weekly. Design team members found it difficult to even locate those assigned as their district coordinators. Elections for new board members were held within the year. NAS returned to meet with the school board and found that not one member had been part of the signing of the original memorandum of understanding.

Going to scale introduced a number of new dilemmas for design teams, staffing being the first and most problematic. Were we going to require that every school have a full-time facilitator devoted to implementing the design? Since we could not provide the financial support for this position, what expectations could we have for this person? How would we staff school support—with experts or generalists? MRSH chose to risk creating a complex set of relationships to ensure expertise in each area. Field managers maintained relations with up to 15 schools and managed the flow of experts into schools. Most designs chose a less complex system of on-site professional development.

Districts in the scale-up phase differed radically in how many additional resources (e.g., computers or time for staff development) they provided to schools adopting a design. Thus, in addition to staffing, the pace and sequence of change in practice varied.

The scale-up phase provided teams with the opportunity to develop staffing and delivery strategies, evaluate the feasibility of their model in real time, and acquire strategies for incorporating district priorities into their support for schools.

FEDERAL EXPANSION

Concurrent with the effort to go to scale in a number of large urban districts, NAS helped the design teams develop strategic plans that would, presumably, allow them to be self-sustaining. During the previous scale-up phase, design teams' overhead costs were covered by NAS funding, but direct costs were assumed by the partnering districts. Now teams, mostly incubated within larger organizations, had to confront organizing their expansion, establishing fees that covered both direct and indirect costs, and creating systems that would ensure quality services were provided.

NAS set expectations for each team's planning and successfully acquired a federal funding stream available to support Title I schools wanting to partner with a design team. Known as the Obey-Porter Comprehensive School Reform initiative, the funding stream emerged from a bipartisan collaboration of lead members of the House Appropriations subcommittee on Labor, Health and Human Services, Education and Related Agencies. Nine components of school change (subsequently expanded to eleven)[5] were identified, and funding was apportioned to states following the Title I system of allocating funds.

States were expected to distribute the funding on a competitive basis, mostly to Title I schools with a minimum of $50,000 awarded to selected schools for each of three years. Applicants were restricted to a subset of Title I schools: those with the weakest track records in student achievement. One complication emerged—those Title I schools in greatest need were also those least capable of providing what might have traditionally been viewed as a competitive proposal. It was not unusual for principals be unable to find state assessment results, to never have heard of academic standards, or to have no clue which reading textbook

series they were using. Such challenges were related not to their dedication, but rather to the great number of crises that fell in their laps.

If urgency was great during scale-up, it approximated panic in the
federal expansion phase. Targeted to the lowest performing Title I
schools, this phase presented teams with schools that justifiably could
not tolerate waiting two years, much less three, before substantial
improvements were evident. Like in most high-poverty, low-
performing schools, faculty turnover was high and teachers were often
inadequately prepared for teaching the students they served (Berends,
Bodilly, and Kirby 2002). Clearly, if designers were to work with such
needy schools, their first obligation was to deliver the necessary tools.

Design teams adapted in a number of ways, introducing yet another
issue—what does it mean to sustain fidelity to the original design?
Training in literacy strategies, managing classrooms, working with
culturally diverse students, and a variety of other essential instructional
skills were greatly needed by teachers in this new cohort of schools.
Should design teams seek to provide support in these areas? Most
teams chose to do so. Should design teams seek exceptions to district
policies to maintain elements of their design, or adjust their design?
Choices varied.

Most designs expanded their capacity to improve teachers' knowledge of reading instruction. Many developed similar support capacities
in classroom management and mathematics instruction. Rather than
combine this new type of support with the activities usually addressed
in the first year of implementation, MRSH chose to add a "readiness"
phase that only addressed the most fundamental issues. Other teams
eliminated aspects of their designs to make the implementation more
feasible over three years; others insisted that school and district officials
commit to five years (two years beyond federal funding) to realize full
implementation.

Educators' substantial needs in this phase were not the only source
of challenges. The CSR grant cycle was more often that not out of sync
with the school calendar. Thus opportunities for teachers to become
immersed, much less proficient, in alternative instructional strategies
were lost. Teachers' enthusiasm for their CSR awards often was no
match for their frustration with the fragmented training they received.

Given the research evidence from early RAND studies, federal guidelines did move to increase districts' support of schools in their adoption
and implementation phases. That, combined with increased focus on
schools in smaller districts, led to much stronger collaboration between
design teams and central office staff. In some cases, design partners
helped schools transition to new texts, consolidate with other schools
or districts, and even adapt other designs. New paradigms for coordination have emerged, where districts such as Atlanta have established

some common strategies across schools, but allow schools to design the instruction and school services that will best fit their students (Kilgore 2005). If there was a new problem in this phase of scale-up, it was the challenge of establishing strong partnerships with school principals. In the most chaotic schools, principals were distracted by constant emergencies, allowing them considerably less time and energy to understand and lead the change.

During this period of federal support, design teams began to find their respective niches. Some are flourishing; some are struggling. Some have maintained strict fidelity to their design but have sought environments, such as charter schools, that are more compatible. Others have sought to serve schools in rural areas or have unbundled their services and provided them districtwide. That said, each design in its own way serves the children in greatest need in this country. Moreover, comprehensive school improvement designs, whether developed inside or outside the NAS umbrella, remain fairly unusual in their capacity to build a professional culture among teachers so they can learn from each other, identify problems for which they need outside assistance or support, and create an environment where good teachers want to stay.

LESSONS LEARNED

The expectations NAS held for design teams can now be viewed after a decade of going to scale and federal expansion. I find some noble visions, some real transformations, and one implausible strategy.

Change Must Be Comprehensive: A Question of Context

The notion of looking comprehensively at how school organization contributes to student learning is now considered commonsensical among educators and policymakers. That is a real transformation. Along with other researchers, Newmann and colleagues (2001) note that for substantial change to occur and remain, all facets of school life must be integrated in pursuit of high levels of student achievement.

Research, however, also suggests that comprehensive change is difficult to implement fully—particularly in complex urban systems within the timeframe provided during federal expansion (Berends, Bodilly, et al. 2002; Bodilly 2001; Evans 1996). In fact, many have been moved to advocate that the district should be the unit of change. I seek to qualify that claim. While district policies are critical to any school improvement effort, certain essential processes must be school-specific if improvement is to be continuous rather than episodic. In particular, a collegial culture that allows for data-driven reflection upon teaching and learning must be embedded in schools. Collegial networks across schools are useful, but not substitutable for school-based expectations that create the press for change—a press that most often occurs in the context of school-based collegial relations. Models exist for integrating districtwide initiatives with school-based comprehensive school improvement, as the case of Atlanta suggests.

The experiences in the federal expansion phase suggest an alternative hypothesis: success in the scale-up phase was compromised as much by the relationships that teams lacked as by the complexity of the systems into which teams were drawn. During the federal expansion phase, design teams functioned without the NAS mediator for district relations. While the districts were typically smaller, the frequency with which design teams partnered with districts (and sometimes teacher associations) increased, harkening back to the pilot phase. While this is undocumented by research, the phase of federal expansion appears to have been marked by smoother transitions and adoptions.

Whether comprehensive approaches to school improvement are the most viable in all circumstances, though, is questionable. For instance, it may be cruel and unusual punishment to engage in comprehensive school improvement when schools enter the phase of "corrective action"—with only a two-year time horizon for success before schools must be reconstituted. Targeted assistance may be more beneficial. The problem is that targeting may do little to stabilize the teaching force or exploit the power of collaboration across grades and classes. Schools under reconstitution, though, may be especially advantaged by comprehensive approaches, if granted some measure of stability in staffing. The usefulness of comprehensive school improvement, as delivered by an external provider, remains, in my mind, contextually specific.

Performance Must Be Benchmarked against World-Class Academic Standards: A Question of Synchronization

Design teams "going to scale" in the mid-1990s, when the evolution of state standards and systems of assessments was at its most chaotic, compromised the commitment to world-class standards in a number of ways. First, offering schools a design-specific framework for academic standards and student assessment could only complicate the lives of teachers and their students, certainly an unnecessary confusion in high-poverty, low-performing schools. On the other hand, helping schools work with state assessments and standards was equally problematic, as states routinely changed from one testing vendor to another, shifted testing periods from fall to spring, and developed standards that were only coincidentally aligned with their assessments. Teachers and many design team leaders were justifiably circumspect about the potential of standards, much less assessments, to provide insights into the real problems of student learning.

Performance results were seldom available to schools in a timely way that would allow staff to identify, much less address, systemic and individual weakness. Teachers working in schools with "failing marks" in this era of confusion were hard pressed to take any proposed remedy seriously, especially one requiring a high investment of their time. The lack of coherence in state standards and testing systems not only cultivated confusion—and sometimes even cynicism—among educators, it also compromised the ability of researchers to assess what was and was not working in all types of school improvement efforts.

One cannot help but wonder how scale-up would have looked had a coherent set of academic expectations and assessment systems preceded it. What if federal resources and regulations had encouraged more thoughtful assessments of student learning? What if assessments were aligned with standards? These are the questions of synchronization.

In particular, the unchallenged press toward specificity in standards signaled to teachers the need to design their instruction in terms of discrete skills and tidbits of knowledge—strategies that render learning more difficult and its application more unlikely. Research evidence is fairly unequivocal in pointing to learners' need for a larger context in which they can organize, synthesize, and otherwise make sense of what they are learning (Bransford, Brown, and Cocking 1999). The press toward rigorous academic standards was intended to raise the bar for those students and parents least likely to know what they need to know. If, in the process, the actualities made it more difficult for them to learn and more difficult for them to apply what they have learned, then we have failed. Herein rests a challenge for all strategies to improve schools and instruction.

Designs Must Be Capable of Going to Scale: Is This Possible?

Going to scale, a plan and timeline for mass adoption or production of a practice or product, deserves more critical scrutiny as a methodology for school improvement. Despite its conceptual appeal, going to scale is not a strategic concept that can be usefully applied to transforming instructional practices and student learning in public-sector schools in the United States. Not only do we lack the fundamental conditions for such, but it exposes a great amount of naiveté about how one changes existing organizations in any sector. Transforming existing schools is entirely different than creating them from scratch. With existing schools, the change agent must help schools *renegotiate* both explicit and implicit rules and perceptions of reality. Creating schools "from scratch" does not require such renegotiations. Instead, the change agent is helping faculty and building administrators *create* instructional, organizational, and cultural norms and practices where none existed.

Change in existing organizations that is sustained, and thereby deeply embedded, has to be driven more organically than "going to scale" can honestly imply. The perceived need and potential benefit of changes has to be perceived among all people in all layers of the bureaucracy. Change involves time to learn new ways of doing things. It requires accepting that people will be less proficient in their roles for a time. For the benefit to outweigh these costs, leaders must ensure that change is addressing their priorities. Anything less leads to compliance-driven behavior, where (in this case) teachers exhibit the desired signals of change but shift few of their instructional practices.

Moreover, substantial change in existing institutions requires substantial investments. Yet providing additional financial resources to induce change always introduces mixed motives—are schools seeking improvement, or better technology and higher salaries? These can be noble motives, but they will, nevertheless, undermine the more substantive goals. Relying on a "going to scale" model distorted the change process accordingly.

Berends, Bodilly, and Kirby (2002) conclude that "externally developed education reform interventions cannot be 'break the mold' and still be marketable and able to be implemented in current district and school contexts." While certainly the scale-up phase of the NAS initiative gives considerable evidence to that claim, two caveats remain. First, the decision to go to scale in large urban systems presented the greatest challenge to the NAS strategy. Second, the time parameters for change in existing schools are universally challenging but untenable in a system that introduces new penalties for each additional year that a school fails to meet a target. In such a high-risk environment, people in any organization revert to the security of time-tested practices, even if they were inadequate all along.

Without a doubt, comprehensive school reform efforts have been tested in the most challenged schools of this nation. Without a doubt, many schools benefited. Without a doubt, many teachers' original passion for educating the young was renewed. At the same time, many were frustrated. A strategy of going to scale in existing organizations was, and is, an implausible strategy.

CONCLUSION

The value of the NAS design effort does not rest solely on the capacity to create "break the mold" schools. It should also be assessed in terms of how well it developed a diverse set of external providers that can support districts and states in measurably improving the quality of education in our most troubled schools—by increasing the repertoire of instructional strategies teachers can use, by fostering a professional learning community that not only builds teachers' capacity but also the stability of the teaching force, and by helping to construct parent and teacher collaborations that improve student learning.

Many of the most challenged schools in this nation needed what these designs initially took for granted: a relatively safe environment for adults and young people, teachers equipped with tools to help students become literate, and a modestly stable policy environment. Design teams did adapt, some changing their approach more than others, to target this population of schools. In doing so, however, some became developmental organizations, not design teams, by concentrating on the schools existing strengths. Others maintained fidelity to their design, choosing to work in environments such as charter schools that could establish new practices and standards more easily and with longer commitments. Other teams helped entire districts with some of the tools they developed for comprehensive school improvement.

Adopting a comprehensive design for school improvement is just one of a variety of intervention techniques available to schools. The nagging question for all intervention strategies is, what is best for which school serving which children? I don't think we're any closer to establishing solid research evidence now than we were 10 years ago. Understanding school improvement in a contextual and developmental perspective may be the next opportunity for researchers.

NOTES

1. In its request for proposals, NASDC wrote "[a] design should enable virtually all students to acquire the skills and knowledge that they need to function and compete effectively in a world that is becoming more complex and demanding. Moreover, designers should recognize that world-class standards are dynamic and can be expected to change through time. Designs should be capable of accommodating such changes." (New American Schools Development Corporation 1991).

2. The 11 designs were Audrey Cohen, ATLAS, Bensonville New American Schools, Community Learning Centers of Minnesota, Co-nect, Expeditionary Learning Outward Bound, Los Angeles Learning Centers, Modern Red School-House, National Alliance for Restructuring Education, the Odyssey Project, and Roots & Wings.

3. Each design's strategy for furnishing on-site coordinators had its strengths and weaknesses. For example, the team-based facilitator's time is more protected than a facilitator who is part of regular staff. On the other hand, a team-based strategy is not easily brought to scale.

4. Within a month of Lam's departure, elementary and middle school teachers were asked to vote whether they wished to continue using the mathematics text series adopted during her tenure. Eighty percent voted to discontinue it. Anticipating a substantial drop in model enrollment and thus funding, the interim superintendent adapted this strategy to other budget choices. Teachers at schools partnering with NAS designs were asked to vote whether or not to continue their relationship with the team. Secret ballots were required; no discussion was permitted. Those schools with at least 90 percent of the teachers voting in the affirmative would be allowed to continue their partnership. Only one team continued their work after this vote (Berends, Chun, et al. 2002).

5. See chapter 4 for a list of the eleven federally mandated components of comprehensive school reform.

REFERENCES

Berends, M., S. Bodilly, and S. Kirby. 2002. "Facing the Challenges of Whole-School Reform: New American Schools after a Decade." Monograph/Report MR-1498-EDU. Santa Monica: RAND.

Berends, M., J. Chun, G. Schuyler, S. Stockly, and R. J. Briggs. 2002. "Challenges of Conflicting School Reforms: Effects of New American Schools in a High-Poverty District." Monograph/Report MR-1483-EDU. Santa Monica: RAND.

Birman, B. 1987. *The Current Operation of the Chapter 1 Program: Final Report from the National Assessment of Chapter 1*. Washington, DC: Office of Educational Research and Improvement, U.S. Department of Education.

Bodilly, S. 2001. "New American Schools' Concept of Break the Mold Designs: How Designs Evolved and Why." RAND Monograph/Report MR-1288-NAS. Santa Monica: RAND.

Bransford, J. D., A. L. Brown, and R. R. Cocking, eds. 1999. *How People Learn: Brain, Mind, Experience, and School*. Washington, DC: National Academy Press.

Coleman, J. S., T. Hoffer, and S. B. Kilgore. 1982. *High School Achievement: Public, Catholic and Private Schools Compared*. New York: Basic Books.

Dreeben, R., and A. Gamoran. 1986. "Race, Instruction, and Learning." *American Sociological Review* 51(5): 660–69.

Evans, R. 1996. *The Human Side of School Change: Reform, Resistance, and the Real-Life Problems of Innovation*. San Francisco: Jossey-Bass.

Garet, M. S., and B. DeLany. 1988. "Students, Courses, and Stratification." *Sociology of Education* 61(2): 61–77.

Glennan, T. K. 1998. "New American Schools after Six Years." Monograph/Report MR-945-NAS. Santa Monica: RAND.

Kilgore, S. 2005. "Comprehensive Solutions for Urban Reform." *Educational Leadership* 62(6): 44–47.

McLaughlin, M. W. 1987. "Learning from Experience: Lessons from Policy Implementation." *Educational Evaluation and Policy Analysis* 9(2): 171–78.

Mickelson, R., and A. Wadsworth. 1996. "NASDC's Odyssey in Dallas (NC): Women, Class and School Reform." *Education Policy* 10(3): 315–41.

Mirel, J. 1994. "School Reform Unplugged: The Bensenville New American School Project, 1991–1993." *American Education Research Journal* 31(3): 481–518.

National Center for Education Statistics. 2000. *NAEP 1999 Trends in Academic Progress, Three Decades of Student Performance*. Washington, DC: Office of Educational Research and Improvement, U.S. Department of Education.

National Commission on Excellence in Education. 1983. *A Nation at Risk: The Imperative for Education Reform*. Washington, DC: U.S. Government Printing Office.

New American Schools Development Corporation. 1991. "Designs for a New Generation of American Schools: A Request for Proposals." Arlington, VA: NASDC, October.

Newmann, F. M., B. A. Smith, E. Allensworth, and T. Bryk. 2001. "Instructional Program Coherence: What It Is and Why It Should Guide School Improvement Policy." *Educational Evaluation and Policy Analysis* 23(4): 297–321.

Ravitch, D. 2000. *Left Back: A Century of Failed School Reforms*. New York: Simon & Schuster.

Schmidt, W. H. 1983. "High School Course-Taking: Its Relationship to Achievement." *Journal of Curriculum Studies* 15(b): 311–32.

Sebring, P. B. 1987. "Consequences of Differential Amounts of High School Coursework: Will the New Graduation Requirements Help?" *Educational Evaluation and Policy Analysis* 9(3): 257–73.

Sizer, T. 1992. *Horace's School: Redesigning the American High School*. New York: Houghton Mifflin.

Wiggins, G., and J. McTighe. 1998. *Understanding By Design*. Alexandria, VA: Association for Supervision and Curriculum Development.

Wilson, B. L., and G. B. Rossman. 1993. *Mandating Academic Excellence: High School Responses to State Curriculum Reform*. New York: Teachers College Press.

3

COMPREHENSIVE SCHOOL REFORM AND STATE ACCOUNTABILITY SYSTEMS

Kerstin Carlson Le Floch and Andrea Boyle

As comprehensive school reform (CSR) gained momentum during the 1990s as an improvement strategy for the nation's neediest schools, state education agencies were in various stages of developing statewide accountability systems to stimulate and track schools' progress toward meeting student performance objectives (Borman et al. 2002; Consortium for Policy Research in Education 1998; Desimone 2000; Education Commission of the States 1999). Studies of CSR often noted the impact of these emerging accountability policies on school-level CSR efforts, describing how school stakeholders frequently cited the desire to raise students' performance on state assessments as their motivation for adopting a CSR model. Later, some perceived inconsistencies arose between schools' CSR outcomes and the demands of accountability testing (Berends et al. 2002; Bodilly 2001; Glennan 1998; Johnston 2002; Mitchell 1995).

While accountability procedures constituted an early state-level influence on the CSR movement, formal state-level policies on CSR typically did not originate until 1998, when the federal Obey-Porter/ CSR Demonstration funding program charged states with administering CSR grants to schools and districts. Federal policy and guidance for the new program allowed states considerable latitude in disbursing the funds; although states needed to comply with certain minimum requirements, they could specify award priorities, application procedures, and funding allotments. As a result, state education agencies created individualized CSR strategies that were shaped by their existing state education agencies (SEAs) and state policy contexts, including their existing accountability mechanisms. As Datnow (2005, 133) explains, "CSR policies at the federal and state levels were latecomers to the larger CSR movement and were laid on top of (or had to exist alongside) state accountability systems."

This chapter probes the types of CSR policy decisions that state education agencies have made within the context of their accountability and school improvement strategies. Specifically, we discuss the extent to which 15 states have actively specified policies at the state level to customize their approach to CSR, thereby leveraging the federal CSR funding opportunity to create a capacity-building program.

THE RELATIONSHIP BETWEEN CSR AND ACCOUNTABILITY: BUILDING CAPACITY FOR REFORM

To orient our discussion of state-level connections between CSR and accountability, we begin with a conceptual framework for understanding the underpinnings of performance-based accountability systems. As accountability systems grew in prominence during the late 1990s, scholars examining these systems often focused on motivational and expectancy theories and highlighted mechanisms such as performance targets, rewards, and sanctions meant to motivate educators to improve student achievement. More recently, O'Day and Bitter (2003) took the literature one step further and offered a useful framework for understanding the interactive components of a comprehensive accountability system. In the context of their evaluation of California's Immediate Intervention/Underperforming Schools Program, they posited a theory of action in which a comprehensive accountability system is comprised of several core components, including mechanisms designed to (1) focus attention on improvement goals, (2) heighten stakeholders' motivation to reach those goals, and (3) develop educators' and schools' capacity to facilitate improvement.

This approach suggests that accountability should not be perceived as one-dimensional and driven only by test scores and sanctions. Rather, a comprehensive accountability system would support building capacity for reform (without which focusing attention and motivating educators would be inadequate stimuli for change). Other scholars highlight the importance of capacity building in accountability systems. Fullan (2001, 10) describes a framework similar to that advanced by O'Day and Bitter and notes that states have often failed to construct a balanced accountability system:

> Large-scale reform requires what I am going to call an "account-ability pillar" and a "capacity-building pillar.". . . These pressure and support pillars must act in concert in order to produce large-scale reform. When done effectively, integrating pressure and support with a focus on results for students creates pride, greater trust, and tremendous motivation and energy. . . . Further, sustained reform is not possible unless the larger state infrastructure is also transformed. Most states have readily taken on the account-ability pillar, few have addressed capacity building.

Federal policymakers seem to have recognized the importance of creating just such a balanced approach to accountability by legislating capacity-building opportunities alongside requirements for measuring and enforcing performance targets. The Improving America's Schools Act (IASA) of 1994, which formally required all states to develop mechanisms to calculate schools' adequate yearly progress (AYP) and to hold schools accountable for meeting those annual performance goals, also placed strong emphasis on capacity-building tools to assist schools in achieving those yearly targets. The IASA provided funding for the use of comprehensive, schoolwide improvement programs in Title I schools and required states to establish a "statewide system of intensive and sustained support and improvement" (Sec. 1117) for high-poverty, low-performing schools, particularly Title I schools identified as needing improvement. These systems of support were required to include such tools as state school support teams that would aid in the implementation of schoolwide programs, as well as distinguished schools and distinguished educator mentoring programs—all of which were aimed specifically toward improving schools' capacity to meet student performance standards.

The establishment of the Comprehensive School Reform Demonstration program (CSRD) in 1998 extended the federal government's support for schoolwide capacity-building reforms by offering grants of at least $50,000 to schools implementing comprehensive school reform models. In 2001, federal lawmakers situated the CSR funding program within the context of accountability when they incorporated it into the No Child Left Behind Act (NCLB), which reinforced the demands for state accountability systems, threatened to impose stiffer sanctions on consistently underperforming schools, and specified more exacting requirements for statewide systems of support. Furthermore, NCLB's new policies for the CSR program explicitly tied it to state accountability mechanisms; for instance, these new CSR policies included requirements that SEAs (1) give priority to schools identified for improvement or corrective action under their accountability systems and (2) annually evaluate the extent to which schools' implementation of CSR has led to improved student performance. Thus, CSR became framed as a capacity-building tool within a model of accountability and school improvement.

Current research on states' implementation of the CSR funding program suggests that, like federal policymakers, SEA staff have been forging connections between CSR and state-developed accountability systems and school improvement procedures. Since federal CSR policy affords states considerable flexibility in deciding how to implement the grant program, many SEAs made key policy decisions to adapt their CSR strategies and fit them into existing state accountability practices, initiatives, reform goals, and institutional contexts (Hamann and Lane 2004; Lane and Gracia 2005). States often relied on their specific accountability designations to identify schools eligible for CSR funds; for example, Datnow (2005) explains how Florida used its school accountability grading system to determine schools' eligibility. In some cases, states have made direct choices to incorporate CSR into other state programs: Hamann and Lane (2004) describe how Maine merged the CSRD funding opportunity into a state-initiated high school reform program by adapting federal CSRD policy to target only high schools and by connecting the application for CSRD funding to the application for the state program funding. Moreover, states have employed components of their systems of support for low-performing schools to facilitate and assist in schools' CSR efforts (Lane and Gracia 2005).

While current research into states' roles in supporting CSR is in rather short supply, this line of inquiry taps into more generalized theories that SEAs are moving away from their traditional roles as compliance enforcers. Instead, it is thought that SEAs are becoming more active facilitators of school and district capacity building, through such activities as building technical assistance and professional development infrastructures, organizing resource allocation, and establishing reform frameworks, standards, and goals (Little and Houston 2003; Lusi 1997; Massell 1998). Additionally, states' decisions to incorporate CSR into broader accountability and school improvement strategies resonate with theories of systemic reform, which advocate integrating state education policies into common set of educational objectives (Elmore 1993; Fuhrman 1993; Lusi 1997; O'Day and Smith 1993). Such integration would presumably promote coherence across all levels of education systems and would replace "the practice of fashioning a separate program for each educational problem" whereby "individual projects, no matter how uniquely worthy, seldom reinforce one another and frequently send different, even conflicting messages to schools" (Fuhrman 1993, 7).

This chapter seeks to build on this line of research into state-level policymaking. Specifically, we explore the extent to which states have taken advantage of a federal opportunity—the CSR grant program—and customized this program as a capacity-building mechanism within the state accountability system. We assert that three core state activities provide evidence of active policy specification: (1) the degree to which states *integrated* the federal CSR program into their own system of support, (2) the ways in which states *support* CSR grantees, and (3) the extent to which states *refine* their CSR policy.

METHODOLOGY

This chapter draws from the National Longitudinal Evaluation of Comprehensive School Reform (NLECSR), a quasi-experimental five-year study funded through a grant from the U.S. Department of Education.[1] To investigate state strategies toward comprehensive school reform, we focused on two primary sources of data collection. The first involved a thorough review of relevant state and federal policy documents. These included the policy and guidance for Title I, Part F, of the No Child Left Behind Act, which reauthorized the federal CSR grant program initially established by the 1997 Obey-Porter amendment. We also examined Consolidated State Applications under No Child Left Behind, in which states were required to detail their approach to the federal CSR program, targeting strategy, and evaluation methods. In addition, we consulted policy documents available from state department of education web sites. Among these were CSR grant requests for proposals, evaluation rubrics for grant applications, CSR component descriptions and crosswalks, and agendas for technical assistance workshops.

Although these documents provided insight into the state role in comprehensive school reform, they lacked the depth necessary to address some of our more fundamental questions. We conducted interviews with state officials who had primary responsibility for administering the federal CSR program. Our sample consisted of 15 of the 16 states that comprise the NLECSR sample; one state CSR coordinator declined to participate in an interview. States in this sample varied widely in size and covered a range of geographic regions within the U.S. We developed an open-ended interview protocol with questions that probed the following:

- history of state involvement in CSR,
- evolution of state strategy for CSR,
- role of CSR in state systems of support for low-performing schools,
- rationale for funding strategy,
- state technical assistance,
- states' role in model adoption, and
- challenges associated with CSR.

Although we had anticipated that each interview would last approximately 30 minutes, respondents often spoke longer, and several interviews lasted 45 minutes. One staff member conducted the interview, while a second listened and took notes on a computer. These notes were later reviewed in conjunction with the audio recording and were supplemented as necessary. From each interview we produced a transcript that was close to verbatim.

We did not believe the use of a qualitative software program was warranted in coding the interview data due to the relatively small number of interviewees. In addition, the staff members who had developed the interview protocol were also those who had conducted the interviews, and so they were familiar with the interview content. First, we reviewed each transcript, highlighting key passages related to states' CSR policymaking decisions. Upon a second review, we began to associate codes with highlighted text and entered passages into an Excel template, which facilitated the comparison of common themes across states.

Through a process of identifying codes, clustering conceptually-linked variables, refining categories, and creating indices, we developed an analytic mechanism for determining patterns in state CSR activities. In short, we identified three dimensions to describe states' CSR policy activities: (1) the extent to which a state has developed policies and activities that *integrate* CSR into other capacity-building strategies and initiatives within the state, (2) the extent to which a state has developed policies and activities to *support* schools' CSR planning and implementation efforts, and (3) the extent to which states have *refined* their CSR policies and activities to better serve schools. We then defined these three dimensions in terms of seven core components designed to cover the range of related state activities:

- The *Integration of CSR* dimension consists of state policies and activities to (1) target certain types of schools for CSR funding and

(2) connect CSR to the state's system of support for low-performing schools. Connections between CSR and a state's system of support might occur through collaboration between CSR coordinators and state school support staff or through states' incorporation of CSR into policies governing their school improvement strategy.

- The *Support for CSR* dimension includes four components: (1) using the CSR planning application/planning process to ensure schools' readiness to implement a CSR plan, (2) allotting funds to schools, (3) providing technical assistance to help schools write successful grant applications, and (4) providing technical assistance to help schools implement their proposed CSR plan.
- The *Refinement of CSR* dimension involves only one component: (1) the degree to which states change their CSR policies to meet state and school needs.

For each of our seven components, we developed a set of categories and descriptors to capture the variation among states' approaches. We ranked these approach categories according to the degree to which each type of approach demanded active policy customization from SEA staff (see the spectrums outlined in figure 3.1). We then assigned each approach category a numeric rating, such that a score of 0 indicated an approach heavily dictated by federal policy and/or guidance, and higher scores indicated approaches that involved higher levels of policy specification and adaptation at the state level. For each component, we gave states the rating that corresponded to their particular approach. For the technical assistance components, we rated states according to the number of technical assistance activities they provided for grant writing and for implementation; we defined states offering the most types of technical assistance as those with the most highly customized approach.

After determining states' ratings for each component, we calculated summative ratings for each of our three dimensions. We then combined states' integration, support, and refinement ratings to determine their customization rating and used these ratings to group states into three clusters. It is important to emphasize here that states' "ratings" are not intended to judge the quality or effectiveness of states' approaches; they are simply meant to indicate the extent to which states customized their approaches to CSR based on state contextual factors.

Clusters of State CSR Approaches

The first cluster consisted of states with the lowest degree of policy customization. They generally treated CSR as a discrete funding program and focused on ensuring compliance with federal requirements

Figure 3.1. Analytic Dimensions of State Comprehensive School Reform Activity

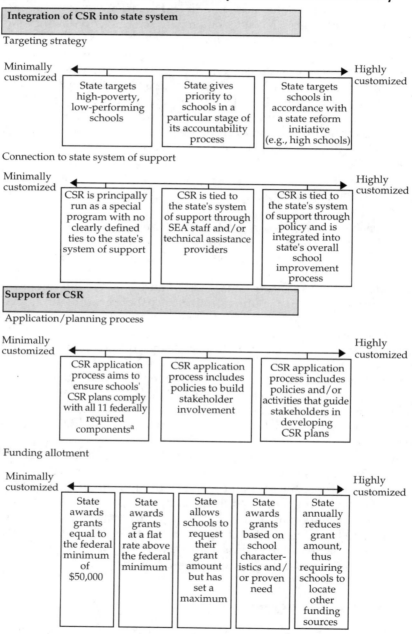

Integration of CSR into state system

Targeting strategy

Minimally customized ← → Highly customized

| State targets high-poverty, low-performing schools | State gives priority to schools in a particular stage of its accountability process | State targets schools in accordance with a state reform initiative (e.g., high schools) |

Connection to state system of support

Minimally customized ← → Highly customized

| CSR is principally run as a special program with no clearly defined ties to the state's system of support | CSR is tied to the state's system of support through SEA staff and/or technical assistance providers | CSR is tied to the state's system of support through policy and is integrated into state's overall school improvement process |

Support for CSR

Application/planning process

Minimally customized ← → Highly customized

| CSR application process aims to ensure schools' CSR plans comply with all 11 federally required components[a] | CSR application process includes policies to build stakeholder involvement | CSR application process includes policies and/or activities that guide stakeholders in developing CSR plans |

Funding allotment

Minimally customized ← → Highly customized

| State awards grants equal to the federal minimum of $50,000 | State awards grants at a flat rate above the federal minimum | State allows schools to request their grant amount but has set a maximum | State awards grants based on school characteristics and/or proven need | State annually reduces grant amount, thus requiring schools to locate other funding sources |

Technical assistance for the application process

State staff coordinates regional meetings/workshops on the application process

State assists schools in applying for CSR during regular
(not specifically CSR-related) site visits

State staff intervenes when schools encounter problems in applying for CSR

State staff works one-on-one with schools to assist in the application process

Technical assistance for implementation

State staff coordinates regional meetings/workshops on issues related
to implementation

State helps schools implement CSR during regular
(not specifically CSR-related) site visits

State staff intervenes when schools encounter problems in implementing CSR

State staff works one-on-one with schools to assist in CSR implementation

Refinement of CSR policy

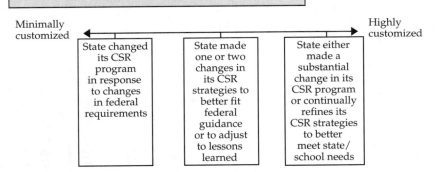

Minimally customized ← → Highly customized

| State changed its CSR program in response to changes in federal requirements | State made one or two changes in its CSR strategies to better fit federal guidance or to adjust to lessons learned | State either made a substantial change in its CSR program or continually refines its CSR strategies to better meet state/ school needs |

CSR = comprehensive school reform
SEA = state education agency
[a] For a list of the 11 federally required CSR components, see chapter 4.

and guidance. For this reason, we refer to this cluster as those states with a *programmatic approach*.

The second or middle cluster—where the majority of states in our sample fell—featured a range of strategies for CSR. These states often scored high on one or two of the dimensions but lower on others. Because these states are less consistent in their strategies, we have opted to call these states those with a *varied approach*. For example, some states in this category provided relatively high levels of support to CSR schools but did little in terms of integrating CSR into their system of support for schools identified for improvement.

Each of the states in our third cluster articulated a vision of CSR as integrated into a clearly defined, cohesive state strategy to build capacity among underperforming schools. We refer to this cluster of states as those with a highly *customized approach*. These states generally provided high levels of support throughout the CSR process and were also more likely to refine their approach to CSR based on lessons learned. Figure 3.2 depicts the clusters of states and their relative ratings on each of these three core components.

To gain further insight into these approaches, we analyzed these clusters in relation to other core components of accountability systems.

Figure 3.2. States' Comprehensive School Reform Model Customization Ratings, as Composites of Their Dimensional Ratings

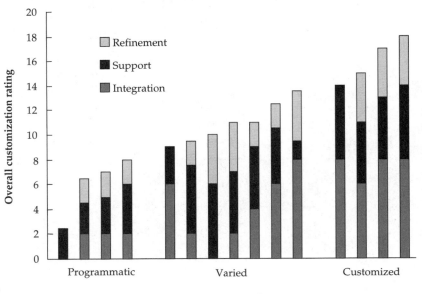

State approach

Source: Author's calculations.

These variables included the presence of a state-specific accountability system (in addition to NCLB-mandated accountability) and historic variables, such as the presence of a performance-based accountability system prior to NCLB.

One notable difference between states with a *customized* approach to CSR and those with a *programmatic* or *varied* approach was the stability of their systems of support for low-performing schools. Drawing from profiles of state accountability systems (Goertz, Duffy, and Le Floch 2001), we identified states that had a separate system of support for Title I schools, states that provided additional support for Title I schools, and states that had an integrated system of support for both Title I and non-Title I schools prior to NCLB. The states with a *customized* approach generally were those that had an integrated system of support in 1999–2000, while those with separate support for Title I schools were those that had a *programmatic* approach to CSR. This suggests that states that now seek to tailor the federal CSR program to meet their schools' needs were also those that proactively integrated Title I program improvement into their comprehensive approach to school improvement nearly six years ago.

There was one exception however: the state that ranked the highest on all indicators was also one that had a separate system of support for Title I schools in 1999–2000, distinguishing it from all other states in this category. In this case, it appears that the state's high marks are due to the activities of a particularly engaged CSR state director. Indeed, other studies of CSR activities at the state level have underscored the importance of state officials' leadership (Buechler 1999; Hamann and Lane 2004; Lane and Gracia 2005). No other accountability-related measures served to distinguish the clusters of states, although all of those in the *customized approach* category had accountability systems prior to NCLB and still maintain separate state systems. Overall, we believe these clusters are distinguishing between important differences in state approaches to CSR, but our sample size does not permit us to identify other features that could further delineate or explain the clusters.

We suggest that states developing a customized approach to the CSR program are also those in which schools are less likely to perceive conflicts between CSR and the targets, tests, and sanctions most frequently associated with state accountability systems. States that weave CSR into school improvement, provide support, and continually seek to improve their practice are also those in which CSR is most likely to strengthen the "capacity-building pillar" of state accountability systems.

Because we have assured confidentiality to all participants in our study—from the state to the local level—we cannot describe any accountability system in a way that would reveal its state. However, because there are commonalities among the states in our study, and indeed throughout the country, we can outline general trends and "types" of states. In the following sections, we will describe the variation in how states adapted the federal CSR policy to their state and SEA contexts, and the degree to which such adaptations resulted in greater integration with states' improvement strategies. We focus specifically on each of the seven components used in our analyses of state CSR policy.

Integration of CSR into the State System

State System of Support: Connections with CSR

Under No Child Left Behind, all states are required to establish a system of support for schools identified for improvement under Title I. Frequently, these systems extend services beyond Title I to encompass non-Title I schools, schools determined to be low performing under the state accountability system, and schools that do not make AYP for only one year. NCLB provisions articulate specific structures that states should establish to support identified schools, including school support teams, distinguished teachers, and distinguished principals. Despite relative uniformity of federal guidelines, states vary greatly in how they have conceptualized their systems of support. While some centralize supports at the state level, others are anchored in regional education agencies. Likewise, states vary in the degree to which such systems are embedded, coherent, and comprehensive.

Among the states in our study are several that have spent many years developing comprehensive support systems. Often, these systems include both tools and structures that together encompass an overarching improvement process. These tools are designed to assist schools in needs assessment, data analysis, developing a school improvement plan, aligning funding streams, and monitoring implementation. The structures may consist of school support teams, school improvement coaches, or regional agencies that provide assistance to schools as needed. The core of such systems is a coherent vision for school improvement, generally grounded in research on school reform. States that have such systems weave new federal grant opportunities into their approach to school improvement—and such was the case with the federal CSR program in nearly half the states in our study, generally those states in the *customized approach* category.

Let us consider an example of a state with a coherent and comprehensive system of support for identified schools. Often, a state with such a system conducts a triage of schools based on core accountability measures, determining which schools had missed the highest number of AYP targets or which had failed to make AYP for several consecutive years. The state then schedules for each of these schools to be visited by a school support team. The team may spend a week at a school, helping administrators and teachers review assessment data or identifying challenging content areas or subgroups of students that could benefit from targeted interventions.

The school support team is most often comprised of SEA school improvement staff, most of whom also have responsibilities for other federal programs, including Title I, Part A, CSR, and perhaps No Child Left Behind's Reading First grants or supplemental educational services. SEA staff assist the school as they identify appropriate improvement strategies and funding opportunities. The SEA support team also helps school staff identify which high-need schools have adequate capacity to benefit from a federal CSR grant, whether the CSR program would integrate well with any existing school-level initiatives, and whether the staff had the capacity to write a CSR grant. As an official in one such state explained,

> CSR falls into and underneath the school improvement division, so we are not only in the same office with all of the low-performing schools, we are also part of the process that goes out and facilitates the assistance to those schools . . . we make sure that school improvement plans are aligned with all of the other initiatives in the school as well as the technical assistance and guidance we provide.

In this context, CSR is perceived as an important support strategy (among others) to be targeted to appropriate schools as part of a broad state vision for school improvement.

At the other extreme are states that have devoted fewer resources to developing a system of support. States have failed to establish such systems for many reasons, such as having insufficient human or financial resources, strong traditions of local control, or relatively few schools identified for improvement. In this context, CSR is merely a funding stream to be administered by the state, rather than an opportunity to be leveraged as part of a broader strategy to address the needs of low-performing schools. These states constituted approximately one-third of those we sampled, most often those in the *programmatic approach* category.

States with varied approaches to CSR may indeed have high levels of integration in their system of support. However, this was counterbalanced by low support ratings. For example, one state in the varied approach category exhibited a relatively integrated system, yet made no efforts to refine its approach to address challenges. Although some states in this middle category do have fairly well-developed systems of support, they do not fully optimize this system in conjunction with the federal CSR program.

Targeting CSR Funds

States also vary in how they target schools for CSR grants, and this variation is often—but not always—associated with the coherence of the system of support. Federal CSR guidance articulates CSR eligibility requirements, but these are relatively broad. Formally, local education agencies apply to states on behalf of Title I–eligible schools, preferably those with the greatest likelihood of promoting schoolwide change and improving student achievement. Among the states in our sample, approximately one-third adopted these fairly general targeting strategies: eligible schools were high-poverty, low-performing schools that had missed AYP or been identified for improvement or corrective action. These states did little to narrow these eligibility requirements.

However, federal guidance also permits states to set their own more explicit eligibility requirements, and many states have further refined their provisions to focus on a specific subset of schools. Such was the case in half of the states in our sample. In states with highly focused eligibility rules, state officials described the evolution of their approach as part of an overall policy refinement, intended to encourage substantive and sustainable reform. Some eligibility restrictions were revised to encourage school-level programmatic coherence: for example, some states limit Reading First schools' participation in CSR to avoid overwhelming them with program requirements. One state official said,

> When you have a low-performing school . . . and we overload them with any number of grants, it may be CSR and Reading First or CSR and 21st Century Schools, there is a limited amount of time in a workweek, and so when Reading First requires or mandates a certain amount of training or requirements, and when CSR has other requirements, one of them just falls by the wayside, and typically, based on my experience, that has been CSR. . . . So I'm trying to coordinate now, and we're going to prioritize those schools that don't have existing reforms in their schools.

Several states elected to focus on schools in "dire need": those identified for restructuring or those at the lowest level of state accountability designations. In contrast, other states focus on schools at the other end of the improvement spectrum, targeting schools that were only recently placed on academic watch or probation. As one state official explained,

"There's a far greater benefit for schools that have had a readiness to benefit as opposed to taking the lowest performing schools, which was what we've done in the past." These schools have not yet been identified for improvement, and CSR is viewed as a mechanism to stave off potential identification in subsequent years.

In a few interesting cases, states opted to target schools that were Title I–eligible (but not receiving Title I funds) and identified for improvement. These schools, while still impoverished, did not benefit from Title I dollars, so CSR was perceived as an effective mechanism to ensure these schools had access to another school improvement strategy and the associated supports. One state official recalled, "This year we said, we're giving a lot of money to Title I schools, so who are we going to address the CSR money to? So this year we decided to give the money to schools which are Title I eligible, but are not Title I served, and in need of improvement under NCLB." Finally, a few states focused eligibility on specific levels—only high schools, or only middle schools—or a specific subject.

Support for CSR

Using the Application/Planning Process to Build Capacity

In addition to formal eligibility requirements, many states were concerned with targeting schools that had at least a minimal level of capacity to support reform, or possessed a "readiness to benefit" from the funds they would receive. High-poverty, low-performing schools, which often lacked the capacity to develop a comprehensive school reform plan that was (1) compatible with their particular needs and (2) capable of being successfully implemented, were one of the states' most common and fundamental challenges. Federal policy restricted use of CSR grants to implementation support only and thereby limited schools' access to resources for needs assessment and planning. In many cases, SEAs found that schools were applying for CSR funds without a clear, well-conceived understanding of how they would actually implement a CSR program and how that CSR program fit into their other efforts. As one CSR coordinator explained,

> They're low-functioning schools, and if they had staff with the skills and capacity to write grants and go through that process on their own, they wouldn't be in CSR—they wouldn't be low performing. So, what happens is, they have an opportunity to apply for money, they have a limited time in which to apply (four, maybe five months), and they slop together a proposal. . . . There

is not a readiness on the part of the school; there's isn't a comprehensive look at what they are doing in a comprehensive way so that they can be good consumers of these funds and technical assistance.

Many SEAs recognized early on that for CSR to serve as an effective capacity-building strategy, the schools they were targeting typically needed assistance in creating an appropriate CSR plan and in preparing school-level stakeholders to implement that plan effectively. To address this issue, some states established policies to promote collective stakeholder support for CSR; such policies included required levels of teacher buy-in and requirements or incentives for district representatives to attend state CSR meetings.

In some states, CSR coordinating staff focused on structuring their CSR application in such a way that it became a meaningful step in school reform planning. Under NCLB, states' CSR applications are required to ensure that schools' proposals adequately address all 11 federally mandated components for CSR.[2] One state CSR coordinator found that her state's grant application, which required narrative accounts of how each component was incorporated into a school's CSR plan, was not having the desired effect of bringing school stakeholders together to develop a comprehensive plan. Instead, principals often assembled committees for each of the components, divided the grant-writing work, and then "cut and pasted" the set of narratives into one proposal. To promote more cohesive planning, this state coordinator developed a customized application that integrated all 11 components into broader categories derived from effective schools research and theory. The application essentially became a professional development tool and required stakeholders to work together to create a clearly outlined plan for their CSR proposal.

Other states are using statewide school improvement planning processes to aid in schools' development of CSR plans. One state coordinator described CSR as part of the state's system for creating Title I schoolwide improvement plans: "All the funding sources and all the efforts are integrated into one plan. CSR is part of that." Because the state connected CSR to this process, applicant CSR schools benefit from state training in identifying the root causes of their achievement gaps and the corresponding needs to be addressed in their CSR strategy. Other states were less successful in their attempts to incorporate CSR into their system for school improvement planning. One state targeted CSR funding toward schools entering its special assistance program, which provided coaching as well as needs assessment and planning assistance to schools identified for improvement. When the requirements for the state program clashed with the requirements for CSR, schools became overwhelmed with excessive mandates and time constraints. This state is now in the process of adjusting this strategy so that schools will create a comprehensive improvement plan through the state planning assistance program first, then have the opportunity to apply for CSR funding to continue those efforts.

Technical Assistance for Grant Writing

In addition to adapting their application procedures, states are creating unique approaches to provide schools with technical assistance for grant writing. Because the targeted schools typically begin the CSR process with low capacity, they often lack access to skilled grant writers to complete the lengthy CSR applications. One CSR coordinator perceived the daunting requirements of these applications to be the principal reason schools were not applying for CSR. "I'd start talking about CSR and what the requirements for that were, [and] people's eyes would glaze over; it was daunting enough for them to write an improvement plan, and CSR just kind of put them over the edge," she explained.

To improve schools' chances of writing successful grant applications, SEAs have developed a range of techniques to both familiarize schools with CSR as a general school improvement technique and to aid schools in writing thoughtful, high-quality CSR proposals. While nearly every state CSR program in the sample answered schools' phone and e-mail requests for information, about two-thirds also held statewide workshops to explain their CSR application requirements. One state with a particularly in-depth approach to grant-writing technical assistance offered a series of workshops to discuss the application requirements, but also how to conduct a needs assessment, how to connect that needs assessment to a school improvement plan, and how to align state standards and policies to that school improvement plan. Several states also encourage schools to bring drafts of their applications and facilitate peer review sessions to improve the applications' quality.

CSR coordinators from about one-third of the states in our sample described working individually with schools to facilitate grant writing. One CSR coordinator explains using individualized assistance as a means of guiding schools in the right direction:

We find that a lot of schools really start out on the wrong foot. They start out telling you all the stuff that you really don't need to know, and it doesn't support anything. The more that you can work with them and say, OK, this is what you are writing, but you need to go back to your staff and you need to do a lot more work. . . . If you can work with people along the way and just get them focused on the right strategies and methods they need to use to even put an RFP [request for proposal] together—the kind of work they need to get stuff in writing down—I find that that's very helpful when they start actually putting pen to paper.

Many SEAs, particularly those conducting CSR competitions with large numbers of applicants, simply do not have the manpower to provide this type of individualized assistance, but some such states are encouraging schools to form partnerships with local universities and/or educational resource centers to provide the grant-writing assistance they cannot.

Technical Assistance for Implementation

State patterns in the provision of technical assistance for CSR often mirror their overall system of support. Among the states in our sample, several had systems of support that relied primarily on decentralized, regional support agencies. States that traditionally centralized most support strategies within the SEA tended to do so for CSR activities as well. A few states collaborated with regional educational laboratories to provide technical assistance to CSR schools, but this was a somewhat less common approach.

While many states provided technical assistance for grant writing, fewer provided technical assistance to support CSR implementation. The most active form of technical assistance consisted of school-level site visits with the explicit purpose of determining progress in model implementation. Approximately one-third of the states in our sample provided direct, one-on-one assistance to schools implementing CSR models through the federal program. A bit more common (approximately one-half of the states in our sample) were states in which SEA staff visited CSR schools in conjunction with another required site visit. Said one, "Every year, I visit each of these schools and I often try to coordinate with other activities, since I'm a Title I consultant."

In addition, the majority of states in our sample conducted workshops to support implementation of CSR strategies. These workshops focused on such topics as principal leadership, sustainability, coaching/reform facilitation, and assessment practices. While the workshops were a less-focused form of technical support, states often worked to ensure they were meaningful for participants. For example one state official noted, "We always have teams come, which is a good thing, we don't ask just one person to participate, we usually have a team that can bring information back to the school. We really encourage whole-school participation that way."

Interestingly, several states engaged directly with model developers when schools encountered problems. Several officials described cases in which model developers were not meeting the terms of the contract, or were not providing the type of support the school needed: "We were kind of the mediators, we worked between schools and model providers in case there were any problems." In another situation, a state official determined that a school should have never opted to implement a specific model, but the model developer had offered to write the grant and the school agreed to go along. However, the school had none of the existing infrastructure necessary to implement the model, putting them in an untenable situation. In this case, the state requested that the model developer sever the contract, and the developer complied.

Most often, states had several layers of technical assistance, each of which provided a slightly different type of support. One CSR director described the set of technical assistance supports that his state provides:

> Let's take what happens after the moment a school gets an award: the first thing we do, prior to the start of their first school year, we do a one-day orientation with them into the comprehensive school reform process. And then, a little later in the summer, for the past several years we have done a two-day data retreat to get them familiar with the potential for data serving them in the decisionmaking process. . . . The goal annually from my part is to then visit at least two-thirds of the schools to make personal monitoring visits to them and to spend an hour and a half or so to discuss with their leadership team members talking about their implementation and concerns and issues. . . . In our office we also have regional consultants. . . . I have asked them in the past to select a couple of schools to shadow and make an occasional visit to get a sense of the quality of implementation and to find out what technical assistance they may need that we can provide.

Finally, some states simply did not have the resources to provide technical assistance for implementation, either because of budget and staffing cuts or because the state had too many CSR schools to provide adequate assistance to all. As one interviewee admitted, "We basically do not do any kind of technical assistance. . . . The only thing that we do is basically when we're on the phone, and they call and ask us questions."

Funding Strategies

States have considerable decisionmaking authority in the way federal grant money is allocated to schools and districts. Federal policy requires that each state-awarded subgrant be at least $50,000 and restricts the amount of funding that can be reserved for states' and districts' administrative costs, but all other policies determining schools' grant size are left to states. Of the states in our sample, only two chose to award schools the federal $50,000 minimum in their 2004–2005 funding cohorts. Four states allowed schools to request their grant amount, as long as it did not exceed a specified maximum. Six states based their funding decision on school characteristics such as size and determined need. Three states chose to reduce the size of their schools' grants over the course of the three-year funding cycle. Such efforts to wean schools from federal funding stem from the intent noted in federal policy that CSR grants be merely start-up funds; by the end of schools' third year of funding, their CSR implementation should be sustainable through other, local funds.

State policies for CSR funding occasionally emphasize sustainability. Several states encourage schools' access to other funding sources during the application process. For instance, one CSR coordinator described using a budget that shows "what they're going to be putting into these initiatives out of all the other funding sources in the school, and then we have totals at the bottom so we can show that CSR is just a small piece of all of the money that is going into that particular school." In some cases, SEA staff perform extensive budget reviews to enforce policies that restrict schools' use of CSR funding. For example, several states restricted large budget items such as literacy or math coach salaries, so that those resources would not be lost once federal funding ended. Some states emphasize sustainability at annual implementation reviews. One coordinator, perceiving that some schools "don't look past tomorrow if you don't make them," personally offers technical assistance in resource allocation and requires schools to report how they will incorporate other funds after federal funding runs out.

Refinement of CSR Policy

While many states have made efforts to adapt CSR to their state contexts, this process continues to evolve. Some states are on a policy trajectory of continuous refinement, but others seem to be more stagnant or in decline. Among the states we interviewed, we can perceive three major themes with their ongoing adaptation of state CSR policy.

First, some states clearly are responding to lessons learned, and are continually refining their approach to CSR. For example, one state's CSR staff came to believe that their model fairs were encouraging schools to simply "try to buy something to fix their problems." The CSR staff then adjusted its model fairs to focus more on the effective strategies incorporated in CSR models and less on the particular models themselves. The state also placed a heavier emphasis on needs assessment and data-based decisionmaking during its application process so that schools were "not just picking something that looks good."

Other states dramatically shifted the direction of their CSR policy. In most cases, such policy revolutions occurred when new SEA staff members assumed the role of CSR coordinator and implemented significant changes to fit their visions for the program. Such changes in CSR leadership occurred in several states in our sample, and in most of these cases, the incoming CSR coordinator had previous experience working in the state's school improvement or accountability division. Two such CSR coordinators made efforts to better align CSR with the state's other school improvement policies after perceiving the state's earlier, less-integrated approach to be ineffective. One of these coordinators described her work as "moving this huge ocean liner here. . . . I took over schools and just couldn't figure out why they weren't going anywhere with this"; she then orchestrated a series of changes in the state's targeting strategy, application process, and technical assistance strategies to create a clearer connection between CSR and the states' other school improvement programs.

Finally, some states have suffered such a reduction in resources that they can do little to adapt CSR to their state context. In these cases, the state official simply hopes to comply with the grant requirements to continue providing the school with resources, but holds little hope that the SEA can provide much support. One such official described CSR as a "marginalized program" and explained, "as long as I keep the reports going, nobody really seems to care what happens with it. In our state, it's viewed as just another source of money for our schools."

CONCLUSION

On the whole, these analyses suggest that states vary a great deal in how they have adapted the federal CSR program to their own context. Recalling the conceptual model discussed earlier, we conclude that states diverge in how fully they leverage CSR as a capacity-building component of their accountability system, working in conjunction with the accountability mechanisms designed to focus attention and motivate educators. Based on how states have specified and adapted their CSR policies, we have identified three main clusters of states: those with *programmatic*, *varied*, and *customized* approaches. The states with highly customized approaches have made full use of flexibility within the federal CSR program to ensure that it suits their policy context. More importantly, these states have worked to ensure state-level coherence in improvement policies. Policymakers in these states ultimately seek to reduce the proliferation of competing reforms at the school level, thus lowering barriers to effective change.

Schools in states that have not encouraged such coordination may still face competing reforms—whether a testing system is not aligned with reforms, or mandates associated with federal programs are layered on top of each other. Unfortunately, some states cannot devote the resources necessary to weave federal programs into a comprehensive vision for reform. Despite their often good intentions, such states are reduced to taking a fairly programmatic approach to comprehensive school reform. At the school level, educators may receive conflicting messages about how reform initiatives fit together. As such, they may perceive an awkward juxtaposition between assessment mandates and CSR strategies.

Our third set of states is most difficult to characterize, so varied are their approaches to CSR. While one state may concentrate particularly on technical assistance for grant writing, another may continually refine its funding and targeting strategies to hone its focus on schools in need. What distinguishes these schools from states taking a programmatic approach is their continued effort to "make CSR their own."

The increasing number of schools identified for improvement will impose more burdens on already stretched-thin SEA staff. Whether states are able to continue their steps toward CSR policy adaptation and refinement, or whether the weight of accountability designations and sanctions will overwhelm SEAs, will be the next phase of research on state-level CSR policy.

NOTES

1. See chapter 1 for more on the NLECSR.
2. See chapter 4 for a discussion of the 11 federally mandated CSR components.

REFERENCES

Berends, M., J. Chun, G. Schuyler, S. Stockly, and R. J. Briggs. 2002. "Challenges of Conflicting School Reforms: Effects of New American Schools in a High-Poverty District." Monograph/Report MR-1483-EDU. Santa Monica: RAND.

Bodilly, S. 2001. "New American Schools' Concept of Break the Mold Designs: How Designs Evolved and Why." Monograph/Report MR-1288-NAS. Santa Monica: RAND.

Borman, G., G. M. Hewes, L. T. Overman, and S. Brown. 2002. "Comprehensive School Reform and Student Achievement: A Meta-Analysis." Report No. 59. Baltimore: Center for Research on the Education of Students Placed At Risk.

Buechler, M. 1999. "Challenges for Comprehensive School Reform: A Working Conference." Presentation, Portland, OR, October 29–30.

Consortium for Policy Research in Education. 1998. "States and Districts and Comprehensive School Reform." Policy Brief RB-24. Philadelphia: University of Pennsylvania, Consortium for Policy Research in Education.

Datnow, A. 2005. "Happy Marriage or Uneasy Alliance? The Relationship between Comprehensive School Reform and State Accountability Systems." *Journal of Education for Students Placed at Risk* 10(1): 113–38.

Desimone, L. 2000. "Making Comprehensive School Reform Work." Urban Diversity No. 112. New York: ERIC Clearinghouse on Urban Education, Teachers College, Columbia University.

Education Commission of the States. 1999. *Comprehensive School Reform: Five Lessons from the Field*. Denver, CO: Education Commission of the States.

Elmore, R. F. 1993. "The Role of Local School Districts in Instructional Improvement." In *Designing Coherent Education Policy: Improving the System*, edited by S. H. Fuhrman (96–124). San Francisco: Jossey-Bass.

Fuhrman, S. H. 1993. "The Politics of Coherence." In *Designing Coherent Education Policy: Improving the System*, edited by S. H. Fuhrman (1–34). San Francisco: Jossey-Bass.

Fullan, M. 2001. "Whole School Reform: Problems and Promises." Paper commissioned by the Chicago Community Trust. Toronto: Ontario Institute for Studies in Education. http://home.oise.utoronto.ca/~changeforces/Articles_01/06_01.htm.

Glennan, T. K., Jr. 1998. *New American Schools after Six Years*. Santa Monica: RAND.

Goertz, M., M. C. Duffy, and K. C. Le Floch. 2001. "Assessment and Accountability Systems in the 50 States: 1999–2000." Research Report No. RR-046. Philadelphia: University of Pennsylvania, Consortium for Policy Research in Education.

Hamann, E. T., and B. Lane. 2004. "The Roles of State Departments of Education as Policy Intermediaries: Two Cases." *Educational Policy* 18(3): 426–55.

Johnston, B. J. 2002. "Absent from School: Educational Policy and Comprehensive Reform." *Urban Review* 34(3): 205–30.

Lane, B., and S. Gracia. 2005. "State-Level Support for Comprehensive School Reform: Implications for Policy and Practice." *Journal of Education for Students Placed at Risk* 10(1): 85–112.

Little, M. E., and D. Houston. 2003. "Comprehensive School Reform: A Model Based on Student Learning." *Journal of Disability Policy Studies* 14(1): 54–62.

Lusi, S. F. 1997. *The Role of State Departments of Education in Complex School Reform*. New York: Teacher's College Press.

Massell, D. 1998. "State Strategies for Building Local Capacity: Addressing the Needs of Standards-Based Reform." Policy Brief RB-25. Philadelphia: University of Pennsylvania, Consortium for Policy Research in Education.

Mitchell, K. J. 1995. "Reforming and Conforming: NASDC Principals Talk about the Impact of Accountability Systems on School Reform." Monograph/Report MR-716-NASDC. Santa Monica: RAND.

O'Day, J. A., and C. Bitter. 2003. "Evaluation Study of the Immediate Intervention/Underperforming Schools Program and the High Achieving/Improving Schools Program of the Public Schools Accountability Act of 1999." Final Report. Palo Alto: American Institutes of Research.

O'Day, J. A., and M. S. Smith. 1993. "Systemic Reform and Educational Opportunity." In *Designing Coherent Education Policy: Improving the System*, edited by S. H. Fuhrman (250–312). San Francisco: Jossey-Bass.

4

THE INFLUENCE OF STATES AND DISTRICTS ON COMPREHENSIVE SCHOOL REFORM

Naida Tushnet and Donna M. Harris

Comprehensive school reform (CSR) is both a concept for an approach to school improvement (Bodilly 1998; Datnow, Hubbard, and Mehan 2002) and a federal program (U.S. Department of Education, 2000a, b; *No Child Left Behind Act, Title I, Part F, Section 1606*) that provides funds for schools to adopt scientifically based strategies that cover curriculum, instruction, school organization, and parent involvement. Comprehensive school reform emerged as a response to some schools' persistent failure to provide students with opportunities to meet high educational standards. As state and federal governments heightened their emphasis on academic standards, they also increased their emphasis on school accountability in a concerted effort to ensure that students meet increasingly high standards. At both the federal and state levels, guidance and funds have been provided to help schools change so that students can succeed and achieve high standards. CSR is one mechanism for providing such assistance.

In 1998, Congress appropriated $145 million for the Comprehensive School Reform Demonstration program (CSRD). This program was designed to encourage schools to engage in a comprehensive effort to better meet student learning needs (U.S. Department of Education 2000a). CSRD definitely was not intended to be an add-on to existing programs and efforts, but instead was designed to encourage schools to integrate local, state, and federal resources to improve student learning (U.S. Department of Education 1999).

CSRD was intended to help schools leverage funds from both public and private sources. While gathering these funds, schools were expected to integrate programs that increased flexibility and accountability for student learning. The unique aspect of this program, relative to other Title I programs and the Improving America's Schools Act (the 1994 version of the Elementary and Secondary Education Act) was the expectation that schools would collaborate with expert partners to implement whole-school reform methods and strategies with a strong research base and a successful replication record (Hale 2000).

As its cornerstone, CSRD stipulated nine criteria that the funded schools' reform programs must meet (U.S. Department of Education 1999). The legislation also offered 17 programs as *examples* of the strategies schools might choose, but allowed schools to select other methods, combine strategies, or create their own reform programs (provided they met the nine criteria). Schools implemented different configurations of the nine components, with some schools focusing on fewer than all nine. In addition, some schools implemented multiple reform strategies such as a "process" model like Accelerated Schools and a content-oriented curriculum such as Connected Mathematics.

The CSRD appropriation spurred dramatic growth in school reform. Even prior to CSRD, more than 2,100 schools were affiliated with one of three schoolwide reform programs: Success for All, the School Development Project, and Accelerated Schools (Consortium for Policy Research in Education 1998). The CSRD initiative was expected to more than double the number of schools embarking on similar reform efforts (Consortium for Policy Research in Education 1998). As of September 2000, 1,800 schools had received CSRD funds (U.S. Department of Education 2000b). The next round of CSRD applications raised the number of funded schools to about 2,000. States such as Colorado, Hawaii, Wisconsin, and North Carolina have used the CSRD model to restructure their reform efforts, providing similar grants to districts in their states. Other states (Oregon, Tennessee, and West Virginia) used the CSRD model to guide how they distribute Title I and state school improvement funds (U.S. Department of Education 2000b).

With the passage of the No Child Left Behind Act (NCLB) in 2001, CSR became a fully authorized program and therefore is no longer considered a demonstration program. NCLB described 11 components of comprehensive school reform (figure 4.1)—two more than the original CSRD stipulated—and did not include a list of model strategies.

Of course, change and reform are complicated and demanding. For change to root itself firmly in improved practice, consistent leadership is needed, as is support from the district (Finnan 2000), as well as support from state policies. School reform is a political process requiring commitment from a broad range of constituencies, including teachers, parents, and the larger community. Developing this concerted commitment takes time. Previous research on comprehensive school reform underscores the need for time to complete implementation and achieve positive outcomes. In Bodily (1998), teachers say it took years

Figure 4.1. The 11 Components of Comprehensive School Reform, as Described in the No Child Left Behind Act

1. **Proven methods and strategies** for student learning, teaching, and school management that are derived from scientifically based research and effective practices, and have been replicated successfully in schools with diverse characteristics.
2. **Comprehensive design** for effective school functioning, that integrates instruction, assessment, classroom management, and professional development, and aligns these functions into a schoolwide reform plan designed to enable all students to meet challenging state content and performance standards and to address needs identified through a school needs assessment.
3. **Professional development for teachers and staff** that is high quality and continuous.
4. **Measurable goals** for student performance and benchmarks for meeting those goals.
5. **Support from staff**, including support from school faculty, administrators, and other staff.
6. **Support for staff**, including support for school faculty, administrators, and other staff (added in 2001).
7. **Parent and community involvement** in planning and implementing school improvement activities.
8. **External assistance and support** from a comprehensive school reform entity (which may be a university) with experience in schoolwide reform and improvement.
9. **Evaluation** of the implementation of school reforms and the student results achieved.
10. **Coordination of resources** (federal, state, local, or private) to help the school coordinate services that support and sustain the school's reform.
11. **Scientifically based research** to significantly improve the academic achievement of students participating in such programs (as compared with students in schools who have not participated in such programs), or strong evidence that such programs will significantly improve the academic achievement of participating children (added in 2001).

Source: No Child Left Behind Act.

before they understood some New American Schools (NAS) comprehensive designs sufficiently to implement them well, and Bodilly and
Berends (1999) find that after three years, many NAS designs still were
not fully implemented. Berends (2000) finds that CSR implementation
increased significantly between years one and two of implementation.

The length of time it takes to implement comprehensive reform
certainly affects outcomes. In a meta-analysis of comprehensive school
reform and achievement, Borman and his coauthors (2003) report that it
was only after the *fifth* year of implementation that student achievement
began to increase substantially. Schools that had implemented CSR
models for five years showed achievement advantages that were nearly
twice those found in CSR schools in general.

This chapter focuses on the roles of districts and states in implementing CSR, reflecting that schools are not independent entities but are
part of district and state systems. In this era of accountability, efforts
at comprehensive reform are increasingly influenced by district and
state policies. States and districts provide motivation for reform and
often provide support during implementation. At the same, these state
and district policies and initiatives may limit CSR implementation. For
example, Ross and Gil (2004) cite the case of Memphis, a city in which
one superintendent phased in the adoption of CSR models in all schools.
The next superintendent thought the reforms ineffective and eliminated the mandate, focusing instead on reading instruction. From a
more theoretical perspective, Smith and O'Day (1991) posit that reform
is most readily achieved when state, district, and school practices and
policies are aligned.

Although changes in federal funding may affect the CSR program,
the concept of comprehensive school reform can be closely tied to
accountability under NCLB. NCLB requires schools receiving Title I
funds to make "adequate yearly progress" (AYP) and prescribes a
progression of actions to be taken when schools fail to make AYP.
States are also required to develop a statewide system of school support
to assist schools that have been identified as requiring corrective action
or in need of improvement, based on their failure to make AYP. States,
therefore, can use the concept of comprehensive school reform, as well
as the CSR program, to help such low-performing schools make the
changes in curriculum, instruction, and school organization needed to
advance student achievement. In fact, in most states, the CSR program
is housed in the state's office for administering Title I, which would
facilitate the use of CSR in helping meet accountability requirements.

We draw from two sources: a national evaluation of the federal
CSR program (the Longitudinal Assessment of Comprehensive School
Reform Implementation and Outcomes—LACIO) conducted by
WestEd and the COSMOS Corporation and an evaluation of one

research-based model for school reform, America's Choice, conducted by the University of Pennsylvania's Consortium for Policy Research in Education (CPRE).

The LACIO evaluation employs multiple methods in a quasi-experimental design. The information reported in this chapter comes from interviews with representatives from 65 local education agencies and all 50 states conducted in 2005. The districts include urban, suburban, and rural districts. In addition, we draw on data from a survey of 500 schools that received CSR funding and a matched sample of 500 schools that had never received such funding at the time of the survey (spring 2004). LACIO also includes case studies of 15 CSR and 15 matched non-CSR schools, implemented in the spring and fall of 2004, as well as an analysis of student achievement outcomes in the 1,000 schools at the end of the 2003–2004 school year. LACIO focused on the following questions:

- How are CSR funds targeted?
- How is CSR implemented in schools receiving CSR funds, in schools receiving Title I funds, and in other schools?
- What is the relationship between CSR implementation and student achievement outcomes?
- What conditions at the state and district level influence the implementation of comprehensive reform programs?

This chapter draws primarily from data related to the fourth question.

The focus of CPRE's evaluation of CSR was to examine to what extent secondary schools were able to implement the America's Choice components and document factors that contributed and detracted from this process. In 2000, CPRE joined the National Center on Education and the Economy (NCEE) in preparing a proposal for a comprehensive school reform development grant from the U.S. Department of Education's Office of Educational Research and Improvement.[1] The proposal was subsequently funded for five years (2000–2004). CPRE's role was to document the development, implementation, and impact of the America's Choice design in middle and high schools.

CPRE's evaluation included ongoing and formative feedback to NCEE and America's Choice schools about emerging trends in the implementation of the design, as well as evidence of the impact of the design. CPRE's evaluation of America's Choice was guided by four questions:

- Were the pilot sites able to implement the design?
- What obstacles or problems were encountered by the schools as they implemented the design?

- How effective was the design support provided by NCEE?
- What were the effects of the design on teaching and learning?

To address these questions, the CPRE research team gathered a broad array of qualitative and quantitative data to develop a rich view of the implementation process over time and to capture the impact of the design on students and teachers. Data sources used in this chapter come from six America's Choice middle schools. Unlike the LACIO evaluation, the CPRE evaluation did not have comparison schools because it was primarily interested in the key factors that promoted and inhibited America's Choice implementation. Middle school data collection took place between fall 2001 and winter 2004 and included interviews with principals, school-level coaches, math and English teachers, guidance counselors, and leadership team members. Annual teacher and principal surveys were sent to a larger universe of America's Choice middle schools to gain a broader understanding about America's Choice implementation. CPRE research team members analyzed the data using appropriate qualitative and quantitative research methodologies to identify patterns of implementation, common problems, intended and unintended consequences, and effects of the design on students, teachers, and schools.

In the LACIO evaluation, explicit attention was paid to state and district policies as they align with the CSR program. States administer the CSR awards, and districts apply for the funds on behalf of the schools. This direct participation by both states and districts provides an opportunity for the proposed CSR activities at any given school to fit both the district's and state's reform-related priorities. Such alignment (e.g., between a district's reform initiatives and the complementary actions that might be supported with CSR in a given school) should increase the strength of CSR implementation. These reform initiatives and other actions might eventually also make the CSR effort more effective. If, on top of such alignment, both a district's and school's plans to implement CSR also embrace their state's standards and assessment practices, comprehensive school reform should promote student achievement even more potently. The America's Choice evaluation complements the portion of LACIO reported here, in CPRE's focus on how schools are affected by state and district policies and initiatives.

STATE AND DISTRICT INFLUENCE ON CSR IMPLEMENTATION

Within the federal CSR program, states are responsible for directing CSR funds to reform programs that include all 11 CSR program components. School districts also have a role in implementing CSR. They identify and support schools applying for CSR funds, provide support during implementation, and monitor outcomes. States decide how to allocate funds and also monitor implementation. These mechanisms ensure that schools meet state standards and advance educational reform. The data in the following section come from interviews conducted in 2004 with staff responsible for the CSR program in the 50 state education agencies, as well as from documents, such as grant announcements and regulations, prepared by those agencies.

CSR Eligibility and Award Criteria

Most states and districts gave priority for CSR funding to low-performing and high-poverty schools. Twenty-nine states (58 percent) targeted schools that were either low performing, high poverty, or both. The remaining 21 states (42 percent) established no priority. Among districts, 62 percent targeted selected schools for reform and 7 percent of those *required* selected schools to apply for CSR funds. The remaining 38 percent of districts identified *all* schools as eligible to apply for funds.

In addition to state policies that determine CSR eligibility, states further targeted funds by the criteria used to award grants. Thirteen states (26 percent) considered only the merit of the CSR proposals when reviewing grant applications. Another 27 (54 percent) awarded CSR funds based on the merit of the CSR proposals, while also weighting applications for schools with demonstrated academic need. Six states (12 percent) funded only schools identified as underperforming. One state, for example, listed all schools identified in need of improvement and provided CSR funds to the most "in need," working through the list until the funds ran out. The remaining four states (8 percent) indicated they had no firm policy on awarding CSR grants.

States' different approaches to determining awards yielded different distributions of the schools receiving funds. When merit was the only criterion, fewer high-poverty schools received CSR awards (38 percent, as compared with 45 percent of all schools receiving CSR funds) (figure 4.2).

As a further effort to ensure that low-performing schools (which frequently have limited capacity to prepare grant proposals) were able to compete successfully for funds, states and districts provided information to schools, a responsibility noted in the federal guidance for CSR. This support largely focused on identifying research-based strategies. Nearly 80 percent of the states (40 states) and 84 percent of districts provided information on research-based reform strategies. Within this group, 19 states (48 percent of the 40 states) reported providing information on how to assess claims about research-based strategies. Fewer (10 states, or 25 percent of the 40) said they provided a list of recommended

Figure 4.2. Effect of Comprehensive School Reform Award Criteria on Targeting to High-Need Schools

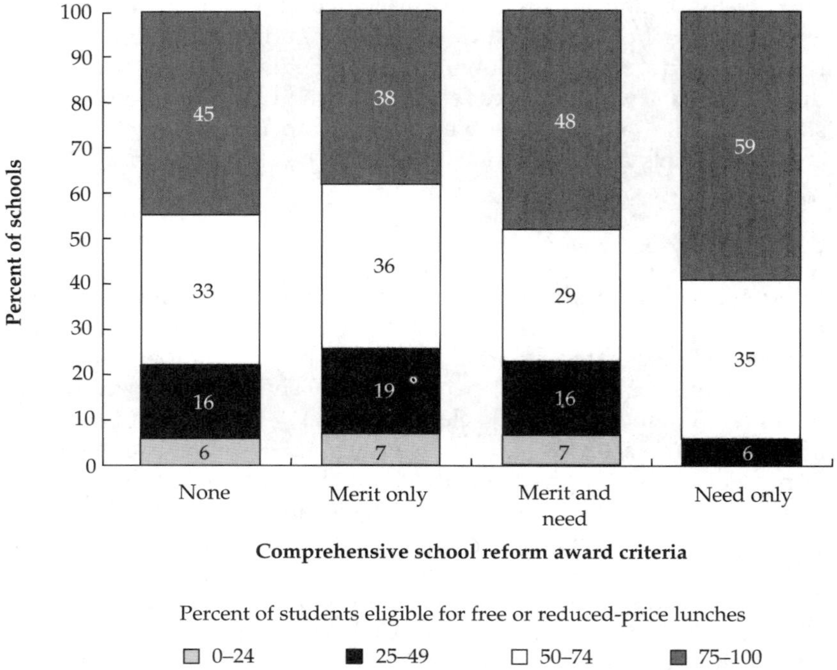

Comprehensive school reform award criteria

Percent of students eligible for free or reduced-price lunches

☐ 0–24   ■ 25–49   ☐ 50–74   ■ 75–100

Source: National Center for Educational Statistics Common Core of Data (2005); Tushnet et al. (2005).

strategies to potential grantees (figure 4.3). In several cases, the list of approved strategies came from the National Clearinghouse for Comprehensive School Reform web site.[2] At least two states, one of which chose America's Choice, selected the reform strategy to be implemented in its low-performing schools. Schools from that state are included in the discussion of America's Choice implementation.

Districts were slightly more likely than states to disseminate information to CSR sites on research-based models, but the type of information provided differed from that provided by states. Districts most often (40 percent) reported giving sites a list of identified or recommended models from which to choose. Only 31 percent of districts provided general information about research-based approaches to potential CSR sites (figure 4.3).

In addition to providing information about CSR, states and districts provided support to schools in preparing proposals. Most states (34, or 68 percent) reported hosting proposal- or grant-writing workshops specifically related to CSR. In a few cases, state employees wrote a

Figure 4.3. Information Disseminated to Comprehensive School Reform Applicants on Research-Based Strategies

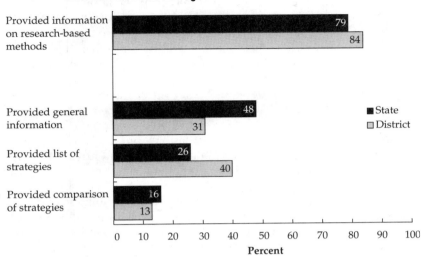

Source: Tushnet et al. (2005).

school's grant application. Districts also provided support to schools, but in different ways. Only 16 percent of districts reported hosting grant-writing workshops, which is not surprising given the high percentage of states that provided such service. District support varied from providing sites with "application templates" and examples of successful applications to reviewing applications before they were submitted to the state. Districts also gave data to schools to use in assessing their needs. As with states, a small number of districts identified a single or limited number of strategies from which schools could choose. Such an approach had effects that were both positive (e.g., increased the district's ability to support school-level implementation, developed a pool of prepared administrators who could continue implementation despite principal turnover) and negative (e.g., lack of buy-in at the school site, delayed or diminished implementation).

One example of district support is a district that helped its schools select a strategy and apply for CSR funds. The district encouraged schools to participate in state workshops on writing a CSR application, so school staff would get a broad understanding of the program and application requirements. The district then worked with individual schools to assess their needs and develop an approach that suited the school and matched the state and district priorities. The district included school board members in the application process.

State and District Roles in Monitoring and Evaluating CSR

Federal guidelines instruct states to monitor and evaluate comprehensive school reform efforts. As a result, all states indicated that they monitored CSR sites. Thirty-two (64 percent) reported that they conducted site visits to CSR schools, while slightly more than half (26, or 52 percent) required "periodic progress reports." Thirty-three states (66 percent) required a formal written evaluation plan to assess the progress of CSR efforts statewide. Nearly all of the evaluation plans (31, or 62 percent) included some student performance indicators. Just under half (24, or 48 percent) of states gathered data on the quality of CSR implementation. Included in evaluations, but at a more modest level, were data on parent participation in reform (addressed by 10 states, 20 percent) and staff development (addressed by 12 states, 24 percent) (figure 4.4).

Many districts also reported that they conducted evaluations of CSR. Over one-half (53 percent) of the districts required local evaluations of CSR sites. Half of these (24 percent of all district respondents) said the evaluation requirements were specific to the district. The remaining districts responded to external requirements, typically a state-mandated evaluation. However, according to respondents, local evaluations were less likely to assess student outcomes than were state evaluations (52 percent, compared with 62 percent). More local evalua-

Figure 4.4. Monitoring and Evaluation of Comprehensive School Reform, According to State and District Respondents

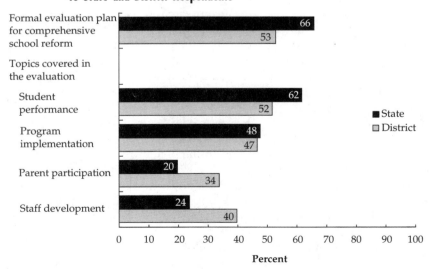

Source: Tushnet et al. (2005).

tions monitored parent participation (34 percent) and staff development efforts (40 percent) than did state evaluations (figure 4.4).

CSR Coordination with Other Reforms

State and district involvement in reform facilitates integration and alignment of CSR with state and district education priorities. However, states differed in the extent to which they used CSR to advance a state reform agenda, and this difference was reflected in the types of activities in which they engaged.

In nearly three-quarters of the states (36, or 72 percent), officials saw CSR as a way to help schools meet state standards and succeed in the state testing program. One state CSR coordinator, for example, noted that the CSR focus on *comprehensive* reform spurred the state to expand its improvement efforts beyond mathematics and language arts. Another noted that the state was using the CSR program to drive other reforms, and that the state had instructed schools implementing other reform programs to consider the 11 CSR components. In such states, CSR was closely tied to the state accountability program.

Thirteen states (26 percent) reported that federal NCLB guidelines drove reform—and CSR—in their state. One state CSR coordinator explained that CSR was beginning to "take a back seat" to concerns over the adequate yearly progress (AYP) requirements of NCLB and the subsequent emphasis on testing. Furthermore, the perceived uncertain future of CSR funding meant this state did not fully integrate CSR efforts with other reforms. Another CSR coordinator noted that the state used federal regulations and guidelines on student achievement, particularly those requiring testing, to determine statewide educational improvement goals and priorities. In contrast with staff in states that viewed CSR as aligned with state and federal accountability, respondents in these states did not view comprehensive school reform as helping schools achieve state and NCLB goals.

District officials often echoed the view that CSR was an important piece of state reform efforts. More than half (52 percent) of the districts indicated that CSR helped schools meet state standards and testing requirements. Only 12 percent of the responding districts saw CSR as primarily serving federal requirements and guidelines.

However, 16 percent of districts developed goals for CSR, mainly guided by local reform concerns that were not always aligned with the state reform program. For example, one school district used CSR to implement its school improvement plan. In another case, the district chose CSR as a vehicle for implementing AVID in all secondary schools.[3] The respondent explained that "we were looking for a program to initiate in the high schools and AVID (through CSR) was it."

There are, then, two groups of districts that did not align CSR with state priorities. One group saw the CSR program simply as a way to provide additional funds to high-priority schools. In such cases, the district played little role in implementation and did not attend to whether the school efforts were aligned with state content standards. A second group of districts had priorities that were not aligned with the state reform program. Those districts provided support to schools, but in many instances the schools were torn between implementing the district program and attending to state standards and assessments. The two types of districts were found both in states that aligned CSR and those that did not. Consequently, we found ruptures in the vertical alignment that mitigated the influence on CSR implementation.

Further, because schools are more closely tied to district than to state policies, changes at the district level were more apt to disrupt CSR implementation. In two large districts in the LACIO sample, for example, a new superintendent was appointed after schools had adopted their CSR strategy. The new superintendent did not abolish CSR efforts, as in Memphis, but mandated particular district strategies. The schools, then, were faced with implementing two challenging reforms—to the detriment of both.

As schools implement a CSR strategy, then, they face decisions about the extent to which they respond to the strategy's requirements or focus primarily on state and district policies. If the strategy and the policies—particularly testing and accountability requirements—are aligned, schools can respond to both. However, in many cases, a disconnect between a particular CSR strategy and state and district policies is perceived, and schools must decide between the two. At the very least, when school personnel perceive differences between the CSR strategy and state and district requirements, they must take time to figure out what to do. That time can detract from CSR implementation, as illustrated by the evaluation of America's Choice.

THE CHALLENGES OF IMPLEMENTING COMPREHENSIVE SCHOOL REFORM

The evaluation of America's Choice provides insight into how six middle schools navigated the path of implementing a CSR strategy and adhering to state and district policies, particularly accountability policies. As LACIO indicates, implementation is easier when the CSR model is aligned with state and district policies. However, schools respond to the immediate press of state and district policies, particularly policies related to accountability, frequently postponing or derailing CSR implementation. Despite the intentions of state and district policies and initiatives, they do not always support the implementation of CSR.

America's Choice, a K–12 comprehensive school reform design developed by the National Center on Education and the Economy (NCEE), has been implemented in hundreds of schools nationwide, many underperforming. According to NCEE, "the America's Choice design was a systematic school design intended to raise ALL students to World Class Standards of performance" (National Center on Education and the Economy 2000).[4] America's Choice provides schools with an English language arts curriculum, mathematics lessons, and an adolescent reading program. All schools are expected to organize students and teachers into teams and follow a block schedule: an opening session mini-lesson; a work period focusing on individual or small-group assignments; and a closing period for students to share their work and the teacher to review key concepts. Large schools are also expected to break up into boarding school–style houses (i.e., intergrade groups of students who associate for their entire careers at the school).

To understand implementation in America's Choice middle schools, CPRE and NCEE initially selected six pilot schools that reflect varying demographics and locations. Most important, pilot schools were required to commit at least three years to the research study. One of the six schools initially selected declined to participate. CPRE did not replace this school during the first year of data collection, as it was unable to find a school that would commit to the three-year involvement. However, a sixth middle school was added in the second year of data collection.

A team of CPRE researchers visited five of the six pilot schools five times between fall 2001 and winter 2004. The sixth school was visited three times over two years. During 2001–2002 and 2002–2003, each school was visited twice during the academic year, usually in the fall and spring. All final visits were completed by early winter 2004. During these visits, teachers and administrators were interviewed, classes were observed, and artifacts (including student work) were examined. In most cases, district and NCEE support personnel were interviewed in person or by telephone. CPRE staff observed professional development sessions and other meetings for middle grades coaches and leadership. In addition, CPRE examined NCEE curriculum and professional development materials and manuals.

The six pilot middle schools were located in Florida, Georgia, and New York. All but one were located in an urban area. The school enrollments varied, with the smallest school serving 314 students and the largest, 1,675 students. All six schools served racially diverse student populations, with two schools serving a sizable population of English-language learners. Across these schools, the majority of students were eligible for free or reduced-price lunches; all students in one school were eligible for this program. Although these six middle schools differed in size, geographical location, and demographics, they shared considerable commitment to, and appreciation for, America's Choice. Within each school, a cadre of the teaching staff seemed aware of the design and was involved with its implementation.

In general, these schools were low performing and adopted the America's Choice model to assist with improving student performance on state tests. During 2001–2002, two schools were designated by their respective state boards of education as needing improvement. One school's involvement with America's Choice was the result of a state-wide policy to target America's Choice to low-performing elementary and middle schools and district leadership's subsequent decision to adopt it. A fourth middle school was at risk of coming under state review. The spring 2001 state test scores for the other two pilot middle schools indicated average student performance. However, the spring 2002 test scores brought a drop in accountability status for one of these schools. As a result, all six of the middle schools had strong incentives to improve student performance.

State Accountability Contexts

The major influence on CSR implementation came from the state accountability systems. All six America's Choice middle schools were located in states with high-stakes accountability systems that required student assessment in reading, writing, and mathematics in the middle grades. Table 4.1 shows assessment requirements by state during the time of data collection, between 2001 and 2003.

Each state developed curricular frameworks and standards to provide all students with a common curriculum and focused instruction to improve student achievement. The pressure to achieve proficiency on state assessments was intended to improve instruction and student outcomes. For example, Florida, Georgia, and New York schools are rated by an index created from student performance. In these three states, schools with low student performance are required to make plans for improvement. In Georgia, a school improvement team may be assigned low-performing schools. In Florida, financial incentives are provided to schools with a D grade. Also, Florida allows students to transfer to other schools in their district if their school received two consecutive grades of F.

As reported in LACIO, states viewed CSR as a vehicle to help schools help students meet standards and prepare them for the state test. Respondents from the six middle schools also shared this belief and

Table 4.1. Middle School Accountability Systems by State

State	Assessment system	School requirements
Florida	Florida Comprehensive Assessment Test Grade 8 Testing in areas of reading, math, writing, and science	Schools required to obtain a school grade (on a scale of A–F) of C or higher.
Georgia	Criterion-Referenced Competency Test Grades 6–8 Testing in areas of reading, English/language arts, math, social studies, and science	Schools required to obtain a school grade (on a scale of A–F) of C or higher. School grades based on absolute student performance and yearly gains from prior years. D or F schools are provided school improvement teams. Long-term low performance could lead to school takeover or closure.
New York	Grade 8 Testing in areas of English/language arts, math, social studies, and science	Middle schools must have 90% of students at or above level 2 and the majority of students must test at level 3 or above. Low school performance leads to registration review. High performance leads to greater flexibility in the use of school resources.

Source: Goertz and Duffy (2001).

indicated that their involvement with America's Choice would help them meet the demands of the state accountability system.

However, though the states and schools agreed that CSR was useful, state and district policies and initiatives often had a contradictory impact on CSR implementation. Schools' adaptation to the accountability policies hindered America's Choice implementation in a number of ways. Responding to the pressure from the state accountability system, district and state entities took actions aimed at assisting low-performing schools. These state- and district-imposed actions also posed considerable challenges to a number of America's Choice middle schools. Although challenges did not prevent the schools from fully adopting all aspects of America's Choice, they either slowed down or modified implementation of the design.

School Responses

America's Choice middle schools had various responses to demands from the state accountability system. Some schools abandoned the America's Choice curriculum to focus on test preparation. At least one of the six middle schools abandoned the curriculum before state test administration in favor of a schoolwide focus on test preparation. CPRE researchers were unable to schedule a visit to this school before the spring's state test, because of the school's focus on test preparation. This school also created temporary groups for students who had not achieved proficiency on the state test, or were at risk of not achieving proficiency. Although test preparation lasted no more than a few weeks, it detracted from America's Choice implementation and limited use of the America's Choice standards-based curriculum.

As with temporary suspension of America's Choice, state accountability policies affected curriculum implementation. Teachers were conflicted about the demands of the accountability system and the America's Choice goals. Some did not have sufficient time to cover the content on the state test and attend to America's Choice standards. Teachers in one New York middle school had difficulty covering both the required state English language arts and America's Choice curricula. Others indicated that, while America's Choice fostered deep conceptual understanding, it did not cover all content tested on their state assessments. In contrast, other teachers indicated that America's Choice concepts could be easily expanded to cover required test content. In short, teachers may abandon America's Choice because state test scores are the ones that count for schools, teachers, and students. However, CPRE's evaluation did not systematically examine the alignment between America's Choice curriculum and standards and the state curriculum frameworks and assessments.

As a result of the high-stakes accountability environment, schools are under tremendous pressure to assess students across grades and subjects. Federal mandates to test in all of the middle grades adds to state pressures. Furthermore, local districts often administer their own standardized assessments. In one district we visited, the yearly Stanford Diagnostic Reading Test was administered in middle schools. Testing multiple times within an academic year and over consecutive years makes it difficult for schools to administer an additional assessment such as the New Standards Reference Exam (NSRE).[5]

The demands of state and local standardized tests and additional costs associated with administering and scoring the NSRE limited its use in America's Choice middle and high schools. Although many of the schools involved with America's Choice during its first three years of scaling up used the NSRE, these schools, including one New York middle school, abandoned it because of cost and lack of alignment with state tests. In addition, the NSRE became irrelevant as state accountability systems imposed school-level and grade-specific consequences for the state tests. The penalties associated with the state assessment prompted teachers and schools to focus on it exclusively. NCEE could do little to compete with federal and state mandates for accountability. As a result, NCEE has modified its expectations for the NSRE and it has become relatively obsolete.

The demise of the NSRE also posed challenges for NCEE, as they lost a source of data to measure impact on student achievement across school districts and states. In partnership with CPRE, NCEE intended to conduct a longitudinal analysis of the America's Choice impact on achievement across many of their schools. Since assessments varied across states, NCEE and CPRE researchers intended to use NSRE as a common assessment. Without these data, no common metric was available to examine the impact of America's Choice on student achievement across schools. As result, they have resorted to conducting state-by-state analysis of achievement (May, Supovitz, and Lesnick 2004; May, Supovitz, and Perda 2004; Supovitz and May 2003; Supovitz, Taylor, and May 2002).

The demands to improve student performance led one district using America's Choice to put their principals on one-month contracts at the end of the 2002–2003 school year. A middle school principal in this district suggested that administrators would be replaced if student performance did not improve. During the following summer, this district made massive changes in school leadership by transferring and replacing principals among its elementary, middle, and high schools. Two principals from the America's Choice middle schools visited by CPRE were transferred. One was transferred to a high school and continued to serve as a principal. However, the second was sent to another school in the district but was not assigned as the principal. This district shake-up had the potential to stifle America's Choice progress throughout the school system. However, the principals selected as replacements had prior experience with America's Choice. One principal was promoted from within the middle school, having previously served as its vice principal. The second principal had been an administrator in a neighboring middle school also involved with America's Choice. Therefore, these schools were able to continue with America's Choice, although teachers had to become accustomed to the new leadership's approach. The continuation of America's Choice illustrates the positive side of districtwide adoption of a CSR strategy.

The state-imposed consequences that result from chronic low performance also hindered CSR implementation. For example, when a school receives two consecutive grades of F, Florida's department of education allows its students to transfer to another district school. A policy such as this can pose serious challenges for any school receiving student transfers, especially schools with average or below-average achievement. Such accountability policies can impede CSR implementation. For example, one middle school CPRE visited in fall 2003 had recently enrolled approximately 100 transfers from low-performing schools in the district. The influx of low-performing students, many of whom had not been exposed to America's Choice, posed teaching challenges. This school's literacy coach stated, "We are having a lot of discipline problems, but they are coming from the opportunity schools [the failing schools in the district] and they don't understand the expectations. It [America's Choice] was absent in the previous school." Therefore, this situation has great potential to limit America's Choice implementation within classrooms, when teachers must simultaneously confront discipline problems and expose students to unfamiliar concepts and curricula. As a result, the influx of students from poorly performing schools could deflate the 2003–2004 schoolwide performance across grades. In fact, in 2002–2003, this school received a grade of C, and during 2003–2004, its grade dropped to a D. Although many factors explain the drop in a school's grade, the presence of students who had performed poorly in their previous school may have contributed.

Statewide Adoption of America's Choice

In their efforts to help low-performing schools improve student outcomes, Georgia and Mississippi state departments of education selected America's Choice. NCEE suggests that Georgia, like many states, lacked the personnel required to provide intensive support to its low-performing schools (National Center on Education and the Economy 2005). A CSR model like America's Choice, adopted statewide for low-performing schools, can provide benefits. First, states can target resources to struggling schools that have the greatest need to improve. In 2001, Georgia allocated state funds to approximately 160 low-performing schools for America's Choice curriculum, materials, and professional development (May, Supovitz, and Lesnick 2004). State department of education employees trained in America's Choice provided in-school support. During 2001–2002, one Georgia pilot school was assigned a state department of education employee as a full-time coach, who assisted with implementing the America's Choice curriculum by working with individual teachers in classrooms and by modeling teaching strategies. Another state employee acted as a liaison between the state department of education, districts, and schools. The liaison supported the work of the leadership team and was also responsible for collecting data about progress in America's Choice schools that was fed back to the district and state department of education.

Although state-level support is important, implementation can initially be hampered when schools have no say in model adoption, because school personnel may not buy into the program. In one middle school, some staff responsible for America's Choice implementation initially resisted. Although the school officials acknowledged the need to improve, they were excluded from the decision to adopt America's Choice. But despite initial hesitation, the school's administration and teachers saw value in implementing the program and had plans to move forward during the second year. This matter was made worse when the state-employed coach and the state-designated school liaison became critical of the school's progress; school personnel were removed at the end of the first year as a result and were replaced by district personnel who were familiar with America's Choice and had a commitment to promoting its implementation.

Like in Georgia, Mississippi education officials selected America's Choice to aid with school improvement. Although CPRE did not collect data in these schools, newspaper accounts indicate that this partnership began during the 2003–2004 academic year and, as of the 2004–2005 school year, approximately 50 elementary and middle schools were implementing America's Choice. Although Mississippi officials promoted the use of America's Choice, low-performing schools and districts had the final say about whether they would implement the design (Richard 2004). Mississippi's strategy of voluntary adoption promoted the likelihood that administrators and teachers would have an initial commitment to employing the design. In situations where sufficient commitment cannot be achieved, schools will drop the design.

OTHER POLICY INFLUENCES ON COMPREHENSIVE SCHOOL REFORM

In addition to state accountability policies, teacher certification requirements, state budgets, and union issues posed challenges to these America's Choice pilot schools and forced them to modify schoolwide implementation.

Teacher Certification and Looping

The America's Choice model expected schools to implement looping, that is, teachers and students would stay together in core subjects from

6th through 8th grade. In some states, teacher certification requirements limited America's Choice schools from fully implementing this component. During the 2002–2003 school year, only 28 out of 105 America's Choice middle school principals who returned surveys indicated they had looping in place. One reason for the slow implementation is likely teacher certification requirements. For example, in Florida, elementary school–certified teachers were ineligible to teach beyond 6th grade. With their middle school (5–9) and secondary school certifications (6–12), 7th and 8th grade teachers were also eligible to teach 6th grade; however, this was not feasible because elementary school certification restrictions locked most 6th grade teachers into teaching grades K–6 only. Because certification varied across subjects and grades, teachers could not stay with their students for three years. Despite this challenge, one of the middle schools CPRE visited was able to implement looping with modifications. Groups of students stayed together from 6th through 8th grades and were taught by the same teachers in core subjects at 7th and 8th grades. This challenge is not limited to America's Choice schools in Florida, because other states have similar certification policies.

State certification regulations were not the only cause of looping's slow implementation. Among 105 America's Choice principals who responded to a 2002–2003 CPRE survey, only 28 had implemented this component. Another 30 principals indicated that they planned to implement looping during the 2003–2004 academic year. For some, this feature of the America's Choice design was not feasible because of the burden of teaching alternative grades and course content. Looping would require teaching new curriculum content and standards over a span of years. This is especially difficult in middle and high schools, where teachers may have expertise in specific subjects such as mathematics and science. Although the idea of having teachers move with students across grades may promote the continuity to create and sustain student engagement and achievement, the burden on teachers may be too high. In the end, the quality of instruction may suffer if teachers must adjust to a new curriculum each year rather than honing their skills at a specific grade and subject.

Budget

Although states and districts may promote the use of CSR models in their schools, state budget issues posed a potential threat to America's Choice implementation. During CPRE's visits to their six America's Choice middle schools, personnel shared their concern about whether funds would be available to continue officially with this CSR model.

However, all six middle schools were able to continue with America's Choice over the course of our evaluation.

Budget limitations became a prominent issue especially after September 11, 2001, when states confronted severe budget deficits that required cuts in such local district line items as travel. During the 2001–2002 academic year, America's Choice schools in one Florida district encountered implementation challenges when prior to the start of the year, funds were cut by almost 50 percent. Schools were unable to expand existing programs and were forced to make budget cuts. In one school CPRE visited, the principal indicated that the school had to cut elective courses with low enrollment, such as band and shop, as result of limited funds. An administrative position was also cut to fund the America's Choice literacy coach, a key person responsible for providing professional development to English teachers and assisting them with implementing the America's Choice English arts curriculum. In addition, no funds were available for travel to America's Choice professional development events and the annual conference.[6] These budget issues had the potential of impeding the America's Choice implementation. However, the school had a resourceful principal, and discretionary funds from the parent-teacher organization paid school representatives' annual conference expenses.

Budget constraints and teacher certification requirements were bothersome for these six middle schools, but they were able to overcome these obstacles. However, if such issues were confronted in schools without a supportive district or parent-teacher organization, their ability to implement specific America's Choice components could have been severely limited.

District Union Contracts

Union contracts in some states like New York prevented consistent professional development among all teachers. The teacher contract in one district did not allow America's Choice professional development to be mandatory during after-school hours. America's Choice schools in this district had to find ways to address contractual constraints while providing the professional development needed to sustain the program. One New York school provided professional development after school but gave stipends for teacher attendance. Attendance was still voluntary, guaranteeing that not all teachers would participate.

Conclusions

The LACIO and America's Choice evaluations provide important insights about how state departments of education, districts, and schools understand and use CSR to meet the demands of state and federal accountability systems. The LACIO data show that state departments of education and districts play a prominent role in CSR selection and funding. Generally, states are responsible for allocating CSR funds and tend to target funds to low-performing and/or high-poverty schools. Both districts and states assist schools with the selection of research-based models, as well as with their formal applications for funds. In a limited number of cases, the state or district selects the CSR models to be used in schools. Also, state departments of education and districts monitor the implementation and impact of these initiatives.

Most states view CSR as a means of helping schools further their accountability agendas and do not intend for testing policies to undermine implementation. Although state departments of education, districts, and schools believe that CSR can help with meeting the demands of state accountability policies, the America's Choice evaluation indicates that schools often feel constrained by such policies. In such cases, state and district policies pose challenges for CSR implementation. Most of the time, the six America's Choice middle schools met the challenge of modifying the America's Choice components. However, sometimes the challenge was met by eliminating an America's Choice component. The America's Choice findings show that support at the time of adoption—and even with implementation—is not sufficient.

Other state policies and programs may hinder rather than facilitate change through comprehensive school reform. As the America's Choice evaluation indicates, for example, no state advocates "teaching to the test." However, the evaluation data show that teachers worried about how their efforts to implement America's Choice would relate to their students' performance on the state test, leading to slippage in implementation. Although the America's Choice staff has worked with several states to align its New Standards performance measures with state standards, the result has not always informed teacher practice.

Other studies, have shown that changes in leadership, particularly at the district and school level, may also hinder CSR implementation. In at least two large districts in the LACIO evaluation, the new leadership has brought in new—and somewhat competing—programs. The middle schools in the America's Choice evaluation were not affected by changes in leadership, perhaps because they were in districts with a concentration of schools involved in the model. Therefore, when school leaders were replaced, the district could draw on a pool of administrators within the system who had experience with America's Choice. Such circumstances are likely to be unusual.

As states and districts strive to meet the NCLB accountability requirements, they continue to seek both funds and intellectual resources to help low-performing schools achieve AYP. If schools are able to align their policies, comprehensive school reform strategies can serve as an important resource. If they do not do so, CSR sustainability will be challenged.

NOTES

1. In 2002, federal legislation reauthorized the Office of Educational Research and Improvement, which is now known as the Institute for Education Sciences.

2. http://www.csrclearinghouse.org/

3. AVID, or Advancement Via Individual Determination, is "an in-school academic support program for grades 5–12 that prepares students for college eligibility and success" (http://www.avidonline.org/info/?tabid=1&ID=548).

4. America's Choice assumes that only students who are severely handicapped will be unable to reach the standards.

5. During the initial development of America's Choice, all schools were expected to administer the New Standards Reference Exam, an assessment aligned with America's Choice curriculum and standards.

6. Although teachers and administrators were able to attend America's Choice professional development held outside the district during the early summer of 2001, they were not able to attend follow-up professional development meetings held the following fall and winter and the 2002 America's Choice national conference. Attendance at the America's Choice professional development follow-up and the national conference were expected for all schools to support continuing implementation of the design. The national conference allowed teachers and administrators to network with peer institutions, attend presentations about approaches to America's Choice implementation, and display students' work.

REFERENCES

Berends, M. 2000. "Teacher-Reported Effects of New American Schools Design: Exploring Relationships to Teacher Background and School Context." *Educational Evaluation and Policy Analysis* 22(1): 65–82.

Bodilly, S. J. 1998. "Lessons from New American Schools' Scale-Up Phase: Prospects for Bringing Designs to Multiple Schools." Monograph/Report MR-942-NAS. Santa Monica: RAND.

Bodilly, S. J., and M. Berends. 1999. "Necessary District Support for Comprehensive School Reform." In *Hard Work for Good Schools: Facts, not Fads, in Title I Reform*, edited by G. Orfield and E. H. DeBray (111–19). Cambridge, MA: Harvard University Press.

Borman, G. D., G. M. Hewes, L. T. Overman, and S. Brown. 2003. "Comprehensive School Reform and Achievement: A Meta-Analysis." *Review of Educational Research* 73(2): 125–230.

Consortium for Policy Research in Education. 1998. *CPRE Policy Briefs*. Philadelphia: University of Pennsylvania.

Datnow, A., L. Hubbard, and H. Mehan. 2002. *Extending Education Reform: From One School to Many*. London: RoutledgeFarmer.

Finnan, C. 2000. *Implementing School Reform Models: Why Is It so Hard for Some Schools and Easy for Others?* Paper presented at the American Educational Research Association annual meeting, New Orleans, April 24–28.

Goertz, M. E., and M. C. Duffy. 2001. "Assessment and Accountability Systems in the 50 States: 1999–2000." Research Report RR-046. Philadelphia: University of Pennsylvania, Consortium for Policy Research in Education.

Hale, S. 2000. *Comprehensive School Reform: Research-Based Strategies to Achieve High Standards.* San Francisco: WestEd.

May, H., J. A. Supovitz, and J. Lesnick. 2004. "The Impact of America's Choice on Writing Performance in Georgia: First-Year Results." Consortium for Policy Research in Education Report. Philadelphia: University of Pennsylvania.

May, H., J. A. Supovitz, and D. Perda. 2004. "A Longitudinal Study of the Impact of America's Choice on Student Performance in Rochester, NY, 1998–2003." Consortium for Policy Research in Education Report. Philadelphia: University of Pennsylvania.

National Center on Education and the Economy. 2000. *National Principals' Academy Notebook, August 2000.* Washington, DC: National Center on Education and the Economy.

———. 2005. "School Profiles: Summerville Middle School." http://www.ncee.org/acsd/results/profiles/summerville.jsp. (Accessed November 22, 2005.)

Richard, A. 2004. "At State's Urging, Mississippi Schools Use Reform Model." *Education Week,* October 13, 1.

Ross, S., and L. Gil. 2004. "The Past and Future of Comprehensive School Reform." In *Putting the Pieces Together: Lessons from Comprehensive School Reform Research,* edited by C. T. Cross (151–74). Washington, DC: National Clearinghouse for Comprehensive School Reform.

Smith, M. S., and J. A. O'Day. 1991. "Systemic School Reform." In *The Politics of Curriculum and Testing,* edited by S. H. Fuhnman and B. Malen (233–68). Bristol, PA: Falmer.

Supovitz, J. A., and H. May. 2003. "The Relationship between Teacher Implementation of America's Choice and Student Learning in Plainfield, NJ." Consortium for Policy Research in Education Report. Philadelphia: University of Pennsylvania.

Supovitz, J. A., B. S. Taylor, and H. May. 2002. "Impact of America's Choice on Student Performance in Duval County, Florida." Consortium for Policy Research in Education Report. Philadelphia: University of Pennsylvania.

Tushnet, N., J. Flaherty, A. Smith, C. Ormbsby, N. Gold, R. Yin, J. Burt, and E. Warner. 2005. *Longitudinal Assessment of CSR Implementation and Outcomes.* Washington, DC: U.S. Department of Education.

U.S. Department of Education. 1999. *Guidance on the Comprehensive School Reform Demonstration Program.* Washington, DC: U.S. Department of Education.

———. 2000a. *CSRD in the Field: Final Update.* Washington, DC: U.S. Department of Education.

———. 2000b. *Early Implementation of the Comprehensive School Reform Demonstration Program: Summary Report.* Washington, DC: U.S. Department of Education.

5

COMPREHENSIVE SCHOOL REFORM AS A DISTRICT STRATEGY

Brenda J. Turnbull

Policy Studies Associates set out to investigate comprehensive school reform as a district strategy for school improvement by drawing on an evolving vision of an effective use of comprehensive school reform models. In this vision, schools would benefit from two mutually reinforcing kinds of intervention: a model, bringing a complete package of new ideas and tested practices to improve instructional coherence throughout the school; and the steady, close-at-hand support and leadership for implementation that the school district would provide. Our study examined whether and how schools would experience something like this vision when districts decided to bring in comprehensive reform models.

For some years, those engaged in the policy and practice of comprehensive school reform have spoken of the district's power to support or undermine (Bodilly 1998; Datnow and Stringfield 2000; Slavin and Madden 2000). They have drawn on research indicating that a district's commitment of resources—including money, staff, and time—contributed to the continuation and institutionalization of initiatives for school improvement (Purnell and Hill 1992; Slavin and Madden 2000).

Our study of comprehensive reform as a district strategy for school improvement evaluated the experiences of schools where district leaders had brought in comprehensive models and had made some commitment to their implementation. We wanted to know how the key elements of models looked from the standpoint of participating teachers and principals, when mediated through district policy and procedures. We wondered to what extent adopters of comprehensive models perceived that district leaders endorsed their aims and approaches. We also wanted to know how teachers and principals experienced tangible support from their districts, such as routine assistance with curriculum and instruction, as they implemented models. In particular, we wondered about the dynamics of trying to implement a model: would guidelines and support from different sources reinforce one another and form a coherent push for reform; would the different sources of support instead present school staff with conflicting signals; or would districts simply cede their support role in some schools to the external assistance providers?

Related to our inquiry into the district role were questions about teachers' and principals' perceptions of the external models. Would teachers and principals think that comprehensive models adopted from outside the district offered something distinctive to their school, qualitatively different from other improvement efforts? And, whether or not they perceived the models that way, would their improvement efforts in fact receive a discernible boost when compared with other improvement efforts that were less comprehensive in design?

Thus, we wanted to understand not only the dynamics of the implementation effort but also its results within schools. We wanted to investigate the extent to which comprehensive models were producing their intended effect—focusing the energies of teachers and school leaders on shared purposes and more uniform instructional practices. This has always been a desired result of bringing in and supporting a well-developed model (Desimone 2002; Fashola and Slavin 1998), although experience has shown that implementation within schools may be uneven (Stringfield 1997). Research has indicated, also, that instructional coherence within a school leads to better results than the adoption of multiple initiatives for improvement (Newmann et al. 2001b). We viewed this conclusion as an important part of our conceptual framework, and we adapted some of our measures from the work of Newmann and his colleagues (2001 a, b).

Our study has spanned times and sites in which model implementation was not, in itself, a district goal. School improvement, however, was said to be important. We followed our districts and schools through the years 2001–2004, a period in which No Child Left Behind and the state policies that predated it were designed to compel a focus on accountability and school improvement. These might or might not be aligned with a school's comprehensive model, yet they were expected to take paramount importance for districts and schools. In this environment, virtually every school was urged to undertake serious improvement efforts of some kind. Our study looked at the ways in which the experience of implementing a comprehensive model was distinctive, when compared with the reform efforts of similar schools in the same districts.

MODELS AND OTHER REFORM EFFORTS

Unlike a good deal of research on comprehensive school reform, this study did not focus on the specific characteristics of particular models. For our purposes, the curricular or organizational approach that distinguishes one model from others was not very important. Schools in this study had adopted Accelerated Schools, America's Choice, Co-nect, Cornerstone, Direct Instruction, MicroSociety, Modern Red School-House, the Comer School Development Program, Success for All, and other externally developed models. We did not focus on the implementation of their particular approaches to school improvement.

Our study instead emphasized the cross-cutting characteristics that distinguish comprehensive school reform itself, as a policy and practice intervention, from other approaches to reform. For identification of these characteristics, we turned to the analysis developed by a predecessor of the Institute of Education Sciences, called the Office of Educational Research and Improvement (OERI), in the U.S. Department of Education. In the OERI analysis, some of the distinguishing characteristics of comprehensive school reform were strategic:

- an integrated set of supportive materials, frameworks, or guidelines;
- the capacity to provide sustained professional development, technical assistance, and other support for teachers, administrators, and others responsible for reform tasks;
- the capacity to support all systems in a school—organization, instruction, professional development, and management;
- the ability to engage all classrooms in implementing a common, articulated strategy to improve teaching and learning for all students; and
- assurances that teachers and administrators are held accountable for the reform and achieving its intended outcomes.

In addition, OERI identified key properties that must be inherent in the models themselves:

- model components are derived from research on effective practice;
- models have been developed and tested in one set of schools and have demonstrated capacity to meet the needs of other schools; and
- evidence has demonstrated the model's effectiveness in increasing student achievement.

The study collected data in schools that had adopted comprehensive models and also in matched comparison schools. The comparison schools were not blank slates during the study, of course. Their teachers were implementing curricula, availing themselves of professional development, and, in most cases, adopting one or more externally developed innovations for their classrooms. Some adapted elements of comprehensive reforms (e.g., the Core Knowledge model); many participated in district-initiated professional development on such topics as classroom questioning strategies or classroom management. Many had grant support for implementing their programs.

DISTRICT PRIORITIES

The study of district strategies followed a sample of schools located in four districts that had taken steps to use comprehensive reform as a district strategy—to a greater degree than most districts nationally. District leaders had expressed support for the comprehensive approach. They had made the support tangible by dedicating staff resources to the effort: each had designated an administrator as the district-level facilitator for comprehensive reform.

At the time of our first visits to districts, in 2002, their policy stances on comprehensive reform ranged from advocacy to tolerance. None had taken the step of requiring every school to adopt a comprehensive model, but three had offered some degree of encouragement for such models, and the fourth had approved of model adoption as part of several schools' required improvement plans.

- District A, with about 20,000 students attending about 40 schools, had a superintendent who believed in the value of comprehensive models and encouraged all the schools to adopt one.
- District B, with about 30,000 students and about 60 schools, supported comprehensive models as a vehicle for improving failing schools and for supplementing the district's admittedly inadequate

professional development. Both the superintendent and another senior central-office administrator championed the use of models.

- District C, with about 50,000 students and 100 schools, took a more eclectic approach to school improvement but helped schools apply for grants from the Comprehensive School Reform Demonstration (CSRD) program.
- District D, with about 50,000 students and 85 schools, placed a high priority on improvement plans for failing schools. Top administrators expressed skepticism about the merits of externally developed programs but encouraged their failing schools to select models and apply for CSRD grants. Some schools that had high student achievement also took the opportunity to adopt models and apply for grants.

RESEARCH APPROACH

The study design was longitudinal and comparative. Repeated measures allowed us to trace the events of implementation and to look at the maturation of comprehensive school reform in districts and schools. We surveyed teachers and principals in three consecutive school years, in spring 2002, 2003, and 2004. All teachers in the study schools (kindergarten through 6th grade) were surveyed. Members of the research team visited all the participating schools in 2002 and 2004. The site visits included individual interviews with principals and district staff, and focus groups with teachers. Questions posed in the surveys and interviews were largely the same from year to year.

The study's comparative approach was primarily geared to assessing what, if anything, proved to be distinctive about adoption of a comprehensive model as a reform strategy. The schools in our study sample were 34 that had adopted a comprehensive reform and 34 comparison schools. Within each of the four districts, each adopting school was paired with a comparison school matched on prior achievement, size, and demographic composition. The questions posed in surveys and on site visits were largely identical for adopting schools and comparison schools, enabling us to learn how the teachers and principals in comparison schools viewed their own journey toward school improvement and how, if at all, this differed from the perceptions and activities found in adopting schools.

REFORM IS ALL AROUND: SOME SURPRISING COMPARISONS

Did teachers in schools that had adopted comprehensive models report a sense that their reform was especially coherent and that they were experiencing a well-integrated system of support? Or, to put it another way, did teachers in the comparison schools have a *lesser* sense of a coherent, schoolwide journey toward improvement?

Principals' reports bore out our belief that in virtually any school, one or more reforms are under way at any given time. To get a gross characterization of our schools' reform landscapes, we asked a simple question of the principals: "How many reform initiatives are currently under way at your school?" In each year, most of the principals in schools that had adopted comprehensive models answered "one," although 35 to 40 percent reported having at least two reform initiatives. Most principals of the comparison schools reported having at least two reform initiatives.

The survey questions posed to teachers in adopting schools and comparison schools were identical, except that for the adopting schools the survey asked about "your reform model" and in comparison schools "your reform effort." We had assumed that in any school, professionals are likely to believe they are engaged in some sort of improvement, and this was apparently the case. Overwhelmingly, teachers in the comparison schools were willing to report on their experience with a "reform effort."

Most of the comparison schools, as just mentioned, reported having two or more reform initiatives under way, whereas the schools with comprehensive models more often reported having only one reform in progress. This difference might suggest a greater degree of focus in the schools with comprehensive models. Nevertheless—and surprisingly—it was the teachers in comparison schools who reported, on average, higher levels of various kinds of coherence in the reform they were undertaking.

Teachers in Comparison Schools Perceived Their Reforms as More Clearly Specified

Because comprehensive reform models had substantial investments in research and development, they were intended to offer the benefits of careful, thorough development. However, our study findings indicated that these benefits were not necessarily perceived by participating teachers. When asked about the instructional plan and goals that their reform offered, it was the teachers in comparison schools who were more likely to agree the reform offered clarity and detail. In 2001–2002, teachers were given a series of statements about their reform. The responses are shown here on a scale from 0.0 (strongly disagree) to 3.0 (strongly agree). The mean response in both sets of schools was close to 2.0 (agree). However, compared with teachers in the schools that had adopted comprehensive models, teachers in the comparison schools expressed greater agreement with two statements (figure 5.1):

- The school reform defines clear instructional goals for students.
- The model/reform provides a detailed plan for improving instruction in our school.

By 2003–2004, those differences remained, and others had emerged (figure 5.2). The teachers in comparison schools were also agreeing in greater numbers with another, related assertion:

- The steps the model/reform provides for improving instruction are carefully staged and sequenced.

The teachers in comparison schools also reported having more complete information; they were *less* apt to agree with the following statement:

- I often have to fill in the gaps in information from the school reform model before I can use it in my classroom.

Teachers in Comparison Schools Reported Learning Opportunities

Not only did the teachers in comparison schools perceive they were engaged in a reform with comparatively clear goals and complete

Figure 5.1. Average Scale Score in 2001–2002 on Clarity of Schools' Plans to Improve Instruction, by School Type

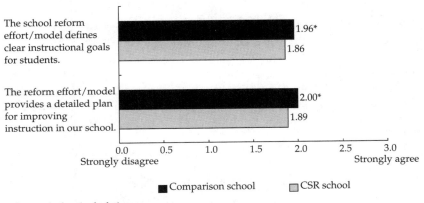

Source: Authors' calculations.
CSR = comprehensive school reform
*p < .05

Figure 5.2. Average Scale Score in 2003–2004 on Clarity of Schools' Plans to Improve Instruction, by School Type

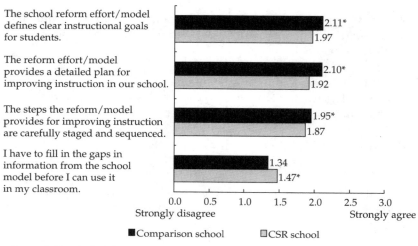

Source: Authors' calculations.
CSR = comprehensive school reform
*p < .05

information, they also reported that their reforms offered them plentiful and useful learning opportunities. In 2001–2002, it was the comparison school teachers (figure 5.3) who agreed more often with these statements:

- I have worked directly with the model developer/others both inside and outside my classroom on implementing the model/reform effort.
- The model developer/others have provided me with many useful ideas and resources for changing my classroom practice.

By two years later, in 2003–2004, comparison school teachers were more likely to agree not only that they received "useful ideas and resources" but also with the following statements about the materials available in support of their reform effort (figure 5.4):

- My participation has exposed me to many examples of the kinds of student work the model is aiming for.
- My participation has exposed me to many examples of the kinds of classroom teaching the model seeks to foster.
- The materials provided by the model have helped me improve my classroom practice.

Figure 5.3. Average Scale Score in 2001–2002 on Learning Opportunities Available to Teachers, by School Type

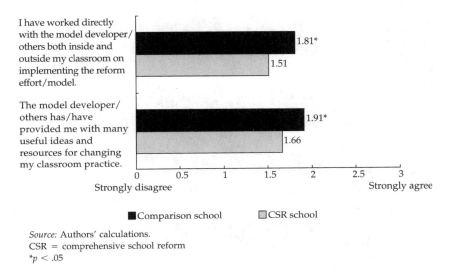

Source: Authors' calculations.
CSR = comprehensive school reform
*$p < .05$

Reporting on the professional development, the teachers in comparison schools were also more apt to say that it was coherently organized in support of their reform and was designed for effectiveness. In the study's final year, with response options ranging from "not at all" (0.0) to "to a great extent" (3.0), teachers in the comparison schools gave higher ratings to the following aspects of their professional development (figure 5.5):

- sustained and coherently focused, rather than short-term and unrelated;
- designed to support the school reform effort under way in their schools; and
- designed to include enough time to think carefully about, try, and evaluate new ideas.

What Could Explain These Differences?

These results do not necessarily prove that the teachers in comparison schools were experiencing reform efforts that were more thoroughly engineered and supported than the comprehensive models in the adopting schools. One possibility is that their perceptions may have reflected the different expectations associated with more modest-scale

Figure 5.4. Average Scale Score in 2003–2004 on Learning Opportunities Available to Teachers, by School Type

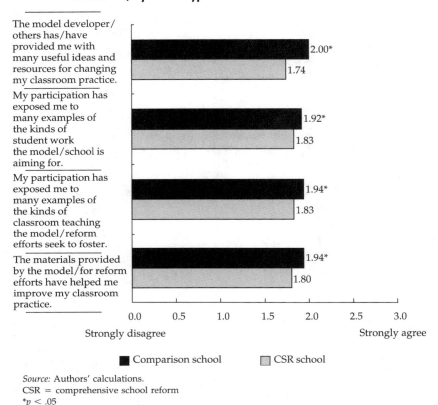

Source: Authors' calculations.
CSR = comprehensive school reform
*p < .05

reforms. The process of undertaking a serious, far-reaching change might have brought teachers in the adopting schools face to face with unexpected complexities, with the result that they were, ironically, more likely to perceive what was lacking than colleagues who were engaged in simpler reform efforts. Schlechty (1997, 215) makes this point: "systemic change does not make things better or easier in the short run; instead, it is likely to create uncertainty, doubt, and confusion."

It is also possible that, over time, teachers in some adopting schools became highly skilled in aspects of their reform and were more able to notice deficiencies in the materials and support—whereas teachers in the comparison schools were working at a more superficial level with newer reforms.

Figure 5.5. Average Scale Score in 2003–2004 on Coherence of Professional Development Available to Teachers, by School Type

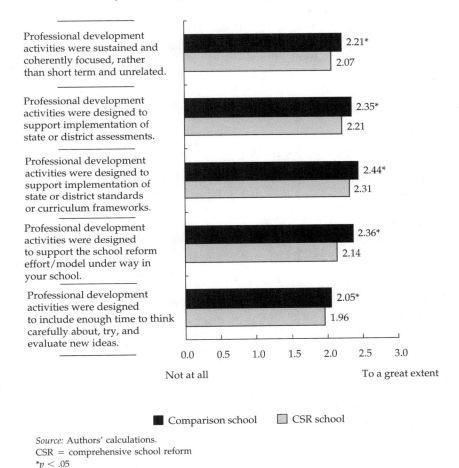

Professional development activities were sustained and coherently focused, rather than short term and unrelated. — 2.21* / 2.07

Professional development activities were designed to support implementation of state or district assessments. — 2.35* / 2.21

Professional development activities were designed to support implementation of state or district standards or curriculum frameworks. — 2.44* / 2.31

Professional development activities were designed to support the school reform effort/model under way in your school. — 2.36* / 2.14

Professional development activities were designed to include enough time to think carefully about, try, and evaluate new ideas. — 2.05* / 1.96

Not at all — To a great extent

■ Comparison school   ☐ CSR school

Source: Authors' calculations.
CSR = comprehensive school reform
*p < .05

Whatever the case, though, these survey results cast a great deal of doubt on any notion that a comprehensive reform model would enable teachers to bask in the comfort of a complete solution to their problems of practice. Instead, comprehensive reform models left many teachers criticizing what they saw as incomplete materials and supports. This means that district support might, as researchers have suggested, play a particularly important role in furnishing the help that teachers want. We turn now to our findings about district support for the adopting schools and the comparison schools.

DISTRICT SUPPORT FOR SCHOOL REFORMS

Each of the districts in this study had launched a sizable proportion of its schools on the adoption of comprehensive models. Although comprehensive reform was not embraced as an end in itself by any of these districts, none set out to discourage or interfere with implementation. In interviews for this study, policymakers in Districts A and B expressed some degree of optimism that comprehensive models would be a good vehicle for school improvement. In District C, policymakers said that the adoption of models was consistent with a local tradition of innovation at the school level. In District D, policymakers were more skeptical about comprehensive models but approved the schools' initiative to bring them in.

Districts could support a reform effort in several different ways. At the outset of this study, each of the four districts had a staff member whose responsibilities included overseeing the implementation of comprehensive models; the presence of such a person was a criterion for district selection. As described by Haslam (1999) in research conducted for New American Schools, the assignment of this responsibility to a district-level facilitator can support implementation and scale-up in the district.

If reform models were being brought into the district as part of a deliberate strategy for improvement, one would expect to see intangible kinds of support as well. District leaders might publicly endorse the reform that the school was undertaking (Bodilly 1998; Haynes 1998). Teachers would be likely to perceive that their reform work was consistent with the district's overall goals and priorities.

We asked teachers about their perceptions of all these kinds of support. Here, we report on the extent to which schools that had adopted models—compared with those that had not—experienced a sense of district support.

Comparison Schools Reported More Help from District Staff

Because this study focused on districts that had committed some central-office staff resources to the implementation of comprehensive models, we thought it quite possible that teachers would report having support for comprehensive model implementation. When asked whether they agreed or disagreed that district staff "provided important information and expertise" to support their reform, most of the teachers in schools with comprehensive models did agree to some extent. However, teachers in the comparison schools were more likely to report this kind of help with their reform effort. This difference held true in both the first and third years of the study (figures 5.6 and 5.7).

Figure 5.6. Average Scale Score in 2001–2002 on Teachers' Perceptions of District Support, by School Type

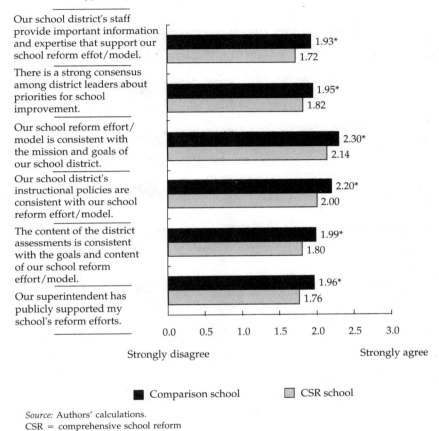

Our school district's staff provide important information and expertise that support our school reform effot/model.
1.93*
1.72

There is a strong consensus among district leaders about priorities for school improvement.
1.95*
1.82

Our school reform effort/model is consistent with the mission and goals of our school district.
2.30*
2.14

Our school district's instructional policies are consistent with our school reform effort/model.
2.20*
2.00

The content of the district assessments is consistent with the goals and content of our school reform effort/model.
1.99*
1.80

Our superintendent has publicly supported my school's reform efforts.
1.96*
1.76

0.0   0.5   1.0   1.5   2.0   2.5   3.0

Strongly disagree   Strongly agree

■ Comparison school   ☐ CSR school

Source: Authors' calculations.
CSR = comprehensive school reform
*$p < .05$

In focus groups, teachers in several schools that had adopted comprehensive models voiced disappointment with district help. Some said they were assigned a liaison who was not knowledgeable about the model or did not agree with it. Others reported that no one from the district office worked with them. Still another theme was the unpredictability of support for professional development, which was sometimes withdrawn.

- "Personally, I feel we get poor marks in all of the support areas. The district people were ill informed about the models. . . . People just didn't know. After the first year, we were assigned a district

Figure 5.7. Average Scale Score in 2003–2004 on Teachers' Perceptions of District Support, by School Type

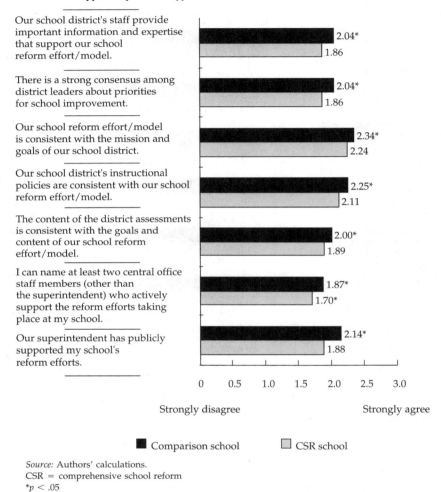

Our school district's staff provide important information and expertise that support our school reform effort/model.
2.04*
1.86

There is a strong consensus among district leaders about priorities for school improvement.
2.04*
1.86

Our school reform effort/model is consistent with the mission and goals of our school district.
2.34*
2.24

Our school district's instructional policies are consistent with our school reform effort/model.
2.25*
2.11

The content of the district assessments is consistent with the goals and content of our school reform effort/model.
2.00*
1.89

I can name at least two central office staff members (other than the superintendent) who actively support the reform efforts taking place at my school.
1.87*
1.70*

Our superintendent has publicly supported my school's reform efforts.
2.14*
1.88

0   0.5   1.0   1.5   2.0   2.5   3.0

Strongly disagree   Strongly agree

■ Comparison school   □ CSR school

Source: Authors' calculations.
CSR = comprehensive school reform
*$p < .05$

coordinator who didn't have any idea what they were doing. The commitment was never there."

- "One of the things with Accelerated was that the district was ready to support us, and had assured us that we would have district support with district coaches. We lost the district coach, and when you don't have that external coach coming in, you don't have someone keeping you on focus. So your cadres were meeting, but we lost the district support, which is in my opinion why we lost impetus."

- "What was most frustrating for us was when we were told, sorry, we're not going to train you any more because the district does not want it. We were scheduled to go to part two [of the School Development Program training], and it wasn't a priority the district wanted."

Comparison Schools Reported More Sense of Congruence with District Priorities

Comprehensive reform models garnered some support from these districts. Most teachers in schools that had adopted models reported that their model was consistent with district goals and policies. However, teachers in the comparison schools were even more likely to perceive that they were undertaking a reform that enjoyed district support. This was true at the outset of the study (despite two of the districts' outspoken advocacy of comprehensive reform models), and it remained true in the study's third year (figures 5.6 and 5.7). The teachers in comparison schools were more likely to report that the superintendent and central office staff supported what they were doing in reform. They were also more likely to perceive that their school's reform effort was in line with district goals and policies.

Thus, teachers in the schools that had adopted comprehensive models apparently experienced less district support in both tangible and intangible forms. Perhaps districts offered them less staff support on the rationale that these schools had access to outside help from the developer organization. Rather than working with the schools to ensure that the outside help was effective, district staff more often seemed to assume that these schools were taken care of, thanks to their grants and their external networks, and that the district could focus more of its own attention on other schools.

Similarly, the reforms under way in comparison schools were more likely to include initiatives more recently introduced into the district, which were well understood and championed by district leaders and staff. Nationally disseminated models may have failed to command as much district allegiance, even though all these districts were at least willing to entertain them as a strategy for reform.

MODELS' CONTRIBUTIONS TO A SENSE OF COHERENCE IN SCHOOLS

Having gathered teachers' reports about the reform strategy in which they were participating, we wanted to know what contributed to their sense that the reform process was moving in a coherent direction. We also wanted to look at the conditions associated with greater coherence in instruction. Using multiple regression methods, we identified variables that contributed to (1) a sense of coherence in a school's reform implementation and (2) reported coherence in curriculum and instruction. The results suggest that these two kinds of coherence, while related to each other, were not exactly the same thing.

Comparison Schools' Teachers Felt Reform Was More Coherently Implemented

Part of the rationale for comprehensive reform is to present a school with a design and a set of supports that operate throughout the school and bring a sense of greater coherence, when contrasted with more piecemeal approaches to reform. As suggested by the above findings comparing the perceptions of teachers in adopting schools and comparison schools, comprehensive reform models did not, in general, work in this way in the schools we studied.

We measured the perceived coherence of reform implementation in the schools and, using multiple regression, built a model to identify variables that contributed to the perception of greater coherence. This analysis indicated that comprehensive models did not make such a contribution. It identified other conditions that did, however.

The measure of coherence in implementation of the model or reform was a scale developed from the responses of all teachers in a school to several questions. They were asked to agree or disagree with the following statements:

- Most teachers support implementation of the school's reform effort/model.
- The reform effort/model is closely coordinated among teachers at the same grade level.
- The reform effort/model is closely coordinated across grades.
- There is a core curriculum that all teachers follow.

Our model explained much of the variance in teachers' perceptions of implementation coherence at the school level, with an adjusted R square of 0.57 (table 5.1).

One predictor of a high rating of implementation coherence, it turned out, was being a comparison school. The schools that had adopted comprehensive models lost 0.10 percentage points in their ratings of implementation coherence. The comparison schools—where principals generally reported having more reforms under way, and where teachers generally perceived stronger district support—were thought to

Table 5.1. Predicting Coherence of Reform Implementation within a School, 2003–2004

Independent variables	β	SE
Whether teacher was in a CSR school	−.10**	.015
District support scale	.08*	.036
Professional development scale	.06*	.027
School climate scale	.04	.024
Instructional coherence scale	.34**	.040
Principal leadership scale	.18**	.033
Teacher influence over school policy scale	.13**	.021
Constant	.10**	.021
R^2	0.57	n.a.

Source: Authors' calculations.
CSR = comprehensive school reform
n.a. = not applicable
Note: Responses were collected from 1,123 teachers in 68 schools. We performed a Huber-White correction to adjust for clustering.
* $p < .05$, ** $p < .001$

have relatively more coordination of the reform efforts within and across grades, and to have core curricula that teachers followed.

The largest contributor to a sense of coherent implementation was a related measure, instructional coherence. This variable (which we discuss below as the outcome variable in another regression analysis) included several questions about consistency in curriculum and instruction, as well as the articulation of different programs within the school. With an increase of a percentage point in the instructional coherence score, a school's reform coherence score rose by 0.34 percentage points.

A measure of principal leadership in reform also emerged from this analysis as an important variable for coherent implementation. Principal leadership was a variable that included a question about the principal's establishment and communication of a vision for the school, and several questions about his or her attention to implementation of the reform (Stringfield et al. 1998). For example, it included teachers' reports that the principal monitored classroom implementation of the reform, rewarded teachers for practices that supported the reform, and informed teachers about the school's progress in meeting the reform goals. For every percentage point increase in this scale, the implementation coherence score rose by 0.18 percentage points.

The variable of teacher influence was also significantly related to implementation coherence. It comprised teachers' reports of how much they influenced the school's goals and mission, budget, curriculum, schedule, promotion and retention policy, and the content and design of their professional development (Bodily 1998). With each percentage point increase in this measure, the scale of implementation coherence rose by 0.13 percentage points.

The district support perceived by teachers also helped to predict implementation coherence. This scale included several questions about the consistency and focus of district policy: for example, it included teachers' reports that the district held high expectations and inspired teachers' best job performance, that priorities were shared and policies were consistent over time, and that the district helped the school focus on teaching and learning. Also included in this variable were teachers' reports on the consistency of their school's reform effort with district goals and policies, and on the information the district provided to support the school's reform. For every percentage point increase in a school's score on this scale, perceived implementation coherence rose by 0.08 percentage points.

Professional development, the final significant variable in this analysis, included teachers' reports of the extent to which professional development was designed to support several sets of priorities—the reform effort or model, state or district standards or curriculum frameworks, and state or district assessments. The variable also included teachers' assessments of the time available to think about and try new ideas, and of the extent to which professional development was sustained and coherently focused. An increase of a percentage point in the score for this scale was associated with an increase of 0.06 percentage points in perceived implementation coherence.

Comprehensive Models Contributed to a Sense of Instructional Coherence

So far, we have discussed the views that teachers reported when asked about the reforms they were undertaking. When compared with the teachers in schools that had adopted comprehensive reforms, teachers in the comparison schools reported enjoying a greater sense that their reforms gave them ample guidance, and they were more likely to perceive tangible and intangible district support for their reform's direction. These findings might suggest that adoption of a comprehensive reform model was, if not actually counterproductive, probably not advantageous for school improvement when compared with the other reform efforts one might find in schools.

However, the aim of a comprehensive reform is to improve student achievement by strengthening the coherence in teaching and learning throughout the school. Although it seems desirable for teachers to report that the reform process is a coherent one that offers them plenty of support, the process is only a means to an end. In supporting comprehensive reform models, policymakers are ultimately more interested in seeing schools where students' learning experiences are consistent across grades and classrooms, driven by a shared vision of teaching and learning. Thus, we wanted to understand what conditions and reform approaches were found in those schools where teachers reported high levels of instructional coherence.

Our outcome measure of instructional coherence combined the responses of teachers within a school to a series of questions about their school in the study's third year. For this analysis, we looked across all the schools, both those that had adopted comprehensive reforms and the comparison schools, all of which had some sort of reform effort under way. This measure was adapted in large part from the work of Newmann and colleagues (2001a, b). Teachers were asked whether they agreed or disagreed with the following statements:

- Curriculum, instruction, and learning materials are well coordinated across the different grade levels at this school.
- There is consistency in curriculum, instruction, and learning materials among teachers in the same grade level at this school.
- You can see real continuity from one program to another in this school.
- Once we start a new program, we follow up to make sure that it's working.
- Most changes introduced at this school help promote the school's goals for learning.

We were able to explain a good deal of the variation in instructional coherence with a multiple regression model (table 5.2); the adjusted

Table 5.2. Predicting Instructional Coherence within a School, 2003–2004

Independent variables	β	SE
Whether the teacher was in a CSR school	.12	.013
District support scale	.16**	.036
Professional development scale	.09**	.022
School climate scale	.20**	.036
Coherence of reform implementation scale	.31**	.040
Principal leadership scale	.15**	.028
Teacher influence over school policy scale	.06*	.030
Constant	−.02	.027
R^2	0.58	n.a.

Source: Authors' calculations.
CSR = comprehensive school reform
n.a. = not applicable
Notes: Responses were collected from 1,123 teachers in 68 schools. We performed a Huber-White correction to adjust for clustering.
* $p < .05$, ** $p < .001$

R square of the model was 0.58. In this model, the independent variables were teachers' reported perceptions of the implementation of reform (whether that reform was a comprehensive model or the reforms in place in the comparison schools), of school and district leadership, and of school climate. That the school had adopted a comprehensive reform was not significantly related to instructional coherence, other things being equal. In other words, these schools held their own in instructional coherence, despite the observed negative effect of the model on reform coherence.

In explaining instructional coherence, the strongest predictor was the scale of implementation coherence discussed above. For every percentage point increase in teachers view of the implementation of the model (or reform effort) as coherent, the instructional coherence score rose by 0.31 percentage points.

Also positively related was our measure of school climate as perceived by the teachers in the school. It combined teachers' reports about the school's shared academic focus, as well as questions about shared beliefs, coordination of content, mutual help among teachers, high standards set by teachers, and analysis of student performance data. A percentage point increase in this scale was associated with a rise of 0.20 percentage points in instructional coherence.

Other variables significant in this model of instructional coherence were similar to those that helped explain implementation coherence. As table 5.2 shows, the regression model for instructional coherence also included district support, principal leadership, professional development, and teachers' influence over school policy.

Thus, we found that a particular combination of conditions could make a powerful contribution to the instructional coherence reported by teachers. If they perceived support and coordination of their reform effort among fellow teachers, a climate of shared focus within the school, support from the district, leadership from the principal, professional development, and influence over school policy, the result tended to be an appreciably greater sense of instructional coherence. This held true with or without a comprehensive model—and having a model did not, in itself, either drive or detract from instructional coherence.

Having reviewed these multivariate analyses of the survey data, we turn next to a more descriptive look at the ways in which schools' experiences did or did not match the combination of conditions associated with greater instructional coherence. In particular, we review what we learned in visits and interviews about district strategy and its relationship with comprehensive school reform.

How Comprehensive Reform Was or Wasn't a District Strategy

According to the teachers' survey responses, these districts did not consistently support comprehensive models as their preferred vehicle for school improvement. The models themselves also fell short of offering teachers a complete package of practical guidance. Instead, the teachers in the matched comparison schools came closer to reporting the kind of coherent reform experience advocated as a benefit of adopting a comprehensive model with district support.

The four districts and 34 model schools in this study were living with limited budgets and growing accountability pressures. Comprehensive models were one of the resources at their disposal, but only as one option within a crowded landscape of imperatives and choices for curricula, instruction, and school organization. Districts' policies and visions evolved over the course of this study, and schools faced shifting pressures. In this context, the use of comprehensive reform models presented schools with challenges.

District Priorities Diverged from a Focus on Implementing Models

At the district level, new leadership and new policy imperatives came to the fore during the two years between our first and last rounds of data collection. Each of the four districts had a change in superintendents during the study period. Superintendents who had been outspoken champions of comprehensive models departed from Districts A and B, an event that has been associated with the loss of support for models in the past (Slavin and Madden 2000). The district-level liaison with comprehensive models left District B (for employment with a model developer); the liaison in District C retired. In District D, the liaison with models—who had expressed skepticism about the effectiveness of models—became the new superintendent.

Budget pressures, already noticeable at the outset of the study, became still more intense by 2004. District C in particular experienced major layoffs of central office staff and of teachers. In all four districts, administrators lamented their lack of resources for improvement initiatives of any kind. In this climate, payments from district funds to the assistance providers for comprehensive models were an expendable budget item. In District C, a moratorium on travel also curtailed the use of existing grant funds, preventing teachers from attending out-of-town professional development for their models.

Other grant opportunities displaced some of the district-level focus on comprehensive reform. Districts A and B both began working with operating foundations under new frameworks that guided the participating schools in planning and improvement. District C won numerous small and large grants for programs in its schools. District D was introducing Reading First grants (funded by No Child Left Behind) in 2004.

The policy influence that loomed largest in our interviews with district administrators, however, was accountability. Under pressure to demonstrate gains in student performance, the districts were trying to direct their schools' attention to state tests (Smith et al. 1998). Changing the tests to align more closely with the comprehensive reform models was not an option; instead, the content and skills emphasized on the tests crowded out the curriculum associated with the models.

In District B, for example, there was always some unresolved tension between the district's policy of encouraging adoption of comprehensive models and its policy of adhering to standards-based reform. The district instituted benchmarks based on state standards and tests that dictated curriculum and instruction for each nine-week period. The benchmarks were not aligned with the curricula of comprehensive models. Whether or not a model would eventually equip students to do well on the test at the end of the year—as some educators in adopting schools said it would—the lack of alignment with the periodic benchmarking tests posed a problem.

Increasingly, the districts centralized their control over the curriculum, claiming that they were responding to accountability pressures. In particular, they cited No Child Left Behind as their reason for instituting a uniform curriculum. This was a trend in the two districts where the former superintendents had been advocates of comprehensive models. By the end of our study, District B had moved beyond simply issuing benchmarks. District policymakers planned to phase out the use of comprehensive school reform models. An assistant superintendent said, "The models seemed to fragment us and pull us in so many different directions." Instead, the district would "standardize the literacy approach across the district," instituting a program that emphasized balanced literacy (using the Accelerated Reader program and the approach of the Consortium on Reading Excellence) and two new frameworks for districtwide professional development. In District A, after the departure of the former superintendent, another top administrator commented diplomatically, "The models themselves don't necessarily line up with what we're being held accountable for right now. So schools aren't necessarily looking for models right now."

In Schools, Models Were in Tension with District Mandates

On our surveys in both 2002 and 2004, the teachers in schools with comprehensive models were relatively less likely than comparison school teachers to say that their reform efforts were consistent with the districts' direction. A few of them, in interviews, cited disparaging comments about their models from district officials. More often, however, their sense of being relatively less in tune with the district probably came from the work that they were doing to reconcile differences between their model and current district initiatives. The district typically left this work in the hands of the schools.

In some schools in District B, for example, teams of teachers worked to align their use of the model with the district benchmarks. In quite a few schools, the teachers simply ran two programs in parallel, teaching reading twice each day with the two different approaches. Some considered and rejected that approach: "We would need to do [Modern Red SchoolHouse] in the morning and district in the afternoon and we can't do both. There were no state standards when we first started looking at [comprehensive models], but now there are."

As the sense of accountability pressure increased, teachers reflected on what would best enable them to reach their performance targets, and in many cases the models did not appear likely to fill that need—a phenomenon that has appeared in past research on model implementation (Stringfield et al. 1998). In a school in District A identified by the state for improvement, a teacher said, "The push is on academics, and we are being judged, and Comer is not on academics."

Time pressures were felt acutely in some of the model schools. Teaching two literacy blocks each day was one obvious source for some teachers. Another was attendance at model-related events as well as district events. Principals in District B were attending meetings for both the district and their models. Three teachers in a District A school participating in Accelerated Schools commented in 2002: "It's a model that requires a commitment of time." "Time is the thing we need most of and we have the least of." "It's competing with extra testing and paperwork, which are mandatory. Teachers get to a point when they have to pick and choose."

As three of the districts increased their control over curriculum, the models became untenable in some schools. District A adopted new textbooks for reading and mathematics in 2003, seeking better alignment with the state standards. Teachers reported in 2004 that they were now following the texts more closely and using fewer supplemental materials. In District B, as mentioned, some teachers with comprehensive models felt they had to teach reading twice a day. In District D, schools using Co-nect in particular experienced tension between their model and an increasingly assertive district role in curriculum. As one teacher described,

Comprehensive school reform didn't work because there was no support from the district. We thought [the district] would back us in our decision to implement the Co-nect model, but they wanted us to do their curriculum their way. We wanted to do project-based instruction and the district wanted us to drill students in reading/language arts and math.

Schools Kept Elements of Their Models Despite the Difficulties

Although the faithful use of a comprehensive model program was not usually seen as the best way to follow district priorities, schools seldom abandoned their models entirely. The accretion of reform initiatives was customary in these schools, in fact. When asked whether they had dropped or discontinued a reform initiative in the past two years (and, if so, for what reason), 81 percent of the principals in the schools with comprehensive models said no in both 2002 and 2004. Similarly, in the comparison schools, 81 percent of the principals said no in 2002, and 70 percent in 2004. Some schools found new funding sources to support their comprehensive models. In many such cases, they decreased the amount of technical assistance and professional development they would purchase.

Because we did not measure the classroom implementation of specific elements of each model, we cannot say exactly how teaching may have changed as a result of the models' introduction. However, this study yielded information about the kinds of organizational innovations that survived over time and some information about instructional approaches. Some schools reportedly had become accustomed to joint planning and intended to continue it. In some cases, the planning was schoolwide. An example of extensive use of new planning approaches can be seen in the way a principal described the legacy of Accelerated Schools, even though the school had formally discontinued use of that model.

We stopped the Accelerated Schools Program [ASP] two years ago, but we're still using their philosophy, still using the inquiry process. We do have . . . a state-funded program [that] features whole-faculty study groups—we use the cadres from ASP. We use these study groups to look at student work, identify best instructional practices, etc. We have a group right now looking at ways to increase students' vocabulary—the group is formulating an action plan (like ASP) and will share that with faculty. What ASP brought our teachers was a sense of collaboration—teachers working harder together. We developed a site-based management system because of ASP—we have teams and teacher leaders. At the beginning of our implementation of ASP, our teachers were used to being told what to do. Now, our teachers want to have input in our decisions. We have good teacher retention in our school—not high teacher turnover. The teachers understand what's needed at the next grade level.

Other principals expressed a similar belief that teachers would continue to meet, at least by grade level and in some cases schoolwide. The principal of a school that had been using the Modern Red SchoolHouse model said, "The concept behind the model will stay; its basic structure will remain. We will still emphasize shared decisionmaking and the structure of leadership teams and task forces will remain." The principal of an Accelerated School said, "We follow the model because we bring all stakeholders together to make a decision. We try to include everyone."

The reported increase in professional conversation among teachers, within grade levels and sometimes across grade levels, seems related to our finding that comprehensive models contribute to a school's instructional coherence. Comprehensive models may have brought teachers together for serious interaction about teaching and learning, and this may have bolstered their sense of having a shared instructional program.

Substantive dimensions of the models were remaining in place as well, according to teachers and principals. Some of those implementing the Comer School Development Program commented that the model's procedures for engaging parents were useful and would continue. In some schools that had implemented Co-nect, principals and teachers spoke highly of its project-based approach to learning. A teacher described the change:

> Teachers learned how to adapt curriculum to make it meaningful and to respond to varied learning needs. We've learned how to make learning real and meaningful (kids made their own store, set their own prices, etc.). We're continuing to do it. Teachers are doing thematic teaching now on the overriding issues they want kids to get.

Finally, several of the models had taught teachers ways of reviewing and using achievement data, a set of skills that they expected to continue to use. A teacher commented, "We analyze test scores really well because of Co-nect. Now test scores have become a factor in instruction—we used to just throw those things away." A principal, describing what remained in place from Accelerated Schools, said, "We're committed to using some elements . . . using data—the good thing about using data to make a decision is that the data don't lie—it's there in black and white."

District Policymakers Said They Assimilated Ideas from the Models

Finally, returning to the relationship between comprehensive reform models and district policy, we found that some district policymakers did claim to have absorbed some of the models' philosophy. District B stood out in this regard. In interviews in 2004, its leaders explained that they were no longer supporting implementation of most of the externally developed models, but that the experience of bringing in models had paved the way for more change, and that their approach to school improvement had been influenced by the experience of model implementation.

Looking back, an administrator in District B cited the power of the models to galvanize change: "What comprehensive school reform allows is organizational change," she said. "We often get teachers who've been teaching 10 to 20 years and are not willing to change. When we bring in a model . . . it lets teachers know they need to change or move on. We can't do it otherwise without the model. Without the structure [of a model], it's difficult for principals to manage everyday work and then lead a reform. . . . We're ready to take this knowledge and move on."

Looking ahead, this district has borrowed elements of its new balanced literacy approach from several of the models (e.g., high expectations, infusion of technology, a strong home-school connection, take-home books for children); peer coaching from Cornerstone; scripted lessons and frequent assessment and regrouping from Success for All; and technology from Co-nect. The district also chose to retain the model facilitators in schools that already had them, but to retrain them. The plan was for facilitators to serve as literacy coaches like those of America's Choice, conducting professional development and supporting teachers' implementation of the new model.

An administrator in District B commented that the value of peer coaching had become visible through the use of the models: "Peer observations and discussions of what the peer has seen in the classroom, the quality of assignments and the quality of teacher-made tests seem to be part of what pulls the school together. If we can replicate that broad-scale across the district, research shows that's how teachers are growing professionally." He also said the district plans to train principals and teachers to use the results of frequent student assessments (the benchmark tests) to adjust and modify instruction, an approach borrowed from Modern Red SchoolHouse and other models.

Summarizing the district's stance on models in 2004, this administrator said,

We are moving away from school reform models—but in a way, that's not true, because what we've done is we've examined several models and taken the best from those models and created our own model. . . . As we roll out our literacy initiative, we will develop a new phase that will create an in-house model.

A similar comment in 2004 came from an administrator in the other district that had initially embraced models most enthusiastically, District A.

The [CSR] models themselves don't necessarily line up with what we're being held accountable for right now. So schools aren't looking for models right now. But we've brought in hybrid models that match what we're being held accountable for. . . . Fidelity to the model isn't so important anymore. An externally developed model was a starting point. . . . Comer has a social element that remained—family and community. I see this as very much what the district [strives for]. . .

The other districts had different stances on the experience of using models. District C, overwhelmed with its financial difficulties and turning its attention to newer grants, was paying little attention at the policy level to that experience. An administrator commented,

In the past two years [in meetings of a high-level policy group], there hasn't been one discussion of comprehensive school reform. There is no talk about it on a districtwide level. . . . I may just be out of the loop, but I think the district isn't terribly aware of the progress of these schools.

Finally, the initial skepticism in District D had not abated at the end of our study. The superintendent had no visible qualms about discouraging further use of the models and moving on to other priorities:

We're not about stuff or programs—we're about methods; we're just trying to get people to change. . . . There were pockets of success. I think some models were put to good use. With all the accountability pressures on top of us, it's hard to do it all. Another problem with comprehensive school reform was that curriculum and instruction were not aligned with the district and state standards. I suppose there were probably ways to help with that. Comprehensive school reform in [District D], however, is not doable. NCLB is layered on top of everything.

Still, some of the superintendent's favored approaches for improvement—planning and coaching—were processes that schools had adopted as part of their models.

> There are certain things that I want every school to do now. For example, developing a school improvement plan is now a requirement that every school must do so that the district can understand what's going on. . . . We're learning to know good teaching when we see it. We're using coaches to convey messages about good schools.

CONCLUSIONS

Rarely, if ever, does policy implementation follow the script written by reform advocates, and these districts' support for comprehensive school reform did not do so. Although they had initially seen potential benefits from the adoption of models, the districts did not maintain allegiance to this strategy when superintendents left, budgets dwindled, and the pressures of No Child Left Behind mounted.

But this study does not just tell a simple story of shifting priorities in school districts. For one thing, it brings into focus the universality of school reform efforts, at least in these sample districts. Teachers in the comparison schools, no less than those in the schools that had adopted models, could describe their reform efforts. Indeed, they were *more* likely to claim that they were engaged in a coherent effort and that they had the necessary support from materials and professional development.

From the perspective of teachers and principals in schools that had adopted comprehensive reform models, the implementation of these models brought visible challenges from the outset. Reconciling the conflicting signals of model specifications and district policies took time and energy, and it was a task largely left up to the schools—even in the first year of this study, when districts nominally supported the use of models. For example, in a number of schools, teachers said they had to teach reading twice a day, once using the model and once following the district's specifications. It is not surprising that teachers in the adopting schools, on average, felt less support from their districts in several respects than the teachers in the comparison schools.

Still, even though teachers in the comparison schools reported more coherence in their reform efforts, they reported no more coherence in their schools' instructional programs. Consistency in teaching and learning was not impaired in schools that had adopted comprehensive models, despite the policy incoherence that surrounded their implementation efforts. Teachers and principals in many schools expected to continue the teamwork practices they had learned in using their comprehensive models. And, coming full circle, one of the districts that had formally reduced its commitment to comprehensive models was articulating a new strategy for reform, one that drew on aspects of the models its schools had implemented.

REFERENCES

Bodilly, S. J. 1998. "Lessons from New American Schools' Scale-Up Phase: Prospects for Bringing Designs to Multiple Schools." Monograph/Report MR-942-NAS. Santa Monica: RAND.

Datnow, A., and S. Stringfield. 2000. "Working Together for Reliable School Reform." *Journal of Education for Students Placed at Risk* 5(1&2): 183–204.

Desimone, L. 2002. "How Can Comprehensive School Reform Models Be Implemented?" *Review of Educational Research* 72(3): 433–80.

Fashola, O. S., and R. E. Slavin. 1998. "Schoolwide Reform Models: What Works?" *Phi Delta Kappan*, January, 370–79.

Haslam, M. B. 1999. *How to Rebuild a Local Professional Development Infrastructure*, vol. 4. Arlington, VA: New American Schools.

Haynes, N. M. 1998. "Lessons Learned." *Journal of Education for Students Placed at Risk* 3(1): 87–99.

Newmann, F. M., B. Smith, E. Allensworth, and A. S. Bryk. 2001a. "Instructional Program Coherence: What It Is and Why It Should Guide School Improvement Policy." *Educational Evaluation and Policy Analysis* 23(4): 297–321.

———. 2001b. "School Instructional Program Coherence: Benefits and Challenges." Chicago Annenberg Research Project Report. Chicago: Consortium on Chicago School Research.

Purnell, S., and P. Hill. 1992. "Time for Reform." Report R-4234-EMC. Santa Monica: RAND.

Schlechty, P. C. 1997. *Inventing Better Schools: An Action Plan for Education Reform*. San Francisco: Jossey-Bass.

Slavin, R. E., and N. A. Madden. 2000. "Roots & Wings: Effects of Whole-School Reform on Student Achievement." *Journal of Education for Students Placed at Risk* 5(1&2): 109–36.

Smith, L., S. Ross, M. McNelis, M. Squires, R. Wasson, S. Maxwell, K. Weddle, L. Nath, A. Grehan, and T. Buggey. 1998. "The Memphis Restructuring Initiative: Analysis of Activities and Outcomes that Affect Implementation Success." *Education and Urban Society* 30(3): 296–325.

Stringfield, S. 1997. *Schools, Programs, and Systemic Support*. Urban and Suburban/Rural Special Strategies for Educating Disadvantaged Children: Final Report. Washington, DC: U.S. Department of Education.

Stringfield, S., A. Datnow, S. M. Ross, and F. Snively. 1998. "Scaling Up School Restructuring in Multicultural, Multilingual Contexts: Early Observations from Sunland County." *Education and Urban Society* 30(3): 326–57.

Appendix

DISTRICT SUPPORT SCALE

Items

1. I feel that our district inspires the very best in the job performance of its teachers (scale: 0–3).
2. Our district holds high expectations for my school (scale: 0–3).
3. I can name at least two central office staff members (other than the superintendent) who actively support the reform efforts taking place at my school (scale: 0–3).
4. There is a strong consensus among district leaders about priorities for school improvement (scale: 0–3).
5. Our district helps my school focus on teaching and learning (scale: 0–3).
6. Our superintendent has publicly supported my school's reform efforts (scale: 0–3).
7. Our school reform effort/model is consistent with the mission and goals of our school district (scale: 0–3).
8. Our school district's instructional policies are consistent with our school reform effort/model (scale: 0–3).
9. Our school district's staff provide important information and expertise that support our school reform effort/model (scale: 0–3).
10. The scheduling and timing of our district assessments do not interfere with our school reform effort/model (scale: 0–3).
11. The content of the district assessments is consistent with the goals and content of our school reform effort/model (scale: 0–3).
12. There is a great deal of turnover in the central office in our district (scale: 0–3).
13. Central office policies and procedures change frequently in our district (scale: 0–3).

Descriptive Statistics

Minimum possible score: 0   Maximum possible score: 39

Alpha: .90, Mean: 25.81, Standard deviation: 6.53, Variance: 42.66

SCHOOL CLIMATE SCALE

Items

1. Teachers coordinate the content of their courses with teachers in their department/grade-level/curricular area (scale: 0–3).
2. Most teachers share the same beliefs and values about what the central mission of the school should be (scale: 0–3).
3. Teachers in this school feel responsible to help each other do their best (scale: 0–3).
4. Teachers are engaged in systematic analysis of student performance data (scale: 0–3).
5. Teachers in this school set high standards for academic performance (scale: 0–3).

Descriptive Statistics

Minimum possible score: 0   Maximum possible score: 15

Alpha: .91, Mean: 10.59, Standard deviation: 3.39, Variance: 11.48

INSTRUCTIONAL COHERENCE SCALE

Items

1. You can see real continuity from one program to another in this school (scale: 0–3).
2. Once we start a new program we follow up to make sure that it's working (scale: 0–3).
3. Curriculum, instruction, and learning materials are well coordinated across the different grade levels at this school (scale: 0–3).
4. There is consistency in curriculum, instruction, and learning materials among teachers in the same grade level at this school (scale: 0–3).
5. Most changes introduced at this school help promote the school's goals for learning (scale: 0–3).

Descriptive Statistics

Minimum possible score: 0   Maximum possible score: 15

Alpha: .86,   Mean: 9.40,   Standard deviation: 2.91,   Variance: 8.46

REFORM COHERENCE SCALE

Items

1. Most teachers support implementation of the school's reform effort/ model (scale: 0–3).
2. The reform effort/model is closely coordinated among teachers at the same grade level (scale: 0–3).
3. The reform effort/model is closely coordinated across grades (scale: 0–3).
4. There is a core curriculum that all teachers follow (scale: 0–3).

Descriptive Statistics

Minimum possible score: 0   Maximum possible score: 12

Alpha: .82,   Mean: 8.00,   Standard deviation: 2.25,   Variance: 5.06

PROFESSIONAL DEVELOPMENT SCALE

Items

To what extent were the professional development activities

1. Designed to include enough time to think carefully about, try, and evaluate new ideas (scale: 0–3).
2. Designed to support the school reform/effort under way in your school (scale: 0–3).
3. Designed to support implementation of state or district standards or curriculum frameworks (scale: 0–3).
4. Designed to support implementation of state or district assessments (scale: 0–3).
5. Sustained and coherently focused, rather than short term and unrelated (scale: 0–3).

Descriptive Statistics

Minimum possible score: 0   Maximum possible score: 15

Alpha: .89, Mean: 11.16, Standard deviation: 3.15, Variance: 9.92

PRINCIPAL LEADERSHIP SCALE

Items

1. My principal monitors the curriculum I use in my classroom to see that it reflects my school's reform effort/model (scale: 0–3).
2. My principal monitors my classroom instructional practices to see that they reflect the school's reform effort/model (scale: 0–3).
3. My principal evaluates my performance using criteria directly related to the school's reform effort/model (scale: 0–3).
4. My principal praises, publicly recognizes, and/or provides tangible rewards to teachers whose instructional practices support the school's reform effort/model (scale: 0–3).
5. My principal knows what kind of school he/she wants and has communicated it to the staff (scale: 0–3).
6. My principal informs teachers (in meetings, through written materials) about our progress in meeting our school reform effort's/model's goals (scale: 0–3).

Descriptive Statistics

Minimum possible score: 0   Maximum possible score: 18

Alpha: .94, Mean: 12.67, Standard deviation: 4.21, Variance: 17.75

6

MANDATES AND SUPPORT OF COMPREHENSIVE SCHOOL REFORM

Daniel K. Aladjem, Anja Kurki, and Andrea Boyle

While the roots of comprehensive school reform (CSR) extend to at least the 1980s, researchers generally trace the origin of CSR as a distinct school improvement strategy to the establishment of New American Schools in the early 1990s (Cross 2004). At the time reformers sought to focus reform efforts at the school level, in accordance with the prevailing wisdom that districts were dysfunctional organizations and obstacles to student learning and school improvement (Appelbaum 2002). Over time, however, interest in and recognition of districts' role in CSR has risen. Increasingly, research on CSR specifically and school reform in general includes analyses of local school district activities.

Part of the theory implicit in CSR has long been that districts were part of the problem facing schools and that the appropriate role for districts was to leave schools alone to implement whole-school programs. In fact, many districts did just that. However, the role of the district has become more diverse; some districts have maintained their hands-off attitude, while others have adopted a more hands-on approach. Many districts have gone so far as to require schools to implement CSR, while others have merely encouraged and supported implementation.

Examining the relationship between district support and school reform is especially relevant in light of the emphasis that the No Child Left Behind Act places on school districts. In cases where schools repeatedly fail to make adequate yearly progress, districts have the primary responsibility for ensuring that schools are implementing appropriate reform strategies. No Child Left Behind (NCLB) endorses district efforts to support implementation of CSR; this chapter examines the relationship between mandated implementation and reform.

Using data from a large-scale, quasi-experimental program evaluation, the National Longitudinal Evaluation of Comprehensive School Reform, we explore the relationship between schools' CSR implementation and districts' mandates, support, and context for CSR. Specifically, we look at whether these district factors are associated with schools' level of CSR model implementation. Our earlier research has shown that schools' level of CSR model implementation is related to the support they receive from their model developer, the quality of their principal's leadership (i.e., site-based leadership), and the quality of their teachers' professional community, as well as the specific CSR model that they adopt (Kurki, Aladjem, and Carter 2005). Specifically, our earlier research provided further evidence to support the claim that more prescribed programs have higher fidelity of implementation.

Here, our goal is to add a district level to our analysis to explore the role that districts' mandates, support, and context for CSR play in CSR model implementation. Composed primarily of items from longitudinal surveys of district administrators and principals, our measures of district context include the prevalence and diversity of CSR models within a district. Our measures of district support include district-sponsored assistance with CSR model selection, professional development for teachers, technical assistance for implementation, and community outreach activities.

Schools in our sample adopted their CSR models under a variety of circumstances: some schools decided to adopt a model of their own volition, while some adopted CSR in response to state or district mandates. Some schools were free to choose their own CSR model or to select from a list of preferred models, while others were forced to adopt a particular CSR model. We hypothesize that districts mandating CSR are more actively engaged in reform and thus assist schools in maintaining fidelity to the models' design.

We pose the following research questions:

- To what extent are districts supportive of CSR, and are districts' levels of support related to whether they mandate CSR?
- To what extent are high levels of CSR implementation a function of districts' mandates, support, or context for CSR?

DISTRICTS' ROLE IN SUPPORTING REFORM

The literature on districts' support for school improvement is large, varied, and growing constantly (Anderson 2003; Elmore 1997; Marsh 2000; McLaughlin and Talbert 2003; O'Day and Bitter 2003; Ross, Hannay, and Brydges 1998; Snipes, Doolittle, and Herlihy 2002; Togneri and Anderson 2003). Less is known about district support in relation to CSR specifically. Current research describes both the characteristics of high-performing districts and those highly supportive of CSR. It also tells us that district preferences about CSR and specific CSR models are associated with the kind and quality of support provided to schools, and that hands-on, model-related support improves schools' quality and level of CSR model implementation.

Bodilly and her coauthors' study of the implementation of New American Schools designs (1998) determined that certain district contexts and activities were associated with higher levels of CSR model implementation. Districts that offered higher levels of support, such as San Antonio and Memphis, had higher levels of implementation, while less-supportive districts such as Dade, Philadelphia, and Pittsburgh had lower levels of implementation. Using interviews in which school staff were asked which actions, policies, and conditions at the district level supported their reform work, Bodilly and her coauthors established the following set of components: leadership support and centrality of the CSR initiative, lack of crises, a culture of cooperation and trust, school-level authority and/or autonomy, availability of resources for transformation, and program-compatible accountability and assessment systems (1998, 87–90).

Berends and his coauthors (2001) later used this framework to create a district support index for a quantitative analysis of New American Schools' scale-up period. Schools located in districts that ranked a standard deviation higher on this index had implementation levels about one-tenth of a standard deviation higher than schools in less-supportive districts. This study also found that, on average, schools reporting more resources for implementation (including materials; professional development; time for planning, collaboration, and development; consultants to provide ongoing support; technology; and funding) had higher levels of implementation, and thus emphasized the district's potential impact as a provider of such resources.

A policy brief by the Consortium for Policy Research in Education (1998; see also Slavin 1998 for a similar list) argues that districts should play several other crucial roles in initiating and sustaining CSR implementations. These include (1) assisting schools in selecting a program design, (2) structuring the CSR approach into schools' and districts' continuing operations, (3) designing a new district operating environment, (4) finding a district-appropriate method of supporting CSR, (5) monitoring and controlling the quality and performance of design teams, and (6) creating an outreach process that engages and informs parents and the school's community. Datnow and Stringfield (2000) echo many of these recommendations, indicating that supportive districts need to establish a distinct set of common goals that are connected to key long-term improvement strategies; create a coordinated effort for disseminating information about reform; facilitate a thoughtful, critical evaluation of what needs to change in a school and why; align policy systems to support reform; and be willing to change to adapt to the needs of the reform.

While researchers generally concur on the types of activities districts can use to support CSR implementation, research into district policies that mandate CSR implementation has produced somewhat varied conclusions. Bodilly and Berends (1999) determined that district policies forcing schools to adopt particular CSR models hindered schools' implementation efforts. But district policies requiring schools to adopt an unspecified model were beneficial in that they encouraged schools to investigate school improvement strategies from several CSR design teams. Other research suggests that district mandates for CSR can weaken schools' chances of reaching and sustaining high levels of implementation, because mandating reform can increase the staff's resistance to change by inhibiting teacher buy-in and by reducing the staff's ownership of the school improvement process (Appelbaum 2002; Asensio and Johnson 2001; Ross 2001). Further, Ross (2001) argues that districts should be selective about using CSR mandates and refrain from requiring all of their schools to adopt CSR; he cites the case of Memphis and the resistance received from its high-performing schools when they, too, were included in a districtwide CSR mandate.[1]

This chapter will further explore the effects of districts' CSR mandates on schools' implementation efforts and will also investigate the relationship between districts' mandates for CSR and districts' support for CSR. In doing so, we focus on the following five types of district support: assistance with program selection, professional development for teachers, technical assistance for CSR model implementation, and district-community outreach activities. We also explore the associations between schools' level of CSR model implementation and three district-level contextual variables: district stability as well as the prevalence and the diversity of CSR models within a district.

Assistance with CSR Model Selection

Much of the literature surrounding comprehensive school reform stresses the importance of choosing a CSR model that will adequately address the needs and conditions of a particular school (Asensio and Johnson 2001; Datnow and Stringfield 2000; Desimone 2000). Additionally, Bodilly and her coauthors (1998) find that schools that obtained more information about their CSR model during their model selection process tended to have higher levels of implementation during their first two years. Given the potential significance of this process, the Consortium for Policy Research on Education (1998, 7) suggests that aiding schools in selecting an appropriate CSR model is one of the district's most important roles, and urges districts to "be aggressive in developing strategies that facilitate informed design selection by schools." Such strategies might include organizing design fairs, funding visits to schools exhibiting CSR models in action, and demanding data and information from model developers. Studies of the assistance districts provided to schools applying for federal CSR grants have found that districts' input and requirements for CSR model selection were "very influential in narrowing choices" (Ross, Hauser, and Workman 2001, 6). However, these studies did not find an apparent effect of district support on implementation differences in the first year of the federal grant program.

Professional Development and Technical Assistance

Elmore and Burney (1998, 1999) emphasize the importance of professional development for reform in their description of the long-term CSR effort in New York City's District #2. New York's reform effort surpassed most in its "depth, consistency, and instructional focus" (1998, 1), having involved substantial investments in professional development for teachers and principals. This professional development "focused on introducing and supporting specific instructional practices in literacy and mathematics" (1998, 1) and "enabled schools to approach instructional improvement in ways that were closely tailored to their situations" (1998, 13). Similarly, Stringfield and his coauthors (1997) find indications that resources for staff in-service time, particularly for a schoolwide program and for teachers' roles in that program, were then tied to successful implementation. Mizell (1999) urges policymakers to evaluate the level of support and professional development schools need for successful reform. Glennan (1998) further explains that several district-sponsored professional development and technical assistance activities—including training in site-based management, budget planning, instructional approaches, and use of technology—may have supported CSR model implementation.

Community Outreach

Marsh (2000) asserts that most studies examining the district's role in school reform treat the district's community as a contextual or background variable rather than as a key participant. Others (such as Firestone 1989, Firestone and Fairman 1998, and Rosenholtz 1991) indicated that community involvement hindered reform efforts. However, Florian, Hange, and Copeland (2000) found that administrators in 10 out of 16 districts cited building relationships with parents and other community members as an important factor in supporting reform. Moreover, Cohen (1995) argues that certain social resources that require parent and community involvement are critical to reform success; these include students willing to collaborate in reform efforts (and families that will support such efforts); students "decently prepared" to go to school and learn (i.e., clothed and well fed, receiving educational support from their families, and lacking burdensome family or social problems); and social and economic incentives and encouragement for academic work (e.g., from colleges or area businesses).

MEASURING IMPLEMENTATION

Level of CSR implementation has been widely studied and measured both qualitatively and quantitatively. Qualitative measures of implementation have often been based on a combination of model developers' benchmarks (Bifulco, Duncombe, and Yinger 2005; Bodilly et al. 1998; Smith et al. 1998); classroom observations (Bloom et al. 2001; Datnow et al. 2003; Engelmann and Engelmann 2004; Smith et al. 1997; Smith et al. 1998); and interviews with teachers, principals, and other staff. Quantitative measures of implementation have included measures based on principals' and teachers' self-reported survey answers, as well as more indirect measures such as the number of years a school has been implementing a CSR model (Barnes et al. 2004; Berends, Bodilly, and Kirby 2002; Berends et al. 2001; Cook et al. 1999; Kirby et al. 2001; Supovitz and May 2003).

Our approach is somewhat different. We measure implementation as *fidelity*: the extent to which the CSR model of interest is delivered to the intended recipients in the intended way (Aladjem 2003; Kurki et al. 2005). The approach we have developed measures what schools are actually doing and compares those activities with the set of activities that CSR model developers consider to be "full" implementation. Measuring implementation becomes an exercise in taking the difference between the empirical reality of school life and the model developer's normative vision.

We initiated this process by asking CSR model developers to fill out the same survey instruments (principal and teacher surveys) as our survey respondents, as if they were a fully implementing school. We compared the survey answers from our principals and teachers to the answers from their respective CSR model developers. Then, we calculated the distance between the ideal developer-specified implementation (the developers' answers) and the actual implementation taking place in schools (the principals' and teachers' answers). Squared euclidean distance was used to calculate the difference between developers' answers and principals' and teachers' answers; this distance measure was transformed into a school's percentage of implementation, to make interpretation of the results more intuitive. Although our implementation measure includes the same survey items for each CSR model, the survey answers by teachers and principals from each CSR model school are compared to the answers given by their respective model developer. As a result, each CSR model has its own individualized "fidelity of implementation" key. Thus, our measure of implementation can be understood as measuring how fully a school is engaged in optimal practices during full implementation of a specific CSR model. (For detailed description, see Kurki et al. 2005.)

The principal and district surveys were administered three times (once for each year of the study, 2002, 2003, and 2004), and the teacher survey was administered twice, during years one (2002) and three (2004). We focus on the full set of possible implementation indices, using the information provided by the CSR model developers in the teacher surveys.

The indices created based on the teacher survey instruments are closely aligned with the 11 components of Title I, Part F, of NCLB.[2] Our implementation indices include 7 general categories—Governance, Technology, Parent/Community Involvement, Professional Development, Assessment, Organization of Teaching/Classrooms, and Instruction—and 12 specific implementation indices—Shared Decisionmaking, Use of Technology in Classrooms, Parent/Community Involvement, Emphasis on Professional Development, Engagement in Informal Professional Development, Influence of Assessments, Use of Assessments, Inclusion, Student Grouping, Time Scheduled for Teaching, Curriculum, and Pedagogy (table 6.1).

Seven CSR model developers returned our principal and teacher surveys; the total number of schools for which we could create imple-

Table 6.1. Descriptions of Implementation Indices for Comprehensive School Reform Programs

Governance	
Shared Decisionmaking	The extent to which decisionmaking authority in a school is shared among faculty, staff, and administrators according to the CSR program developer's ideal. This index uses both principal and teacher survey items.
Technology	
Use of Technology in Classrooms	The extent to which teachers' use of technology in their classrooms matches the CSR program developer's ideal. This index uses both principal and teacher survey items.
Parent/Community Involvement	The extent to which a school's parent-school communication and community involvement match the CSR program developer's ideal. This index uses both teacher and principal survey items.
Professional Development	
Emphasis on PD	The extent to which the PD received by teachers matches the CSR program developer's ideal regarding the type (e.g., all grade-level teachers collectively vs. noncollectively) and emphasis of the PD.
Engagement in Informal PD	The extent to which teachers' engagement in informal PD (e.g., seminars, workshops, conferences) matches the CSR program developer's ideal.
Assessment	
Influence of Assessments	The extent to which different types of assessments influence students' grades, grouping decisions, curriculum adjustments, and the like, according to the CSR program developer's ideal.
Use of Assessments	The extent to which the teacher is using classroom assessments according to the CSR developer's ideal.
Organization of Teaching/ Classrooms	
Inclusion	The extent to which nonnative English speakers and students with disabilities are mainstreamed in general education classes, according to the CSR program developer's ideal.

Student Grouping	The extent to which students are taught in similar- or mixed-ability groups and how often these groups change, according to the CSR program developer's ideal.
Time Scheduled for Teaching	The extent to which the frequency and length of instructional time matches the CSR program developer's ideal.
Instruction	
Curriculum	The extent to which mathematics or English topics are taught according to the CSR program developer's ideal.
Pedagogy	The extent to which teachers engage in different instructional activities according to the CSR program developer's ideal.

CSR = comprehensive school reform
PD = professional development

mentation indices is 255. The actual number of schools or teachers for which we could create implementation scores varies, due to our survey and item response rates. Although we have seven CSR models in our sample, the number of schools implementing each model varies, but the proportion of schools using each CSR model in the sample closely mirrors the proportion of schools using these CSR models in the United States (table 6.2).

Some CSR developers did not provide the survey answers required to create all the indices included in this chapter. For example, the

Table 6.2. Number and Percentage of Schools Implementing Comprehensive School Reform Models

CSR model	Number of schools	% of schools
Accelerated Schools Project	39	15.3
ATLAS Communities	19	7.5
Co-nect	30	11.8
Success for All/Roots & Wings	135	52.9
Expeditionary Learning Schools Outward Bound	10	3.9
Modern Red SchoolHouse	15	5.9
Turning Points	7	2.7
Total	255	100.0

Source: Authors' calculations.
CSR = comprehensive school reform

Success for All/Roots & Wings developer did not return the separate survey for English teachers; therefore, Curriculum and Pedagogy indices could not be developed for English teachers. The Expeditionary Learning Schools Outward Bound developer did not answer survey questions needed to calculate indices for Parent/Community Involvement, Professional Development, Influence of Assessments, Inclusion, Curriculum, and Pedagogy. In addition, we do not have survey answers regarding Use of Technology, Parent/Community Involvement, and Inclusion for Modern Red SchoolHouse, and ATLAS Communities did not provide needed information regarding Curriculum. Consequently, analyses of these indices have lower numbers of total cases.

DATA AND METHODS

The analysis presented in this chapter includes only schools that we know were implementing a CSR program in 2000–2001. Although our approach can create implementation measures for comparison schools, we could not include comparison schools in our district-level analyses because our survey questionnaires were designed to ask about district support for CSR specifically. Thus, we do not have reliable measures of district support in general and cannot analyze whether CSR schools receive more or less district support than schools not implementing a CSR model. We further condensed our sample to include only those schools for which we could create implementation measures. As a result, our sample for descriptive district-level analysis includes 21 districts, and our sample for HLM analysis includes 255 schools and approximately 1,000 teachers. The actual number of observations included in each analysis varies, depending on the survey and the survey item response rates (both from CSR model developers and from teachers).

We use descriptive statistics to describe the level and change in district mandate, support, and context, and we use three-level (teacher, school, and district) HLM models to explore whether district support was related to the level of CSR model implementation by year three of the survey (2004). Ideally, we would relate the change in district mandate and district support to the change in schools' CSR model implementation between year one (2002) and year three (2004). However, due to teacher turnover, relatively few teachers returned surveys both in 2002 and 2004.[3] Therefore, we will focus on testing the association between the levels of district mandate and district support and the level of CSR model implementation in 2004. Further, we will limit our HLM analysis of CSR implementation to those indices with at least 9 percent of their variance at the district level, either in 2002 or 2004.

District support was measured using (1) items from the district survey that asked specifically about the types of support the district provides to CSR schools and (2) items from the principal survey that recorded principals' perceptions of the technical assistance and professional development their school received from their district. The district survey items capture whether a district has mandated CSR and give a comprehensive picture of the district's aid for CSR: is the district actively (1) supporting CSR model selection, (2) providing CSR-related professional development and technical assistance, and (3) engaged in including and informing the community about the CSR efforts? In addition, we have captured principals' perceptions of the usefulness of district assistance for CSR professional development and technical assistance.

RESULTS

To what extent are districts supportive of CSR, and did districts' level of support change between 2002 and 2004?

We explore the variation in district mandate, district support, and district context by descriptive analysis because our sample includes 21 school districts. To show this variation, we present descriptive statistics for both years 2002 and 2004. District support is measured by individual district support scales, as well as a total District Support variable that was created by summing the individual district support measures, except Community Outreach. We left Community Outreach out of the total measure, because it has a different scale and none of the districts offered full support for it (table 6.4).

Table 6.4 shows three distinguishable trends for district support. First, more than half of the districts in 2002 were clearly giving full support for professional development and technical assistance, indicating that districts offered all support activities used to compose these specific scales. In addition, the total District Support variable shows that almost one-fifth of the districts were engaged in all support activities listed in our district survey (omitting Community Outreach), and approximately 62 percent of the districts reported a very high level of support for CSR (more than 2.5 in a scale from 0.0 to 3.0). Similarly, in 2002, more than half of the districts (12 out of 21) had mandated CSR in at least a portion of their schools.

The second observable trend is the decrease in District Mandate co-occurring with stable, continuous district support. In 2002, 12 districts had mandated CSR for at least some of their schools; in 2004, only 4 did. Two districts had increased their support between 2002 and 2004 (i.e., they instituted a mandate or perceived themselves to be more

Table 6.3. Survey Items Used to Measure District Mandate, Support, and Context

District Mandate	
District and Principal Surveys	Which statement best characterizes your district's approach to requiring schools to adopt a comprehensive school reform program?
	(a) The district requires some schools to adopt a comprehensive school reform program.
	(b) The district actively supports the use of comprehensive school reform programs, but has no particular requirements for schools.
	(c) The district does not play a role in the selection of CSR programs.
District Support	
Principal's Perception of Technical Assistance (scale, $\alpha = 0.81$)	What types of technical assistance did the district provide to you as you were beginning to implement a comprehensive school reform program? ($1 =$ not provided by the district, $2 =$ not useful, $3 =$ slightly useful, $4 =$ moderately useful, $5 =$ extremely useful)
	TECH_A: The district provided instructional leadership to the teaching staff throughout the implementation of our comprehensive school reform program.
	TECH_B: The district facilitated negotiations with the comprehensive school reform program.
	TECH_C: The district provided coaching for me and other staff members in school-program relations.
	TECH_D: The district helped us to secure additional resources for implementation.
	TECH_E: The district required that our school improvement plan focus on program implementation and assisted us in the process of developing the plan.
Principal's Perception of Professional Development (scale, $\alpha = 0.57$)	The following questions address whether your district did any of three items to support the professional development of teachers during the CSR implementation process.
	PROF_A: The district provided a central office staff member who provided professional development to our faculty as needed.
	PROF_B: The district encouraged or required our teachers to participate in teacher support networks or mentoring programs.
	PROF_C: The district involved teachers in the development of assessments, curriculum, scoring rubrics, etc., in order to build professional capacity.

District Technical Assistance (scale, α = 0.91)	What types of technical assistance does the district provide for schools as they are beginning comprehensive school reform programs?

(a) The district provides instructional leadership to teaching staff throughout the implementation of comprehensive school reform.

(b) The district facilitates aspects of negotiations with comprehensive school reform programs.

(c) The district coaches principals and other staff to assist in school-program relations.

(d) The district negotiates with program or program developers for training and assistance.

(e) The district assists schools in securing additional resources for implementation.

(f) The district requires that school improvement plans focus on design implementation, and assists in this process.

District Professional Development (scale, α = 0.79)	Does your district do any of the following to support the professional development of teachers during the CSR implementation process?

(a) The district designates central office staff to rotate among schools to provide professional development as needed.

(b) The district employs staff members who are assigned to one school to provide continuous, on-site assistance.

(c) The district designates classroom teachers to provide information or support to their colleagues on specific innovations.

(d) The district has brought in external consultants to work specifically on school reform issues.

(e) The district encourages or requires the establishment of teacher support networks or mentoring programs.

(f) The district involves teachers in the development of assessments, curriculum, scoring rubrics, etc., in order to build professional capacity.

Community Outreach (scale, α = 0.77)	To what extent has the district engaged in any of the following activities to familiarize community members with school reform programs?

(a) The district discussed the comprehensive school reform process in a public forum prior to program selection.

(b) The district provides regular communication to the community about our reform efforts (through newsletters, web site information, press releases, etc.).

(c) The district makes efforts to actively involve community members in the reform process.

(d) The district provides information on findings from reform evaluation and monitoring in a public setting.

(continued)

Table 6.3. *(continued)*

Model Selection (scale, $\alpha = 0.81$)	What types of assistance does the district provide as schools are selecting a comprehensive school reform program?
	(a) The district assists schools in conducting a formal needs assessment that will allow them to select an appropriate program.
	(b) The district organizes "program fairs" during which schools can visit with design teams.
	(c) The district provides travel funds for school teams to visit school reform programs "in action."
	(d) The district provides written documentation on comprehensive school reform.
	(e) The district provides one-on-one facilitation to assist in selecting a comprehensive school reform program.
	(f) The district requires CSR developers to provide data on design impacts in different contexts.
	(g) The district helps schools to identify programs that are aligned with district standards and assessments.
District Context	
Prevalence of CSR (CSR concentration)	Standardized proportion of CSR schools and total number of schools in district, based on responses to district surveys.
Diversity of CSR	Standardized proportion of CSR programs and total number of CSR schools in district, based on responses to district surveys.
Principal's Perception of District Stability: District Policy and Leadership	To what extent is the following a problem for your school? (1 = not a problem, 2 = minor problem, 3 = moderate problem, 4 = major problem) (a) Frequent changes in district policy and reform priorities. (b) Changes in district leadership.

CSR = comprehensive school reform

supportive of CSR), while 11 districts either removed the mandate or decreased their support. However, the level of district support does not change significantly; key dimensions of support, technical assistance, and professional development remain stable over time.

The stability of district support is mirrored in our principal-level analysis. Principals in CSR schools perceived their schools to be receiving more professional development and more useful technical assistance in 2004 than in 2003. A paired *t*-test that included 134 schools indicates that the increase in principals' perceptions of the usefulness of technical assistance is statistically significant (at an 0.05 level). These results are

Table 6.4. Descriptive Statistics for District Mandate and Support Variables, 2002 and 2004

District Support N = 21	2002 Full support	2004 Full support	2002 Mean	STD	2004 Mean	STD
Model Selection	6 (31.6%)	6 (31.5%)	0.80	0.26	0.87	0.12
Technical Assistance	14 (66.7%)	13 (61.9%)	0.90	0.16	0.85	0.28
Professional Development	11 (52.4%)	11 (52.4%)	0.88	0.19	0.81	0.31
Community Outreach	0 (0.0%)	0 (0.0%)				
Total District Support	4 (19.0%) 13 (61.9%)[a]	4 (19.0%) 10 (47.6%)[a]	2.52	0.67	2.47	0.81

Perceived district support by principals

District Support N = 174	2002 Full support	2004 Full support	2002 Mean	STD	2004 Mean	STD
Professional Development	73 (40.5%)	60 (33.7%)	2.03	1.00	2.13	0.87
Technical Assistance	5 (2.8%)	5 (2.8%)	2.91	1.29	3.28	1.08

District Mandate N = 21	Mandated CSR	Mandated CSR				
Mandate	12	4	n.a.	n.a.	n.a.	n.a.

Source: Authors' calculations.

CSR = comprehensive school reform

n.a. = not applicable

Notes: Possible values for total District Support range from 0 (no support) to 4 (full support). *Full support* refers to having the highest value for each item in the district support scale.

[a] When a cut-off point of 2.6 instead of 3.0 is used for full total District Support.

consistent with our earlier finding that shows high levels of professional development and technical assistance support both in 2002 and 2004. These results together imply that the effects of a district policy change on mandates do not negatively affect the level of technical assistance or professional development received in schools implementing CSR.

To see whether district mandates and district support are associated with one another, we conducted a chi-square test between the District Mandate and District Support variables. Although our sample size is only 21, some of the individual scales measuring district support, such as district support for Technical Assistance and Professional Development, had significantly different levels depending on the type of district mandate in 2002 (i.e., whether the district mandated, supported, or played no role in CSR, significant at a 0.01 or higher level). Moreover, District Mandate was significantly related to total District Support both in 2002 and 2004. The District Mandate variable is not associated with principals' perceptions of professional development and technical assistance in 2003, but in 2004, significant associations can be found. In 2004, principals in districts that mandate CSR report higher usefulness of technical assistance (a mean of 3.5 in districts that mandated CSR, versus 2.98 in districts that played no role in CSR, significant at a 0.05 level). The trend regarding professional development is less clear: districts that report having no role in CSR have a bipolar distribution, implying that some districts provide very low levels of CSR-related professional development while others still provide high levels. This could again be because changes in district policy on CSR mandates do not necessary affect the level of professional development in schools that have already adopted a CSR model, or that the effect of a district's policy change is delayed. However, in general, principals in districts mandating CSR report higher levels of professional development than principals in districts that only support or have no role in CSR.

Although our descriptive results indicate that district mandates and district support could be associated, it is possible that district mandates affect schools through mechanisms other than district policy. For instance, districts that mandate CSR possibly have more schools adopting CSR models, and hence are required to build the supporting infrastructure. Alternatively, it might not be a mandate per se that makes districts more likely to provide more support, but the stability of policies and leadership.

Table 6.5 shows two interesting trends regarding the context in which CSR is taking place over time. First, districts in our sample clearly diverge on CSR between 2002 and 2004. Although the average CSR concentration (percentage of schools implementing a CSR model) increases over time, so does the standard deviation—some districts in our sample decided to drop CSR, while all schools in other districts are implementing it. Our analysis shows a significant relationship between CSR concentration and district mandate in 2004: districts that continue

Table 6.5. District Context for Comprehensive School Reform

| District Context | 2002 | | 2004 | |
n = 21	Mean	STD	Mean	STD
CSR diversity	0.28	0.27	0.13	0.12
CSR concentration	0.31	0.26	0.36	0.36
Perceived district instability by principals				
Instability in district policy	2.51	1.03	2.28	1.10
Instability in district leadership	2.63	0.88	2.46	0.95

Source: Authors' calculations.
CSR = comprehensive school reform

to mandate CSR also have higher concentrations of CSR schools, as would be expected. Interestingly, our measure of CSR diversity (the number of CSR programs in a district divided by the number of CSR schools in that district) decreases over time, implying that the districts that still embrace CSR have higher concentrations of CSR schools using fewer CSR models. This could be due to districtwide adoption of a few specific CSR models. Secondly, our principal-reported measures of district instability show that changes in district policies or district leadership became less of a problem in 2004 than in 2002 (a paired t-test shows that this difference is significant at the 0.05 level). To test whether it is the prevalence of CSR or the general district stability, and not the district mandate, that is driving the level of district support, we ran a similar descriptive analysis but could not find a significant relationship between district context measures and district support measures.

Our descriptive analysis of district mandates and support shows that many districts became less hands-on with CSR between 2002 and 2004. Support for CSR remains stable in most of the districts included in our sample. However, the district mandate appears in simple cross-sectional analysis to be related to the level of support districts provide for CSR. Consequently, if district mandates and support are related to schools' level of CSR program implementation, we would expect to find that districts' mandate or support for CSR is related to the level of CSR model implementation in 2004. We will address this question by conducting a three-level HLM analysis that appropriately acknowledges our nested data structure (e.g., teachers within schools, schools within school districts) and can simultaneously control for both teacher- and school-level factors likely to affect the change in CSR program implementation.

To what extent is the level of implementation of CSR a function of district support, change in mandate, or context? We started our exploration of the district's role in CSR model implementation by running two sets of unconditional three-level HLM models to see what proportion of variance is located at the district level. The proportion of variance at the district level is in itself an indicator of the district's importance: a small proportion of variance implies that (1) specific district CSR policies that would differentiate districts in CSR implementation do not exist, (2) CSR policies are similar across districts, or (3) district CSR policies are not effectively modifying principals' and/or teachers' behavior.

Our results are similar to those of Berends and his coauthors (2001), who find that approximately 80 to 90 percent of variation in CSR implementation resides at the teacher level. The exceptions are Shared Decisionmaking, Inclusion, Time Scheduled for Teaching, and Peda-

Table 6.6. Location of Variance in Comprehensive School Reform, Teacher vs. School vs. School District (percent)

Implementation indices	Teacher		School		School district	
	2002	2004	2002	2004	2002	2004
Governance						
Shared Decisionmaking	63.5***	84.6***	27.4***	11.8***	9.0***	3.6**
Technology	87.1***	91.1***	7.3***	5.9***	5.6**	2.9**
Parent/Community Involvement	78.6***	80.9***	16.7***	16.8***	4.7**	2.3*
Professional Development						
Emphasis on PD	91.9***	88.8***	4.7***	6.4***	3.8**	4.8**
Engagement in Informal PD[a]	81.7***	78.7***	15.5***	16.4***	2.7**	4.8**
Assessments						
Influence of Assessments	90.9***	94.0***	4.4***	5.9***	4.7**	~0.0
Use of Assessments	89.8***	91.9***	5.9***	6.5***	4.3**	1.5*
Organization of Teaching/Classrooms						
Inclusion	28.2***	63.7***	48.3***	26.3***	23.5**	10.0**
Student Grouping	96.8***	94.3***	3.2**	5.3***	~0.0	0.3
Time Scheduled for Teaching	54.0***	33.84***	38.2***	59.5***	7.8**	6.6**
Instruction						
Curriculum	78.3***	88.4***	19.9***	13.1***	2.1*	2.9*
Pedagogy	50.9***	43.9***	35.7***	42.8***	13.4***	13.4**

Source: Authors' calculations.
PD = professional development
[a] Informal professional development includes seminars, workshops, conferences, and the like.
* $p < 0.1$, ** $p < 0.05$, *** $p < 0.01$

gogy, each of which has a significant proportion of variance to be explained either at the school or district level. The first three indices—Shared Decisionmaking, Inclusion, Time Scheduled for Teaching—are quite clearly school- or even district-level phenomena; teachers do not usually have the power to decide the length of their lessons, whether ESL students or students with disabilities are mainstreamed, or how decisions are made in schools. The Pedagogy index, which measures teachers' self-reported classroom practices, has a surprisingly high proportion of variance at the school and district levels. This could be due to school- and district-level professional development in instruction. Interestingly, the Curriculum and Assessment indicies (use of specific curricula and programs and use of assessments in classrooms, respectively), which arguably could be determined by school districts, have most of their variance at the teacher level, showing how much the use and application of assessments vary by classroom. In general, a trend of increased variance at the teacher level seems to exist over time, which corresponds to the trend of school districts having a less hands-on approach to CSR that we found in our descriptive analysis.

For the purpose of this chapter, the most interesting outcomes are for Shared Decisionmaking, Inclusion, and Pedagogy, all of which have 9 percent or more of their variation at the district level (in both 2002 and 2004). In the subsequent analysis, we will focus on these outcomes to test whether changes in district policy affect the level of schools' CSR implementation.

To examine the association between district support and schools' level of CSR model implementation, we built a three-level HLM model in which the level of CSR implementation in 2004 is predicted by teacher-, school- and district-level variables. We expected higher levels of district support to be associated with higher levels of CSR implementation. The effect of district support was tested by adding different measures of district support one at a time to the base model. This approach was adopted due to the small number of school districts ($N = 20$; one district included in the study only has comparison schools that are not implementing a CSR model). To include the highest possible number of cases in the HLM analysis, we imputed for missing contextual variables by using multiple imputation.[4]

Our earlier research has shown that school-level contextual variables were less important predictors of CSR model implementation than those related to the actions of relevant CSR participants. Specifically, we found that a school's level of CSR model implementation is related to the model developer's support, the principal's instructional leadership, the quality of teachers' professional community, and the specific CSR model that the school adopts (Kurki et al. 2005). The level of implementation in 2004 may be affected by both the level of and change in our predictors. We examined our independent variables to assess whether large changes took place between 2002 and 2004. Because the school-level variables measuring school characteristics did not change significantly between 2002 and 2004, we decided to use the mean values from 2002 and 2004 in our analysis. For instance, we hypothesized that the change in implementation is affected by the mean level of poverty, not by the change in the level of poverty between 2002 and 2004. Although we wanted to use both the level of and change in variables that are likely to fluctuate more over time, such as teacher-level reports on Teacher Community, Usefulness of Developer's Assistance, and

Principal's Instructional Leadership, we could not because a small number of teachers returned surveys in both 2002 and 2004.

Thus, we include the following predictors in the base model:

- A set of dummy variables identifying schools implementing specific CSR models (school-level variables); the largest, Success for All/Roots & Wings, is used as a reference point.
- District Mandate, a dummy variable measuring whether a school was mandated to adopt a CSR model in 2002 (school-level variable) and changes in the district mandate variable (district-level variable).
- District support variables at the school level: Principal's Perception of Technical Assistance (scale, $\alpha = 0.81$) and Principal's Perception of Professional Development.
- Contextual variables describing school districts: CSR Concentration (district-level variable) and District Policy and Leadership Stability (school-level scales).
- Variables controlling for school context: Percentage of Students Receiving Free/Reduced-Price Lunch, Percentage of Non-English-Speaking Students, School with Middle Grades, and School's AYP Status in 2002 (school-level variables).
- Principal leadership: Principal's Instructional Leadership scale (an average of 2002 and 2004, teacher-level scale, $\alpha = 0.93$), a dummy variable recognizing new principals with one year of experience or less in their current school (school-level variable).
- Teacher background: a dummy variable identifying new teachers with one year of experience or less in their current school, a dummy variable distinguishing between English and mathematics teachers, a Teacher Community scale measuring the quality of teachers' professional community (average of 2002 and 2004, teacher-level scale, $\alpha = 0.89$).
- Usefulness of Developer's Support scale (2004) (teacher-level scale, $\alpha = 0.89$).
- Years of CSR implementation: dummy variables for three to five years and for more than five years of implementation (school-level variables).

To this base model we will add our district-level support measures.

District-Level Support: Mean Technical Assistance, Professional Development, Model Selection, and Community Outreach

The HLM model can be summarized as

$$Y_{ij} = \beta_{0j} + \sum B^* X + \varepsilon_{ijk} + \gamma_{jk} + \delta_k$$

where Y_{ij} is the implementation index; the units of analyses are i teachers that are nested within j schools and k districts; a data matrix X contains values for the predictors; while B is a set of coefficients to be estimated; and errors—district-level error δ_k, school-level error γ_{jk}, teacher-level error ε_{ijk}, and district-level error—are normally distributed, with a mean of zero.

Shared Decisionmaking

Most of the variance in Shared Decisionmaking is explained by the variables that designate different CSR models. Success for All/Roots & Wings, the omitted reference group, has consistently higher levels of implementation than other CSR models (approximately 4 to 10 percent higher). Our earlier research (Kurki et al. 2005) has shown that the vast differences among CSR models in schools' level of implementation are partially an artifact of the way in which implementation is measured; those CSR models that require unusual practices are likely to have lower levels of implementation because they are simply more difficult to implement with fidelity.

It is also clear that many variables related to the actors involved in CSR model implementation (i.e., principals, teachers, and developers) are also significant; Principal's Instructional Leadership and Usefulness of Developer's Support are positively related to schools' level of implementation, while being a new teacher has a negative association with schools' implementation of Shared Decisionmaking. The level of implementation of Shared Decisionmaking decreases the longer a school implements its CSR model, implying that CSR models' governance dimensions may be more important in the early phases of implementation. Of the contextual variables, the English teachers have a significantly higher percentage of implementation than the mathematics teachers.

District Mandate, measured either by 2002 school-level reports as to whether schools were required to adopt a CSR model or by district-reported policy changes in their mandate requirement for CSR, is not statistically significant related to schools' implementation of Shared Decisionmaking. Of the district support variables, principals' reports on the usefulness of the district's technical assistance or the types of professional development provided by the district are not associated with schools' level of implementation. However, the average level of technical assistance support is negatively related to the implementation of Shared Decisionmaking, while the district support regarding Model Selection is positively related to the fidelity of implementation. This positive relationship could be due to better model fit: district staff may consciously encourage principals and teachers to recognize and select CSR models with a significant governance element consciously. None of the measures of district context are significantly related to the level of Shared Decisionmaking implementation.

Pedagogy

As with Shared Decisionmaking and Inclusion, most of the variance in Pedagogy is explained by the CSR model variables. As before, our omitted Success for All/Roots & Wings variable has the highest level of implementation, ranging from 5 to 30 percent higher than the other CSR models. In addition, Pedagogy is implemented with higher fidelity in schools that have recently adopted a CSR program, perhaps highlighting the importance of instructional elements in many of the CSR models included in the study. Of the teacher-level variables, Teacher Community is positively related to the level of implementation of Pedagogy in five out of the six models, while English teachers have consistently higher levels of implementation than mathematics teachers.

Of the district support variables, only Community Outreach is significantly and positively related to the level of implementation. From the district-level contextual variables, Frequent Changes in District Leadership is negatively related to the level of implementation, but the effect of instability in the level of implementation remains small (approximately 1 percent).

Inclusion

Of the three implementation indices selected for HLM analysis, Inclusion is the most difficult to predict. As with Shared Decisionmaking, the level of implementation for Inclusion is mostly predicted by CSR model variables. Again, the Success for All/Roots & Wings model clearly has higher implementation levels (approximately 6 to 40 percent higher) than other CSR models. Inclusion is also negatively associated with the Percentage of Non-English-Speaking Students variable, as would be expected. This is likely due to our sample, which mostly includes urban schools with high percentages of minority students.

As with Shared Decisionmaking, district mandate variables are not significantly related to the level of implementation of Inclusion. From the district support variables, principals' perception of the usefulness of district-provided technical assistance is positively related to implementation with borderline significance, but its effect size is rather small (less than 2 percent). None of the district support variables have a significant relationship to the implementation of Inclusion.

DISCUSSION

Our descriptive analysis of district mandates and support for CSR reflects the reality in many school districts: policy positions do change, and often quite rapidly. These changes can be fostered by many factors such as district-level leadership change, or changes in state or federal policy. An example of the former happened in Memphis, which had a superintendent who supported CSR. Once the superintendent left, the CSR effort quickly faded. Similarly, federal policies such as Reading First and No Child Left Behind, which may compete and conflict with CSR, can cause districts to reduce their support for CSR. These policies may cause, for instance, districts to introduce new curricula that do not match ongoing CSR models. However, school districts could also possibly choose CSR as their main strategy for meeting the demands of federal policies such as No Child Left Behind, and opt for a mandated CSR strategy for struggling schools.

Several interesting trends can be seen in our descriptive analysis. First, districts mandated CSR less often in 2004 than in 2002: more than half of the districts that mandated CSR in 2002 had stopped doing so in 2004. Furthermore, district supports for CSR, especially those related to professional development and technical assistance, remain stable over time, implying that districts' mandate and support for CSR are not related over time in our sample of school districts (although we could find statistically significant relationships between District Mandate and District Support both in 2002 and 2004). Secondly, districts seem to diverge over the study period. In a subsample of districts in our study, CSR has institutionalized itself as a credible policy alternative and the number of schools adopting CSR models has increased, while some districts have stopped endorsing CSR and consequently have a lower concentration of CSR schools.

Although our descriptive analysis seems to have captured clear changes in districts' positions toward CSR, our HLM analysis reminds us about the relative importance of the district in the implementation of CSR models. Our unconditional three-level HLM model confirms results by Berends and coauthors (2001) that 80 to 90 percent of variance in CSR model implementation is located at the teacher level. These results imply that districts' chances of affecting CSR model implementation, perhaps even under the best possible circumstances, may be limited.

This finding is confirmed by our HLM analysis, which shows that the level of district support is not consistently related to three implementation measures chosen for closer examination: Shared Decisionmaking, Inclusion, and Pedagogy. For instance, for Shared Decisionmaking, the level of Model Selection support is positively related to the level of implementation, while the district's level of Technical Assistance has a negative effect on the fidelity of implementation. Only for the Inclusion outcome is the principal-reported usefulness of district technical assistance positive and significant. In addition, District Mandate, which in our descriptive analysis seems to be related to the level of district support, is not significantly associated with these outcomes. From the district-level contextual variables, district stability measures (i.e.. the lack of frequent changes in district policy and leadership) predict implementation of Pedagogy, but the effect is small.

If district mandate, support, and context do not predict the level of CSR model implementation, then what does? The level of implementation is mostly predicted by the CSR model being implemented. In our study, the Success for All/Roots & Wings model is consistently implemented at higher levels than most of the other CSR models. Not surprisingly, the Success for All/Roots & Wings model is often described as highly prescriptive. Our earlier research, however, has also shown that not all CSR models are equally easy to implement, which at least partially explains the differences in implementation among CSR models in our study. In addition to CSR model variables, the level of implementation is predicted by variables related to those who participate in CSR model implementation, such as being a new teacher in the school (teacher turnover), the quality of school-based leadership (specifically teachers' perceptions of their principal's instructional leadership), and the quality of teacher community.

NOTES

1. For more on a similar occurrence in San Antonio, see chapter 2 in this volume.

2. For a list of the 11 federally mandated components of the No Child Left Behind Act, see chapter 4.

3. The national average of teacher turnover in high-poverty urban schools is approximately 15 percent per year. We expect the turnover in our sample of high-poverty urban schools to be similar to or higher than the national average. We fully acknowledge that a high level of teacher turnover makes implementation of school-based programs such as CSR difficult. However, for a CSR model to improve a school, it must include the ingredients of sustainable change in an environment with high teacher turnover.

4. All variables used in the HLM models were included in the multiple imputation model. Multiple imputation created 15 datasets, which were analyzed. Results from each of the 15 data runs were combined to create final estimates and standard errors. Multiple imputation and meta-analysis were done by using SAS PROC MI and PROC MIANALYZE procedures.

REFERENCES

Aladjem, D. K. 2003. "Measuring Implementation across Multiple Interventions." Paper presented at the Association for Public Policy Analysis and Management Annual Research Conference, Washington, DC, November 6–8.

Anderson, S. E. 2003. "The School District Role in Educational Change: A Review of the Literature." ICEC Working Paper No. 2. Ontario: International Centre for Educational Change.

Appelbaum, D. 2002. "The Need for District Support for School Reform: What the Researchers Say." Research Brief. Washington, DC: National Clearinghouse for Comprehensive School Reform.

Asensio, M. L., and J. Johnson, 2001. "Comprehensive School Reform: Perspectives from Model Developers." WestEd Workshop for Model Developers Report. San Francisco: WestEd.

Barnes, C., E. Camburn, J. Kim, and B. Rowan. 2004. "School Leadership and Instructional Improvement in CSR Schools." Paper presented at the Annual Meeting of the American Educational Research Association, San Diego, CA, April 12–16.

Berends, M., S. Bodilly, and S. N. Kirby. 2002. "Facing the Challenges of Whole-School Reform: New American Schools after a Decade." Monograph/Report MR-1498-EDU. Santa Monica, CA: RAND.

Berends, M., S. N. Kirby, S. Naftel, and C. McKelvey. 2001. "Implementation and Performance in New American Schools: Three Years into Scale-Up." Monograph/Report MR-1145-EDU. Santa Monica, CA: RAND Corporation.

Bifulco, R., W. Duncombe, and J. Yinger. 2005. "Does Whole-School Reform Boost Student Performance: The Case of New York City." Journal of Policy Analysis and Management 24(1): 47–72.

Bloom, H. S., J. Rock, S. Ham, L. Melton, and J. O'Brien. 2001. "Evaluating the Accelerated Schools Approach." Report. New York: MDRC.

Bodilly, S., and M. Berends. 1999. "Necessary District Support for Comprehensive School Reform." In Hard Work for Good Schools: Facts, Not Fads, in Title I Reform, edited by G. Orfield and E. DeBray (113–21). Cambridge, MA: Civil Rights Project, Harvard University.

Bodilly, S., B. R. Keltner, S. W. Purnell, R. Reichardt, and G. Schuyler. 1998. "Lessons from New American Schools' Scale-Up Phase: Prospects for Bringing Designs to Multiple Schools." Monograph/Report MR-942-NAS. Santa Monica, CA: RAND.

Cohen, D.K. 1995. "What is the System in Systemic Reform?" Educational Researcher 24(9): 11–17.

Consortium for Policy Research in Education. 1998. "States and Districts and Comprehensive School Reform." CPRE Policy Briefs. Philadelphia: Consortium for Policy Research in Education, University of Pennsylvania.

Cook, T. D., F. Habib, M. Phillips, R. A. Settersten, S. C. Shagle, and S. M. Degirmencioglu. 1999. "Comer's School Development Program in Prince George's County: A Theory-Based Evaluation." American Educational Research Journal 36(3): 543–97.

Cross, C. T., ed. 2004. Putting the Pieces Together: Lessons from Comprehensive School Reform Research. Washington, DC: National Clearinghouse for Comprehensive School Reform.

Datnow, A., and S. Stringfield. 2000. "Working Together for Reliable School Reform." *Journal of Education for Students Placed at Risk* 5(1 and 2): 183–204.

Datnow, A., G. Borman, S. Stringfield, L. Rachuba, and M. Castellano. 2003. "Comprehensive School Reform in Culturally and Linguistically Diverse Contexts: Implementation and Outcomes from a Four-Year Study." *Educational Evaluation and Policy Analysis* 25(2): 25–54.

Desimone, L. 2000. "Making Comprehensive School Reform Work." Urban Diversity Series No. 112. New York: ERIC.

Elmore, R. F. 1997. "Accountability in Local School Districts: Learning To Do the Right Things." In *Advances in Educational Administration*, vol. 5, edited by Richard C. Hunter (59–82). Greenwich, CT: JAI Press.

Elmore, R. F., and D. Burney. 1998. "Continuous Improvement in Community District #2, New York City." Unpublished, Learning Development Center, University of Pittsburgh.

———. 1999. "Investing in Teacher Learning: Staff Development and Instructional Improvement." In *Teaching as the Learning Profession: Handbook of Policy and Practice*, edited by L. Darling-Hammond and G. Sykes (263–91). San Francisco: Jossey-Bass.

Engelmann, S. E., and K. E. Engelmann. 2004. "Impediments to Scaling Up Effective Comprehensive School Reform Models." In *Expanding the Reach of Education Reforms: Perspectives from Leaders in the Scale-Up of Educational Interventions*, edited by T. K. Glennan Jr., S. Bodilly, J. Galegher, and K. A. Kerr (107–33). Santa Monica, CA: RAND.

Firestone, W. A. 1989. "Using Reform: Conceptualizing District Initiative." *Educational Evaluation and Policy Analysis* 11(2): 151–64.

Firestone, W. A., and J. C. Fairman. 1998. "The District Role in State Assessment Policy: An Exploratory Study." Paper presented at the annual meeting of the American Educational Research Association, San Diego, CA, April 12–16.

Florian, J., J. Hange, and G. Copeland. 2000. "The Phantom Mandate: District Capacity for Reform, McREL at Aurora, CO; AEL at Charleston, WV; SEDL at Austin, TX." Paper presented at the annual meeting of the American Educational Research Association, New Orleans, LA, April 1–5.

Glennan, T. K. 1998. "New American Schools after Six Years." Monograph/Report MR-945-NAS. Santa Monica, CA: RAND.

Kirby, S. N., M. Berends, S. Naftel, and J. S. Sloan. 2001. "Schools Adopting Comprehensive School Reform Demonstration Models: Early Findings on Implementation." Santa Monica, CA: RAND.

Kurki, A., D. Aladjem, and K. R. Carter. 2005. "Implementation: Measuring and Explaining the Fidelity of CSR Implementation." Paper presented at the annual meeting of the American Educational Research Association, Montreal, April 11–15.

Marsh, J. A. 2000. "Connecting Districts to the Policy Dialogue: A Review of Literature on the Relationship of Districts with States, Schools, and Communities." CTP Working Paper W-00-1. Seattle: Center for the Study of Teaching and Policy, University of Washington.

McLaughlin, M., and J. Talbert. 2003. "Reforming Districts: How Districts Support School Reform." CTP Research Report R-03-6. Seattle: Center for the Study of Teaching and Policy, University of Washington.

Mizell, H. 1999. "What Key Reformers Have Learned about Reform." Panel presentation at the annual conference of the National Staff Development Council, Dallas, TX, December 4–8.

O'Day, J., and C. Bitter. 2003. "Evaluation Study of the Immediate Intervention/ Underperforming Schools Program and the High Achieving/Improving Schools Program of the Public Schools Accountability Act of 1999." Washington, DC: American Institutes for Research.

Rosenholtz, S. J. 1991. *Teachers' Workplace: The Social Organization of Schools.* New York: Teachers College Press.

Ross, J., L. Hannay, and B. Brydges. 1998. "District-Level Support for Site-Based Renewal: A Case Study of Secondary School Reform." *Alberta Journal of Educational Research* 44(4): 349–65.

Ross, S. M. 2001. "Creating Critical Mass for Restructuring: What We Can Learn from Memphis." AEL Policy Brief. Charleston, WV: AEL Inc.

Ross, S. M., B. A. Hauser, and C. Workman. 2001. "Regional Educational Laboratories' Studies on State and District Roles in the 1999–2000 CSRD Program: A Synthesis of Findings from CSRD Research and Evaluation." Paper prepared for the OERI Symposium on Comprehensive School Reform Research and Evaluation, Denver, CO, July 18.

Slavin, R. E. 1998. *Effective Methods: School District Strategies to Support School Change.* Baltimore, MD: Center for the Social Organization of Schools, Johns Hopkins University.

Smith, J., S. Maxwell, D. Lowther, D. Hacker, L. Bol, and J. Nunnery. 1997. "Activities in Schools and Programs Experiencing the Most, and Least, Early Implementation Successes." *School Effectiveness and School Improvement* 8(1): 125–50.

Smith, L., S. Ross, M. McNelis, M. Squires, R. Wasson, S. Maxwell, W. Weddle, L. Nath, A. Grehan, and T. Buggey. 1998. "The Memphis Restructuring Initiative: Analysis of Activities and Outcomes that Impact Implementation." *Education and Urban Society* 30(3): 296–325.

Snipes, J., F. Doolittle, and C. Herlihy. 2002. "Foundations for Success: Case Studies of How Urban School Systems Improve Student Achievement." Report prepared for the Council of the Great City Schools. New York: MDRC.

Stringfield, S., M. A. Millsap, R. Herman, N. Yoder, N. Brigham, P. Nesselrodt, P. Schaffer, E. Karweit, M. Levin, and R. Stevens. 1997. *Urban and Suburban/ Rural Special Strategies for Educating Disadvantaged Children: Final Report.* Washington, DC: U.S. Department of Education.

Supovitz, J. A., and H. May. 2003. *The Relationship between Teacher Implementation of America's Choice and Student Learning in Plainfield, New Jersey.* Philadelphia: Consortium for Policy Research in Education, University of Pennsylvania.

Togneri, W., and S. E. Anderson. 2003. *Beyond Islands of Excellence: What Districts Can Do to Improve Instruction and Achievement in All Schools.* Washington, DC: The Learning First Alliance and the Association for Supervision and Curriculum Development.

7

COMPREHENSIVE SCHOOL REFORM VS. NO CHILD LEFT BEHIND

Elgin L. Klugh and Kathryn M. Borman

This chapter addresses the challenges facing large city school districts presented with both a reform agenda in the context of comprehensive school reform (CSR) models and accountability requirements associated with No Child Left Behind (NCLB). Of particular interest in this analysis are the challenges to CSR adoption, implementation, and sustainability, as they are perceived by district administrators and others closely engaged in district-level decisionmaking. Using data from interviews with district administrators, university researchers, nonprofit agency workers, teacher organization administrators, and school principals, challenges are identified and grouped into seven thematic areas that form the framework for the district case studies included in this chapter.

CSR models were developed to focus on school-level changes (Rowan, Camburn, and Barnes 2004). As there are in excess of 800 different "models" or "designs," ideally, each school is able to choose a model with design features helpful to the school environment, faculty, and student population in question (Rowan et al. 2004). However, the current context of national and state policies emphasizing accountability and high-stakes testing for all public school students has compelled many schools and districts to make adjustments in the ways that they take on whole-school reform (Datnow 2005).

To adhere to accountability requirements, districts discussed in this chapter have created districtwide instructional programs that align with state and federal standards and assessments. One might assume that these efforts would be the death knell to school-based approaches such as CSR. However, research presented here describes at least four urban school districts that have not abandoned CSR, but instead have found ways to incorporate and align models into a standards-based, high-accountability environment.

The five medium and large urban school districts we discuss in this chapter (called here Eastwicker, Oceanway, Riverton, Everville, and Dodgeland) were selected based upon the number and variety of models they were using. Each district is racially and ethnically diverse, although dominated by a large African American student population, and administrators must deal with problems common to many urban schools, including budgetary constraints, declining physical facilities, and a host of issues associated with low-income student populations. To gain an understanding of the context in which district administrators operate, we first turn to an exploration of the literature on school districts in general, literature concerning NCLB, and challenges relating to CSR in particular.

DISTRICT CONTEXT

The district context is a critically important mediator of reform at the school level (McLaughlin and Talbert 2003; Spillane 1996). By *context*, we refer to the set of both school district demographic characteristics and those policies affecting district-level involvement in school reform. Both sets of factors are important because they influence CSR adoption, implementation, and sustainability.

Corcoran and Lawrence (2003, 1) describe school districts as "uniquely American institutions" representing our cultural emphasis on the importance of local control over education, and further define districts as entities positioned between state authorities and schools, with responsibilities to "interpret and buffer state policies and initiatives" and to engage in policymaking. Thus, "local policies, priorities, and capabilities continue to exert powerful influences on teaching and learning, on the selection and implementation of reforms, and, therefore, on the improvement of academic outcomes." Given the American preference for local control, and the recent intrusions (or advances) made by the federal government into educational policy areas tradition-ally not within their purview (Borman et al. 2004), districts can be seen as the central points of an ongoing "tug-of-war" between advocates of school-based reform and reform initiatives prescribed by governmental authorities that tend to emphasize a "one size fits all" approach.

Viewing CSR from the perspective of its role in this power struggle is informative. In the face of questions about districts' competence in orchestrating reform and improving student achievement (Chubb and Moe 1990; Hess 1999; Hill and Celio 1998), it is has been argued that implementing CSR has been a way for educational researchers and CSR model and program developers to "bypass the district governance structure to work directly with schools" (Corcoran and Lawrence 2003, 1). However, a critical look at CSR reveals that district personnel are instrumental to CSR efforts (Borman et al. 2004; Consortium for Policy Research in Education 1998; Massell and Goertz 1999; Spillane and Thompson 1997) and are often aware of challenges associated with the various thematic areas we discuss below.

No Child Left Behind

The No Child Left Behind Act (NCLB) was overwhelmingly passed by both houses of Congress in 2001, then subsequently signed into law by President George W. Bush in 2002 (Popham 2004). Specific provisions of the law support varied items such as the following.

- **Title I funding:** the law increases Title I funding "for students in high-poverty schools."
- **Teacher qualifications:** "under *No Child Left Behind*, all teachers must be highly qualified by the end of the 2005–06 school year."
- **Language instruction:** NCLB provides funds and expands "educational opportunities for all students, including students who are learning the English language and students who are new to this country."
- **Parental choice:** under NCLB, "students who attend Title I schools that do not make adequate yearly progress, as defined by the states, for two consecutive years have the option of transferring to a higher-performing public school or charter school within their district."
- **Accountability:** "every state is required to (1) set standards for grade-level achievement and (2) develop a system to measure the progress of all students and subgroups of students in meeting those state-determined grade-level standards."

- **Responsiveness to local needs:** NCLB "provides unprecedented levels of flexibility regarding the management of federal funds" so that "states and school districts have the flexibility to pursue educational excellence by the means that best meet their needs."
- **Reading:** a goal of NCLB is to have "every child reading by 3rd grade."
- **Children with disabilities:** "The 1997 reauthorization of the Individuals with Disabilities Education Act (IDEA) required that students with disabilities be included in state- and districtwide assessment programs. *No Child Left Behind* builds on this requirement by ensuring that these assessments measure how well students with disabilities have learned required material in reading and mathematics" (U.S. Department of Education 2004, 14–21).

Though primarily associated with the George W. Bush administration, NCLB's design predates it. Noting the tendency of critics to associate NCLB solely with the current Republican administration, Chenoweth (2004, 42) writes,

> Although George Bush took a lot of credit for it, and his secretary of Education, Dr. Roderick Paige, has put some teeth into it by refusing to grant waivers, NCLB really had its start in the 1994 reauthorization [of the Elementary and Secondary Education Act of 1965] under President Bill Clinton and was shepherded along its way by such Democratic politicians as Sens. George Mitchell and Edward Kennedy.

These ideologically varying proponents of NCLB call into question any simplistic, partisan criticisms.

Bracey (2004, 79) reports that criticisms concerning NCLB stem from "four discrete sources." These are (1) "state legislatures like Virginia that resent the federal intrusion" and see NCLB as an unfunded mandate, because the actual costs of implementing the law exceed the money provided by the federal government—"often by a great deal"; (2) "members of AASA [the American Association of School Administrators] as well as other organizations who perceive NCLB to be based on a flawed strategy for organizational change—punishment"; (3) "teachers and experts in various fields of instruction who perceive that the educational assumptions about learning embedded in NCLB are all wrong"; and (4) "independent scholars . . . who in various publications have called attention to the role of social class and poverty in producing the 'achievement gap'." Each of these groups has its own set of circumstances and constituencies, but all share a common concern about the capacity of schools and districts to successfully achieve adequate yearly progress (AYP) targets.

Concerning AYP, Bracey (2004, 70) writes,

> AYP is not a new concept, having been part of the reauthorization of the Elementary and Secondary Education Act in 1998 (which, technically, is what NCLB is, too). But NCLB throws in two new curves: (1) schools that fail to make AYP for two or more consecutive years are subject to increasingly harsh sanctions, and (2) all children must score at the "proficient" level or better by 2014. And pigs will fly.

Though his discussion of NCLB may be faulted as politically charged, serious concerns about AYP targets and the requirement of 100 percent proficiency for all subgroups of students by 2014 are echoed elsewhere (e.g., Popham 2004).

Implications for District Administrators

Education in the United States has a strong tradition of local control, thus elevating the importance, and local impacts, of district administrators. However, it may be argued that NCLB has altered freedom, flexibility, and traditional district roles long taken for granted.

The pressures of accountability are real, and potentially severe. Popham (2004, 43) reports,

> If a district fails AYP for four consecutive years, then the state must take one of several—quite severe—corrective actions regarding the district. For example, the state can (1) replace district personnel deemed to be responsible for the district's failure; (2) authorize students to transfer to schools in another, higher-performing district if that district agrees to accept such transfers; or (3) shut down the district altogether.

The U.S. Department of Education explains that NCLB provides unprecedented levels of flexibility with federal funds so that "states and school districts have the capacity to pursue educational excellence by the means that best meet their needs" (U.S. Department of Education 2004, 19). However, the prescriptions of NCLB, and the severe sanctions if requirements are not met, arguably narrow the focus and decrease the flexibility of district administrators. In fact, as this research shows, though NCLB officially recognizes and provides for CSR in Title I, Part F, of the 2002 Elementary and Secondary Education Act (U.S.

Department of Education n.d.), district administrators are often engulfed in efforts to meet AYP targets at the expense of dedicating time, energy, and funds toward CSR.

EMERGENT THEMES

On the surface, CSR and NCLB appear to conflict. CSR is a school-based strategy that lends itself to uniqueness and creativity, while NCLB is a federal government–mandated mega-reform (targeting all levels of educational practice and professionalism) aimed at increasing standards, accountability, and uniformity. An analysis of 91 district administrator, community stakeholder, and principal interviews across the five districts revealed seven major thematic areas that represent the most frequently occurring challenges associated with the adoption, implementation, and sustainability of CSR in the current climate of NCLB:

- **administrative mandates:** the extent that top-down decisions impede or change the focus of local reform efforts;
- **instability of leadership and policy:** how lack of continuity among district, state, and federal educational leaders, and shifting priorities affect ongoing efforts at reform;
- **model fit:** how to make sure a given CSR model at the school level aligns with instructional goals, and the culture and vision of the district and the school;
- **teacher buy-in:** the extent to which teachers resist or accept model practices;
- **teacher and student mobility:** how high teacher turnover and student mobility affect district efforts to coordinate and organize curriculum and instruction;
- **resources:** concerns associated with securing adequate funding for successful implementation and sustainability of CSR; and
- **developer limitations:** obstacles faced by districts in securing necessary professional development and technical support from developers.

As illustrated by our findings, these seven themes represent varying degrees of challenge when analyzed across districts, and when viewed from the perspective of district personnel as opposed to community stakeholders and principals. We turn now to an exploration of existing literature to establish a foundation for understanding these thematic areas.

Administrative Mandates

When district administrators make decisions, school personnel responsible for reform, particularly principals, may be resentful; however, the press of policies emanating from the state or federal levels compel district administrators' decisions. Borman and her coauthors (2004, 110) discuss the hierarchy of educational authority in which districts exist, and the complications this hierarchy may have for CSR implementation. They write, "District policies may be undercut by state-mandated requirements, and both districts and states are required to address federal legislative controls."

District administrators act as filters, or midlevel management, for state and federal policy. At the same time, they have authority to establish their own policy agendas. Thus, the way in which district administrators understand, interpret, and disseminate policy is critical in any reform process (Marsh 2000; Spillane 1996). District administrators have the ability to support, undermine (Rosenholtz 1991), or even abandon CSR (Colgan 2002). In a study of the CSR models under the rubric of New American Schools, Berends and his coauthors (2002) present evidence to show the importance of focused district leadership intent on providing adequate resources and professional development for successful reform. Likewise, McLaughlin and Talbert (2003) explain that sharing responsibility for carrying out and supporting CSR "across levels within district offices promotes effective reform," and can mitigate against potentially disruptive turnover in district leadership (Borman et al. 2004, 115). Conversely, these researchers explain that lack of district support for CSR negatively influences outcomes.

Districts' decisions to support reform can make a positive difference (Elmore and Burney 1997). However, a test of dedication to supporting CSR may be a district's efforts to build its reform-managing capacity. Fullan (2004) discusses district offices as "silos" that are narrowly organized to carry out their specific responsibilities. However, research (e.g., McLaughlin and Talbert 2003), shows that organizational coherence and shared responsibility are basic ingredients for "district capacity" to successfully manage CSR (Borman et al. 2004, 114–15). Thus, it is no surprise that reformers and researchers intent upon promoting CSR have begun to ask how school districts can be transformed into "effective agents of improvement," especially given that NCLB legislation has increased pressure to show timely districtwide improvement (Corcoran and Lawrence 2003, 1).

An extreme example of top-down decisionmaking detrimental to CSR happened in Memphis. Colgan (2002, 10) writes,

Few local education stories were bigger in summer 2001 than the decision made by Johnnie Watson, superintendent of Memphis

City Schools, to end his district's six-year implementation of district-wide comprehensive reform models. The reform was begun in 1995 by Watson's predecessor, Gerry House, who had gained acclaim for her work in a struggling district and was named national superintendent of the year in 1999.

Despite his predecessor's claims of improvement, bolstered by supportive data on student achievement and teacher satisfaction, the new superintendent, himself bolstered by research (prepared after the former superintendent's departure), claimed CSR was a liability for the district and instituted his own curriculum program (Colgan 2002, 10–11). Despite a third-party evaluator stating that the latest district study "was based on flawed design and analyses" and an offer by former New American Schools president Mary Anne Schmitt "to invest funds in a joint [New American Schools–Memphis City Schools] evaluation on the state of CSR on a school-by-school basis," the new superintendent was unwilling to keep CSR (New American Schools n.d., 1–3). Given the potential of such politically based changes, which tie directly into how unstable leadership and policy can negatively affect CSR implementation and sustainability, it is not at all surprising that district officials and school principals might hesitate to commit significant resources and efforts to CSR districtwide.

Instability of Leadership and Policy

Several researchers have presented evidence demonstrating that unstable district leadership has adverse effects on reform and district performance (Berends et al. 2002; Manpower Demonstration Research Corporation 2002; Murphy and Hallinger 1986). Corcoran and Lawrence (2003, 3) point to work by Murphy and Hallinger (1986; 1988) that "examined the role of superintendents in the improvement process and concluded that stability of leadership and focus were key factors in district performance." Likewise, findings from Berends and his coauthors' (2002) study on New American Schools show that unstable district leadership and incoherent policies have adverse effects on districts' ability to carry out successful comprehensive school reform.

Datnow (2005, 122–23) discusses how changing state and district policy environments affect the sustainability of CSR models. She writes,

A longitudinal study of the implementation of six externally developed school reform models in 13 schools in one urban district provides an interesting opportunity to investigate reform sustainability under changing environmental conditions. . . . After 3 years, reform expired in 6 of the 13 schools we studied; two other schools were still implementing reforms but at very low levels. Only 5 of the 13 schools were still continuing to implement their reform designs with moderate to high levels of intensity. During this period, significant policy and political shifts occurred at the district and state levels.

Datnow (2005, 147) posits that these "policy and political shifts" adversely affected schools' ability to focus on sustaining CSR until model practices could achieve institutionalization. Noting that most reforms do not last, and citing these shifts as a contributing factor, she goes on to explain,

> Policy systems need to become aware of how they are influencing comprehensive school reform efforts and decide whether these are the effects they desire. More than 6,000 schools have received federal funding for reform through the federal Comprehensive School Reform Demonstration (CSRD) program. Meanwhile, states are simultaneously implementing high stakes accountability systems. Districts are also now increasingly promoting their own change efforts. In other words, change vectors are coming at schools from several directions, which may or may not be well synchronized.

New regimes, an apparent constant in urban school districts where superintendents serve an average of two to five years in a given superintendency (Council of the Great City Schools 2003), may interpret policy directives differently and also often desire to implement their own aggressive policies. The corresponding shifts in support (financial and professional development) and instructional priorities make proper reform model implementation problematic, and lead many schools to abandon models or to put them on the "back burner" (Datnow 2005, 136).

Model Fit

Given the array of CSR models and their varying pedagogical and organizational approaches, success may depend on how well selected models align with district goals and/or mandates. O'Day and Bitter (2003) explain how implementing a districtwide instructional program in one California district led to problems in schools using differently focused models. In response to such issues, model developers and district personnel are paying closer attention to how model design features align with district goals.

In April 2004, the "From Whole-School to Whole-System Reform" conference was convened in Chicago by the National Clearinghouse for Comprehensive School Reform, the Annenberg Institute for School Reform, the Consortium for Policy Research in Education, and New American Schools to explore the impacts of whole-school reform, and "what actions will be required to take reform efforts to the next level" (Martinez and Harvey 2004, 1). Several suggestions emerged on creating a "balance" between model providers and schools' and districts' capacity to successfully utilize models.

- Model developers and intermediaries must recognize that many complex activities occur simultaneously within individual schools and their districts; these need to be reconciled to maintain coherence when new initiatives are adopted.
- All participants must recognize the importance of partnerships. The most effective reform designs promote a team-based approach for building local competence, rather than allowing each entity to act independently by importing expertise that may be impervious to the local district context in which the school is embedded.
- Reform models must have the capacity to adapt to the local district context, a characteristic that should be developed alongside the capacity of the school and district to carry out further reforms.
- An alternative support infrastructure must be established to provide direct guidance and consultation to schools in the autonomous selection of their reform models.
- Districts must find ways to sustain multiple school reform programs—by maintaining a so-called "portfolio of schools"—in an era when districts demand greater alignment across professional development, the curriculum, and instructional practice (Martinez and Harvey 2004, 2).

These suggestions, while focusing on model developers' flexibility and districts' willingness to take a "teamwork" approach to addressing CSR, hearken back to earlier suggestions about the district's responsibilities for CSR model design alignment:

- help schools make matches,
- embed the comprehensive school design approach into the district's and school's continuing operations,
- design a new district operating environment,
- find an approach to supporting comprehensive school reform that fits the district,
- monitor and control design teams' quality and performance, and

- create a public engagement process that informs parents and the community about comprehensive school reform (Consortium for Policy Research in Education 1998).

These are ideal roles and responsibilities for district personnel in addressing CSR model design alignment; however, negotiating these in an environment of shifting policy directives (as discussed later in this paper) has proven to be quite a challenge.

Teacher Buy-In

The best-planned reforms cannot achieve success without teachers committed to altering their practices and learning new approaches. David and Shields (2001) explain that changes in practice do not result by simply putting components of a program in place. Instead, they stress the importance of on-site guidance and continued professional development for teachers in creating successful reform. Datnow (2001) explains that perceived district support for reform is also a key factor in teachers' accepting and internalizing its value. Borman and her coauthors (2004, 119) report,

> The current literature on buy-in suggests that three elements are critical to promoting buy-in and commitment by teaching staff. These include (1) the process by which teacher support for reform is obtained; (2) alignment of teacher's perceptions of the school's main problems and the strategies proposed to address them; and (3) the amount of professional development and technical support provided by the developer.

Among the literature Borman and her coauthors (2004) reference are studies by Datnow and others (1998) and Ross and others (1997). According to these researchers, model developers are aware of the importance of teacher buy-in. This, accordingly, is the primary reason for most models requiring "that at least 80 percent of the faculty support the model adoption" (Borman et al. 2004, 119).

Since teachers' initial attitudes about models are so important (Le Floch, Zhang, and Herrmann 2005), it is a concern that teachers may be pressured to work with models they do not accept and continually undermine after adoption. Pressure may come from the principal or may emanate from the district (Datnow 2000). Despite the 80 percent positive faculty vote most model developers require, Datnow (2000, 362) reports that teachers often saw the voting process as meaningless and quotes one individual who explained, "It was a vote, but we voted until they got their way."

Even teachers who willingly accept models may, unwittingly, be an obstacle to successful implementation. Spillane (2002) explains that teachers may not clearly understand the extent of change needed to implement reform, and instead make only minor adjustments to their established methods. This issue points to the importance of professional development, not only in the initial stages of reform, but continued throughout the reform process (Borman et al. 2004). Another caution is that teachers interested in model adoption but unwilling to change their established practices may undercut reform by choosing models similar to their established routines (Borman et al. 2004, 21; Datnow and Stringfield 2000).

Teacher and Student Mobility

Literature that speaks directly to the impacts of teacher and student mobility on CSR is sparse. However, teacher turnover is a potential obstacle for CSR's sustainability in schools, given that new teachers would have to constantly be trained about the models (Haynes 1998, 91). This training may be superficial (limited to procedural rather than transformative knowledge) if teachers did not participate in initial model implementation. Meanwhile, teachers who were committed to, vested in, and the most knowledgeable about the transformative aspects of models may be lost.

"Moderately higher rates" of teacher turnover are a fact of life in most urban districts and affect the district's ability to organize effective districtwide improvement (Ingersoll 2001, 3). Likewise, students moving between schools with different models may present instructional challenges. Despite the threats posed by these factors, districts that adopt a well-articulated program of reform can sustain improvements over time. As an example, District #2 in New York City was effective in systemically implementing standards-based reform in literacy, improving student achievement dramatically (Elmore and Burney 1997; Resnick and Harwell 2000).[1] In this case, "the district adopted a clear vision of good practice in literacy instruction, mobilized its resources to focus on its enactment, and sustained its focus over a number of years" (Corcoran and Lawrence 2003, 4). However, after personnel change at top administrative levels and organizational changes, District #2 looks more like comparable schools in terms of activities and performance.

Research by the Manpower Demonstration Research Corporation (2002) compared urban districts that had made relatively fast progress in reforms and student achievement against those with slower progress. Among characteristics of the rapidly improving districts, this research identified political and organizational stability, efforts to adopt "district-wide curricula and instructional approaches rather than allowing schools to devise their own strategies," and efforts to support "these district-wide strategies through professional development and technical assistance" (Corcoran and Lawrence 2003, 5). These district-level efforts at coherence militate against adverse effects of teacher and student mobility.

Resources

Districts' resources often make or break school reform efforts. In some cases, districts have used their resources or budgets and professional development activities to support certain CSR models and discourage others. For example, Datnow (2000) tells of a district that decided to fund Success For All schools. Similarly, Yonezawa and Datnow (1999) describe a district that actively supported schools using New American Schools with funds for training and full-time facilitators, while passively responding to support requests from schools using other models. Districts may provide resources for CSR through "assistance with program selection, provision of coaches in schools, professional development for teachers, technical assistance for implementation, and district community outreach activities," and by adjusting budgets and/or relaxing regulations to accommodate CSR (Aladjem et al. 2005, 2).

In fall 1997, Congress authorized $150 million to support comprehensive reform models.[2] This money was known as the Comprehensive School Reform Demonstration program (CSRD) or the Obey-Porter program (Consortium for Policy Research in Education 1998). This money gave cash-strapped urban schools and districts an additional source to augment budgets and implement progressive programming. However, governmental shifts in educational priorities (and associated funding programs) have left districts "holding the bag" and facing hard decisions about funding priorities (Borman et al. 2004, 111). Likewise, changes in leadership and priorities at the district level and consequent "withdrawal of financial support" for CSR models have left schools burdened with finding funding for existing reforms (Datnow 2005, 140).

Developer Limitations

Logic dictates that proper implementation of CSR models should involve input and assistance from model developers. However, the extent of assistance may differ according to the complexity of the model and the developer's capacity to provide technical assistance and professional development.

The primary way that developers support reform models is through professional development (Cotner et al. 2005, 6). On-site developer presence is a crucial support source for model implementation (Desimone 2000, 20), and the continued presence of developers or design teams positively impacts model sustainability (Haynes 1998). As explained in the earlier section on teacher buy-in, continued professional development assistance greatly increases the likelihood of successful reform.

Cotner and her coauthors (2005, 28) discuss the importance of ongoing developer support, explaining that it "was discussed as a challenge to implementation when school stakeholders perceive that they did not receive adequate assistance from the developer." This lack of assistance may result when the developer does not have the capacity to provide promised services, or from district budgetary issues that prevent a developer from working in the school. However, with models designed to "internalize" support by using district staff as coaches, districts have erred by appointing coaches without reducing their other responsibilities.

Methodology

Methods informing data collection and subsequent analyses were designed to allow (1) coherence of methods across study analyses, through reliance upon the construct key designed during the project; and, *most importantly*, (2) development of a set of comparative case studies involving each of the five districts in the present study.

District Selection

Districts analyzed in this chapter are those comprising the subject matter of the larger, five-year National Longitudinal Evaluation of Comprehensive School Reform conducted by the American Institutes for Research. For this study, urban school districts of similar size throughout the country were selected based upon the number of CSR models operating in the district, and the economic and social diversity of their student populations.

Data Collection

Data were collected over a two-week period in each of the five districts of interest in two waves. The first wave of data collection occurred in all five of the districts during the 2002–2003 school year, with the second occurring in 2004. Eighty-two interviews with all participants whose data are considered here occurred in the first wave, with an additional nine taking place in three districts. While the research questions and the analytic approach are aimed at understanding the districts' perspectives on CSR, our data analysis also relied upon supporting evidence gathered from other research participants who had a perspective on the district's role in CSR. Thus, we also take into account the interview data provided by community members and school principals. In all but a few cases, interviews were undertaken by the second author. All interviews were open ended and lasted 45 minutes on average.

District-Level Participants

Identification of key individuals at the district level was undertaken using a modified reputational approach. In other words, beginning at the level of the superintendent or CEO of the district, we endeavored to contact those in key school district positions identified as most knowledgeable about school reform generally and about implementation of CSR specifically. This process was repeated in each of the districts in question and generated a list of 5 to 10 people in each district administrative office. Subsequently, each of those identified was contacted and appointments for interviews during the course of our stay were arranged.

Community Participants

In addition, members of the districts' communities were contacted. Individuals with links to the district's school reform efforts, generally, and CSR, specifically, were identified. This was done primarily in consultation with each principal, to determine if there were community members (in social service agencies, for example) who supported implementing and sustaining the model in question. Where appropriate, we use information from community interviews, although they are not central to the analyses presented here.

Principals

The 34 principals whose interview data were analyzed for this chapter were working for the schools included in the study.

Analysis

Once data were collected during the research period (2002–2004), they were transcribed by experienced transcriptionists familiar with the goals of the project. All totaled, 91 interviews with district administrators, community members, and principals were transcribed.

Table 7.1 shows the array of the data across the five districts, indicating the individual's role or position in the district management structure. District personnel positions are summarized in two occupational categories, *senior-level administrators* and *midlevel administrators.* Senior-level administrators are those whose positions are closely associated with the superintendent's office and are central to policymaking within the district. Examples of these positions are chief academic officer and associate superintendent. Examples of positions labeled midlevel administrators are testing coordinator, program associate, and director of research.

Community interviews were done with individuals associated with various entities involved with schools and school reform. These are summarized using the occupational categories *university researcher, nonprofit worker*, and *teachers union administrator.* University researchers are those associated with universities, in teaching and/or research capacities, who are actively engaged in school reform. Nonprofit workers represent organizations working either directly with schools and students (such as GEAR UP, a federal competitive grant program "designed to increase the number of low-income students who are prepared to enter and succeed in postsecondary education"),[3] or organizations engaged in implementing and researching school reform, such

Table 7.1. Number of Individuals Interviewed, by Study Site

	Study site					
Occupational category	*Eastwicker*	*Oceanway*	*Riverton*	*Everville*	*Dodgeland*	*Total by category*
District	6	1	9	8	4	28
Senior-level administrator	2	1	4	2	1	10
Midlevel administrator	4	0	5	6	3	18
Community	5	5	10	6	3	29
University researcher	1	1	2	1	0	5
Nonprofit worker	4	4	7	4	2	21
Teachers union administrator	0	0	1	1	1	3
Principal						
School principal	4	8	7	5	10	34
Total by district	15	14	26	19	17	91

Note: Study site names are pseudonyms.

as the National Clearinghouse for CSR. Teachers union administrators are individuals actively engaged in representing teacher concerns and informed on local district politics as they relate to reform.

Construct Tables

Following the transcription of the data, detailed analyses were undertaken. The first step in this process was a preliminary data sort, done by closely reading each transcript. As transcripts were read, relevant excerpts were entered into construct tables collaboratively designed to facilitate this analysis.

Each construct table is composed of five sections relating to the leading district analysis research questions: district context; leadership, organization, and governance; the CSR models; professional development; and resources (such sections are labeled as outline categories in table 7.2). Each section consists of more detailed items from the coding construct key, used by both the larger quantitative and qualitative studies (i.e., the district context section contains a construct labeled "culture/climate; leadership stability/instability"). A total of 58 constructs were used in the formation of the tables.

Fifteen construct tables were developed, three for each district (i.e., Dodgeland district interviews, Dodgeland community interviews, Dodgeland principal interviews). This enabled the researchers to iden-

Table 7.2. Sample Construct Table

Outline category	Constructs	Eastwicker district interviews
District context	Culture/climate; leadership stability/ instability	"We're in the throes of transformation, indeed we are. In 2002 [the previous superintendent] left the school system and Ralph Watkins, Dr. Watkins took her—is now at the helm of [Eastwicker] public schools."
		"Since 1997, we have had five superintendents."
		"Yes, we're in the process of looking for a new superintendent now. Dr. Watkins, he resigned . . . had one interim who left . . . and we have an interim now as they finalize . . . hopefully they're anticipating that the person will be in place by June."
		"I've been here for two years now and this will—the next superintendent would be the fourth superintendent that I've served under in that two-year period. So you know I'm looking for stability."

tify areas of greatest concern (constructs with the largest percentages of associated responses) in each district. Table 7.2, a sample from a construct table, demonstrates how we sorted data according to their corresponding construct.

From the evidence presented in this construct table, we see that four of the district administrators interviewed in the Eastwicker district voiced concerns about the numerous administrative changes at the superintendent level. In actuality, this construct, edited here for size and confidentiality, contains similar concerns voiced by 100 percent of the district administrators interviewed in Eastwicker, thus emerging as a prominent area of concern for this analysis.

Constructs with the largest percentages of associated responses were then analyzed collaboratively, revealing the seven themes associated with district personnel's perceptions of challenges related to CSR: top-down decisionmaking, instability of leadership and policy, model fit, resources, teacher buy-in, teacher and student mobility, and developer limitations. Analysis was first done individually by the first author, with the data for two of the districts.

After establishing prevailing themes based on comparisons of data from two districts, the remaining three districts were analyzed according to those themes—with careful attention to the potential emergence of other themes. Although districts differed in the percentage of responses to certain themes, analyses of the three remaining districts revealed no thematic areas containing response rates higher than those already identified. Instead, one theme, developer limitations, was lacking in the remaining districts. However, it was kept for the purposes of this analysis because of the high response rate in the districts where it applied.

Case Studies

In all qualitative analyses of this kind, researchers endeavor to locate exemplars among the data analyzed. For the discussion of our findings, each theme is discussed using case studies informed by exemplars selected to typify the experiences, voices, and views of respondents. The districts from which exemplars are chosen for discussion were those with the largest percentage response rate for the particular theme.

FINDINGS

Administrative Mandates

In the mid-1990s, schools in the Everville district applied for and successfully received funding to implement CSR models through three primary sources of funding: (1) a local foundation, (2) CSRD funding from the state board of education, and (3) a large national foundation. Excited about the potential of CSR and new sources of federal funding, the district required schools to apply on a competitive basis.

By the time interviews were conducted in December 2002, the pressure of organizing districtwide instructional improvement to show student achievement on state examinations (a result of pressures associated with NCLB) had placed the CSR school-by-school approach in jeopardy. In addition, a recent evaluation by a district researcher had argued that CSR models had not effectively boosted student achievement. Thus, despite an evaluation by an external organization with findings to the contrary, and over the objections of some schools with models in place, a decision had been made to stop CSR in the district to fully focus on a districtwide reading initiative.

Reflecting on the district's decision to abandon CSR, a school principal commented,

> But the unfortunate part—we, our staff, has worked so hard and we've had numerous hours of in-service on developing curriculum and really pulling apart the curriculum to actually see what it is that we're supposed to be teaching and aligning it with state standards and district standards and national standards and we had really come up with a piece, a document that, by grade level, that we could probably sell. However, the district kind of abandoned all of our school reform models and we were just kind of chopped off at the knees and so we're just kind of reeling from that.

Given these kinds of sentiments and ongoing activity, the decision to halt CSR in the Everville district was eventually reversed.

A midlevel district administrator involved in accountability explained,

> There was a decision at one time not to do any reform, but they [the district] rethought that and did decide to continue because, number one, the schools had already applied, had been awarded CSR funding and then the [local foundation] funding has been going on, and [funding from a large national foundation] has been going on for a while, so you had all this going on so the decision was finally made to continue this. The schools were really pleased when they were told that they could continue with their school reform models.

To coordinate the reimplementation of CSR in a way that would align with ongoing efforts in the district, the district created a position for a CSR expert as manager.

The decisions to discontinue CSR and focus on implementing district-wide standards, and then to again allow CSR to operate provided it aligns with district standards, illustrate how district officials can be pulled between advocates of school-based reform and pressures to orchestrate uniform, districtwide instructional practices. When CSR was stopped, one principal noted, "it usually takes about five years before you actually see the results. And so with it being cut off that abruptly, I would say we really have not seen it to its fruition."

However, commenting on pressure from state and federal mandates, another midlevel district administrator explained the context of districts' impatience with reform.

> We are expected to make adequate yearly progress every year by the state and now by the federal government. And they expect that every year, every kid is gonna learn to the maximum—now be that sane or insane it doesn't matter. We cannot step back and say, well, charter schools haven't been in business that long and CSRDs haven't been around that long. Either it is something which can be used to help kids' achievement this year, or forget it.

This quote illustrates how the pressure of new state and federal mandates can undercut already-established efforts, and the position of district officials caught in the middle. How district officials understand and make changes to implement new initiatives is crucial to the existence of CSR, and in the case of the Everville district almost resulted in CSR's permanent demise.

Instability of Leadership and Policy

To illustrate challenges associated with instability, we focus on the Eastwicker and Riverton districts. Neither is unique, in the sense that they are urban districts experiencing changes in central office administrations. However, the comments of those observing, and affected by, these changes are insightful.

The Eastwicker district, in particular, has experienced several changes at the superintendent level. At the time of our discussion in May 2004, a midlevel administrator commented, "I've been here for two years now, and this will—the next superintendent would be the fourth superintendent that I've served under in that two-year period. So you know I'm looking for stability." Given that each superintendent will potentially change a district's instructional priorities, the large number of superintendents in such a short time indicates that CSR would be in jeopardy.

Principals we spoke with explained that a previous administration strongly encouraged the adoption of CSR models, and even required them for low-performing schools. However, decreasing support for CSR models, and a corresponding emphasis on a districtwide reading curriculum, resulted from changes in administration (and as a response to new NCLB requirements). Discussing the impact of central office instability on a particular model's sustainability, another midlevel administrator explained,

> Maybe it started in 2000–2001 under a previous administration. Most of the contracts were for three years. We started off initially with three years. Little gain was seen and the advantage of maintaining those comprehensive school reform models—the wisdom of that was not embraced by our, our last superintendent.

Another district administrator commented, "I think that probably the reform model effort is one that has died. And I think that it's died because we were never concerned with the reform model." It appears here that the district's decisions to not support CSR were made before the longitudinal effects of implementation could be adequately evaluated. And, from the numerous changes in leadership, it also appears that district officials' ability to embrace models was impaired.

Riverton district personnel have been subject to far-reaching changes in leadership and policy. Successive administrations and a state takeover of low-performing schools have left officials looking for stability. Concerning these changes, one midlevel administrator commented,

> So the reform as it's happening now over the last two years, you could best describe the system as being unstable because of lack of leadership. I think we're still suffering from that so until things really get straightened out, people just don't know.

On learning to adapt to an unstable leadership environment, a senior-level district administrator stated,

> I think whenever you go through change it tends to be stressful, chaotic. But in that chaos and stress there is a pattern, and I think that we are beginning to identify a pattern and that pattern is to provide more focus on instruction.

However, this instability can cause confusion and frustration for those counting on district support to implement reforms at the school level, as evidenced by a school principal:

> You know most people say a minimum of five years to see real change; three to five, so if the funding stops after three years— especially if you started it slower as I did, so that you had time to make it effective. So that would be my—why did they stop?

In spite of the instability, CSR models that align with district standards remain active in Riverton, likely because prior district leadership (with a longer tenure than was the case in Eastwicker) had been supportive, and district administrators were more knowledgeable about CSR models and what they can do for schools and students.

Similar to other districts, Riverton's primary concern is making sure that schools meet AYP guidelines as set forth by NCLB. When asked in 2004 about their responsibilities, two district administrators commented that they were practically living and breathing NCLB. However, this primary shift in focus has not impelled the district to abandon CSR models, but to carefully utilize select models that align with the district's instructional priorities.

Model Fit

Interviews were first done in Dodgeland in October 2002. At that time, community stakeholders in particular were candid about what they perceived as a forced and flawed model selection process. Speaking about schools placed on probation and instructed to choose a model, a Dodgeland nonprofit worker explained,

> These schools did not choose to undergo the process of reform. They in most cases did not really write the proposals that were submitted. The proposals were really written by someone else, and there was no widespread buy-in to the whole process. And that means that, in addition, I don't think that funding was rationalized around the idea of comprehensive school reform. I think rather what happened is that you went through and you looked for things that were already being funded and you said, oh well, that's part of this project.

The president of the teachers union in the district commented,

> Probation schools were encouraged to find an external partner. So they would link up with, you know, anybody they know—a university, a consultant selling a project. So they just were willy-nilly, you know, linking up with external partners.

These comments do not bode well for the likelihood that the selected models were those most appropriate for the schools.

Principal interviews in October 2002 reveal that this selection process resulted in at least some principals, though interested in positive model benefits, not pursuing models that would involve aggressive change. One principal stated that her school went for a specific model because it "was so close to what we were already doing that we said, hey, this is a way to go." As Spillane (2002) points out, using reform to make only minor adjustments to established methods may stem from not understanding the extent of change needed to implement reform. This understanding should come through proper district support and professional development during selection, which early evidence does not demonstrate for Dodgeland.

However, later interviews, done in March 2004, show a more concerted, district-level effort at model alignment. A senior administrator for the district reported,

> We're really trying to see which ones are really aligned with our new district priorities. I think that there are probably situations where we may actually adopt for some of our lowest-performing schools who don't have the internal capacity to support the rigorous work that we want occurring. I think that we're looking to see if, you know—which of the models would be more appropriate.

Likewise, a principal interviewed at this time talked about her collaborative efforts with model developers to improve student scores on state tests:

> We're working with [a model developer]. He's from the [CSR model] and he's helping us with the data analysis, and [to] see how we can use the data to predict how the students . . . are going to do on the [state assessment], and to try to target students who need that extra push.

Between 2002 and 2004, the Dodgeland district underwent a restructuring with goals that included a focus on professional development and promoting the whole notion of a professional learning community. These efforts appear to have been beneficial for efforts to successfully align CSR models with districtwide instructional goals.

The story of efforts to align models in the Everville district is similar to that of Dodgeland. In December 2002, a senior administrator in Everville expressed her frustration with multiple, misaligned models in the district—likening it to a cluttered Christmas tree:

I've heard it likened to a Christmas tree with bulbs on it—and Regina comes to me and she's a vendor and she says, I've got this project, I've got this program, if you buy it, it's the greatest thing since sliced bread and your kids will learn. So I buy it, okay, so I've got that project going and then someone else comes and someone else and everybody's got the saving grace and you know, I feel that how can I—how can I refuse someone who's telling me here that this is the saving grace? So you end up with really a very cluttered school program.

However, by 2004 the district had engaged in efforts to align CSR efforts with districtwide instructional goals. Another senior administrator described her personal involvement in alignment efforts:

Under the last [senior administrator], I worked on the curriculum side of the house and pulled together all of the schools that had models, and said to them that we were going to make sure that any school with a model focused the improvement effort on the [districtwide instructional program] and to see how the model, the components, worked to support that improvement effort. So it didn't matter if they were Comer, it didn't matter if they were Different Ways of Knowing, anything. It had to wrap itself around the [districtwide instructional program], which was the district's reading effort. Then we charged the model provider with the same mandate.

She goes on to say that "models are being woven right into the fabric of the district." Similarly, the newly appointed district administrator in charge of coordinating CSR commented, "Well, I would say that what we've done is we've really done a great job of making sure that the schools and the model providers understand how they—what they do in the district supports the district's goals." These focused efforts on model alignment are likely a result of pressures from NCLB and demonstrate how district personnel have decided not to abandon, but to utilize, existing programs to address new policy mandates.

Teacher Buy-In

Literature shows that teachers' attitudes about CSR are critical to successful reform (Borman et al. 2004). In cases where there is little district support for reform efforts, teacher buy-in can make the difference between CSR being implemented in schools or not. A mid-level administrator in the Eastwicker district explained, "We had two schools that were able to manage, both schools that were able to find the time for professional development—find the money—were the most successful in implementing. And those [were] schools where teachers really bought into the program." Describing reasons for differing levels of implementation in schools with the same models, a senior administrator in the Eastwicker district observed, "Two sets of faculty go into the same reform model; one executes, the other one doesn't, and that's the difference. The reform model is not immune to the ways in which faculties embrace or don't embrace them." Differences in model acceptance between schools may point to issues of individual school culture and leadership. However, they also bring into question the levels of support and encouragement received from the district.

The Eastwicker district's initial heavy-handedness encouraged low-performing schools to adopt a model from a list of 13 suggested designs. However, shifts in administration and policy have led to a decrease in focus on reform models, leaving schools frustrated with mounting costs for models they do not feel are a district priority. This frustration is only magnified in schools that implemented models out of perceived pressure from the district, and never truly had an opportunity for faculty buy-in.

In Dodgeland, although more recent interviews demonstrate effective district professional development efforts, earlier (2002) interviews indicate the district did little to achieve teacher buy-in. A teachers union administrator in the district stated,

> Comprehensive school reform models have never been promoted here in [Dodgeland]. Accelerated Schools Project was here, ATLAS Communities was just here because of people that have gone out on their own to find them. I can speak about the Co-nect model. A network of schools that really on their own went out, found a model that could help them, brought it in and despite a disinterest in—on the part of the central office—were able to find the money and make it work. There was very little interest from the central office to see any of these models work, so those that work have done so because of the, you know, the initiative and the commitment of the people in the building.

These examples show that, in individual schools, successful CSR can be achieved without district support. However, districtwide support helps create a less-chaotic, higher-achieving environment wherein, presumably, the wheel would only have to be invented one time.

Teacher and Student Mobility

Teacher and student mobility present a challenge for district administrators dealing with multiple models operating in various schools. In particular, a highly prescriptive model may present a challenge when having to train a constant influx of teachers with no prior experience with the model. Speaking from his observations in the Oceanway district, a university researcher explained,

> [The] second problem is high teacher turnover. For example, in the more prescriptive models, if you have high teacher turnover then you're constantly redoing what you should only have to do once or twice. And once teachers are trained, if they stay there they can then train new teachers. But if you have a 30 percent, you know, attrition rate each year, there's very little transfer from year to year, and you go over the same things.

Extending the concern about mobility to students, this same researcher asked, "What happens when one student is in a school for one year under one model and then moves to another model?"

These concerns are echoed by a university researcher in Everville. When commenting about the impact of teacher and student mobility on CSR, he stated,

> One of the most significant facts about urban schools is that poor children in urban areas move a lot. All right? So if you have a situation like New American Schools in vision, where you have, you know, a Roots & Wings, a Slavin model over here and you have the—an Essential Schools model here and you have an Expeditionary Learning model over there, that's fine on one level if you have different approaches that can, you know, address different kinds of things that kids might be interested in, different learning types, all that. But if you don't have a common, comprehensive curriculum, that means that kids will move from one school to another and constantly have to be just like you described those teachers, trying to figure out the system.

In the face of increasing accountability measures, wherein student test scores are paramount, these are questions district officials must address.

In a 2004 interview, a midlevel district administrator explained how the district had responded to concerns over student mobility:

> We have standardized the curriculum because of the mobility of our students. And they cannot be at one place doing [a CSR model] and then move to [the district-wide instructional program] around the district.

This change, while directed at creating stability for students, also creates instructional stability for teachers who may move from school to school.

Similar to the Everville case, in an earlier (2003) interview a Riverton midlevel district administrator commented on teacher mobility, saying, "We have fairly high mobility among our teachers; teachers are trained in one school and go to another school, so it's really hard to keep the programs alive because of that mobility." In a later (2004) interview, a school principal commented on what she saw as the district's strategy to decrease the adverse affects of student mobility:

> So the goal across the district is to make sure that we have a lot of transient students, so when they move—if I move across the city and I am in 6th grade, am I getting the same, you know, the same skills, acquiring the same skills that I would if I came from this side of town?

Again, as in Everville, decreasing the differing instructional models used districtwide is viewed as a useful strategy, given high rates of student mobility.

Resources

Funding for CSR has become a real challenge for many districts, as cycles end for the CSRD grants that caused many districts to encourage CSR adoption (Consortium for Policy Research in Education 1998). And, as state and federal priorities have changed, much CSR funding is no longer available. Given the cost of some models and focus on districtwide instruction, in some cases, models have to be stopped.

A midlevel Eastwicker district administrator noted the expense associated with maintaining CSR:

> And so the CSR models were discontinued. They were very costly and the training—a lot of the training was outside of the city. It didn't result in the kinds of movement or the kinds of reform at the local school that was thought that it would. As a matter of fact, now with our No Child Left Behind Title II money, one of the responsibilities that I had is to change the culture to ensure that professional development is no longer going to chips and, you know, taking junkets and learning, you know, participating in two- and three-day workshops—but rather professional development is designed and geared toward local schools, it's facilitated at local schools.

Another midlevel Eastwicker administrator described his unsuccessful experiences in budgetary negotiations with a model developer:

> We took a look at it. It's a very well thought-out program but it is extremely expensive and what we wanted to negotiate with them was the talent search part at the early grades of the 9th grade—that we would purchase that. But we already had developed the academy model which is on the backhand of that program, but we couldn't get them to look at breaking up the model and selling us the half that we needed to go with the one that we had.

Instead of CSR, district administrators are focusing limited financial resources and professional development on districtwide instructional programs they feel are more congruent with NCLB.

A midlevel administrator in the Everville district also spoke about budgetary concerns in keeping CSR: "Just keeping the process alive with funding is becoming a major problem because people are saying, you know, this is money we could use for other things." Likewise, a university researcher in the Oceanway district observed,

> You know, if they say cut this much out of the budgets and you can opt out of whole-school reform and keep 20 teachers or you can lose 20 teachers and have a reform model, [a principal will] say, I want the teachers first, I need them in the classroom. And under strict budgetary constraint those are the choices that may have to be made.

Given these budgetary concerns, the fact that some models are kept is a testament to their perceived value by teachers, principals, and district administrators.

Developer Limitations

Though most districts in this analysis did not report serious issues with model developers overstretching their ability to provide services, individuals in the Oceanway district, in particular, expressed this concern. A senior administrator described the problems:

> These developers were not prepared with staff to provide the service. I mean, it looks very nice when you start saying come in and do this, you know, dollar signs start ringing up. But you have to remember you have to provide a service.

She went on to explain her frustrations with the quality of service that model developers were able to provide in the implementation stage:

So many times you walk into schools where the person who was delivering the—quote—the service had never taught, didn't know anything about children, didn't know anything about the topic because they had memorized a script and the minute you had a question they couldn't even answer it. I think they needed to say, we have to phase this in, we can only do whatever, we can't provide—some of them, some of them never sent things to schools. We had schools that were e-mailed presentations and told to do it themselves.

Her sentiments were echoed by a school principal who stated, "We could have gotten more assistance from the model consultants. I think that when we took on the model they promised more than what they produced. They promised us that there would be on-site consulters for our needs. That did not materialize."

Although not to the same extent, individuals in the Everville district also expressed concern over model developers' lack of service capacity. One principal reported,

We also met with the regional [CSR model] manager and one of the CEOs because that was one of our main thrusts and we let them know that we thought we were let down. They did not have our backs because they—we thought that they were going to follow up on the technology.

Likewise, a nonprofit worker explained,

A lot of it—I mean, frankly, we found that some model providers were really not equipped to provide the kind of assistance that schools really needed and of course those—those schools turned out to not be very high implementers and so what—one of the things that we've learned is that the capacity of the model providers themselves is critical.

These kinds of frustrations poorly affect teacher buy-in and proper model implementation. These kinds of constraints also contribute to decisions to stop using certain models.

DISCUSSION

Much of the CSR research is confirmed when district administrators and other individuals aware of districts' responsibilities toward reform express their views of the challenges they observe and experience. Unfortunately, some factors, such as administrative instability and politically based changes in instructional focus, are beyond the control of district administrators and will likely continue to challenge future reform efforts. These particular challenges can be addressed, however, through efforts to distribute leadership roles, lessening the impact of changes in individual leaders on school reform efforts (Spillane and Sherer 2004).

The challenges emerging from this research that have not often appeared in existing literature are those associated with teacher and student mobility and developer limitations. In this study, these were two of the thematic areas with the lowest percentage of response, but the opinions that informants voiced about these issues reveal that they have critical impacts on the sustainability of the reform process.

Perhaps the largest challenge revealed by our research is balancing CSR with NCLB. Depending on the extent to which CSR is embedded in the district and on the extent to which district administrators have developed an allegiance to working with the models, a district may decide either to utilize and align CSR models to achieve goals associated with NCLB, or to abandon CSR.

The case of Everville is interesting because it shows a district that first responded to NCLB by getting rid of CSR and adopting a districtwide instructional program. Then, in the face of objections from those involved in CSR implementation (e.g., schools, funding agencies, and some district administrators), the district decided to support CSR as long as it could be aligned with the districtwide instructional program—even appointing a district administrator to facilitate this alignment process.

In fact, in all but one of the districts analyzed in this study (Eastwicker), adjustments in standards and curriculum to meet the NCLB accountability requirements resulted in efforts to align CSR with districtwide instructional initiatives. This is a testament to the buy-in for and perceived value of CSR models and their usefulness in raising student achievement. However, future research will have to be done to assess how models are altered away from developers' original intentions, and how heavily models, or model components, are being used in districts.

When discussing the climate of these districts, it is interesting to note the fixation on AYP as revealed through the district administrator interviews. Though disaggregation of the data is a strength of NCLB because it does not allow schools and districts to hide the lack of achievement by subgroups (such as minorities and individuals with disabilities) in averages, the linking of the disaggregation to AYP has caused quite a bit of difficulty. Specifically, rules that label a school as "failing" because not enough students showed up to take a test, or because a particular subgroup showed substandard proficiency, are seen as harsh and sometimes unfair.

Although various aspects of NCLB have been amply criticized, particularly AYP, potential positive impacts in respect to the challenges described in this paper should be noted. Concern about NCLB has heightened district administrators' involvement in various aspects of instruction. In districts that continue to retain models, administrators have vested interests in creating positive relationships with model developers, increasing their knowledge about the usefulness of particular models, and making sure that models are achieving district goals.

The higher level of involvement on the part of district administrators should be beneficial for resolving challenges relating to (1) teacher buy-in (teachers may be more likely to buy in to a district-supported model that clearly helps to achieve AYP goals); (2) model fit (district administrators can make sure that models used align with state testing standards, and can negotiate with model developers to make alterations to model designs); (3) resources (district administrators are more likely to dedicate financial resources and professional development for models they advocate and see as in line with district priorities); (4) teacher and student mobility (in cases where models are implemented district-wide, teachers and students moving from one school to another within the district will have a less adverse effect on model implementation and sustainability); and (5) developer limitations (districts may be more successful than individual schools in making sure that model developers provide what they promise).

NCLB may also have the effect of creating a more stable environment that will lessen the impact of administrative mandates, and unstable leadership and policy. Given the prescriptions of NCLB, new superintendents may be less likely to drastically change a district's focus. However, if districts are repeatedly unsuccessful in achieving AYP, the state's power to shut them down could produce an unprecedented level of instability.

CONCLUSIONS

The findings in this paper provide insight into predictions offered by Borman and their coauthors (2004, 143). In their discussion of the potential impacts of NCLB on CSR, they write:

> The full impact of policies governing schools and districts under the No Child Left Behind Act has yet to be realized, but is certain to have an impact on CSR implementation and sustainability. One

likely outcome is that district and state policies will become more tightly aligned as policies regarding support for low- and high-performing schools are determined. If funds are provided to support CSR implementation—a scenario we see as unlikely because CSR emphasizes *whole*-school reform—CSR models are likely to flourish. On the other hand, the more likely outcome—one that seems to be anticipated by the coalition of model developers—is that districts and schools will opt to determine districtwide strategies that may or may not be compatible with aspects of some CSR models.

Certainly some CSR models will clash with districtwide instructional programs; however, the developers' flexibility in adapting to new instructional environments will determine whether models continue to operate in districts. As models change, it will be interesting to see if they are able to maintain an emphasis on *"whole*-school reform," or instead get cut up into components deemed useful, and more affordable, by district administrators.

In the midst of procedural debates over district, state, and federal educational jurisdiction, that the goal of reform is to improve education for our children must never be forgotten. Properly implemented, both CSR and NCLB can significantly advance achievement. And in both cases, poor implementation can create a situation worse than when reforms were first deemed necessary.

NOTES

1. Reform in District #2 may been particularly successful because the district includes the Upper East Side, one of the wealthiest areas of New York City.

2. House Res. 2264, 105th Cong., 1st Sess. (1997), which earmarked competitive grants of $50,000 per school for the first year of funding and additional funding in the next two years.

3. This quote was taken from http://www.ed.gov/programs/gearup/index.html.

REFERENCES

Aladjem, D., A. Kurki, J. Taylor, K. Uekawa, and Y. Zhang. 2005. "Compulsory School Reform? What Mandated Program Implementation Means for District Support for CSR." Paper presented at the 2004 Association for Public Policy Analysis and Management Annual Research Conference, Atlanta, GA, October 28–30.

Berends, M., J. Chun, G. Schuyler, S. Stockly, and R. J. Briggs. 2002. "Challenges of Conflicting School Reforms: Effects of New American Schools in a High-

Poverty District." Monograph/Report MR-1483-EDU. Santa Monica: RAND.

Borman, K. M., K. Carter, D. K. Aladjem, and K. Le Floch. 2004. "Challenges to the Future of Comprehensive School Reform." In *Putting the Pieces Together: Lessons from Comprehensive School Reform Research*, edited by C. T. Cross (109–50). Washington, DC: National Clearinghouse for Comprehensive School Reform.

Bracey, G. W. 2004. *Setting the Record Straight: Responses to Misconceptions about Public Education in the U.S.*, 2nd ed. Portsmouth, NH: Heinemann.

Chenoweth, K. 2004. "50 Years Later: Can Current Education Policy Finish the Work Started with *Brown*?" *Black Issues in Higher Education* 22(9): 40–44.

Chubb, J. E., and T. M. Moe. 1990. *Politics, Markets, and America's Schools*. Washington, DC: Brookings Institution Press.

Colgan, C. 2002. "Memphis Blues." *Principal Leadership* (High School Edition) 2(5): 10–15.

Consortium for Policy Research in Education. 1998. "States and Districts and Comprehensive School Reform." CPRE Policy Brief. Philadelphia: University of Pennsylvania, Consortium for Policy Research in Education.

Corcoran, T., and N. Lawrence. 2003. "Changing District Culture and Capacity: The Impact of the Merck Institute for Science Education Partnership." Research Report. Philadelphia: University of Pennsylvania, Consortium for Policy Research in Education.

Cotner, B. A., S. Herrmann, K. M. Borman, T. Boydston, and K. Le Floch. 2005. "A Developer Look at Implementation: School-Level Stakeholders' Perceptions of Comprehensive School Reform." Paper prepared for the annual meeting of the American Educational Research Association, Montreal, Canada, April 11–15.

Council of the Great City Schools. 2003. "Urban School Superintendents: Characteristics, Tenure, and Salary (4th Biennial Survey)." *Urban Indicator* 7(1).

Datnow, A. 2000. "Power and Politics in the Adoption of School Reform Models." *Educational Evaluation and Policy Analysis* 22(4): 357–74.

———. 2001. "The Sustainability of Comprehensive School Reform in Changing District and State Contexts." Paper presented at the annual meeting of the American Educational Research Association, Seattle, April 10–14.

———. 2005. "The Sustainability of Comprehensive School Reform Models in Changing District and State Contexts." *Educational Administration Quarterly* 41(1): 121–53.

Datnow, A., and S. Stringfield. 2000. "Working Together for Reliable School Reform." *Journal of Education for Students Placed At Risk* 5(1&2): 183–204.

Datnow, A., B. McHugh, S. Stringfield, and D. J. Hacker. 1998. "Scaling up the Core Knowledge Sequence." *Education and Urban Society* 30(3): 409–32.

David, J. L., and P. M. Shields. 2001. "When Theory Hits Reality: Standards-Based Reform in Urban Districts." Final Narrative Report. Menlo Park, CA: SRI International.

Desimone, L. 2000. "Making Comprehensive School Reform Work." Urban Diversity Series No. 112. New York: ERIC Clearinghouse on Urban Education, Institute for Urban and Minority Education.

Elmore, R. F., and D. Burney. 1997. "Investing in Teacher Learning: Staff Development and Instructional Improvement in Community District #2, New York City." Report. New York: National Commission on Teaching and America's Future / Philadelphia: Consortium for Policy Research in Education, University of Pennsylvania.

Fullan, M. 2004. "Whole-School Reform." Paper presented at the "From Whole-School to Whole-System Reform" Conference, Chicago, April 26–27.

Haynes, N. 1998. "Summary and Conclusions: Lessons Learned." *Journal of Education for Students Placed at Risk* 3(1): 87–99.

Hess, F. 1999. *Spinning Wheels: The Politics of Urban School Reform*. Washington, DC: Brookings Institution Press.

Hill, P. T., and M. B. Celio. 1998. *Fixing Urban Schools*. Washington, DC: Brookings Institution Press.

Ingersoll, R., 2001. "Teacher Turnover, Teacher Shortages, and the Organization of Schools." CTP Research Report R-01-1. Seattle: Center for the Study of Teaching and Policy, University of Washington.

Le Floch, K., Y. Zhang, and S. Herrmann. 2005. "Exploring the Initiation of CSR Models." Paper presented at the annual meeting of the American Educational Research Association, Montreal, Canada, April 11–15.

Manpower Demonstration Research Corporation. 2002. *Foundations for Success: Case Studies of How Urban School Systems Improve Student Achievement*. Washington, DC: Council of the Great City Schools.

Marsh, J. 2000. "Connecting Districts to the Policy Dialogue: A Review of the Literature on the Relationship of Districts with States, Schools, and Communities." Working Paper. Seattle: Center for the Study of Teaching and Policy, University of Washington.

Martinez, M., and J. Harvey. 2004. "From Whole-School to Whole-System Reform: Report of a Working Conference." Washington, DC: National Clearinghouse for Comprehensive School Reform.

Massell, D., and M. E. Goertz. 1999. "Local Strategies for Building Capacity: The District Roles in Supporting Instructional Reform." Paper prepared for the annual meeting of the American Educational Research Association, Montreal, Canada, April 11–15.

McLaughlin, M., and J. Talbert. 2003. "Reforming Districts: How Districts Support School Reform." CTP Research Reports R-03-6. Seattle: Center for the Study of Teaching and Policy, University of Washington.

Murphy, J., and P. Hallinger. 1986. "The Superintendent as Instructional Leader: Findings from Effective School Districts." *Journal of Educational Administration* 24(2): 213–36.

———. 1988. "Characteristics of Instructionally Effective Districts." *Journal of Educational Research* 81(3): 175–81.

New American Schools. n.d. "What Worked? What Didn't Work? Memphis City Schools, Comprehensive School Reform, 1995–2000." http://www.naschools.org/contentViewer.asp?highlightID=8&catID=320. (Accessed November 10, 2005.)

O'Day, J., and C. Bitter. 2003. "Evaluation Study of the Immediate Intervention/Underperforming Schools Program and the High Achieving/Improving Schools Program of the P.S. Accountability Act of 1999." Final Report. Palo Alto: American Institutes for Research.

Popham, J. W. 2004. *America's Failing Schools: How Parents and Teachers Can Cope with No Child Left Behind*. New York: RoutledgeFalmer.

Resnick, L., and M. Harwell. 2000. *Instructional Variation and Student Achievement in a Standards-Based Education District*. CSE Technical Report No. 522. Los

Angeles: National Center for Research on Evaluation, Standards, and Student Testing, University of California–Los Angeles.

Rosenholtz, S. J. 1991. *Teachers' Workplace: The Social Organization of Schools.* New York: Teachers College Press.

Ross, S. M., D. Henry, L. Phillipsen, K. Evans, L. Smith, and T. Buggey. 1997. "Matching Restructuring Programs to Schools: Selection, Negotiation, and Preparation." *School Effectiveness and School Improvement* 8(11): 45–71.

Rowan, B., E. Camburn, and C. Barnes. 2004. "Benefiting from Comprehensive School Reform: A Review of Research on CSR Implementation." In *Putting the Pieces Together: Lessons from Comprehensive School Reform Research,* edited by C. T. Cross (1–52). Washington, DC: National Clearinghouse for Comprehensive School Reform.

Spillane, J. P. 1996. "Districts Matter: Local Educational Authorities and State Instructional Policy." *Educational Policy* 10(1): 63–87.

———. 2002. "Local Theories of Teacher Change: The Pedagogy of District Policies and Programs." *Teachers College Record* 104(3): 377–420.

Spillane, J., and J. Sherer. 2004. "A Distributed Perspective on School Leadership: Leadership Practice as Stretched over People and Place." Preliminary Draft for Presentation at the Annual Meeting of the American Education Association, San Diego, April 12–16.

Spillane, J., and C. Thompson. 1997. "Reconstructing Conceptions of Local Capacity: The Local Education Agency's Capacity for Ambitious Instructional Reform." *Educational Evaluation and Policy Analysis* 19(2): 185–203.

U.S. Department of Education. n.d. "Comprehensive School Reform Program." http://www.ed.gov/programs/compreform/2pager.html. (Accessed May 19, 2005.)

———. 2004. *A Guide to Education and No Child Left Behind.* Washington, DC: U.S. Department of Education, Office of the Secretary, Office of Public Affairs.

Yonezawa, S., and A. Datnow. 1999. "Supporting Multiple Reform Designs in a Culturally and Linguistically Diverse School District." *Journal of Education for Students Placed at Risk* 4(1): 101–25.

8

IMPLEMENTING COMPREHENSIVE SCHOOL REFORM MODELS

Georges Vernez and Dan Goldhaber

This chapter describes the process by which schools decide to engage in comprehensive school reform (CSR) and select a comprehensive school reform model (CSRM). It also describes and assesses the process of implementation of four comprehensive school reform models that have been widely implemented throughout the nation: Accelerated Schools, Core Knowledge, Direct Instruction, and Success for All.

The study is based on detailed longitudinal case studies of 12 schools that have sought to implement one of these four models. These qualitative case studies were meant to complement a broader quantitative study that seeks to understand (1) the model, district, school, and classroom factors that may lead to effective CSR implementation; and (2) the effects that the models have on student achievement.[1] Little is known about the process of model selection, and while more is known about the process of implementation, we wanted to provide a deeper understanding of how these processes may differ across models. Although caution should be exercised in generalizing from a few qualitative case studies, the findings are consistent enough across schools and models to suggest specific actions that model developers and school and district administrators could take to ensure successful school implementation of CSRMs.

The remainder of this chapter is divided into six sections. The first describes the conceptual framework used for the study, characteristics of the specific schools in our sample, and the key components of the four comprehensive school reform models included in the study. The second discusses the process by which schools decided to engage in CSR and select a specific CSRM. The third reviews the support infra-structure the schools put in place to facilitate implementation of the models, including teachers' commitment, initial training, resources, and internal and external assistance. The fourth discusses, respectively, specifics on how the schools selected and implemented the respective models and the factors affecting implementation. The final concludes with a set of recommendations designed to increase the probability of successful implementation of comprehensive school reform models.

CASE STUDY DESIGN

Conceptual Framework

Much research has been devoted to understanding the implementation of educational reforms and to the factors that determine the reforms' success or failure.[2] More specifically, early experience with CSR suggests that successful implementation depends on such factors as a model's specific features; the model's consistency with school, district, and state policies; the type and level of assistance provided to the school; the stability of the school environment; and principal and teacher buy-in. (For instance, see Berends 1999; Berends et al. 2002; Bifulco, Duncombe, and Yinger 2003; Bodilly 1998; Desimone 2002; Glennan 1998).

Drawing on this extensive literature, figure 8.1 provides a framework for understanding the process of selecting and implementing compre-hensive school reform models. As shown, the process starts with a district or a school decision to engage in comprehensive school reform. The school (with or without district inputs) engages in a search for the appropriate model and eventually selects one with or without teachers' involvement and with or without a vote of the faculty.

Upon selecting a model, the school prepares for implementation. This process may be more or less involved: resources have to be

Figure 8.1. Framework for Analysis of Process of Comprehensive School Reform Model Selection and Implementation

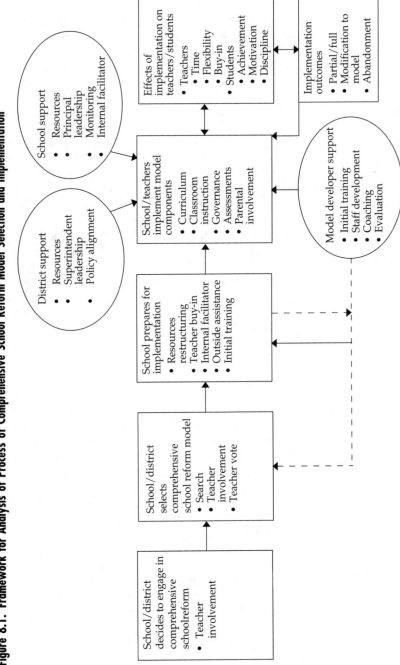

acquired, teacher buy-in may be sought, school scheduling and structure may have to be modified and new materials acquired, staff may
need to be hired or reallocated to new functions, and initial training
must be provided. Only after these activities have been performed can
the school and its teachers begin in earnest to implement the model.
As indicated in figure 8.1, the process of implementing the model's
components (including curriculum, instruction, governance, student
assessment, parental involvement, and the like) interacts with and is
influenced by support from the district, school, and model developer.
All three may provide necessary—albeit possibly different—kinds of
support, including financial resources, in-kind resources, leadership,
coaching, monitoring, and progress evaluations.

As implementation proceeds, either all at once or in phases, the
principal and teachers assess the model's effects on them and, through
them, on the students. Teachers come to understand the level of effort
required to implement the model, the flexibility it offers in the classroom, and the ways in which students respond to the new curriculum
or instructional practices. Changes in students' motivation, discipline,
and achievement—either perceived (initially) or actual (later)—affect
teachers' and principals' attitudes and buy-in. These changes, in turn,
influence how fully the model is implemented and, ultimately, it is the
school's decision to stick with, adapt, or abandon the model.

School Selection and Characteristics

To conduct in-depth case studies, we selected 12 schools from the
broader study sample of 169 schools known to be implementing Accelerated Schools (AS), Core Knowledge (CK), Direct Instruction (DI), or
Success for All (SFA) in Florida and Texas. To the extent feasible, we
selected elementary schools that were in their first year of implementation and similar in size and poverty level to the overall sample of
schools implementing each model. We succeeded in doing so for a
majority (eight) of the schools, including three AS schools, three CK
schools, one DI school, and one SFA school (table 8.1). For DI and SFA,
there were no other "start-up" schools in 2001 and 2002 in our overall
sample. Thus, for these models we selected schools that had most
recently started model implementation; these schools were typically
in their third and fourth years of implementation during our first visit.
In these latter schools, we collected retrospective information about
their first and other early implementation years (see below). Nine of
our case study schools are located in Texas and three in Florida.[3]

Select characteristics of the 12 schools are shown in table 8.1. Most
of the case study schools serve disadvantaged children. DI and SFA
schools are high poverty (with one exception, 85 percent or more of

their students are eligible for the federal free and reduced-price lunch program) and the majority of the students are members of a racial or ethnic minority. By contrast, 20 to 60 percent of the students at all but one of the AS and CK schools can be classified as poor, while 22 to 38 percent are members of a racial or ethnic minority. Most of the case study schools are located in urban areas: three are located in a large central city, three in the urban fringe of large cities, and three in the urban fringe of midsize cities. Of the remaining, two are in small towns and one is rural. Although the case study schools vary in size, most are midsize with enrollments ranging from 400 to 700 students.

The DI and SFA schools were typically low-achievement schools, with student scores in 2003 below their respective state averages. Nevertheless, the Texas DI and SFA schools met the state's 2003 Adequate Yearly Progress target, though the Florida schools did not. By contrast, two of the AS and two of the CK schools performed above state average.

The selected schools are located in districts of various sizes. Three schools, AS_1, AS_2, and DI_3, are located in small districts of about 3,000 students. The first two are located in the same district, in which all elementary schools applied for Comprehensive School Reform Demonstration (CSRD) funds in the same year. The third school is located in a predominantly rural district.

Six schools are located in suburban districts of varying sizes: AS_3 in a district of about 3,600 students, CK_1 and CK_2 both in the same district of about 19,000 students, DI_2 in a district of about 45,000 students, SFA_1 in a district of about 43,000 students, and SFA_3 in a district of about 5,000 students.

The remaining three schools, CK_3, DI_1, and SFA_2, are all located in the same large urban district of slightly more than 200,000 students.

All but one of the districts in our study retained their superintendents for the duration of the study. The only change in the superintendent occurred at the beginning of year three in the district where AS_1 and AS_2 are located.

All schools were visited at least twice, and some were visited three times. All but one school were visited in the springs of 2003 and 2004. In addition, half of the schools were also visited in the spring of 2002. A team of two researchers initially visited each school for one day. At each school, the team interviewed the principal and two focus groups of teachers (typically 1st and 4th grade teachers). The team also observed instruction in 1st and 4th grade reading classes and reviewed available written materials about the school. Each participating school received an incentive of $100, while those staff interviewed each received $10.

To facilitate uniform data collection across sites, the teams used protocols that covered the topics and elements included in our analytic

Table 8.1. Characteristics of Case Study Schools

School characteristic	Accelerated Schools			Core Knowledge			Direct Instruction			Success for All		
	AS_1	AS_2	AS_3	CK_1	CK_2	CK_3	DI_1	DI_2	DI_3	SFA_1	SFA_2	SFA_3
Fall of model implementation	2001	2001	2001	2001	2002	2001	1999	1998	2001	1999	2002	1998
Demographics (2002) Enrollment	445	601	598	561	673	394	705	570	415	796	411	640
% eligible for free/ reduced-price lunch	42	42	67	35	20	86	98	94	66	98	94	79
% minority[a]	31	33	22	37	38	100	100	88	1	94	97	25
% meeting state standards (2003) Math	88	93	92	95	95	88	93	42	35	83	85	53
Reading	91	94	88	94	94	77	89	44	31	88	82	53
Met AYP (2003)	Yes	Yes	Yes	Yes	Yes	Yes	Yes	No	No	Yes	Yes	No
Location	Small town	Small town	Suburb, midsize city	Suburb, large city	Suburb, large city	Large central city	Large central city	Suburb, midsize city	Rural	Suburb, large city	Large central city	Suburb, midsize city

Source: Authors' calculations on data from the National Center for Education Statistics Common Core of Data for the 2002–2003 school year (2005), the RAND/ University of Washington survey of model schools (2003), the Texas Education Agency 2003 Adequate Yearly Progress Campus Data Tables (2005), and the Florida Department of Education Accountability Data for 2003 (2005).

AYP = adequate yearly progress

Note: The following schools are located in the same district: AS_1 and AS_2; CK_1 and CK_2; CK_3, DI_1, and SFA_2.

[a] Includes African Americans, Hispanics, and Asians.

framework. Respondents were probed about the decision to engage in comprehensive reform, the selection of the model, the implementation of each component of each model, any modifications the school made to the model, and the nature and level of support received from the district, school, and model developers. Staff were also asked about their experiences with the model and their perceptions of its effects. Model-specific protocols for classroom observations were also used to allow assessment of potential variations in implementation of models within schools. Finally, all principals and six teachers per school were asked to respond to a survey questionnaire.

Overview of Model Characteristics

The four models included in the study—Accelerated Schools, Core Knowledge, Direct Instruction, and Success For All—were chosen for a variety of reasons. All have been widely used and implemented throughout the nation since the early 1990s; however, they differ in significant ways. Accelerated Schools emphasizes governance and a specific mode of instruction called Powerful Learning. Core Knowledge offers primarily a general curriculum designed to provide students with a core foundation of facts and knowledge. Direct Instruction provides a highly structured curriculum and a fully scripted mode of classroom instruction. Finally, Success For All provides a structured program emphasizing cooperative learning and offering strategies designed to assist at-risk students, including tutoring and regular home reading assignments. Table 8.2 provides a brief description of each of these models.

SELECTING A COMPREHENSIVE SCHOOL REFORM MODEL

Deciding to Engage in Comprehensive School Reform

The decision to engage in comprehensive school reform has often been associated with a desire to improve students' performance in such areas as reading and mathematics. The majority of our case study schools followed this pattern, citing a desire to improve students' performance, particularly in reading, as the primary reason for engaging in reform; this was particularly true for those schools performing below state average. All but two of these low-performing schools eventually adopted a highly prescriptive reading model, either Direct Instruction or Success for All. But an interest in improving student performance was not the only reason given for pursuing change, particularly for

Table 8.2. Comprehensive School Reform Models Included in the RAND/University of Washington Assessment

Accelerated Schools (AS)	The primary goal of AS is to bring children in at-risk situations to at least grade level by the end of the 6th grade. The model emphasizes three important components: an integrated curriculum that emphasizes language development in all subjects; a mode of instruction, Powerful Learning, that focuses on problem solving, cross-age tutoring, and cooperative learning; and collaborative decisionmaking involving administrators, teachers, parents, and students. AS emphasizes higher-order skills, interdisciplinary/thematic instruction, and a full range of electives. The curriculum applies to all students. Teachers are to take the role of learning facilitators rather than instructors. The school's decisionmaking is supported by cadres or small groups of school stakeholders that focus on the school's most pressing needs: a steering committee and a body called School as a Whole that approves all major decisions on curriculum, instruction, and resource allocation. The model is implemented in sequence with an initial "taking stock" period to assess the current situation and develop a shared vision and set priorities in the first year. Solutions to identified issues are developed in the second year and are implemented in the third year. To support schoolwide change, AS trains a designated coach (usually not from the school) and an internal school facilitator. In turn, the coach trains teachers. Total annual costs are estimated at about $65,000 yearly, including the AS fees of $45,000 but excluding teachers' release time.
Core Knowledge (CK)	Core Knowledge is based on cognitive psychology findings that children learn based upon what they already know. It provides all students with a core foundation of facts and knowledge through a sequentially structured and systematic grade-by-grade curriculum. Although CK specifies topics that are to be covered in monthly or weekly time periods, it is designed to cover 50 percent of the curriculum, allowing schools to supplement the CK sequence with the school's existing curriculum. While CK specifies content, it does not specify how it ought to be taught. CK curriculum can be phased in over time or implemented all at once. Increased parental involvement is encouraged. To support implementation, teachers are to be provided with common planning time to research topics and develop curricula and daily lesson plans. CK provides training in developing lesson plans and helps schools integrate CK content with district and state requirements. A school-based CK coordinator should be appointed to receive intensive training on CK and to serve as liaison with the CK foundation. CK staff is to make three school visits per year. CK fees are about $45,000 in the first year and $37,000 in the second and third years. In addition, schools are expected to allocate a minimum of $1,000 per teacher for CK materials and to provide teachers' release time.

Direct Instruction (DI)	Direct Instruction is based on the theory that clear instruction and eliminating misinterpretation can greatly improve and accelerate teaching. It provides a curriculum for reading, language, writing, and mathematics that details activities for each lesson. Curriculum material is available commercially and includes a teacher's guide or presentation book for each subject. DI lessons are fully scripted and the teacher is expected to closely follow the script. Students' errors are to be corrected immediately and consistently. Students should be taught each subject in a small, academically homogeneous group of six to nine students (typically for 30 minutes daily) and should be regularly assessed and regrouped at least three times a year. All reading classes are to be scheduled at the same time so that students can be grouped across classes. Extra reading or math periods should be provided to students functioning below grade level. DI consultants provide 24 hours of initial training and 60 hours of in-service training. They should also visit the school for 30 to 50 days during the year. An internal school coach should be designated to work with the external DI consultant. DI costs from $194,000 to $245,000 in the first year, including the $75,000 DI fees, up to $210 per student for materials, release time for teachers, and a full-time facilitator.
Success for All (SFA)	Success for All is based on the premise that cooperative learning is most effective when integrated with instruction and curriculum. SFA is a highly structured 90-minute daily reading program for pre-K to grade 5. In early ages, it focuses on language development, then on building reading skills through phonics and whole-language methods and, in later grades, emphasizes reading comprehension, language fluency, and writing skills. Students should be grouped across grades by reading ability in classes of about 20, and special education students should be mainstreamed to the greatest extent possible. SFA also includes a social problem-solving curriculum, Getting Along Together. SFA expects all low-performing students and at least 30 percent of 1st graders to receive daily tutoring. Students are to be assessed every eight weeks and regrouped as needed. Parental involvement is encouraged via the assignment of 20 minutes of reading homework daily and the establishment of a family support team made up of school staff. SFA provides three days of initial training, and its staff is to visit the schools two to four times a year. A full-time school staff should be appointed to serve as a facilitator responsible for coaching teachers, presiding over component meetings (to be held every two weeks), and helping test and regroup students. Success for All costs about $270,000 in the first year to cover training, including teacher release time, materials, a full-time facilitator, and three tutors. If current staff are reallocated to fill the facilitator and tutor functions, the cost lowers to about $70,000.

those four schools in our study performing above the state average. For two of these schools, the decision to adopt a school reform model was opportunistically related to the availability of federal CSRD funds. For the two others, the main reason was to take part in one of the suburban district's "Schools of Choice" strategy, which aims to "keep well-to-do families" in the district.[4] These four schools chose models that provided them with greater flexibility—Accelerated Schools and Core Knowledge, respectively.

In our case study schools, the impetus for reform was either *district driven* or *principal driven*. In half of the schools, the decision to engage in reform followed an initiative taken by the district, while in the other half the decision was the principal's alone with no reported input from the district. Among those schools in which the district led the reform effort, the nature of the initiative and the motivation behind it varied significantly. In one district, the superintendent encouraged schools "to take advantage of the availability" of CSRD funds; in another, the superintendent felt that reform would provide incentives for middle class families to stay in the district; and in another, school reform was part of a comprehensive initiative (Project GRAD)[5] to increase student achievement and improve public support and confidence.

Selecting a Model

Regardless of whether the district or the principal was the primary driver behind reform, the decision to adopt a specific model was made at the school level, typically by the principal. In a few instances, principals actively sought the help of a school committee of teachers and other staff. However, regardless of the staff's level of engagement, the model's ultimate selection was based primarily on the principal's knowledge of or prior experiences with it, or on the recommendation of a consultant or a school or district stakeholder. This finding is consistent with the existing literature that describes the tendency of teachers and administrators to base decisions on anecdotal information received from their colleagues instead of findings reported in research or informational materials (Corcoran 2003; Finnigan and O'Day 2003; Huberman 1983).

In most cases, the model adopted was the only one considered. Even when a committee was charged with conducting a search, that search appeared to be limited to a few models and typically was carried out via the Internet, where objective, independent information on the hundreds of potential models is not readily available. A comprehensive search for a model that appropriately fits the context of a particular school is bound to be time consuming, and time is a scarce resource. Given limits on teachers' time, access to information, and knowledge about potential resources—given, too, the pressures of accountability—we were not surprised that most low-performing schools in our sample did not find plausible a systematic effort to evaluate multiple alternatives; this finding is consistent with Gross and colleagues (2005).

Although model developers assert that staff buy-in is key to the eventual success of any school reform attempt, teachers were typically *not* involved in the decision. The choice of model was often presented to them as a fait accompli they could choose to support or not, and in three schools (two CK and one SFA), teachers were simply told that the program would be implemented.

The reasons given for selecting a particular model were specific to that model. Principals choosing Accelerated Schools singled out its philosophy of teaching all students "as if they were gifted." They also appreciated the model's focus on teaching staff how to assess their school's strengths and weaknesses, its use of research to address identified issues, and its relatively low cost. Perhaps more importantly, two principals saw these process-related features as a way to further their own agendas: in one case, toward the adoption of a new curriculum and in another, to change the school's philosophy and teaching methods.

Core Knowledge was chosen by two schools for its emphasis on building equitability through a common knowledge foundation that grows by grade. In the third school, Core Knowledge was chosen primarily because the schools believed that it would improve reading comprehension.

Direct Instruction was reportedly chosen for its phonics-based approach to reading, "appropriateness for language dependent students," and/or its grouping of students by ability. Principals also thought that its scripted lessons would make it easier for new teachers to teach reading, of particular relevance because schools that selected it had high levels of teacher turnover.

Finally, two schools selected Success For All because of its reputation for increasing student achievement. In the third SFA school, respondents could not remember why the model had been adopted, since the principal who was a driving force behind its adoption left before implementation.

SECURING TEACHERS' COMMITMENT TO AND ASSISTANCE FOR MODEL IMPLEMENTATION

Teachers' commitment, as well as support from model developers, districts, and other external sources, are all believed to be critical for effective model implementation. In this section, we describe activities taken by principals to secure teachers' commitment, the initial training for teachers, the source and level of resources available to the schools, and the external and internal assistance schools secured to support implementation.

Securing Teachers' Commitment

None of the case study schools prepared intensively for the shift from their previous curricular and instructional practices to those specified by the adopted model. After the principals had selected a model, they sought staff buy-in by arranging for model developers to brief teachers on the model's general features and evidence of its effectiveness. In interviews, teachers complained that developers downplayed the level of effort required of them to implement the model, instead using these briefings to "sell" the model to the staff.

Aside from providing the opportunity for some teachers to visit schools that had adopted the same model, or to attend the model developer's national or regional conference, our case study schools went no further in preparing teachers for implementation until the initial training just before or at the beginning of the school year.

In 9 of 12 case study schools, teachers were given the opportunity to vote whether to adopt the model and in all cases, more than 80 percent did so, thereby meeting one of the model developer's requirements. These positive votes, however, did not necessarily equate to teacher buy-in; rather, they signaled more of a recognition that the school "would go ahead with the model anyhow." Teachers reported levels of acceptance ranging from resignation to "feeling pressured" to "feeling some anger." In four schools, the prospect of receiving additional funds under CSRD provided an incentive to vote for the model. However, in none of these schools was the staff made aware that the CSRD funds could have been used for any comprehensive school reform model other than the one chosen. Two CK schools and two SFA schools offered staff the opportunity to transfer, and a considerable number of teachers reportedly did so, or retired.

Teachers' self-reported commitment to the models typically remained the same or declined over time. Asked their level of agreement that "teachers are committed to using the model," on a five-item scale ranging from 1 (strongly disagree) to 5 (strongly agree), teachers ratings ranged between 3.0 (neither agree nor disagree) and 5.0. The average ratings of teachers' commitment declined in 6 of the 12 case study schools (1 AS, 1 CK, 2 DI, and 2 SFA), and remained constant or rose in the others (table 8.3). Principals typically rated their teachers' commitment to the model higher than teachers themselves did. Likewise, teachers also tended to rate their principals' commitment to the model higher than their own (table 8.3).

Providing Initial Training

Staff at seven of our case study schools received the amount of initial training prescribed by the respective model developers. Of the remaining five, staff at one CK school received two days of training and at another, received none.[6] Similarly, staff at two DI schools and one SFA school received two days of initial training instead of the five days recommended by the model developers.

Teachers' assessments of the adequacy of training depended on the model. Teachers generally thought that CK and DI initial training was adequate, although some noted that the DI training was "overwhelming" and that the CK training required "changing one's mind-set." By contrast, teachers reported that training related to AS and SFA was, respectively, "overwhelming" and "insufficient." There was consensus among the AS teachers that the AS trainers had not been adequately prepared to address teachers' questions. Teachers also criticized AS initial training for "not giving the full picture" and "being too broad," leaving many questions unanswered. Teachers who received SFA initial training indicated that they were not fully prepared to use SFA in the classroom. They wished that the training had included more modeling of instructional techniques and opportunities to practice these techniques.

All internal facilitators indicated that the training they received was inadequate to prepare them fully for their roles. This was particularly the case for AS facilitators, who had to guide teachers in "taking stock" of the school and in developing implementation plans, as well as train them in the Powerful Learning instructional protocol.[7] Internal facilitators at SFA schools expressed the need for more "how-to" assistance, especially concerning how to place students in groups. One facilitator also said that the SFA "jargon" constituted a barrier to effective communication. Thinking that a guide to translate the SFA jargon would have been helpful, this individual eventually developed her own.

Securing the Resources[8]

As noted in table 8.2, the out-of-pocket costs for the study's four models varied in the first year from a low of $45,000 (AS and CK) to a high of $75,000 (DI and SFA), and were somewhat less in subsequent years. These costs cover initial training provided by model developers, their follow-up visits to the schools, and some materials. Schools must also cover (with additional resources or the reallocation of existing school resources) teacher release time for training and meetings, a part-time or full-time internal coach or facilitator, tutors (in the case of SFA), and books. With these additions, total costs in the first year may increase two- to fourfold, depending on the staffing requirements.

Table 8.3. Principals', Teachers', and Districts' Support of Their Comprehensive School Reform Model, by Years

Survey item	AS₁		AS₂		AS₃			CK₁			CK₂		DI₁			DI₂		DI₃		SFA₁			SFA₂		SFA₃		
	2ᵃ	3	2	3	1	2	3	1	2	3	1	2	3	4	5	5	6	1	2	3	4	5	2	3	4	5	6
Teachers agree, "most teachers are committed to using the model."ᵇ	3.0	3.0	3.0	3.0	4.4	3.6	3.6	n.a.	4.6	5.0	4.4	4.2	3.0	n.a.	4.2	3.4	2.6	4.2	3.2	4.6	4.2	3.4	1.6	1.8	4.4	4.4	3.4
Principals agree, "most teachers are committed to using the model."ᵇ	3.0	3.0	3.0	3.0	5.0	5.0	5.0	5.0	5.0	5.0	5.0	5.0	5.0	n.a.	4.0	n.a.	n.a.	5.0	3.0	5.0	n.a.	4.0	0.0	2.0	5.0	5.0	4.0
Teachers agree, "their principal is committed to using the model."ᵇ	3.4	4.4	4.0	4.0	5.0	4.6	3.6	5.0	5.0	4.6	5.0	4.6	5.0	n.a.	4.6	4.4	3.4	4.4	3.4	5.0	5.0	3.4	3.2	3.2	5.0	5.0	4.0
Principals agree, "the district gave the school all the support needed to implement the model."ᶜ	1.0	1.0	1.0	1.0	1.0	1.0	1.0	n.a.	2.0	1.0	2.0	2.0	1.0	n.a.	2.0	n.a.	n.a.	1.0	1.0	n.a.	2.0	1.0	2.0	2.0	n.a.	1.0	1.0

Source: Responses from principals and teachers to the RAND/University of Washington surveys of model schools (2002, 2003, 2004).

AS = Accelerated Schools
CK = Core Knowledge
DI = Direct Instruction
SFA = Success for All
n.a. = not available (DI₁ did not participate in the second wave of the survey.)

ᵃ Number indicates year of implementation: 1 is the first year of implementation, 2 is the second year, and so on.
ᵇ Respondents were asked to indicate their level of agreement on a five-item scale ranging from 0 (strongly disagree) to 5 (strongly agree).
ᶜ Principals were asked whether the district provided none (0), some (1), or all (2) the support their school needed to implement the model.

Four of our case study schools received ample federal CSRD funds to cover the full cost of model implementation over the first three years. The other schools used a combination of district and school (including Title I) funding and/or funding donated by school-based organizations such as a parent organization.

District contributions appear to have been particularly important for keeping schools on track with implementation. Of the three schools that did not receive tangible resources from their districts, two abandoned their efforts within two years. However, even with tangible district support, the combined funds from all sources were inadequate to fully cover the costs of supporting the model. Consequently, schools reallocated staff and/or did not meet all staffing requirements recommended by the models. In addition, some opted against upfront funding for all of the staff and materials recommended by the model developers.

Table 8.4 provides more details on how schools in our case study sample met the resource requirements to implement their respective models. As noted earlier, four of our study schools (three AS and one SFA) applied for and received federal CSRD funds for a period of three years. The CSRD grants all exceeded $120,000 per year, with one reaching $200,000 per year. The schools reported that these funds were more than adequate to cover all model implementation costs, including staff time to attend training and pay for substitute teachers, with some surplus funds remaining. After three years, one AS school is planning to continue the program using its own funds. The SFA school is similarly now using Title I funds. In the latter case, the amount used for model maintenance decreased to about $3,000 annually. This school no longer has a contract with SFA and sends fewer staff to SFA annual conferences. The other two AS schools abandoned the program at the end of the three-year CSRD grant.

All other case study schools obtained the needed resources from multiple external and within-school sources. Five schools (two CK, two DI, and one SFA) received tangible dollar and/or in-kind support from their respective districts. At the two CK schools in the same district, the district provided each school $20,000 a year for materials and funded a part-time district staff member to serve as the "school-based coordinator." At one DI school, the district paid for the services to be provided by DI, and at the other DI school, the district provided the funds for initial training and ongoing staff development. At the SFA school, the district paid for all SFA-related costs. Some of the schools supplemented the district contributions with their own resources, using either Title I or regular funding, or contributions from school-based organizations such as a parent organization. These contributions were reportedly small, ranging from $2,000 to $15,000.

Table 8.4. Schools' Methods of Meeting Comprehensive School Reform Model Resource Requirements

	AS₁			AS₂			AS₃			CK₁			CK₂		CK₃			DI₁				DI₂				DI₃		SFA₁				SFA₂		SFA₃		
	1[a]	2	3	1	2	3	1	2	3	1	2	3	1	2	1	2	3	1	3	4	5	1	4	5	6	1	2	1	3	4	5	1	2	4	5	6
Funds																																				
CSRD	x	x	x	x	x	x	x	x	x																											
Federal grant																						x							x							
District funds										x	x	x	x	x				x	x	x	x	x	x	x	x											
District in-kind										x	x	x	x	x																						
Title I funds															x																					
Regular school funds																		x	x	x	x	x	x	x	x		x			x	x			x	x	
SBO funds										x	x	x																								
Private grant														x	x	x																				
Staff time reallocation															x	x	x	x	x	x	x				x			x	x	x	x	x	x	x		
Not all staffing requirements met										x	x	x	x		x	x	x	x	x	x	x							x	x	x	x	x	x	x	x	x

Sources: Responses from principals to RAND/University of Washington surveys of model schools, and school visits (2002, 2003, 2004).
AS = Accelerated Schools
CK = Core Knowledge
CSRD = Comprehensive School Reform Demonstration
DI = Direct Instruction
SBO = student body organization
SFA = Success for All
[a] Number indicates year of implementation: 1 is the first year of implementation, 2 is the second year, and so on.

Only 3 of our 12 case study schools (one CK, one DI, and one SFA) funded CSR model implementation exclusively with school resources, using Title I or regular funds.

Getting External Assistance

All but one of the case study schools hired an external facilitator/coach (typically staff from the model developer), who generally visited schools at the frequency recommended by the model developers (table 8.5). The three Accelerated Schools hired a consultant who visited the schools about once a week, as required by AS. Two of the Core Knowledge schools eventually shared a part-time coach paid by the district and trained in Core Knowledge. This coach visited one of these two schools only once and the other six days a year. The third CK school did not hire an external coach. Visits by DI coaches varied widely across schools, with one school being visited by its consultant once a week (as recommended by the model developer), and the other two, three times a year. Finally, Success for All schools were all visited by coaches at least two or more times a year as required by the model developer.

With few exceptions, principals met with the external coach at each visit and indicated that the level of support provided by the consultants was adequate. By contrast, teachers rarely met formally with the external coaches (except at AS schools, where teachers reported meeting with the consultant 5 to 11 times a year per teacher). Nonetheless, teachers generally agreed with their principals' assessments of the adequacy of the external coaching. They typically indicated that the consultants were responsive to their questions, and, with SFA, found the consultants particularly flexible in agreeing to adjust the program to fit the schools' needs. However, not all teachers were satisfied with the external coaching. Teachers at one AS school, one DI school, and one SFA school said that the model developers were inflexible and disapproved of the adjustments teachers wanted to make to the respective programs.

Principals varied in their assessments of how well their respective districts had supported their school's efforts. Asked whether they had received all, some, or none of the support their schools required, by 2004, principals at three schools indicated that they had received all the support their school needed (table 8.3), while seven indicated they had received "some support." Those who said their district had provided all the support needed had received district support in dollars; one school also received in-kind support (table 8.4).

Table 8.5. Schools' Fulfillment of Requirements for Internal Facilitators and External Coaches

	AS_1	AS_2	AS_3	CK_1	CK_2	CK_3	DI_1	DI_2	DI_3	SFA_1	SFA_2	SFA_3
Internal facilitator	2	2	2	0	0	0	0	2	1	2	2	2
External coach	2	1	2	1	2	0	2	1	1	2	2	2

Source: RAND/University of Washington surveys of model schools (2002, 2003, 2004).
AS = Accelerated Schools
CK = Core Knowledge
DI = Direct Instruction
SFA = Success for All
Note: 2 = model requirements fully met; 1 = partially met; 0 = no one was designated to fulfill this function

Internal Support

The schools' principals recognized the value of having an internal facilitator/coach, as recommended by the model developers. Eight of the 12 schools either hired or designated one or more existing staff members to function as an internal facilitator. At DI and SFA schools, the designated facilitator was typically a reading specialist. The three Accelerated Schools divided this function among several teachers, two at one school and three at the other two. In most schools, these facilitators were allocated the time prescribed by the model developers (table 8.5).

Some schools chose not to designate an internal facilitator. One DI school was said to receive sufficient support from its external coordinator, and one CK school left use of the program to the discretion of individual teachers. In two other CK schools without a formal internal facilitator, the principals said that they and their associate principals fulfilled this function. The latter were mainly responsible for aligning CK with state standards at one school, and for identifying materials and other resources needed to support CK at another.

The level of effort provided by internal facilitators generally met model requirements. In SFA schools, the internal facilitators spent 100 percent of their time helping group students by skill level, tracking and reviewing assessments, identifying students in need of tutoring, observing classrooms and providing feedback to teachers, presiding over component meetings, and in a few schools, tutoring. At the Accelerated Schools where this function was divided among several staff members, facilitators spent their time presiding over committee and cadre meetings and providing on-the-job training. The internal facilitators constituted in aggregate one full-time employee at one school and about 75 percent of a full-time employee at the other two. Only one of the three DI schools had a full-time facilitator, while another had a quarter-time facilitator and the third had none.

Interactions between the internal facilitators and principals on the one hand and teachers on the other varied significantly across models. Principals at the AS, DI, and SFA schools reported that they met with their respective internal coaches from 20 to 70 times a year. Formal meetings between teachers and internal coordinators, however, were typically much less frequent and ranged from an average of four to five times a year per teacher at the DI and SFA schools and up to 10 times a year per teacher at the AS schools during the second year, and less frequently thereafter.

IMPLEMENTING THE MODELS

In this section, we broadly describe schools' implementation of the models' key curriculum, instructional, and/or governance components, and discuss principals' and teachers' assessments of their experiences using the respective models. Because each model's key components are unique, we focus separately on the process of implementation for each.

Accelerated Schools

All three AS schools sought to implement the program over the specified phase-in period of three years. They started by "taking stock"—assessing the current situation and identifying priorities—which took the entire first year of implementation. At the beginning of the second year, all three schools formed up to three *cadres* (or committees) to address the issues that had been identified and develop action plans. None of the schools, however, was able to complete the action plans as scheduled. The cadres continued to function in the third year, although meetings were held less frequently. In the meantime, the Powerful Learning instructional practices, including problem solving and cooperative learning, were gradually introduced in classrooms with varying degrees of success.

"Taking Stock"

As prescribed, committees were formed at the three schools to review each school's current activities, with teachers allowed to join the committee(s) of their choice. For instance, one school set up five committees, for school organization, instruction and achievement, curriculum and assessment, culture and climate, and family and community. In addition to gathering data on such items as test scores and attendance rates, two of the schools also surveyed teachers, parents, and students. All three schools reported seeking parents' involvement as encouraged by AS, but had only limited success. This lack of participation was attributed to working parents' difficulty in attending midafternoon meetings.

The committees met regularly and in at least one school, weekly, for about four months and then less frequently throughout the year. The issues identified in meetings ranged from the broad (e.g., "inadequate math curriculum") to the specific (e.g., variations in the time allotted to math teaching across grades or teachers' competency in using technology).

At the end of the year, one school produced a written "taking stock" report as specified by AS, while two schools presented results to staff during an in-service day.

Setting the Governance Structure and Developing the Action Plan

Guided by the outcome of the taking stock process, all three schools established three cadres each to develop action plans: one cadre each for math and reading in all three schools, a cadre for instructional practices in two schools, and a cadre for parental involvement in the third. Most teachers reported participating in at least one cadre as prescribed by AS. To support and review the cadres' progress, the schools also set up a steering committee that included the principal, the external and internal coordinators, and the cadre leaders.

The cadres met weekly for an hour, whereas the steering committees met twice monthly, also for one hour (at least at the beginning). Again, the schools indicated that they were unable to involve parents in cadre and steering committee activities as encouraged by AS.

Each school's cadres appeared to progress at different rates, but none was able to complete their work as expected by the program (i.e., by the spring of the second year). One school did not complete its action plans until the end of the second year; the second school, until the beginning of the third year; and the third school, until the end of the third year. The latter school is planning to implement its action plans in its fourth year of using the Accelerated Schools model.

The two schools that completed their action plans by the beginning of the third year continued convening their respective cadres during the third year, but less frequently. The two schools reported making various improvements, although we could not ascertain clearly whether these changes were all products of the cadres' deliberations. Both schools implemented a new math curriculum, but this was a districtwide curriculum different from that recommended by one of the cadres. Both schools focused on English as a Second Language (ESL) students: one school stopped pulling ESL students out of mainstream classrooms, instead assigning them to ESL teachers, and the other developed new instructional strategies for ESL students consistent with Powerful Learning. Both schools established a writing initiative for teachers.

Powerful Learning

Powerful Learning, a form of instruction described as "authentic, interactive, collaborative, learner-centered, inclusive, and continuous," was introduced gradually in all three schools over the first year. By year two, all teachers were expected to use it in their classrooms. Training in Powerful Learning was ongoing, reportedly taking place both in formal training sessions and in cadre and grade-level meetings. Teachers occasionally presented examples of the desired mode of instruction or shared lesson plans with each other at these meetings. One school set up a mentor program to train new teachers in Powerful Learning.

Teachers indicated that they rarely got feedback on their teaching. At two schools, the principals observed classes regularly, but did not provide feedback to individual teachers unless requested to do so. In the third school, the internal facilitators visited classrooms every two months, evaluating teaching practices against the Powerful Learning matrix. They used the best teachers to demonstrate their lessons to other teachers.

Principals' and Teachers' Assessments

Teachers described the "taking stock" process as one of "trial and error." Staff in at least two of the schools expressed frustration at the lack of direction they were receiving from AS staff. Some also expressed their frustration at having identified "what was wrong with the school and yet not being able to look for positive solutions until the following year." At all three schools, staff said they were unprepared for the amount of time they would have to devote to the process, adding to the frustration of not seeing tangibly where this process would eventually lead.

School staff generally found developing action plans difficult despite the assistance provided by the external and internal facilitators and, more generally, the members of the steering committees.[9] Nearly all staff mentioned the time required by the process as the most important impediment to its success. Staff complained that they spent more time doing research than lesson plans. Eventually all schools cut down on the frequency of cadre meetings, moving from meeting once a week to once a month or less frequently. Lack of "know-how" was also an issue. As one internal facilitator said, "Teachers don't know how to use data and do research." The details required in action plans also created a problem for teachers "who are not used to making decisions."

Teachers had difficulty developing action plans that clearly defined the steps to be taken, the resources needed, and other requirements.

Although frustrated by the length and deliberate pace of the process, staff had generally favorable views of the outcomes. Staff in all three schools said that the process made their school more reflective, leading to significant changes in school vision and culture. One school indicated that, in addition to the specific improvements mentioned above, it had shifted from a focus on discipline to a focus on academics. Staff at all schools thought the process had increased interaction across grades and facilitated grade-level coordination. Another positive outcome for all schools was a change from top-down to collaborative decisionmaking, which increased cohesion, trust, and the sharing of ideas.

Teachers admitted that making the transition to Powerful Learning instruction had been difficult and gradual, and that by the end of the third year of implementation, they still didn't use all of its components all of the time.[10] They identified as "most difficult" the transition from teacher-centered to student-centered instruction and the use of authentic instruction in reading. Our classroom observations toward the end of the third year of AS implementation generally confirmed these teacher self-assessments.[11] Nevertheless, teachers spoke positively of the effect of Powerful Learning instruction on students, stating that it "gets kids more involved in learning," "helps kids communicate," and "increases students' involvement and motivation."

In the end, two of the schools we observed decided to terminate their relationships with Accelerated Schools. Both schools believed that AS staff had not been as helpful as they could have been and had not been sufficiently sensitive to their needs. Clearly, the end of the three-year federal CSRD grant was a key consideration in their decisions. Nevertheless, both schools expected to continue using Powerful Learning, and at least one of these two schools expected to continue using the governance structure put in place, including the math and the reading cadres and a modified "just do it" cadre meant to work on solutions that could readily be implemented. The third school expected to continue its association with Accelerated Schools, because unlike the other two schools, it found AS staff "supportive and helpful." The school went into its fourth year of using the model with the intent of implementing its action plans, but also with the concern that the district might not give it the autonomy it desired.

Core Knowledge

Curriculum Implementation

All three schools phased in Core Knowledge gradually; two did so over a two-year time period, while the third was still in the process of phasing in the program well into its third year of implementation. Teachers at the first two schools were mandated to use the program, whereas use at the third school was voluntary.

In the first year, the first two schools set the goal of implementing 50 percent of the CK curriculum in all grades and in all subjects except mathematics.[12] Having contributed to the development of the yearlong plan (a key CK component), teachers were expected to follow it closely using a checklist to track what they were covering. Principals at both schools held teachers accountable for implementing the program by regularly observing classrooms and requiring teachers to submit weekly reports on their progress. All teachers in a grade level had the same time period to write lesson plans, thereby helping assure horizontal integration of the curriculum. However, the 45 minutes provided for this purpose daily were also to be used for meetings with parents, correcting tests, and completing other tasks as needed.

Two to three times a year, during in-service days, the grade-level teams looked at the CK sequence and coordinated to assure vertical integration. To do so, teachers at these schools divided into two groups, with teachers of grades K–3 in one group and teachers of grades 4–6 in another. Facilitators moderated the proceedings. Core Knowledge was aligned with state standards during the second year of implementation at both schools. By the end of the second year, teachers at both schools reported that they were covering 80 to 100 percent of the Core Knowledge sequence, one year ahead of the timeframe suggested by the developer. One of these two schools was certified an official CK school by the end of its third year of implementation; the second expected to become similarly certified, also at the end of its third year of implementation.

At the third school, little progress was made in implementing the program, which was voluntary. The school was primarily focused on improving students' results on the state test, and therefore concentrated its efforts on implementing Project CLEAR, a districtwide improvement program, with Core Knowledge seen as a means to support this effort. Hence, implementation proceeded slowly, at the initiative of individual teachers. We were told that in year one only a few teachers, at grades 1 and 5, had fully embraced the program. In year two, a yearlong plan was developed along with a mapping of the state standards against Core Knowledge requirements. The CK sequence was seemingly used more often in the lower grades (K–2), which are not tested, than in the upper grades, which are. In the upper grades, teachers said they implemented the CK units they identified as supporting Project CLEAR. The principal was confident that, with time, teachers would learn how to integrate CK instruction into state testing preparation. To this end, she organized grades 4 and 5 into an arts/social studies department and a math/sciences department. She required teachers to indicate in monthly plans which topics they covered, but she did not hold them accountable for using CK or review their checklists.

Principals' and Teachers' Assessments

Teachers reported that implementing Core Knowledge was a "challenge," especially during the first year, but that "things got easier with time." Teachers raised two issues about the start-up process. First, they thought the time needed to research and write lessons exceeded the time allocated by the school. Although aware that lesson plans were available on the CK web site, teachers insisted that they preferred to make the lessons their own. They partially addressed this problem by dividing the task of writing lessons among all teachers from the same grade.

Teachers were also challenged by their unfamiliarity with the CK material, especially in social sciences and history. Teachers had to engage in self-directed learning about some topics, which they saw as cutting two ways: on the one hand, acquiring this new knowledge necessitated more time to prepare and develop lessons, but on the other hand, it motivated them because "they were learning too."

Teachers also reported some problems in aligning subject matter and in sequencing topics from the CK curriculum with the newly established state standards. For example, the state's history needed to be covered in greater depth than specified by CK. The CK science curriculum was reportedly not well aligned with the state standards, and in social studies, the CK sequence required some units to be covered in grades different than those specified by state standards. As the district pressured the schools to increase students' performance, the schools responded by altering the sequence and shifting some topics to different subject areas while continuing to cover most of the CK curriculum. Teachers also believed that some of the CK material was beyond the students' vocabulary levels. One example cited was *Don Quixote*, thought to be beyond the appropriate level for 5th graders.

In spite of these challenges, both principals and teachers were generally enthusiastic about Core Knowledge. They said Core Knowledge had "sparked more excitement in learning," and that students "were made better problem solvers," had become "more inclined to do research on their own," and "really drank up the vocabulary." In sum, as one teacher put it, "children like the stuff." In addition, teachers reported that Core Knowledge allowed for "more creativity" and made it "easier to make connections between subjects." Teachers also remarked that implementation of Core Knowledge had helped open lines of communication and facilitated sharing between teachers and students.

Direct Instruction

Curriculum Implementation

Only one of the three schools initially implemented Direct Instruction in all grades, only to limit its use to grades K–2 after the first year of implementation. One school limited use of the program to grades K–2 from the beginning, and the third piloted the program in grade 1 before expanding its use to all grades. The schools did so because the program "does not adequately address reading comprehension in the elementary upper grades." The one school still using the program in all grades has adapted it to reinforce reading comprehension; another school abandoned the program altogether in the second year of implementation.

In the two schools continuing to use the model, teachers and other staff met its prescribed requirements in spirit, although not to the letter. Teachers adapted the program and complied unevenly within and across schools. All teachers implemented a 90-minute reading/language arts block as prescribed. Most were comfortable with the 30-minute group sessions per class; however, some preferred to have 45 minutes per group, and hence were working with two instead of three groups.

Students were typically grouped by level of achievement as prescribed by DI, although some classes had three groups ranging from 5 to 9 students, while others were split into two larger groups of 10 to 12 students. Regrouping typically occurred less frequently than the three times a year recommended by DI, although the frequency varied across schools and across teachers within a school.[13] The mastery tests were administered every 10 lessons as prescribed.

In all schools, the classrooms we observed were organized so that the teachers could see all students, as recommended by the program. However, in half the classrooms we visited, students' desks were not cleared of all materials other than those pertinent to the lesson, as prescribed. Nor did any of the classrooms we observed place low-achieving students up front, closer to the teacher. Most of the classrooms also appeared to ignore DI's recommendation to post subject lessons, student records, and critical rules.

Few teachers reported following the scripts to the letter, although the extent of departure varied across teachers more than across schools. Teachers sometimes diverged from the script to emphasize more comprehension, to make the program "more interesting," or to correct workbooks with their students rather than by themselves. Some teachers corrected students unevenly or not at all. Finally, in all three schools we observed that teachers had difficulties managing their students, especially those on independent work tasks.

Some teachers also found the pace of lessons challenging. This was particularly the case at the one school that had been required by the district to cover two lessons rather than one per day. However, teachers in that school adjusted the pace to their students' level, some completing the two lessons on the same day, some not.

The extent to which teachers were held accountable for using DI as prescribed was uneven across the schools. At one school, the principal made sure that teachers were using DI by frequently visiting classrooms and holding faculty accountable. He reviewed the weekly log of classroom reports prepared by the external coach. He also checked teachers' workbooks to see if they were adhering to the lesson schedules. At another school, each teacher filled out a card indicating how far each student had progressed in the program by the end of the school year; this report formed the basis for assigning students to classes and groups for the following year.

Two of the schools visited are now Direct Instruction "maintenance" schools; they have used the program in excess of four years and plan to continue doing so. The third school abandoned the program in its second year of implementation.

Principals' and Teachers' Assessments

In the two schools continuing to use the program, both principals and teachers perceived that students benefited in several ways. Principals and teachers generally agreed that the program "works for students, especially low-achieving students." They thought the program not only helped students increase their scores on state tests, but also kept students "on task." They noted that the program improved students' behavior and that grouping students by ability level increased students' self-esteem because, within a group, "they don't feel like low achievers." Finally, several teachers indicated that their expectations for students have increased and that they can push their students further than they did in the past.

Teachers, in turn, said that DI "can't be made much easier . . . everything is there . . . materials are there," and that it promotes "security in their life." They also reported that the program increased coordination within and across grades.

Not all teachers viewed the program positively, however. Implementation was reportedly difficult, at least at first. Some teachers found the program repetitive and restrictive. But most importantly, they identified items they would like to see added to the program. As noted above, a primary concern with DI was that "it teaches children to read, but not necessarily to comprehend what they are reading." They also complained that students "get bored." Two schools were shifting to DI's Reading Mastery Plus component to partially address this issue. Some teachers and one principal also suggested that DI add a literature component.

Success for All

Curriculum Implementation

All three schools acted to put in place two key SFA components: a 90-minute schoolwide reading block and the assignment of students to classes by achievement level. Two of the schools allocated students to reading classes by level of achievement across grades. To create reading class sizes as recommended by SFA, one school renovated spaces previously used for storage and hired new certified teachers. The third school also assigned students by level of achievement but within—rather than across—grades, resulting in classes with a reportedly broad ability span. The principal of this school did not want to use ancillary staff to teach reading classes and could not hire additional teachers; hence, not enough reading classes of the appropriate size were established.

The schools differed significantly in the extent to which they implemented the many other SFA components. One school fully put in place all SFA components in the first year of the program, including the GAT curriculum,[14] component meetings, a family support team, daily home reading assignments, and mainstreaming of special education students. It also hired tutors for the 1st grade and continued to use the HOSTS mentoring program for other grades.[15] Finally, it aligned state standards with SFA lessons.

The other two schools were more selective in the components they put in place. Both established 20 minutes of home reading, tutoring for some students, and a family support team (although one school's functions fell short of those recommended by SFA). Neither school chose to implement GAT, hold component meetings, or mainstream special education students. While one school aligned its state standards with the SFA lessons, the other made no attempt to do so.

Schools also differed in the extent to which their teachers used SFA materials in the classrooms. Whereas one school used SFA materials nearly exclusively during the first year, the other two used them as a supplement to other reading materials.

Teachers in all three schools agreed that they faced challenges during the first year. As one teacher declared, "the first year was an unbelievable struggle." Even though not all teacher respondents assessed their experiences so dramatically, they all said their adjustments to SFA were impeded by a lack of time to prepare lessons and fill out the paperwork, as well as by their inability to complete lessons within the time prescribed by SFA. Teachers had much to get used to, such as teaching reading across grades and using cooperative learning. To prepare for lessons, they had to create flash cards, word maps, and other visuals. They also learned that SFA required a significant amount of paperwork, including maintaining a daily log of students' homework completion.

These problems were alleviated but not fully eliminated during the second and subsequent years, as teachers could reuse materials and had become more familiar with the lessons' content. At the same time, the schools reported that SFA became less strict about pacing in subsequent years, recommending that teachers skip some components of lessons or extend the days spent on others when necessary.

As the schools became more familiar with the program, they also increasingly modified it to meet their needs and their students' needs as they saw fit, generally with the approval of SFA staff. One school began testing students at the end of the year instead of the beginning. This allowed them to finish assigning students to classrooms before school convened. The school also stopped automatically mainstreaming Spanish-speaking students in the 3rd grade. If these students were not deemed ready, they continued to receive instruction in Spanish and completed the state assessments in Spanish. The school also set up special classes for dyslexic students, taking a modified approach in which SFA techniques were used only half of the time, while techniques specially designed for such students were used for the other half.

Over the years, teachers at this school made various adjustments to the pacing and content of lessons. They skipped activities with students whose abilities exceeded the level of the lessons and/or took fewer or more days than recommended to cover lessons and activities. Changes in the state testing standards prompted the school to add instructional supplements to promote reading comprehension and higher-order skills, and lessons plans were expanded to expose students to analytical questions.

After initially resisting SFA implementation, the other two schools took diverging paths. At one school, teachers continued to resent the "imposition" of the program and continued to mainly use other reading materials—which they believed more effectively addressed the language arts components of the state standards—supplementing them with SFA materials at each teacher's discretion. Teachers reported that they felt even less pressure from the principal and the facilitator to use SFA materials in the second year than they had in the first. They thought that SFA did not adequately address many of the state standards, and said they would do "what it takes to get their kids to pass the tests."

By contrast, teachers at the third school developed a liking for SFA and eventually sought to comply with its requirements. Like teachers in SFA_1, they kept within the SFA framework by adjusting the pacing and content of lessons to meet what they perceived to be their students' needs. Based on the results of its students' achievement test results, this third SFA school decided to focus tutoring on 4th grade students rather than 1st graders. Additionally, the school grouped students by achievement level within grades rather than across grades as recommended by SFA, reportedly because teachers preferred to remain closer to their homeroom students. After five years of using SFA, the school considered itself an SFA school.[16]

Principals' and Teachers' Assessments

Schools credited SFA with improving student achievement on state tests. One school reported that students' proficiency in reading increased by 10 percentage points between the first and fourth year of using SFA. Teachers from all three schools generally agreed that the increased frequency of testing provided teachers with useful information on students' weaknesses and individual performance, and also helped them focus on students' progress. They saw the grouping of students by ability across or within grades as a plus that encouraged collaboration among teachers and joint conferences with parents. They also indicated that the program provided structure for new teachers who otherwise would have difficulties adjusting. Finally, the only school that used GAT throughout the years credited it for helping the school introduce new discipline policies and intervention mechanisms to address ongoing problems.

Teachers also agreed about the program's drawbacks. They unanimously said that SFA demanded too much time for lesson preparation (which included developing posters, charts, and word maps), especially at the beginning. Principals and teachers also unanimously thought that SFA did not focus adequately on comprehension, higher-skills development, or writing. (The schools' need to address this problem grew when the state standards changed to emphasize these skills.) Finally, concern was also raised that students left behind were not well served by having to repeat the same material a second time.

Individual schools noted a few other issues. One school saw SFA's high cost as a problem after its federal CSRD grant expired, forcing the school to cut back on the number of teachers sent to SFA conferences and to limit its interactions with SFA staff. Staff also noted that SFA does not work well for schools unless they have enough teachers to create the appropriate number of reading classes. Finally, some teachers said that use of SFA limited their creativity in the classroom due to the lessons' prescribed content.

Factors Affecting Implementation

All case study schools initially sought to implement their selected model in the way prescribed by their developers, and while none succeeded fully, the extent of implementation varied significantly. As has been seen in previous studies, schools often exercise some control over the changes requested by external agents and adapt the models to their own resource constraints, needs, and expectations (Datnow, Borman, and Stringfield 2000; Finnigan and O'Day 2003; Muncey and McQuillan 1996; Spillane, Reiser, and Reimer 2002). In this sample, after initial experience with the model, schools and teachers made adjustments to meet their own needs, their students' needs, and their time availability. In the end, 4 of our 12 case study schools eventually discontinued their association with the model developers. Partial implementation was related to inadequate initial training and, in several instances, inadequate ongoing training and support from external and internal coaches. However, as we discuss below, the primary reasons for partial implementation and, for some, the decision to discontinue model use varied across models and to a lesser extent, across schools implementing the same model.

Lack of "know-how" was the primary reason for partial Accelerated Schools implementation in our three case study schools. The model requires teachers to engage in activities they are not prepared for, including doing a comprehensive school needs assessment, conducting research, and developing plans of action. Training was not sufficient, and reportedly too disjointed, to overcome teachers' skills gaps. Time required for these activities was too demanding, especially as teachers could not see how these efforts would pay off in the classroom. After three years of implementation, two of the schools that were located in the same district decided to no longer contract with Accelerated Schools and to abandon much of the model's committee and cadre structure. Although this decision coincided with the end of their respective CSRD grants, the difficulties mentioned above and the schools' general dissatisfaction with AS training and support seemed to have been more compelling reasons.[17] The third AS school planned to continue, even though its CSRD grant was ending (also after three years). This school indicated that it was working well with AS staff and receiving all the assistance it needed, and that it had the flexibility to adjust the timetable for the AS-prescribed products.

Perceived lack of alignment between the DI curriculum and state standards, and difficulties in following the prescribed pacing of lessons and scripts were the main reasons for partial DI implementation in our three case study schools. All respondents indicated that the program does not adequately address reading comprehension. For this reason, two schools limited its use to the lower grades (K–2). These two schools chose not to align the program with state standards, contributing to their decision to use DI only in untested grades. The third school that did align the program with state standards used DI in all grades, but supplemented it with another reading program in the upper grades. Teachers in all schools indicated having difficulty following the lessons' pace and therefore made adjustments according to their students' capabilities. Most teachers reported that both they and their students found the lessons "boring," and as such, teachers departed from and complemented them in various ways. These adjustments and teachers' overall satisfaction with the program contributed to its maintenance at two of our three case study schools. By the time of our last visit in spring 2004, the schools were, respectively, in their sixth and fifth years of using DI and planned to continue. The third school decided to discontinue the program at the end of its second year. Several factors seemed to have coincided to lead to this decision. This school had a rough, slow start, having responded negatively to its first external coach. The internal coach felt unprepared and provided little ongoing support and coaching. As a result, the teachers' and principal's commitment plummeted after the first year. The school also had to use its own funds to cover program costs, after having financed the program with a small federal grant in the first year.

In contrast to our other case study schools, two of our three Core Knowledge schools came the closest to full program implementation. Principals at these schools made clear what was expected of the staff and held teachers closely accountable for keeping with the yearlong plan. Teachers who were not committed were allowed to transfer. In turn, the district superintendent monitored these schools closely, as the Core Knowledge implementation was critical to his strategy of offering some measure of parental choice. One of these two schools was officially assessed by the Core Knowledge foundation at the end of its third year of implementation and became recognized as an official Core Knowledge school. The principal of the other school expected that it would be similarly recognized at the end of the third year. Nevertheless, both schools indicated that, in spite of their efforts to align the program with state standards, they still had to make adjustments in the program's sequence and in some of its content. Even as supportive as the district superintendent of these two schools was,[18] he nevertheless made clear to the schools that meeting the state proficiency standards came first.

Voluntary implementation at the third Core Knowledge school appears to have doomed reform efforts. Indeed, this school's experience offers an illustration of everything a school ought not to do when embarking on comprehensive school reform. Teachers and other staff received no training and no external support. Although an internal coordinator was appointed, her time and functions were limited and teachers were left on their own to gather material and prepare lessons.

The primary reasons for partial Success For All implementation ranged widely from openly hostile staff to tougher state testing requirements and inadequacy in meeting perceived school needs. Openly hostile staff was the reason for partial implementation at two of the three schools. The district imposed the program on one school, and at the other school, the principal had committed the school and its staff to adopting Success For All just as he was retiring. Both schools decided not to implement all components of the program, such as GAT or tutoring, and only partially implemented the Family Support Team. Similarly, both schools did not exclusively use SFA materials that teachers said they did not like in the first place. After the first year, however, the two schools' paths diverged, with one school continuing its resistance to SFA in spite of its district's support and the requirement that the school use the program. By contrast, the second school had a new principal dedicated to making the program work, the staff grew to like the program and the SFA materials, and implementation of its multiple components broadened over time. At the same time, the school implemented some modifications to the program, such as altering groupings of students within rather than across grades. By the fifth year, this school was considering itself an "SFA school."

Tougher state testing standards and perceived school needs were the main reasons for partial implementation at the third SFA school. The school started to use instructional supplements to promote reading comprehension, altered the pace of some lessons and skipped some others, and discontinued the automatic mainstreaming of Spanish-speaking students at the 3rd grade. These changes were reportedly made with the approval of the SFA staff.

In conclusion, program characteristics were the primary reason for partial implementation in 7 of our 12 schools, lack of alignment with state standards in 2, openly hostile staff in another 2, and voluntary implementation in the last. Other factors, including principal leadership, teacher buy-in, district support and policy alignment, and resources identified in the literature as affecting implementation, played varying roles in most of our case study schools. Principals' commitment and leadership was key not only for model selection but for implementation as well. Where this leadership was missing from the start or dwindled (as it did in four of our case study schools), these schools eventually abandoned the program or continued to resist implementation.

Teacher buy-in affected the long-term viability of the programs. In several of our schools, teacher buy-in was not sought during the program's initial implementation. Indeed, in two of our case study CK schools, the staff was not even consulted; in other schools, staff agreed only reluctantly to follow the program. However, sustaining a reform program over time required staff to eventually accept, and even come to like and support, it. In schools where teachers' support for the program did not develop or dwindled along with the principal's, the program was abandoned or was weakly implemented.

District support seems to have had a positive benefit on those schools that received it. Five of seven schools received active district support, although some only during the first couple of years. Obviously, district funding and/or training for model implementation, even if partial, was important to the schools that benefited from it; all of these schools are continuing to use the model even though one continues to resist implementation. By contrast, schools that did not benefit from district material support have not faired equally well with the model. Out of these seven schools, three have abandoned the model, one has not implemented the model, and only three are still using the model.

CONCLUSIONS AND RECOMMENDATIONS

Caution should be exercised in generalizing from this limited number of case studies. Although many of our findings are consistent with those of previous studies as noted, we cannot reject the possibility that some of our findings are idiosyncratic to the experiences of the schools and districts in which they are located. Still, our findings are sufficiently consistent across schools and across models, regardless of their differences, that they do suggest a number of measures that model developers, schools, districts, and federal education administrators should consider in facilitating and improving implementation of comprehensive school reform models.

Recommendations for Model Developers

Provide Additional Practical Training for Teachers

Teachers interviewed in our case study schools overwhelmingly said that the initial training did not fully prepare them to implement the model their school had adopted. Their reasons varied across models. For example, teachers were unprepared to use the specific prescribed instructional practices required by three of the models. They could have benefited from more modeling of instructional techniques and expanded opportunities for practice. For the one model that required research, more training on how to conduct research would have been useful. Because schools already have difficulties providing the necessary release time, we are not suggesting that the length of initial training should be increased (although certainly teachers would benefit from it). Instead, we are suggesting that training should place more emphasis on the model's practical applications in and out of the classroom. Schools might also benefit from additional training focused specifically on how model components can be modified to meet the needs of their specific contexts (e.g., state standards); this is discussed further below.

Increase Training for Internal Coaches

The internal coaches we interviewed said unanimously that they were not prepared to fully meet the expectations for their functions as defined by model developers, a finding confirmed by most of the teachers interviewed. Internal coaches play a crucial role in implementing comprehensive school reform models, regardless of the model, and serve as ongoing trainers, moderators, promoters, and leaders of within- or across-grades meetings. To a large extent, they are the only providers of ongoing "training" for school staff. Our case studies suggest that teachers do not receive training commensurate with the responsibilities they are to assume. Some models provide these coaches with no more training than received by other teachers; others provide only a few days of additional training. Regardless, coaches were not adequately prepared to answer teachers' questions, serve as leaders and solve problems in meetings, or in some cases, even communicate what the model expects teachers to do in the classroom. Given the critical role of the coaching function, model developers ought to reassess internal coaches' training needs for their respective models.

Recognize Limitations on Teachers' Time

The one teacher complaint common to all models was that it was time intensive (at least in the first year) to participate in additional meetings, realign the curriculum with state standards, coordinate within and across grades, learn new materials, and prepare new lessons. Some teachers perceived a lack of candor about the effort required to implement the model. Although some schools provided teachers with additional time, teachers nevertheless either had to do some tasks on their own time or reallocate time from other functions that then went neglected. Some model developers have explicitly recognized this issue and designed their program to be implemented over two or more years. Others, however, recommend implementing all parts of the program at once. But any change requires making a mind shift, acquiring new knowledge, altering teaching techniques, and preparing new materials and lessons and mastering them. Either model developers need to explicitly accommodate this reality and lighten the load for teachers in the first year, or districts and schools need to provide teachers with more time. Failure to acknowledge these considerations contributes to partial model implementation and the high frequency with which schools abandon models shortly after implementation.

Provide for Flexibility in Implementation

As previous research has found, schools and teachers will adjust programs to their needs, resources, and level of comfort. Some model developers recognize this reality and are willing to work with schools to modify their programs to meet schools' needs. Other model developers are less willing to accommodate modifications that schools want or are making to their models, regardless of their nature. In both instances, it seems that model developers should identify and communicate to schools those components or aspects of the programs that can be modified, and the specific ways in which they can be modified, without unduly affecting the program's effectiveness. We believe that it does not suffice to argue that a model was not effective because a school did not implement all of its aspects to the letter. Achieving true fidelity is the exception rather than the rule in program implementation. As such, developers should take it upon themselves to guide schools in making modifications in a way that is not only consistent with the philosophy of the model, but that is neutral—if not beneficial—to its effectiveness.

Align Model Requirements with State Standards

Related to flexibility is the need to better align school reform models with state standards. Several of our case study schools undertook the effort to do so on their own while others did not, contributing in the latter case to partial implementation of their model. Changes in state standards and increasing pressures on schools to meet state proficiency requirements under the No Child Left Behind Act are forcing schools to make adjustments that may not be consistent with their models' philosophies and integrity. Some model developers have been working with individual schools to align their model with district standards, while others are aligning their models relative to the standards of individual states. Model developers who do not will most likely be cast aside.

Respond to Schools' Criticisms of the Model's Weaknesses

As amply suggested by our case studies, "shortcomings" in model content or design were key reasons for partial implementation. In two of the models observed, problems lay in inadequate emphasis on reading comprehension, while in a third it was incompatibility of some parts of the curriculum with state standards, and in a fourth it was an assumption that teachers could effectively engage in research and problem-solving practices for which they were not trained. In every instance, the schools responded to these problems by modifying—in some cases significantly—the model content or design and/or shifting the grades in which the model was implemented, rendering the model no longer comprehensive and, in some schools, contributing to the model's abandonment. As noted above, pressures to meet state proficiency standards are such that schools can no longer ignore these problems. We suggest that neither can model developers.

Recommendations for Schools

Make Principals' Leadership and Accountability Key

In nearly all of our case study schools, the principals selected the model and set the extent to which they wanted teachers to implement the model curriculum and instructional practices. Our observations suggest that where the principals made clear they expected all staff to use the model—by regularly monitoring teachers' progress with implementing the yearlong plan and by accounting for individual teachers' adherence to the model—the model was used more faithfully and with greater uniformity within and across grades. Whether this was done in a consensus-oriented or more authoritarian leadership style did not seem to matter much. In the latter case, however, it helped if teachers who disagreed with the model were given the option to change schools.

Provide Internal Coaches with Adequate Time to Fully Perform Their Function

Principals should ensure that internal coaches be provided with adequate time to fully perform their tasks. As already emphasized, the coach's role in implementation can often be critical. But in the majority of our case study schools, the internal coach was not provided with the time model developers deemed necessary for this function, one that requires sufficient opportunities for conducting classroom observations, providing feedback and ongoing training, chairing meetings, and assembling materials.

Plan to Provide Adequate Resources to Implement and Maintain the Model

A school should not implement a CSR model unless it has acquired or is willing to allocate all resources necessary for its implementation and eventually, its maintenance. The costs of initial implementation and model maintenance can be high: first-year costs ranged from $45,000 to $75,000 for the four models in the study, not including staff time. Those case study schools that did not benefit from a generous federal CSRD grant generally underfunded implementation. As a result, teachers were not provided adequate release time for lesson preparation and committee meetings, were not given the latest model material, did not receive adequate training, and had limited opportunities to attend regional or national model conferences. Similarly, insufficient time was typically allocated for the internal coach.

Tell Staff What to Expect

One of the most common complaints we heard from teachers was that developers did not adequately prepare them for the effort required to implement the model. In a few of our case study schools, this eventually generated resentment against the model staff, contributed to the development of a negative view toward the program, and played a role in its eventual abandonment.

Recommendations for Districts

Ensure that District Support is Provided

Consistent with previous research, we found that tangible support from the district is needed to sustain comprehensive school reform efforts. About half of our case study schools received tangible support to implement their adopted models, while the other half did not. While district support does not appear absolutely necessary for a school to initially engage in comprehensive school reform, our case studies suggest that such support is important for efforts to be sustained over time. More than half of our schools that did not benefit from tangible district support eventually discontinued implementation after two or three years. The lesson we draw from this observation is that districts should not allow schools to adopt a model unless they are themselves willing to support implementation in a tangible and visible way.

NOTES

We acknowledge the contributions of Alissa Anderson and Jacqueline Raphael, formerly at the Urban Institute; Rita Karam, Sheila Murray, and Ron Zimmer at RAND; and Bethany Gross and Laura Stuhr at the University of Washington, all of whom participated in site visits and contributed to the analysis. This research was sponsored by the U.S. Department of Education under grant ED-00-CO-0087. The opinions and conclusions drawn in this chapter are those of the authors alone.

1. Conducted by RAND and the University of Washington, this broader study has collected survey data from principals and teachers over three years (2002 to 2004) from a dual sample of public elementary schools in Florida and Texas: a sample of "model" schools that are implementing one of our selected models and a sample of "comparison" schools that were not implementing one of these models. For the study design, refer to Vernez and his coauthors (2004).

2. Several recent studies have reviewed implementation research on education programs and need not be repeated here. For instance, see Glennan and colleagues (2004, 15–27); and Berends and colleagues (2002, 8–17). See also Stringfield, Millsap, and Herman (1997) and Tyack and Cuban (1997).

3. A higher percentage of recent implementers of the four models included in the study were located in Texas than in Florida.

4. In school year 2001–2002, the district choices included (1) 2 of 19 elementary schools, one using Core Knowledge and the other using Spanish immersion; (2) the Suzuki Strings music-based program in several elementary schools; and (3) the International Baccalaureate Diploma Program in one of the district's high schools. In subsequent years, two additional Core Knowledge schools were added to the selection, and the district is planning to go "all Core Knowledge" in year 2004–2005.

5. Project GRAD combines SFA for reading, "Move It Math," and the management program Consistency Management and Cooperative Discipline.

6. Core Knowledge did not start providing five days of training until after 2002. Both CK_1 and CK_3 began implementation in 2001.

7. We discuss Powerful Learning further below.

8. In interpreting our discussion about resources below, the reader should be aware that while schools could generally account for non-school funds or in-kind inputs associated with model implementation, they could not fully account for their own funds spent on model implementation or for the reallocation of teachers' time and/or functions. Our findings below represent our best interpretation of the information provided by multiple respondents from each school visited and from responses to our surveys of principals in these schools.

9. As noted earlier, external and internal facilitators thought they were not adequately trained to help the process along.

10. A few teachers indicated, however, that this was the way they were trained to teach, and that they had been using the techniques before the shift to Accelerated Schools.

11. In making our classroom assessments, we used the Accelerated School Project assessment sheet listing a total of 25 practices that define the five components of Powerful Learning (3 practices for authentic, 8 for interactive/collaborative; 6 for student centered; 5 for inclusive; and 3 for continuous).

12. With Core Knowledge's approval, the two schools continued to use the same math program they used before.

13. At one school, grouping was done at the beginning of the year only.

14. That is, the Getting Along Together curriculum, a system for maintaining order and resolving disputes in the classroom.

15. HOSTS, Help One Student to Succeed, provides one-on-one tutoring for 3rd–5th grade students with low standardized test scores.

16. However, the establishment of new state standards and the district's decision to no longer support SFA "since it had not met the expectations for improvement in students' achievement" was leading this school to consider terminating its contract with SFA.

17. The cost of contracting with Accelerated Schools (less than $45,000 annually) is not a substantial amount. Indeed, one of the reasons these schools had selected AS was its low cost.

18. This superintendent is having all elementary schools in the district implement Core Knowledge in school year 2004–2005.

REFERENCES

Berends, M. 1999. "Assessing the Progress of New American Schools: A Status Report." Monograph/Report MR-1085-EDU. Santa Monica: RAND.

Berends, M., S. J. Bodilly, and S. N. Kirby. 2002. "Facing the Challenges of Whole School Reform: New American Schools after a Decade." Monograph/Report MR-1498-EDU. Santa Monica: RAND.

Bifulco, R., W. Duncombe, and J. Yinger. 2003. "Does Whole-School Reform Boost Student Performance? The Case of New York City." CPR Working Paper No. 55. Syracuse: Center for Policy Research, SUNY.

Bodilly, S. J. 1998. "Lessons from New American Schools' Scale-Up Phase: Prospects for Building Designs to Multiple Schools. Monograph/Report MR-1228-NAS. Santa Monica: RAND.

Corcoran, T. 2003. "The Use of Research Evidence in Instructional Improvement." Policy Brief RB-40. Philadelphia: Consortium for Policy Research in Education, University of Pennsylvania.

Datnow, A., G. Borman, and S. Stringfield. 2000. "School Reform through a Highly Specified Curriculum: Implementation and Effects of the Core Knowledge Sequence." Elementary School Journal 101(2): 167–91.

Desimone, L. 2002. "How Can Comprehensive School Reform Models Be Successfully Implemented?" Review of Educational Research 72(3): 433–79.

Finnigan, K., and J. O'Day. 2003. "External Support to Schools on Probation: Getting a Leg Up?" CPRE Report. Philadelphia: Consortium for Policy Research in Education, University of Pennsylvania.

Glennan, T. K., Jr. 1998. "New American Schools after Six Years." Monograph/ Report MR-945-NAS. Santa Monica: RAND.

Glennan, T. K., Jr., S. J. Bodilly, J. R. Galegher, and K. A. Kerr. 2004. "Expanding the Reach of Education Reforms: Perspectives from Leaders in the Scale-Up of Educational Interventions." Monograph MG-248-FF. Santa Monica: RAND.

Gross, B., M. Kirst, D. Holland, and T. Luschei. 2005. "Got You Under My Spell? How Accountability Policy is Changing and Not Changing Decision Making in High Schools." In *Holding High Hopes: How High Schools Respond to State Accountability Policies*, edited by B. Gross and M. Goertz (43–79). Philadelphia: Consortium for Policy Research in Education, University of Pennsylvania.

Huberman, M. 1983. "Recipes for Busy Kitchens: A Situational Analysis of Routine Knowledge Use in Schools." *Knowledge: Creation, Diffusion, Utilization* 4(4): 478–510.

Muncey, D. E., and P. J. McQuillan. 1996. *Reform and Resistance in Schools and Classrooms: An Ethnographic View of the Coalition of Essential Schools*. New Haven: Yale University Press.

Spillane, J. P., B. J. Reiser, and T. Reimer. 2002. "Policy Implementation and Cognition: Reframing and Refocusing Implementation Research." *Review of Educational Research* 72(3): 387–431.

Stringfield, S., M. A. Millsap, and R. Herman. 1997. "Urban and Suburban/ Rural Special Strategies for Educating Disadvantaged Children: Findings and Policy Implications for a Longitudinal Study." Research Report. Baltimore: John Hopkins University.

Tyack, D., and L. Cuban. 1997. *Tinkering toward Utopia: A Century of Public School Reform*. Cambridge, MA: Harvard University Press.

Vernez, G., R. Karam, L. T. Mariano, and C. DeMartini. 2004. "Assessing the Implementation of Comprehensive School Reform Models." Working Paper WR-162-EDU. Santa Monica: RAND.

9

SCHOOL-LEVEL FACTORS IN COMPREHENSIVE SCHOOL REFORM

*Geoffrey D. Borman, Robert E. Slavin,
Alan C. K. Cheung, Anne M. Chamberlain,
Nancy A. Madden, and Bette Chambers*

Current federal policies focus on the replication and scale-up of research-proven educational programs. In several important ways, Success for All provides a compelling model of the type of programs these policies aim to support. Of 33 comprehensive school reform programs reviewed in a recent meta-analysis, Success for All was one of only three that had positive and statistically significant achievement effects across a large number of rigorous quasi-experimental studies (Borman et al. 2003). Even during the original development of the program's core components (summarized in the appendix), the developers conceived of them entirely from their own and others' research on "what works" in education reform (Slavin and Madden 2001). Since the program's development in the late 1980s, the Success for All developers have built the capacity to disseminate and maintain implementations at a national scale—currently more than 1,200 schools in 46 states.

First at Johns Hopkins University and now at the nonprofit Success for All Foundation, Success for All is one of only a few programs capable of adding more than a hundred schools to its network each year.

Success for All is purchased as a comprehensive package, which includes materials, training, ongoing professional development, and a well-specified "blueprint" for delivering and sustaining the model. Schools that elect to adopt the program implement a whole-school reform strategy for students in grades pre-K–5 that organizes resources to ensure every child will reach 3rd grade on time with adequate basic skills and will continue to build on those skills throughout the later elementary grades.

The program focuses on prevention and early, intensive intervention designed to detect and resolve reading problems as early as possible, before they become serious. Students in Success for All schools spend most of their day in traditional, age-grouped classes, but are regrouped across grades for reading lessons targeted to specific performance levels. Using the program's benchmark assessments, teachers assess each student's reading performance at eight-week intervals and make regrouping changes based on the results. Instead of being placed in special classes or retained in grade, most students who need additional help receive one-on-one tutoring to get them back on track.

The use of cooperative learning methods also helps children develop academic skills and encourages them to engage in teambuilding activities and other tasks that deal explicitly with the development of interpersonal and social skills. In addition, a Success for All school establishes a solutions team, serving to increase parents' participation in school generally, to mobilize integrated services to help Success for All families and children, and to identify and address particular problems such as irregular attendance, vision correction, or problems at home. Finally, each Success for All school designates a full-time program facilitator who oversees the daily operation of the program, provides assistance where needed, and coordinates the various components. These are the main features of Success for All, both as originally conceived in 1987 and as currently disseminated (see this chapter's appendix for more details concerning the Success for All program components).

The research evidence reviewed by Borman and his coauthors (2003) from 46 separate quasi-experimental comparison group evaluations of Success for All and its sister program, Roots & Wings, from across the United States reveals an achievement effect of one-fifth of one standard deviation ($d = .20$). In addition, quasi-experimental evidence from a study by Borman and Hewes (2002) demonstrates that students' multi-year participation in Success for All was associated with notable gains in reading and other school-based outcomes that were sustained through the completion of 8th grade, several years after they had left the Success for All elementary schools.

Though compelling in terms of its scope and results, this prior research has several limitations. First, the vast majority of these previous studies of Success for All have used a quasi-experimental matched comparison group design, in which experimental and control schools were matched on pretests and other demographic characteristics and then compared each year on the subsequent posttests. In recent years, an increasing body of evidence has emerged suggesting that such comparison group studies in social policy (e.g., employment, training, welfare-to-work, education) often produce inaccurate estimates of an intervention's effects, because of unobservable differences between the intervention and comparison groups that differentially affect their outcomes (Glazerman, Levy, and Myers 2002).

With regard to the typical Success for All quasi-experiment, there always may be some systematic reason that the experimental group implemented the program while the comparison group did not. Schools whose staffs expressed interest in Success for All and achieved the required 80 percent majority vote to adopt it may have greater motivation and interest in improving their schools than the control schools' staffs, who did not seek out the program. Indicated by the 80 percent agreement among staff, these schools may have strong cohesion among the teachers or have better leaders. Perhaps the experimental schools have better funding or fewer demands on their resources or energies. These potential artifacts make it difficult to know whether it was the characteristics related to selection of Success for All or the actual components of the program that caused the improvements in the schools. Most studies of Success for All have been well-designed matched experiments that have minimized selection bias—for example, by designating control schools in advance and by avoiding the use of control schools that rejected the program—but selection bias cannot be ruled out without random assignment.

Second, the authors of nearly all previous studies of Success for All have employed designs that attempt to match program and control schools, but have specified the student as the unit of analysis in statistical comparisons of program and control outcomes. Though this unit-of-analysis problem does not necessarily bias the impact estimates, it does underestimate the standard errors of the estimates and leads the researcher to overreject null results. Finally, because the early studies by the developers and by many of the third-party evaluators have involved small numbers of treatment sites, much of the prior work on Success for All may correspond with that which Cronbach and his coauthors (1980) termed the "super-realization" stage of program development. That is, with the researchers actively involved in assuring that they are studying high-quality implementations in a select number of schools, some of these earlier evaluations may represent assessments of what Success for All can accomplish at its best. The extent to which these results may generalize across broader implementations, though, is of some concern.

In 2000, the Success for All Foundation received a grant from the U.S. Department of Education to carry out a three-year study intended to address these limitations of the prior research base. The study reported here was designed as a cluster randomized trial (CRT), with random assignment of a relatively large sample of high-poverty schools from across the United States. A distinguished group of scholars, including C. Kent McGuire, Stephen Raudenbush, Rebecca Maynard, Jonathan Crane, and Ronald Ferguson, was appointed as an oversight committee to ensure that all study procedures were appropriate. After initial difficulties recruiting the sample, 41 elementary schools were recruited from across 11 states. The design primarily compared baseline kindergarten and 1st grade students nested within schools that were randomized into a grade K–2 Success for All treatment condition to kindergarten and 1st grade students whose schools were randomized into a grade 3–5 Success for All treatment condition. Thus, the kindergarten and 1st grade students within the former schools received the Success for All intervention—and served as the treatment cases—and the kindergarten and 1st grade students within the latter schools continued with their current reading programs—and served as the controls.

An analysis of the first-year achievement data for the main kindergarten and 1st grade sample was carried out by Borman and his coauthors (2005). Using hierarchical linear modeling techniques, with students nested within schools, Borman and colleagues reported school-level treatment effects of assignment to Success for All on four reading measures. They found statistically significant positive effects on the Woodcock Word Attack scale,[1] but no effects on three other reading measures. The effect size for Word Attack was $d = 0.22$, which represents more than two months of additional learning gains. In this chapter, we track the second-year impact estimates for the main sample from this three-year study.

THE SUCCESS FOR ALL PROGRAM THEORY

Beyond the applied and empirical evidence supporting Success for All, the central features of the program's theory of action—its comprehensive approach to school reform and its focus on high-quality literacy instruction—can be understood on the basis of two distinct conceptual frameworks. A review by Ramey and Ramey (1998) of the major findings from rigorous evaluations of early interventions revealed the features associated with those programs that exhibited the strongest and most persistent effects on children's outcomes. The framework, *biosocial developmental contexualism*, derived from this review predicts that early interventions focused on education and child development are not likely to succeed unless they are intensive, high-quality, and ecologically pervasive efforts. The Success for All program design exemplifies this comprehensive and intensive approach to early intervention in two important ways.

First, rather than a targeted (and potentially fragmented) remedial approach for improving the school outcomes of children placed at risk, Success for All emphasizes a schoolwide focus on reform and improvement. Though components, such as one-on-one tutoring, are in place to target children who need extra help, the program theory emphasizes the school as the critical unit of intervention and espouses a comprehensive school-level reform plan to help meet the needs of all children attending high-poverty schools. Second, the learning experiences offered through Success for All are delivered to students directly, efficiently, and effectively in classrooms that are regrouped according to students' current achievement levels. The intensity of these services is reflected by characteristics such as students' daily exposure to an uninterrupted 90-minute reading period and the program's emphasis on a multiyear approach to literacy instruction and learning.

Beyond the comprehensiveness and intensity of Success for All, the core focus of the program is on literacy. The importance of literacy can be understood through research demonstrating that reading skills provide a critical part of the foundation for children's academic success (Whitehurst and Lonigan 2001). Children who read well read more and, as a result, acquire more knowledge in various academic domains (Cunningham and Stanovich 1998). The specific sequencing of literacy instruction across the grades is a defining characteristic of the Success for All instructional program, which can be understood through a larger body of empirical research and theory on beginning reading.

The Success for All reading program in kindergarten and 1st grade emphasizes the development of language skills and launches students into reading using phonetically regular storybooks and instruction that focuses on phonemic awareness, auditory discrimination, and sound blending. The theoretical and practical importance of this approach for the beginning reader is supported by the strong consensus among researchers that phonemic awareness is the best single predictor of reading ability, not just in the early grades (Ehri and Wilce 1980, 1985; Perfetti et al. 1987) but throughout the school years (Calfee, Lindamood, and Lindamood 1973; Shankweiler et al. 1995). As this awareness is the major causal factor in early reading progress (Adams 1990), appropriate interventions targeted to develop the skill hold considerable promise for helping students develop broader reading skills in both the short and long term.

During the 2nd through 5th grade levels, students in Success for All schools use school- or district-provided reading materials, either basals or trade books, in a structured set of interactive opportunities to read, discuss, and write. The program offered from 2nd through 5th grade emphasizes cooperative learning activities built around partner reading; identification of characters, settings, and problem solutions in narratives; story summarization; writing; and direct instruction in reading comprehension skills. Through these activities, and building on the early phonemic awareness developed in grades K–1, students in Success for All schools learn a broader set of literacy skills emphasizing comprehension and writing.

IMPLICATIONS AND HYPOTHESES

The evidence and theory supporting Success for All suggest several important implications for the current study. First, Success for All is best understood as a comprehensive school-level intervention. Accordingly, we designed the study as a cluster randomized trial, with 41 schools randomized to a treatment or control condition, and we specified school-level analyses of the treatment effects of Success for All within a multilevel framework, nesting students within the school-level clusters. Second, given the importance of program intensity and Success for All's multiyear approach to literacy instruction, we hypothesized that the program effects estimated for the longitudinal sample of students who had experienced the full program across two years would be larger in magnitude than those effects found for the sample of all students, which included both the longitudinal sample and the group of students who had moved into the schools between the time of the pretest and year two posttest.

Third, consistent with the program theory related to the sequencing of the literacy instruction (which focuses on phonemic awareness skills initially and broader reading skills later), we hypothesized that the second-year program effects would spread into other tested literacy domains beyond the Word Attack subtest.[2] Unlike the first-year impacts, which were restricted to the Word Attack subtest, we hypothesized that we would begin to find treatment effects on the Letter and Word Identification and Passage Comprehension subtests as well. Again, though, due to the importance of program intensity, the multi-year sequencing of literacy instruction, and the general importance of learning phonemic awareness skills early, we assumed that the effects across the tests of broader reading skills would be most pronounced for students from the two-year longitudinal sample.

METHOD

Sample Selection

The total sample of 41 schools was recruited in two phases. The initial pilot efforts focused on reducing the cost to schools of implementing Success for All, which would ordinarily require schools to spend about $75,000 in the first year, $35,000 in the second year, and $25,000 in the third year. During spring and summer 2001, a one-time payment of $30,000 was offered to all schools in exchange for participation in the study. Those schools randomly assigned to the control condition could use the incentive however they wished, and were allowed to purchase and implement any innovation other than Success for All. The schools randomized into the Success for All condition began implementing the program in grades K–5 during fall 2001 and applied the incentive to the first-year costs of the program. During the pilot phase, only six schools were attracted by this incentive, with three randomly assigned to the experimental condition and three to the control condition. This sample was far from sufficient.

A second cohort of 35 schools was recruited to begin implementation in fall 2002. In this cohort, all participating schools received the Success for All program at no cost, but 18 received it in grades K–2 and 17 in grades 3–5, determined at random. Grades K–2 in the schools assigned to the 3–5 condition served as the controls for the schools assigned to the K–2 condition, and vice versa. As discussed by Borman and his coauthors (2005), this design, which included both treatment and control conditions within each school, had advantages and disadvantages.

The design proved to provide a sufficient incentive for the successful recruitment of schools, and it produced valid counterfactuals for the experimental groups that represented what would have happened had the experiment not taken place. The limitation of the design, though, was that the instructional program in the treatment grades might influence instruction in the non-treatment grades. Observations of Success for All treatment fidelity, though, have failed to document contamination of this kind, but to the extent it may have taken place, it would have depressed the magnitude of the treatment impacts. In addition, having the two treatments in the same school may have reduced the estimated effectiveness of school-level aspects of Success for All, such as family support, because both control students and treatment students could have come forward to take advantage of these services. Though these limitations of the design would result in underestimation, rather than overestimation, of the treatment effects, the treatment fidelity observations have suggested that materials and instructional procedures in the Success for All grades were distinct from non–Success for All grades, and that few, if any, control students benefited directly from school-level Success for All services.

During both phases of the study, the random assignment was carried out after schools had gone through the initial Success for All buy-in and adoption process, which all schools go through when applying to implement Success for All. After the schools had hosted an awareness presentation by an authorized Success for All program representative, and after 80 percent of the school staff had voted affirmatively by secret ballot to move forward with the Success for All program adoption, they were eligible for the study. As a final requirement, all schools agreed to allow for individual and group testing of their children, to allow observers and interviewers access to the school, and to make available (in coded form, to maintain confidentiality) routinely collected data on students, such as attendance, disciplinary referrals, special education placements, retentions, and so on. The schools were required to agree to allow data collection for three years, and to remain in the same treatment condition for all three years of the study. The schools that went through this initial process and that agreed to these conditions were randomly assigned by the members of the oversight committee to experimental or control conditions.

After the first year, three schools in St. Louis, selected during the second phase of recruitment, were closed due to insufficient enrollments. These included one school implementing Success for All in grades K–2 and two implementing in grades 3–5. In addition, a school in Chicago refused to implement its assigned treatment in grades 3–5, but did allow continued assessment. Because this school was implementing the 3–5 treatment rather than the K–2 Success for All treatment, it does not have a highly important consequence for the current analysis of K–2 treatment effects. In future analyses of grade 3–5 program effects, this school will be included as an intent-to-treat case. The loss of the three St. Louis schools reduced the second-year analytic sample to 38 schools, 20 implementing Success for All in grades K–2 and 18 in grades 3–5 (hereafter, K–2 schools will be referred to as "experimental" and 3–5 as "control").

The experimental and control schools included in the year two analyses of outcomes are listed in table 9.1. The sample is largely concentrated in the urban Midwest (Chicago, St. Louis, and Indianapolis) and the rural and small-town South, though there are some exceptions. The schools are situated in communities with high poverty concentrations,

Table 9.1. Schools Participating in Randomized Evaluation of Success for All, Grouped by Assignment

School	District	State	Enrollment	% White	% African American	% Hispanic	% Female	% ESL	% Spec Ed	% Free lunch
Northwood[a]	Mooreseville	IN	424	94.70	0.00	0.00	49.50	0.00	4.00	26.00
Jefferson[a]	Midland	OH	315	98.50	2.00	0.00	49.00	0.00	16.00	29.00
Bertha S. Sternberger	Guilford	NC	381	62.00	30.00	5.00	50.00	4.00	20.00	30.00
Pleasant Garden	Guilford	NC	698	76.00	13.70	4.56	49.50	3.50	16.00	33.00
Waveland	S. Montgomery	IN	152	99.00	0.00	1.00	46.00	0.00	15.00	34.00
James Y. Joyner	Guilford	NC	454	41.80	42.90	5.00	48.50	0.05	38.00	35.00
Laurel Valley	Ligonier Valley	PA	409	99.98	0.01	0.01	47.00	0.00	9.00	51.00
Wood	Tempe	AZ	642	19.60	9.60	40.10	49.70	37.50	11.00	51.70
Cesar Chavez	Norwalk	CA	589	6.00	3.00	88.00	47.00	39.00	5.00	71.00
Haven[a]	Savannah	GA	373	0.00	99.00	0.00	65.00	0.00	5.00	85.00
Brian Piccolo	Chicago	IL	1,069	0.10	79.50	20.10	48.00	11.40	11.60	85.60
Robert H. Lawrence	Chicago	IL	635	0.00	98.60	0.02	60.00	0.00	11.30	89.00
Harriett B. Stowe	Indianapolis	IN	174	28.71	25.74	43.56	38.00	40.59	17.80	90.59
Linden	Linden	AL	291	1.00	97.00	1.00	49.00	0.00	15.90	91.00
Lafayette	St. Louis	MO	297	13.20	72.80	9.40	49.70	25.00	12.00	94.00
Benjamin E. Mays	Chicago	IL	263	0.00	95.00	5.00	49.00	0.00	10.00	95.00
Paramount Jr.	Greene	AL	493	0.00	100.00	0.00	41.00	0.00	11.00	97.00
Farragut	St. Louis	MO	350	0.00	100.00	0.00	44.00	0.00	4.00	98.00
Gundlach	St. Louis	MO	365	0.00	100.00	0.00	48.00	0.00	4.40	99.00
Earl Nash	Noxubee	MS	509	1.00	98.00	1.00	51.00	0.20	6.50	100.00
Treatment school means			444	32.08	53.34	11.19	48.95	8.06	12.18	69.24

(continued)

Table 9.1. *(continued)*

School	District	State	Enrollment	% White	% African American	% Hispanic	% Female	% ESL	% Spec Ed	% Free lunch
Newby[a]	Mooresville	IN	252	98.00	0.00	0.00	53.00	0.00	10.00	35.00
Jamestown	Guilford	NC	516	41.00	47.00	3.40	45.00	8.00	15.00	39.00
Central	Central	KS	194	87.00	1.00	5.00	46.00	0.00	10.00	40.00
Walnut Cove[a]	Walnut Cove	NC	355	79.00	17.00	1.00	51.00	0.01	26.00	41.00
Bluford	Guilford	NC	420	9.50	86.70	1.20	48.00	0.00	13.00	42.00
Greenwood	Bessemer	AL	375	13.00	75.00	10.00	52.00	11.00	13.00	76.00
Gulfview	Hancock	MS	590	95.00	3.00	1.00	49.00	0.00	6.70	80.00
Eutaw	Greene	AL	338	0.57	98.50	0.00	49.00	0.00	4.00	86.00
C. F. Hard	Bessemer	AL	619	0.20	99.70	0.00	46.00	0.00	6.00	90.00
Daniel Webster	Chicago	IL	671	0.00	100.00	0.00	44.00	0.00	5.00	95.00
Augustin Lara	Chicago	IL	616	0.50	0.40	98.60	50.00	54.00	8.70	95.70
Edward E. Dunne	Chicago	IL	531	0.00	100.00	0.00	48.00	0.00	3.80	96.00
Bunche	Chicago	IL	643	0.00	100.00	0.00	68.00	0.00	9.70	98.00
Dewey Elem.	Chicago	IL	616	0.00	98.00	0.00	65.00	25.00	6.30	98.00
M. E. Lewis[a]	Sparta	GA	631	1.16	97.67	0.00	50.60	0.16	17.30	99.00
Sigel Elem.	St. Louis	MO	340	8.10	85.30	1.80	45.00	18.00	16.00	100.00
South Delta	South Delta	MS	769	5.00	94.00	1.00	53.00	0.00	4.00	100.00
Stanfield	Stanfield	AZ	757	19.40	1.00	67.70	50.30	50.00	19.00	100.00
Control school means			512	25.41	61.35	10.59	50.72	9.23	12.18	78.59

Source: Authors' calculations.

[a] Denotes the schools selected in the first phase of the study.

with just a few rural exceptions. Approximately 74 percent of the students participate in the federal free lunch program, which is similar to the 80 percent free lunch participation rate for the nationwide population of Success for All schools. The sample is more African American and less Hispanic than Success for All schools nationally. Overall, 57 percent of the sample is African American, compared to about 40 percent within the typical Success for All school, and 11 percent of the sample is Hispanic, compared to the national average of 35 percent. The percent of white students, 29 percent, is similar to Success for All's 25 percent.

Table 9.2 compares the baseline characteristics of the experimental and control schools included in the analyses of year two outcomes. As the results suggest, the 18 control and 20 treatment schools were well matched on demographics, and there were no statistically significant school-level aggregate pretest differences on the Peabody Picture Vocabulary Test. As demonstrated in Borman and others (2005), the original sample of 21 treatment and 20 control schools was also well matched, with no statistically significant differences on demographics or pretest scores.

Treatment Fidelity

Trainers from the Success for All Foundation have made quarterly implementation visits to each school, as is customary in all implementations of the Success for All program. These visits established each school's fidelity to the Success for All model and provided trainers an opportunity to work with school staff in setting goals toward improving implementation. Many efforts were made to ensure fidelity of the experimental treatment. As is the case in all implementations, teachers in Success for All schools received three days of training and then about eight days of on-site follow-up during the first implementation year. Success for All Foundation trainers visited classrooms, met with groups of teachers, looked at data on children's progress, and gave feedback to school staff on implementation quality and outcomes. These procedures, followed in all Success for All schools, were used in the study schools to attempt to obtain a high level of fidelity of implementation.

As of January 2005, all K–2 classes in schools were implementing their assigned treatments. There was some variability in implementation quality, which will be the subject of future analyses. For instance, several schools took almost one year to understand and implement the program at a mechanical level and others embraced the program immediately and have done an excellent job. Difficulties in recruiting schools and last-minute recruitment significantly inhibited quality

Table 9.2. Comparison of Characteristics for Success for All Treatment Schools and Control Schools

Variable	Condition	N	M	SD	95% CI for difference		t
					Lower bound	Upper bound	
PPVT	Control	18	89.82	9.45	-8.30	4.27	0.65
	Treatment	20	91.84	9.62			
Enrollment	Control	18	512.00	172.00	-58.31	195.90	1.10
	Treatment	20	444.00	209.00			
% female	Control	18	50.72	6.38	-2.03	5.60	0.91
	Treatment	20	48.95	5.68			
% minority	Control	18	74.59	36.96	-18.83	32.16	0.53
	Treatment	20	67.92	40.18			
% ESL	Control	18	9.23	17.17	-9.30	11.64	0.23
	Treatment	20	8.06	14.61			
% special education	Control	18	10.75	6.12	-6.08	3.22	0.62
	Treatment	20	12.18	7.81			
% free lunch	Control	18	78.59	25.80	-9.00	27.56	1.02
	Treatment	20	69.24	28.97			

Source: Authors' calculations.
ESL = English as a Second Language
PPVT = Peabody Picture Vocabulary Test

implementation; Success for All schools would have typically done much planning before the school year, which many of the study schools (especially in Chicago, St. Louis, and Guilford County, North Carolina) did not have time to do.

In the non–Success for All grades, teachers were repeatedly reminded to continue using their usual materials and approaches, and not to use anything from Success for All. During implementation visits, trainers also observed classrooms from control grades. Specifically, these observations focused on whether the environment, instruction, and behaviors in the control classrooms resembled the characteristics of the Success for All classrooms. In no case did the trainers observe teachers in non–Success for All classes implementing Success for All components. It is possible that some ideas or procedures from Success for All did influence instruction in the non-treatment control grades, but any such influence was apparently subtle. Instructional materials and core procedures were clearly distinct from each other in the treatment and control grades.

Measures

Students in grades K–1 were pretested on the Peabody Picture Vocabulary Test (PPVT III) and then individually posttested on the Woodcock Reading Mastery Tests–Revised (WMTR). The six schools from the first phase of recruitment were pretested in fall 2001 and posttested during spring 2002 and spring 2003. The 35 schools from the main sample were pretested in fall 2002 and posttested in spring 2003 and spring 2004. The pilot and main samples were combined for the analyses. Because the metrics of the tests varied, and to aid in interpretation of the impact estimates, we standardized the pretest and the posttests to a mean of 0 and standard deviation of 1.

Pretests

All children were individually assessed in fall 2001 (first phase) or fall 2002 (second phase) on the PPVT III. The few children who spoke Spanish primarily were pretested in Spanish on the Test de Vocabulario en Imagenes Peabody.

Posttests

During spring 2002 and 2003 (first phase) and spring 2003 and 2004 (second phase)—and during each subsequent spring through 2005—students in the main longitudinal cohorts (which started in K–1) were individually assessed on the four subtests of the WMTR: Letter Identification, Word Identification, Word Attack, and Passage Comprehension. The WMTR was normed on a national sample of children; the internal reliability coefficients for the four subtests were 0.84, 0.97, 0.87, and 0.92, respectively. Children in the initial cohorts are being followed into any grade as long as they remain in the same school; retention does not change their cohort assignment. They are also being followed into special education. Children who entered Success for All or control schools after fall 2002 are also posttested each year and included in analyses that combine the baseline cohorts and in-moving student cohorts. Children who are English-language learners but taught in English are posttested in English each year. In this analysis, we focused on the outcomes for the year two posttests, which were administered to students in the pilot schools during spring 2003 and students in the main sample of schools during 2004.

Results

The prior review of baseline data for the school-level sample revealed no important differences between treatment and control schools; also, the sample of schools was geographically diverse and generally representative of the population of Success for All schools. In discussing the results of our second-year analyses of achievement outcomes, we begin by assessing whether there was differential data and sample attrition between treatment and control schools, or systematic attrition from the analytical sample that may have changed its characteristics relative to those for the baseline sample.

The final analytical samples were composed of 1,672 students from the 20 Success for All treatment schools and 1,618 students from the 18 control schools. Listwise deletion of student cases with missing posttest data did not cause differential attrition rates by program condition,[3] leaving 56 percent of the baseline sample of 2,966 treatment students and 58 percent of the 2,770 baseline controls for the preliminary analyses. The data and sample attrition occurred for three reasons. Of the students excluded from the analysis, 1,195 (49 percent), were dropped because they had moved out of the school before the year two posttests were administered and, thus, had no outcome data, and 1,021 (42 percent) remained in the treatment and control schools but were missing either pretest, posttest, or other important demographic data. Finally, the closure of three participating schools prevented posttesting of 230 students (9 percent) in year two.

We compared the pretest scores of those treatment students dropped from the analyses to the pretest scores of the control students dropped from the analyses. No statistically significant difference was found between the treatment and the control students,[4] suggesting that the baseline achievement levels of the treatment and the control group students dropped from the analyses were statistically equivalent.

To address the issue of external validity, we also compared those students who were retained in the analysis to students who were not retained. Those students who were retained had higher pretest scores than those who were not retained.[5] Also, not surprisingly, mobile students who had left the Success for All and control schools were overrepresented among those with missing data.[6] Thus, both low-achieving and mobile students from the sample schools were underrepresented in the analyses. This does compromise the external validity of the study in two ways. First, because past quasi-experimental evidence has consistently shown that Success for All tends to have the largest educational effects on academically struggling students (Slavin and Madden 2001), the omission of low-achieving students with missing posttest data who remained in the Success for All schools is most likely to result in downward biases of the treatment effect estimates. Second, because the primary missing data mechanism was mobility from the study schools, analysis of this longitudinal sample limits generalization to students who remained in the baseline treatment and control schools.

While conceding these limitations, there is no conflict in this experiment between random assignment of treatment and data missing at random. That is, among the complete data observations, those assigned to control have similar covariate distributions to those assigned to treatment. As noted by Rubin (1976) and Little and Rubin (1987), the missing data process is *ignorable* if, conditional on treatment and fully observed covariates, the data are *missing at random*.

In addition to the analyses of impacts for the longitudinal sample, we conducted a second set of analyses of treatment effects for the combined longitudinal and in-moving student samples. These analyses included the longitudinal sample of 3,290 students, who remained at the Success for All and control schools from baseline through the second-year posttest, and 890 additional students who had moved into the experimental and control schools after the baseline assessments. Though the in-moving students did not benefit from the full Success for All intervention, this combined longitudinal and in-mover sample does comprise the complete enrollments of the targeted grade levels in the treatment and control schools at the time of the year two posttest. In this way, the sample affords a type of school-level intent-to-treat analysis of the program.

Hierarchical Linear Model Analyses of Year Two Treatment Effects

This cluster randomized trial (CRT) involved randomization at the level of the school and collection of outcome data at the level of the student. With such a design, estimation of treatment effects at the level of the cluster that was randomized is the most appropriate method (Donner and Klar 2000; Raudenbush 1997). We applied Raudenbush's (1997) relatively recently proposed analytical strategy for the analysis of CRTs: the use of a hierarchical linear model. In this formulation, we simultaneously accounted for both student- and school-level sources of variability in the outcomes by specifying a two-level hierarchical model that estimated the school-level effect of random assignment. Our fully specified level 1, or within-school model, nested students within schools with an indicator of the student's baseline grade level (-0.5 = kindergarten and 0.5 = 1st grade). The linear model for this level of the analysis was expressed as

$$Y_{ij} = \beta_{0j} + \beta_{1j}(\text{GRADE})_{ij} + r_{ij}$$

which represents the spring posttest achievement for student i in school j regressed on grade level plus the level 1 residual variance, r_{ij}, that remained unexplained after accounting for the grade level of the students.

In this model, each student's grade level was centered around zero. In this way, we controlled for school-to-school differences in the proportions of kindergartners and 1st graders. With grade coded as -0.5 for students in kindergarten at baseline and 0.5 for students in 1st grade at baseline, the level 2 school-specific intercept represented the average school performance of students from across both grade levels. We treated the within-school grade-level gap—the difference between the posttest scores of baseline kindergarten and 1st grade students in school j—as fixed at level 2 because it was intended only as a covariate and we have no empirical or theoretical reason to model this source of between-school variability as an outcome.

At level 2 of the model, we estimated the cluster-level impact of Success for All (SFA) treatment assignment on the mean posttest achievement outcome in school j. As suggested by the work of Bloom, Bos, and Lee (1999) and Raudenbush (1997), we included a school-level covariate, the school mean PPVT pretest score, to help reduce the unexplained variance in the outcome and to improve the power and precision of our treatment effect estimates.[7] The fully specified level 2 model was written as

$$\beta_{0j} = \gamma_{00} + \gamma_{01}(\text{MEANPPVT})_j + \gamma_{02}(\text{SFA})_j + u_{0j},$$
$$\beta_{1j} = \gamma_{10}$$

where the mean posttest intercept for school j, β_{0j}, was regressed on the school-level mean PPVT score, the SFA treatment indicator, plus a residual, u_{0j}. The within-school posttest difference between baseline kindergarten and 1st grade students, β_{1j}, was specified as fixed, predicted only by an intercept.[8]

Outcomes for the Longitudinal Sample

The multilevel models shown in table 9.3 assessed student- and school-level effects on the four literacy outcomes as measured by the Woodcock-Johnson year two posttests. Across the four outcomes, the impact estimate for Success for All assignment ranged from a standardized effect of approximately $d = 0.12$ for Passage Comprehension, to $d = 0.25$ for the Word Attack subtest. Three of the four treatment effects were statistically significant: the impact on Word Attack of 0.25 at the $p < .01$ level of confidence, the impact on Letter Identification of 0.18 at the $p < .05$ level, and the treatment effect on Word Identification of 0.16 at the $p < .10$ level of confidence. In all four models, the school-level mean pretest covariate was an important predictor of the outcome, and the fixed within-school posttest difference between baseline kindergarten and 1st grade students was between nearly half of one standard deviation and more than three-quarters of one standard deviation.

Outcomes for the Combined Longitudinal and In-Mover Sample

In table 9.4, the multilevel models estimate student- and school-level effects on the four year two literacy outcomes for the combined longitudinal and in-mover sample. The Success for All impact estimates across these multilevel models were relatively smaller in magnitude than the effects found for the longitudinal sample in table 9.3. Across the four outcomes, the impact estimate for Success for All assignment ranged from a standardized effect of approximately $d = 0.09$ for Passage Comprehension, to $d = 0.19$ for Word Attack. In addition to the somewhat smaller effects, the impacts were estimated with greater uncertainty, as indicated by the larger standard errors for the treatment coefficients. The smaller impacts and greater uncertainty of the impact estimates are, in part, explained by the greater variability among students in their exposure to the Success for All treatment. In this sample, students' participation in the Success for All treatment ranged from two years to several months.

DISCUSSION

The second-year results of the randomized evaluation of Success for All show school-level impacts of assignment to the intervention that

Table 9.3. Multilevel Models Predicting Student and School Literacy Outcomes for the Longitudinal Sample of the National Randomized Field Trial of Success for All

	Literacy outcomes test											
	Word Attack			Letter Identification			Word Identification			Passage Comprehension		
Fixed effect	Effect	SE	t	Effect	SE	t	Effect	SE	t	Effect	SE	t
School mean achievement												
Intercept	-0.02	0.04	-0.53	-0.02	0.05	-0.35	-0.03	0.03	0.50	-0.03	0.04	-0.67
Mean PPVT pretest	0.16***	0.04	4.07	0.24***	0.06	4.28	0.20***	0.03	6.62	0.26***	0.04	7.09
SFA assignment	0.25***	0.09	2.85	0.18**	0.08	2.23	0.16*	0.09	1.85	0.12	0.08	1.42
Grade												
Intercept	0.48***	0.05	10.36	0.88***	0.09	9.36	0.85***	0.04	19.01	0.82***	0.04	22.67
Random effect	Estimate	χ^2	df	Estimate	χ^2	df	Estimate	χ^2	df	Estimate	χ^2	df
School mean achievement	0.06	221.16	35	0.07	442.71	35	0.06	278.58	35	0.06	284.54	35
Within-school variation	0.84			0.65			0.72			0.72		

Source: Authors' calculations.

PPVT = Peabody Picture Vocabulary Test

SFA = Success for All

$*p < .10$, $**p < .05$, $***p < .01$

Table 9.4. Multilevel Models Predicting Student and School-Level Literacy Outcomes for the Combined Longitudinal and In-Mover Sample

	Literacy outcomes test											
	Word Attack			Letter Identification			Word Identification			Passage Comprehension		
Fixed effect	Effect	SE	t	Effect	SE	t	Effect	SE	t	Effect	SE	t
School mean achievement												
Intercept	−0.02	0.06	−0.48	0.00	0.05	0.09	−0.01	0.04	0.50	−0.00	0.04	−0.01
Mean PPVT pretest	0.20**	0.06	3.29	0.24**	0.06	4.25	0.20**	0.04	5.38	0.25**	0.04	6.79
SFA assignment	0.19	0.12	1.56	0.18*	0.09	2.09	0.15	0.09	1.55	0.09	0.09	0.34
Grade												
Intercept	0.44**	0.04	10.38	0.87**	0.08	10.50	0.81**	0.04	21.67	0.79**	0.03	23.21
Random effect	Estimate	χ^2	df	Estimate	χ^2	df	Estimate	χ^2	df	Estimate	χ^2	df
School mean achievement	0.13	508.69	35	0.08	546.52	35	0.08	451.40	35	0.07	431.37	35
Within-school variation	0.81			0.66			0.72			0.72		

Source: Authors' calculations.
PPVT = Peabody Picture Vocabulary Test
SFA = Success for All
$*p < .05, **p < .01$

are extraordinarily consistent with key aspects of the program theory and with past meta-analytic evidence on program effects. The cluster randomized trial provided strong evidence that the Success for All comprehensive school reform strategy is capable of producing school-level effects of both statistical and practical importance. The magnitude of these effects across the four literacy outcomes is summarized in table 9.5 as effect sizes and months of additional learning relative to control schools. When converted to additional months of learning, the practical effects of the program appear substantial for Word Attack and relatively large for the other literacy measures. For Word Attack, the longitudinal sample's learning advantage relative to the controls exceeds half of one nine-month school year.

Consistent with the program theory related to the sequencing of the literacy instruction, which focuses on phonemic awareness skills initially and broader reading skills later, we found that the program effects began to spread into other tested literacy domains beyond the Word Attack subtest. Unlike the first-year impacts, which were restricted to the Word Attack subtest, we found statistically significant treatment effects on the Letter and Word Identification subtests as well.

The reliability and magnitude of these effects, though, are sensitive to the amount of exposure students had to the intervention. As the program theory suggests, due to the importance of program intensity, the multiyear sequencing of literacy instruction, and the general importance of learning phonemic awareness skills early, the effects across the four reading skills tested are greater and more reliable for the sample of students from the two-year longitudinal sample. Therefore,

Table 9.5. Success for All Impact Estimates Expressed as Effect Sizes (d) and Additional Months of Learning

Outcome	Longitudinal sample		Combined sample	
	d	Months of learning	d	Months of learning
Word Attack	0.25	4.69	0.19	3.89
Letter Identification	0.18	1.84	0.18	1.86
Word Identification	0.16	1.69	0.15	2.22
Passage Comprehension	0.12	1.32	0.09	1.03

Source: Authors' calculations.

Note: The additional months of learning were computed by dividing each of the coefficients for the Success for All treatment effect on the four outcomes by the respective coefficients for the grade-level intercepts shown in tables 9.3 and 9.4. This one grade-level difference expressed by the intercept approximates the amount of growth that occurs across one school year. By dividing the coefficient for the Success for All treatment effect by this grade-level coefficient, we calculated the percentage of one grade level that the treatment effect represents. Next, we estimated the duration of one school year as 9 months. Multiplying by 9 the figure derived from the first step, we converted the treatment effect coefficient into an estimate of additional months of learning.

although Success for All is a comprehensive schoolwide intervention, which may theoretically advance the academic outcomes of the whole school, students seem to need longitudinal exposure to the program to make the largest and most reliable gains. When one considers literacy achievement as the primary outcome, the multiyear sequencing of literacy instruction and the initial skill development in the area of phonemic awareness appear to be important mechanisms that drive broader improvements in reading.

Interestingly, the effect sizes reported in table 9.5 are quite similar to the average effect size of $d = 0.20$ estimated by Borman and his coauthors (2003) in their synthesis of the quasi-experimental evaluations of Success for All and Roots & Wings. This result is consistent with findings reported by Heinsman and Shadish (1996) and Lipsey and Wilson (1993), who concluded that the mean value of the findings of a large number of nonexperimental studies tends to approximate that of experiments that address the same question. In the context of the current study, the meta-analytic summary of the results of 46 quasi-experimental studies of Success for All produced an effect size estimate that was essentially the same as the impact estimates from this randomized experiment.

The effects are smaller, though, than those found in the early small-scale matched comparison group studies performed by the developers using the same individually administered measures as those used in the present study. The earlier quasi-experimental studies, such as those reported by Madden and her coauthors (1993) and Slavin and Madden (2001), found effect sizes ranging from approximately $d = 0.30$ to $d = 0.50$. The difference in the impact estimates from the current study and these earlier studies of Success for All are most likely explained by two points drawn from Lipsey's (2003) examination of meta-analytic data concerning the effects of intervention programs to prevent or reduce juvenile delinquency.

First, Lipsey's (2003) analysis demonstrates that studies employing random assignment designs are associated with smaller mean effects than those using quasi-experimental designs. Second, Lipsey finds that the program type—that is, a research and demonstration project versus a routine practice program—is also an important moderator for understanding differences in study outcomes. Similar to the concept of the super-realization stage of program development articulated by Cronbach and his coauthors (1980), research and demonstration projects typically involve a small-scale pilot of an intervention designed by the developers to show the effects of the program when it is operating at its best. Not surprisingly, Lipsey's (2003) meta-analytic data reveal that the research and demonstration programs are associated with larger mean effects than routine practice programs. Therefore, both the methodological design and the program type may have important implications for understanding the differences between the achievement impacts estimated by the early Success for All quasi-experiments of demonstration programs and by the current national randomized field trial of the program operating at scale.

Putting the Results in Context

Similar recent efforts to study widespread implementations of educational interventions through a randomized design have yielded few promising outcomes. For instance, the evaluation of 44 schools implementing 21st Century Community Learning Centers programs, which help schools and districts partner with community organizations to provide after-school programs, revealed no positive impacts on academic outcomes, homework completion, student behavior, or parent involvement (James-Burdumy et al. 2005). Similarly, the experimental study of 18 Even Start family literacy programs revealed no treatment effects on literacy and other measures for the children and parents served by the programs (St. Pierre et al. 2003). Indeed, aside from the Tennessee Student/Achievement Ration class-size reduction study (Finn and Achilles 1999), few examples of substantial field trials in education have yielded positive effects of practical and statistical significance across a large number of sites.

Given the relatively high costs associated with implementing Success for All, though, it is reasonable to ask whether the impacts are worth the investment. One answer comes from an earlier cost-effectiveness study by Borman and Hewes (2002), who drew on quasi-experimental evidence from the original implementations of the program in Baltimore. The authors found that those students who had attended Success for All elementary schools completed 8th grade at a younger age, with better reading and math achievement outcomes, fewer special education placements, and less frequent retentions in grade, at a cost that was essentially the same as that allocated to educating their comparison group counterparts. Across the longitudinal period from 1st through 8th grade, the more frequent retentions and special education placements for those from the comparison group wound up costing the same amount as the additional per pupil expenses of implementing Success for All. As these outcomes suggest, the educational practices of prevention and early intervention, as modeled by Success for All, were more effective, and equally expensive, relative to the traditional remedial educational practices of retention and special education.

CONCLUSION

Statistically significant positive achievement effects from a large-scale implementation of a randomized field trial of a routine practice program are unusual for studies in education. A study of this kind, with 38 schools serving more than 20,000 children in districts throughout the United States, provides a rigorous assessment of the impact that can be expected when a program is scaled up in a real-world policy context. The effects may be interpreted as those likely to be obtained in broad-based implementations of Success for All, with all the attendant problems of start-up and of maintaining quality at scale. The research includes schools with good and poor implementations, and with school and district staffs potentially less committed to the program than is usual (because they were not paying for it). In the vast majority of experimental schools, it also included a design that required implementation of the instructional program across only three grades rather than across the whole school. In the remaining six pilot schools included in the study, the control schools were provided the same supplemental funds offered the experimental schools and were permitted to engage in any reform other than Success for All. For these reasons, we believe that the impact estimates are realistic but also somewhat conservative.

Though large-scale cluster randomized trials in field settings are rare in education and though findings of widespread treatment effects are rarer still, these outcomes attest that such studies are possible and can produce unbiased estimates of program effects. Future reports will illuminate many other aspects of the implementation and program impacts. These will include studies of the quality of program implementation, effects for subgroups, and effects in the upper elementary grades.

NOTES

The authors thank Steven Ross, Alan Sterbinsky, Daniel Duran, Michael Reynolds, Shoba Shagle, Margarita Calderon, Dewi Smith, and Dana Andrews for their assistance with data collection and analysis. We also thank the members of the oversight committee for this study: C. Kent McGuire, Stephen Raudenbush, Rebecca Maynard, Jonathan Crane, and Ronald Ferguson.

This research was supported by grants from the Institute of Education Sciences, U.S. Department of Education (R305P030016, R117D40005, and R305A040082). However, any opinions expressed are those of the authors, and do not necessarily represent IES positions or policies.

1. The Word Attack scale measures the ability to convert graphic symbols (e.g., letters) into intelligible language; word attack is also known as decoding.

2. The decoding of non-words is considered the most appropriate measure of phonological recoding (Hoover and Gough 1990; Siegel 1993; Wood and Felton 1994). It provides an indication of the capacity to transfer the auditory skill of phonological awareness to the task of decoding print. The degree to which students are able to use their developing phonemic awareness is directly assessed using the Word Attack subtest, Woodcock Reading Mastery Tests–Revised, which is composed of test items that ask the child to decode nonsense words.

3. χ^2 (1, $N = 5{,}736$) $= 2.02$, $p = 0.67$

4. t (0.50), $p = 0.62$ (two-tailed)

5. t (-6.74), $p < .05$ (two-tailed)

6. χ^2 (1, $N = 5{,}736$) $= 3457.99$, $p < .001$

7. We formulated other multilevel models that included the broader array of school-level covariates listed in table 9.3. After including the school mean pretest covariate, though, these more complex models did not explain appreciably more between-school variance and did not improve the precision of the Success for All treatment effect estimates. For these reasons, we used the more parsimonious models presented.

8. The statistical precision of the design can be expressed in terms of a minimum detectable effect, or the smallest treatment effect that can be detected with confidence. As Bloom (2005) noted, this parameter, which is a multiple of the impact estimator's standard error, depends on whether a one- or two-tailed test of statistical significance is used; the α level of statistical significance to which the result of the significance test will be compared; the desired statistical power, $1 - \beta$; and the number of degrees of freedom of the test, which equals the number of clusters, J, minus 2 (assuming a two-group experimental design and no covariates).

The minimum detectable effect for our design is calculated for a two-tailed t-test, α level of $p < .10$, power, $1 - \beta$, equal to 0.80, and degrees of freedom equal to $J = 38$ schools minus 3 (a two-group experimental design with the school mean PPVT pretest covariate). Referring to tables 9.3 and 9.4 for the Success for All impact estimators' standard errors, which range from .08 to .12, and employing Bloom's (2005) minimum detectable effect multiplier, we calculated minimum detectable effects of approximately $d = .20$ to $d = .30$. That is, our design had adequate power to detect school-level treatment-control differences of at least .20 to .30 standard deviations.

REFERENCES

Adams, M. J. 1990. *Beginning to Read: Thinking and Learning about Print*. Cambridge, MA: MIT Press.

Bloom, H. S., ed. 2005. *Learning More from Social Experiments: Evolving Analytic Approaches*. New York: Russell Sage Foundation Publications.

Bloom, H. S., J. Bos, and S. Lee. 1999. "Using Cluster Random Assignment to Measure Program Impacts: Statistical Implications for the Evaluation of Education Programs." *Evaluation Review* 23(4): 445–69.

Borman, G. D., and G. M. Hewes. 2002. "Long-Term Effects and Cost Effectiveness of Success for All." *Educational Evaluation and Policy Analysis* 24(4): 243–66.

Borman, G. D., G. M. Hewes, L. T. Overman, and S. Brown. 2003. "Comprehensive School Reform and Achievement: A Meta-Analysis." *Review of Educational Research* 73(2): 125–230.

Borman, G. D., R. E. Slavin, A. Cheung, A. Chamberlain, N. Madden, and B. Chambers. 2005. "Success for All: First-Year Results from the National Randomized Field Trial." *Educational Evaluation and Policy Analysis* 27(1): 1–22.

Calfee, R. C., P. Lindamood, and C. Lindamood. 1973. "Acoustic-Phonetic Skills and Reading: Kindergarten through Twelfth Grade." *Journal of Educational Psychology* 64(3): 293–98.

Cronbach, L. J., S. R. Ambron, S. M. Dornbusch, R. D. Hess, R. C. Hornik, D. C. Phillips, D. F. Walker, and S. S. Weiner. 1980. *Toward Reform of Program Evaluation: Aims, Methods, and Institutional Arrangements.* San Francisco: Jossey-Bass.

Cunningham, A. E., and K. E. Stanovich. 1998. "Early Reading Acquisition and its Relation to Reading Experience and Ability 10 Years Later." *Developmental Psychology* 33(6): 934–45.

Donner, A., and N. Klar. 2000. *Design and Analysis of Group Randomization Trials in Health Research.* London: Arnold.

Ehri, L. C., and L. S. Wilce. 1980. "The Influence of Orthography on Readers' Conceptualization of the Phonemic Structure of Words." *Applied Psycholinguistics* 1: 371–85.

———. 1985. "Movement into Reading: Is the First Stage of Printed Word Learning Visual or Phonetic?" *Reading Research Quarterly* 20: 163–79.

Finn, J. D., and C. M. Achilles. 1999. "Tennessee's Class-Size Study: Findings, Implications, Misconceptions." *Educational Evaluation and Policy Analysis* 21(2): 97–109.

Glazerman, S., D. M. Levy, and D. Myers. 2002. "Nonexperimental Replications of Social Experiments: A Systematic Review." Interim Report/Discussion Paper. Princeton, NJ: Mathematica Policy Research.

Heinsman, D. T., and W. R. Shadish. 1996. "Assignment Methods in Experimentation: When Do Nonrandomized Experiments Approximate Answers from Randomized Experiments?" *Psychological Methods* 1(2): 154–69.

Hoover, W. A., and P. B. Gough. 1990. "The Simple View of Reading." *Reading and Writing: An Interdisciplinary Journal* 2(2): 127–60.

James-Burdumy, S., M. Dynarski, M. Moore, J. Deke, W. Mansfield, and C. Pistorino. 2005. "When Schools Stay Open Late: The National Evaluation of the 21st Century Community Learning Centers Program." Final Report. Washington, DC: U.S. Department of Education, Institute of Education Sciences, National Center for Education Evaluation and Regional Assistance.

Lipsey, M. W. 2003. "Those Confounded Moderators in Meta-Analysis: Good, Bad, and Ugly." *Annals of the American Academy of Political and Social Science* 587: 69–81, May.

Lipsey, M. W., and D. B. Wilson. 1993. "The Efficacy of Psychological, Educational, and Behavioral Treatment: Confirmation from Meta-Analysis." *American Psychologist* 48(12): 1181–1209.

Little, R. J. A., and D. B. Rubin. 1987. *Statistical Analysis with Missing Data.* New York: John Wiley.

Madden, N. A., R. E. Slavin, N. L. Karweit, L. J. Dolan, and B. A. Wasik. 1993. "Success for All: Longitudinal Effects of a Restructuring Program for Inner-

City Elementary Schools." *American Educational Research Journal* 30(1): 123–48.

Perfetti, C. A., I. Beck, L. Bell, and C. Hughes. 1987. "Phonemic Knowledge and Learning to Read are Reciprocal: A Longitudinal Study of First Grade Children." *Merrill-Palmer Quarterly* 33: 283–319.

Ramey, C. T., and S. L. Ramey. 1998. "Early Intervention and Early Experience." *American Psychologist* 53(2): 109–20.

Raudenbush, S. W. 1997. "Statistical Analysis and Optimal Design for Cluster Randomized Trials." *Psychological Methods* 2(2): 173–85.

Rubin, D. B. 1976. "Inference and Missing Data." *Biometrika* 63(3): 581–92.

Shankweiler, D. P., S. Crain, L. Katz, A. E. Fowler, A. M. Liberman, S. Brady, R. Thornton, E. Lundquist, L. Dreyer, J. Fletcher, K. K. Stuebing, S. E. Shaywitz, and B. A. Shaywitz. 1995. "Cognitive Profiles of Reading-Disabled Children: Comparison of Language Skills in Phonology, Morphology, and Syntax." *Psychological Science* 6(3): 149–56.

Siegel, L. S. 1993. "The Development of Reading." *Advances in Child Development and Behavior* 24: 63–97.

Slavin, R. E., and N. A. Madden, eds. 2001. *One Million Children: Success for All.* Thousand Oaks, CA: Corwin.

St. Pierre, R., A. Ricciuti, F. Tao, C. Creps, J. Swartz, W. Lee, and A. Parsad. 2003. *Third National Even Start Evaluation: Program Impacts and Implications for Improvement.* Washington, DC: U.S. Department of Education, Planning and Evaluation Service.

Whitehurst, G. J., and C. J. Lonigan. 2001. "Emergent Literacy: Development from Prereaders to Readers." In *Handbook of Early Literacy Research*, vol. 1, edited by S. B. Neuman and D. K. Dickinson (11–29). New York: Guilford.

Wood, F. B., and R. H. Felton. 1994. "Separate Linguistic and Attentional Factors in the Development of Reading." *Topics in Language Disorders* 14(4): 42–57.

Appendix

MAJOR ELEMENTS OF SUCCESS FOR ALL

Success for All is a schoolwide program for students in grades pre-K–6, which organizes resources to attempt to ensure that virtually every student will acquire adequate basic skills and build on this basis throughout the elementary grades, so that no student will be allowed to "fall through the cracks." The main elements of the program are as follows.

Schoolwide Curriculum

Success for All schools implement research-based reading, writing, and language arts programs in all grades, K–6. The reading program in grades K–1 emphasizes language and comprehension skills, phonics, sound blending, and shared stories that students read to one another in pairs. The shared stories combine teacher-read material with phonetically regular student material to teach decoding and comprehension in the context of meaningful, engaging stories.

In grades 2–6, students use novels or basals, but not workbooks. This program emphasizes cooperative learning and partner reading activities, comprehension strategies such as summarization and clarification built around narrative and expository texts, writing, and direct instruction in reading comprehension skills. At all levels, students are required to read books of their own choice for 20 minutes at home each evening. Cooperative learning programs in writing/language arts are used in grades 1–6.

Tutors

In grades 1–3, specially trained certified teachers and paraprofessionals work one-to-one with any students failing to keep up with their classmates in reading. Tutorial instruction is closely coordinated with regular classroom instruction. It takes place 20 minutes daily during times other than reading periods.

Quarterly Assessments and Regrouping

Students in grades 1–6 are assessed every quarter to determine whether they are making adequate progress in reading. This information is used to regroup students for instruction across grade lines, so that each reading class contains students of different ages all reading at the same level. Assessment information is also used to suggest alternate teaching strategies in the regular classroom, changes in reading group placement, provision of tutoring services, or other means of meeting students' needs.

Solutions Team

A solutions team works in each school to help support families in ensuring the success of their children, focusing on parent education, parent involvement, attendance, and student behavior. This team is composed of existing or additional staff such as parent liaisons, social workers, counselors, and assistant principals.

Facilitators

A program facilitator works with teachers as an on-site coach to help implement the reading program, manages the quarterly assessments, assists the solutions team, makes sure that all staff are communicating with each other, and helps the staff as a whole make certain that every child is making adequate progress.

10

PARTNERSHIPS IN MIDDLE GRADES COMPREHENSIVE SCHOOL REFORM

H. Dickson Corbett, Cheri Fancsali,
Pritha Gopalan, Alexandra Weinbaum,
and Bruce L. Wilson

Bringing an educational reform effort to scale and sustaining it past
the period of funding remain challenging issues in the field of
comprehensive school reform (CSR). This chapter emphasizes features
of partnerships such as shared resources, expertise, and responsibility,
which add value to the work that individual schools, districts, and
educational organizations may accomplish on their own. The chapter
suggests that educational partnerships can positively influence scale-
up and sustainability as initiatives mature.

Despite the several initiatives sprung from the 1989 report on middle
grades education "Turning Points: Preparing American Youth for the
21st Century" in 1989 (Carnegie Council on Adolescent Development
1989), and the efforts of the National Forum to Accelerate Middle-

Grades Reform, the field of middle grades education is still at a relatively early phase of its development; it stands to benefit from educational partnerships that widen the pool of knowledge and resources available to schools and districts, and that provide a platform or infrastructure for scaling up and sustaining promising initiatives.

There are few detailed studies of educational partnerships in the school reform literature, although forms of educational partnerships such as technical assistance or school-level coaching (Neufeld and Roper 2003) and ongoing, job-embedded professional development (National Staff Development Council 2001) are well documented. Researchers and model developers within the CSR field have also published several articles and manuals on partnerships between educational organizations and schools and districts (Northwest Regional Educational Laboratory 2006; U.S. Department of Education 2002). Kasak (2004, 237), reflecting on changes in middle grades educational reform, writes of "a realization that collective action across organizational boundaries was proving more effective than individual efforts for affecting change."

School reform has long grappled with ways of bringing successful initiatives to scale and sustaining them over the long run (Cuban 1990; Fullan 2002; Tyack and Cuban 1995). In this chapter we focus on educational partnerships that echo Ames's (2004, 141) statement that "it's a partnership, not an 'intervention'." We draw on studies of three middle grades reform efforts that illustrate the potential of collaborative, long-term partnerships of educational organizations, schools, and districts for improving teaching and learning, and addressing issues of scale and sustainability. We conclude that educational partnerships, though complex to convene and conduct, do have the potential to provide an infrastructure that allows successful initiatives to gain wider implementation and be sustained over the long term.

The first example, drawn from a three-year qualitative study of a large urban school, discusses an ongoing collaboration between a school and a CSR model to improve teaching, learning, and school culture, and the challenges faced in engaging the entire school in the reform effort. It highlights the role that external partners can play in supporting schoolwide engagement and helping staff sustain the reform in the long term; and calls for a reform infrastructure that provides long-term intellectual, financial, and institutional support for such arrangements.

The second example, based on a long-term mixed-method study of a large urban district, investigated the role of district-level partnerships such as university-district alliances and cross-district sharing in whole-school reform. This case suggests that such associations need to have a clear mission and a shared focus on improving teaching and learning to bring the reform to scale within the district, and to have a substantial impact on students' learning and achievement. The case also concludes that partnerships must support the district in developing its capacity in policymaking and implementation to further improve promising trends in middle grades education fostered by the reform.

The third example stems from a qualitative study of the formation and functioning of an educational partnership. The study addresses comprehensive school reform, capacity building of districts and teacher education institutions, and policy and public engagement efforts to support middle grades education throughout a region. This case highlights the promises of a regional coalition for building an infrastructure to sustain reform support, and establishes the complexity inherent in establishing an infrastructure for reform. The three studies portrayed in this chapter are descriptive and are used to illustrate the potential for educational partnerships, as well as highlight their complexities, challenges, and shortfalls.

THE SIGNIFICANCE OF EDUCATIONAL PARTNERSHIPS IN THE MIDDLE GRADES

Research on middle grades education states that the challenges faced by schools with middle grades are often related to the complexity of educating young adolescents, whose academic interests and needs are closely integrated with their developmental and social experiences (Anfara 2001; Davis 2001). Accordingly, the National Forum to Accelerate Middle Grades Reform upholds three goals for middle grades educational improvement: academic excellence, developmental responsiveness, and social equity—thereby promoting not only academic achievement, but also a nurturing school climate and equitable access to high-quality learning environments for all students, regardless of their gender, background, or ability (National Forum to Accelerate Middle Grades Reform, "Vision").

The need for comprehensive school reform in the middle grades is well documented (Jackson and Davis 2000; Juvonen et. al. 2004; Lipsitz 1980). Jackson and Davis (2000) write that the middle grades movement, begun in the 1970s, put a spotlight on developmental responsiveness as a key goal of reform at the middle level. School reformers followed with organizational and curricular innovations that addressed students' social, developmental, and academic interests and needs at the vulnerable stage of early adolescence. Small learning communities of teachers and students, project- and theme-based learning, cooperative learning, and other approaches were seen to better speak to the interests and needs of students entering adolescence (Jackson and Davis 2000).

However, some of these innovations took the form of pullout programs and brief experiments, and did not evolve into comprehensive and sustainable programs that consistently improved the students' academic and developmental outcomes (Jackson and Davis 2000). Furthermore, such approaches were critiqued for diluting academic rigor to benefit developmental outcomes (Lipsitz et al. 1997). Middle school reformers have increasingly adopted and adapted comprehensive school reform as a large-scale, sustainable approach for promoting middle grades educational reform at the school, district, and even national level. Promising CSR models such as Talent Development, Turning Points, and Middle Start have been developed to help schools at this level meet the challenges of addressing students' academic and developmental needs in an equitable manner (National Forum to Accelerate Middle Grades Reform, "Schools"). These models have worked with dozens of schools and are demonstrating success in helping schools better meet the needs of their middle graders (Ames 2004; Northwest Regional Educational Laboratory 2006).

However, achieving success in individual schools falls short of the sweeping changes needed to ensure that all adolescents have access to high-quality learning environments. A middle grades expert, Deborah Kasak (2004, 238), writes, "Widespread implementation of high-quality middle grades practices has not been fully realized." Our illustrations show that educational partnerships, despite their challenges, can support schools and districts in improving teaching and learning on a wider scale and sustain improvements through coherent planning and policymaking.

METHODOLOGY OF THE STUDIES

The three examples reported in the chapter were derived from longitudinal studies of the respective initiatives. Researchers from the Academy for Educational Development and independent third-party evaluators affiliated with Middle Start conducted the studies. The first case is drawn from a qualitative study funded by the W. K. Kellogg Foundation and conducted by the Academy for Educational Development (AED) of a cohort of 12 schools undertaking Middle Start, an accredited CSR model for the middle grades (see Northwest Regional Educational Laboratory 2006), between 1999 and 2004. AED conducted classroom observations, interviews, and a review of site documents collected from this school over a period of three years. AED researchers typically spent two to three days per semester at the school and conducted semiannual interviews with the principal and all three assistant principals, annual interviews with the district superintendent and assistant superintendent, semiannual interviews with over 75 percent of teachers in the school (including core, special education, and related arts), and semiannual interviews with about 10 percent of the student body (including all grade levels and ability groupings). Researchers conducted semiannual classroom visits, covering almost all classrooms in the school. Each observation lasted the duration of a class and was conducted using an observation protocol. They also conducted annual follow-up phone interviews with members of the school leadership team in the (unfunded) fourth year of implementation (Gopalan 2001; Gopalan and Jessup 2001). The case described in this chapter is derived from one of the 12 schools in the larger study.

The second case was derived from AED's five-year external evaluation of the New York City Middle School Initiative (MSI), funded by the New York City Department of Education. The study was conducted from 1996 to 2000. For the evaluation, AED collected data to assess school staff's awareness of middle grades practices, student outcomes, and progress in the school-district-university partnerships. To measure the extent to which schools were implementing middle grades practices, AED surveyed teachers and 7th grade students from a demographically representative selection of 15 schools in 1997 and 18 schools in 1999. AED also surveyed all principals in MSI schools in 1997 and 1999. In 1997, AED received responses from 688 teachers; 4,043 7th grade students; and 50 MSI principals. A total of 5,369 7th grade students, 587 teachers, and 57 principals completed surveys from participating schools in 1999. AED also conducted in-depth interviews with 10 district coordinators, 12 university partners, and the MSI director regarding the accomplishments and challenges of MSI; the roles of the university partner, the district, and the department of education; and recommendations for the future of the initiative. In addition, AED attended MSI initiative-wide meetings and professional development offerings. Finally, AED collected extant student achievement data from the New York City Department of Education for students enrolled in MSI schools in 1996–1997.

The third case study was an external evaluation of the Michigan Middle Start Partnership (MMSP), a collection of diverse organizational partners representing school systems, institutions of higher education, and other nonprofit social and educational service agencies dedicated to academic excellence and healthy development for all students. This work was funded by the W. K. Kellogg Foundation.

The purpose of the evaluation was to document the development and accomplishments of Middle Start work in Michigan. The full evaluation (Corbett and Wilson 2005) portrayed how the partnership operated in a thematic rather than chronological way, with the development of three themes—shared commitments, a layered structure, and the flexibility to act in the present while continuing to plan for the future. The qualitative methodology of the evaluation included attending all the quarterly meetings over four years; monitoring ongoing listserv dialogue between formal meetings; reviewing relevant documents and other external evaluation reports of the partnership's work; and interviewing partnership members (both formally and informally) over the course of our work. It also involved the evaluators playing five roles over the five-year period from 2000 through 2004: (1) reviewing reports and materials prepared by various partners and outside evaluators; (2) facilitating the development of a set of outcomes and indicators by which the ultimate value of Middle Start would be determined; (3) helping formulate the theory of action partners used to enact a systemic approach to reform; (4) conducting occasional special studies that shed additional light on the systemic evolution of Middle Start; and (5) acting as an active participant and critical friend in the Middle Start Partnership (which involved regular attendance at quarterly partnership meetings).

A SCHOOL-CSR MODEL PARTNERSHIP

"You can't miss the school on your right," the woman at the gas station says. "It is huge!" Morningside Middle School, located in Harding, a midsize city in Michigan, has the distinction of being the only public middle school in the Harding district. In 2000, more than 800 students in grades 6, 7, and 8 attended. The student body was racially and ethnically diverse, representing Harding's mixed socioeconomic makeup. Morningside approached Middle Start in spring 2000 when administrators and teachers first discussed applying for a CSR grant through the Michigan Department of Education to improve teaching and learning schoolwide and evolve into a "true middle school."

Through the Middle Start National Center at the Academy for Educational Development and its regional collaborators, Middle Start (1) provides teachers and administrators with school-site professional development to improve teaching and learning; and (2) organizes regional networks of schools, districts, universities, and advocacy organizations to provide support and accountability. The combination of on-site and regional support is intended to spread and sustain successful practices. Middle Start assists schools in undertaking reflective review and self-assessment; establishing small learning communities; aligning instruction and assessment with rigorous curricula; sharing leadership; and engaging staff, families, and community organizations in supporting students. Each area of work is based on critical practices highlighted in the research on middle grades education and school improvement.

Morningside is one of several schools that have partnered with Middle Start in undertaking comprehensive school reform over the last decade. The case seeks to illustrate the processes by which a school embeds comprehensive school reform within existing structures and capacities, to improve academic, developmental, and equity outcomes for its students. It also shows the challenges encountered by a school in taking reform to scale, although the school's partnership with Middle Start enabled the school to accomplish a higher level of implementation than with previous reforms. We do not seek to generalize our findings from Morningside to the population of Middle Start or middle level schools under reform; the case study shows the influence of contextual variables such as district policies, past reform efforts, and other variables in shaping the process and outcomes of its current reform effort. Models may bring considerable levels of quality and consistency to school's reform efforts, but contextual variables within each school contribute to making their reform experience unique.

Goal Setting and Planning the Implementation

Morningside won a CSR grant through a statewide competition to work with Middle Start, a comprehensive school reform program that upholds four principles: reflective review and self-assessment; effective small learning communities; rigorous curriculum, instruction, and assessment; and distributed leadership and sustainable partnerships (National Middle Start Center n.d.). As a first step in the implementation, a team consisting of Middle Start coaches and Morningside staff tailored the school's improvement plan to address improved student literacy; equitable participation of students in the school's instructional programs; and improved student behavior. Their grant application, emphasizing these three areas, won funding for a consecutive period of three years to carry out this work in partnership. Two Middle Start coaches worked with the school over the three years. One coach, a former principal of a Middle Start school, served as a leadership coach, developing and working closely with a leadership team within the school to steer the implementation. The second coach, a former teacher from a Middle Start school, served as an academic coach and worked closely with grade-level teams on professional development in varied instructional approaches appropriate for middle grades.

Building Leadership

The leadership team at Morningside consisted of the principal; three assistant principals (each served as a grade-level principal as well);

and teacher leaders from each grade level, special education, and electives. The leadership team participated in a series of monthly seminars along with the leadership coach and representatives from other Middle Start schools. The seminars provided teams with training in democratically developing school goals, planning and implementing reforms to attain the goals, assessing implementation of the goals continuously, and addressing critical teaching and learning issues through the implementation.

Morningside's leadership team quickly developed into partnership leaders, winning schoolwide acceptance partly because staff recognized that the team was representative and inclusive in its composition and was receptive to staff's suggestions and needs. The composition of the leadership team, however, changed significantly over the three years, as the principal left Morningside for an extended medical leave during the second year and ultimately retired, and two assistant principals left the district for positions as principals in other districts. Despite these setbacks, the leadership team sustained their focus and ensured that the Middle Start implementation did not stray off course. A core member of the leadership team attributes their staying power to having "a guide on the side." She describes the leadership coach as a constant presence who helped staff keep up their morale and continue to focus on reform efforts, despite the daily issues that crop up in schools.

During interviews, the district superintendent of Harding explained that the district had been committed to the "middle school philosophy" for more than seven years before Morningside won a grant to work with Middle Start. As a result, the school had grade-level interdisciplinary teams with common planning time. However, the superintendent stated that the "structures needed to be refined," and "teachers needed to revisit important middle grades concepts and practices, in order to use teaming well." He endorsed the school's choice of Middle Start, based on the program's positive reputation in Michigan and its compatibility with the school's improvement priorities.

Engaging Staff in the Implementation

Staff at Morningside fell along a continuum in describing their perceptions and involvement, and ultimately, the changes in the school through their partnership with Middle Start. Over half the interviewed staff reported being aware of the school's priorities; felt instrumental in carrying out critical pieces of professional development, classroom instruction, and data collection and analysis related to the priorities; and judged the three-year effort a productive one they hoped to sustain with district and administrator support.

Less than half the staff reported being less involved and somewhat critical of the efforts, especially those focused on teaming; they were not in favor of reassignment and feared that concepts and practices they had not found helpful (as part of the district's middle school initiatives over the last seven years) were, in one teacher's words, "making a comeback." However, even these staff members were supportive of the literacy initiative and many described it as the best example of what they had accomplished as part of Middle Start.

About a tenth of the staff, mostly composed of special education teachers, reported that the move to bring about inclusion went against their wishes, and that they had tried mainstreaming special education students in previous efforts and found it did not work. They described these previous efforts as being top-down approaches that did not provide adequate professional development or in-class support for doing inclusion well. Again, special education teachers reported being engaged in the literacy initiative and stated that the new strategies were interesting and that their students responded well to them. Their classrooms, too, showed evidence of their students' participation in the "literacy across the curriculum" initiative, as the walls were decorated with student work responding to schoolwide assignments based on the novel they were all reading.

The implementation of the literacy initiative at Morningside was characterized by high levels of engagement by administrators and staff, strong professional development in key instructional areas, democratic decisionmaking by teachers based on varied sources of data (including surveys of the entire staff), and a keen sense of accountability for student outcomes on the part of coaches and school staff alike. Over three years, the school made impressive strides in improving student literacy through innovative, equitable, and ultimately sustainable strategies.

For example, the coaches helped the school institute a daily reading period during which the entire school, including students, teachers, administrators, and staff, read the same book and engaged in quizzes, writing, and drawing activities, and created newsletters and other materials to share their learning from the book with parents and others. On one visit, the entire school was reading the novel *Holes*, and the hallways of the school were covered with drawings, writing, and posters by students responding to varied assignments based on the novel. As part of their leadership training, administrators did regular walkthroughs of the building to monitor the implementation of the literacy initiative.

During one such walkthrough, an assistant principal spent a class period observing students writing letters to one of the main characters in the selected novel. She noted her observations and informally conversed with the teacher and some of the students to better understand the class content. The administrator explained that her walkthroughs usually took her through the school a few times every semester. The data she compiled during walkthroughs helped her communicate better with grade-level teams about the implementation of the initiative and made them more receptive to her feedback. She also noted that the walkthroughs helped her gain the "big picture" of the school, and enabled her to work better with coaches on ongoing planning and assessment of implementation of reforms.

Addressing Obstacles to the Implementation

However, the school, given the socioeconomic diversity of its student body, had developed a covert system of tracking students (often along class and race lines) into high-performing and low-performing teams at every grade level. Additionally, special education students and their teachers formed isolated pods within the school that could not, and sometimes would not, participate in schoolwide initiatives because of previous negative experiences. During interviews, special education teachers, as a group, stated that past initiatives had expected them to adopt new instructional practices without adequate professional development. "I'm afraid the same thing will happen this time," a veteran teacher admitted. "I don't want history to repeat itself." Although Morningside's literacy initiative was truly inclusive of all teams, the efforts to make team assignment equitable and bring special education staff and students into the mainstream proved challenging, even at the end of three years of sustained effort. Coaches, fully aware of the politics of student assignment, tried to address it head-on in the first year, only to find that this put the school's partnership with Middle Start in jeopardy. The leadership coach said, "The first thing we wanted to do was to reassign the teams. But there was so much resistance from teachers, parents, and even some in the district, that we feared we would waste an entire year fighting this issue. We decided to tackle equitable reassignment through other means." After intensive discussions with the school leadership team, and with the full endorsement of the principal, coaches then decided to emphasize a "literacy across the curriculum" goal, intending to address critical equity issues through a schoolwide literacy initiative launched as the cornerstone of the implementation.

Developing School Capacity through Partnership

School reform research has long underscored the importance of school capacity (Newmann, King, and Rigdon 1997). Coaches typically discuss their efforts to help schools as a process of "finding points of entry" and "picking our battles." They point out that the schools that qualify for special CSR funding are usually in difficult straits and may not be able to meet stringent nonnegotiables, even after three years of sustained effort. Research and practice within the field of school reform define it as a long-term process, rather than a set of one-time interventions (Center for Comprehensive Reform and Improvement n.d.). The challenge and promise of school reform may lie in its longitudinal nature. At Morningside, what remained at the end of three years were stellar schoolwide literacy practices and a representative leadership team with the capacity to independently consult and present data, engage the staff in democratic decisionmaking, maintain their focus on student learning, and facilitate ongoing professional development to sustain good teaching.

The coaches succeeded in inculcating a deep awareness of schoolwide equity among leadership team members and providing them with the resources to continue to address these issues after the three-year period of their intensive involvement. Follow-up interviews in the unfunded fourth year of implementation showed that the school continued to follow through on developing literacy and building internal accountability for student learning through the walkthroughs and other self-assessment practices. However, only some of the teams were fully reassigned and served heterogeneous groups of students.

It is clear that Morningside and schools like it need long-term partnerships with school improvement programs, such as Middle Start, to build on the foundations developed during the three years of intensive contact. While CSR funding has provided unprecedented support to struggling schools through sizable three-year grants, not all schools are in a position to meet important nonnegotiables such as social equity in instructional and organizational arrangements by the end of this period. CSR programs serving these schools can build staff awareness of equity issues over the three years and build their capacity to continue to address them after the period of funding.

A District-Level Partnership

In 1994, the New York City Department of Education launched the Middle School Initiative (MSI), designed to restructure middle schools and improve teaching and learning for middle grade students. Developed and implemented by the department of education, MSI was initially based on "Turning Points" (Carnegie 1989), as well as knowledge drawn from best practices around New York City and the country.

Specifically, "Turning Points" and many middle grade reformers advocate the following:

- creating small communities for learning;
- teaching a core of common knowledge;
- ensuring success for all students;
- empowering teachers and administrators;
- preparing teachers appropriately for teaching the middle grades;
- improving academic performance through better health and fitness;
- reengaging families in the education of young adolescents; and
- connecting schools with communities.[1]

More recently, middle grades reform has focused on three areas: high academic standards for all students; equity in learning opportunities and outcomes; and strong supports for young adolescents in their development (as cited in National Forum to Accelerate Middle Grades Reform, "Vision").

Using qualitative and quantitative evaluation data from AED's five-year external evaluation of MSI (Academy for Educational Development 1997, 2000), we first describe how the initiative provided support for reform through partnerships among universities, districts, and schools, and the roles played by key participants at each level. Then, we discuss challenges encountered and lessons learned that can inform other reform efforts.

The initiative, directed by a New York City Department of Education staff person, involved all schools in 24 participating city districts in a three-year cycle of learning about, planning, and implementing exemplary middle grades practices. Each district was partnered with a local university to assist and support the planning and implementation. District- and school-level teams, composed of administrators, teachers, parents, and United Federation of Teachers representatives in collaboration with the university partners, were expected to coordinate the change process; districts designated one person in the district office with primary responsibility for coordinating the initiative. An advisory council consisting of department of education staff, district and university representatives, outside experts in educational reform and middle grades restructuring, and foundation representatives guided MSI. MSI provided opportunities for networking and learning among district-university partners as well as across cohorts, through cohort meetings and conferences.

At the time of MSI, the New York City school system was organized into 32 community school districts overseen by the city's board of education. More recently the system has been organized into 10 regions, each containing two to four community school districts. Under direct control of the city's mayor, the system is now overseen by the New York City Department of Education. The three phases of the initiative are briefly described below.

In the six-month learning phase of the initiative, district teams were created to learn and exchange ideas about young adolescents, the type of learning environment they needed, and the changes schools would have to implement to meet these needs. The composition of teams varied by district, but typically included principals of middle schools, district staff representatives (such as a middle school coordinator), teachers, guidance counselors, a union representative, some parents, and a university partner. Frequency of district team meetings varied from biweekly to monthly to once or twice during the learning phase, with a subset of team members meeting more frequently with the university partners. The learning phase included essentially the same types of activities in each district—lectures by consultants and university faculty, and hands-on workshops facilitated by university and district staff on selected topics related to middle grades practice. Topics included young adolescent psychology, school-change processes, team teaching, advisories, service and cooperative learning, and interdisciplinary curricula. In addition, members of all district teams conducted visits to schools where they could observe aspects of exemplary middle grades practice. The learning phase concluded with a summer institute in each district, open to all school staff and some parents and district staff and coordinated by the university partner.

Data from teacher and principal surveys and interviews with partners[2] indicate that the learning phase was successful in raising awareness and knowledge about middle grades reforms. Widespread agreement with many of the practices advocated by middle grade reformers was evident in interviews with partners, as well as survey findings from teachers and principals. For example, 71 percent of surveyed teachers and 93 percent of principals reported that grouping students in small units (such as teams or houses) was an important characteristic of middle grades reform.[3] In addition, teachers who participated in MSI professional development activities (such as the summer institute, workshops, or lectures) reported greater agreement than those who did not participate in MSI-related professional development, indicating that the activities of the learning phase had an impact on teachers' support for practices being advocated by MSI.

The summer institutes launched the second phase of the initiative, the planning phase. The institute included high-quality workshops provided by university staff and other practitioners and time for each school team to meet together to develop an implementation plan. The institutes provided participants with a concentrated, uninterrupted period of time to focus on middle grades research and to plan changes in their schools. The one-year planning phase focused on assessing each school's strengths and needs and bringing other staff and parents into the planning group. Continuing into the school year, school-level teams met regularly with the help of their university partner to plan how they would institute organizational changes.

The third phase of the initiative was implementation, lasting another year. At the start of the initiative, schools in each district were in different stages of implementing middle school practices—some having implemented many before MSI began and others only beginning with the initiative itself. MSI was intended to bring about substantial—not cosmetic—change: districts and schools were asked to rethink instruction, organization, governance, and accountability to maximize learning opportunities for all middle grade students. Districts and schools had great leeway in how they implemented middle grades practices and in what sequence; no two schools within a district were expected to be alike. Some schools focused on restructuring into inter-grade houses or teams, others focused on implementing interdisciplinary curricula, still others focused on implementing cooperative learning and other pedagogical changes. In addition, while most schools were either organized in teams or houses before the initiative or restructured as part of the initiative, some were organized by grade levels; others were interdisciplinary or focused around themes such as social justice or technology.

Infrastructural Supports for Reform

An important outcome of MSI was the development of institutional supports for middle grades reforms—what we call here an infrastructure for middle grades improvement. The following section discusses the elements that comprise this infrastructure, where and how they were implemented, and how they were used to support change. The elements include districts, principals, universities, and the New York City Department of Education.

Districts

Districts were required to undertake a number of steps to create an infrastructure for supporting middle grades improvement. This included having an individual devoted part- or full-time to coordinating MSI; creating a districtwide team that would undertake the initial learning phase of the initiative; and developing school teams that would coordinate the initiative at each school.

District Coordinator. Only 2 districts out of 24 had a full-time middle school coordinator and, even in these districts, this individual had multiple responsibilities. In 3 districts, special consultants were hired who focused exclusively on the initiative, usually for two or three days a week. The district staff and consultants coordinated district meetings, communicated with other district staff, visited schools, and coordinated districtwide activities, such as a middle school newsletter or fair. All the people hired as consultants were former administrators, usually from the district in which they were working. Their inside status helped them be successful in coordinating the work on both the school and district level. In several other districts there was frequent turnover in this position, which generally had a depressing effect on the initiative. For example, in two districts the newly appointed person was not knowledgeable either about MSI or middle school reform and the district's momentum was undermined by the turnover.

District- and School-Level Teams. After the learning and planning phases, most district teams ceased meeting and the initiative devolved to the school level. In many districts, regular meetings of middle school principals replaced the role of the district team. Only one district maintained district-level teams: one team focused on policy issues concerning middle schools and the other, composed of the chairs of school teams, focused on implementation. In this district, the initiative maintained a high level of visibility. In the majority of districts, without a district-level team or someone in the district office primarily committed to middle schools, the visibility of the initiative and the importance the district attached to it were reduced.

School teams, on the other hand, remained in place in most schools throughout the initiative, except where there was substantial turnover of leadership. Most school teams met weekly and provided continuity in the design and implementation of middle grades practices.

Much work on the district level was in raising awareness about exemplary middle grades practices and the needs of young adolescents. Little work was done relating to policy, for example, planning districtwide professional development with middle grades needs in mind, or providing support for interdisciplinary teams and effective use of common planning time. The press of district initiatives meant that professional development choices by individual schools were frequently superseded by district priorities. However, the beginnings of the infrastructure were in place and provided good starting points for further work in many districts.

Principals

Principals often saw themselves as more committed to middle grades reform than many of their staff. However, many partners cited lack of leadership from middle grades principals as a major obstacle to middle grades reform. Among the issues raised by partners were lack of knowledge about leading change efforts and lack of capacity for instructional leadership. MSI sought to remedy these challenges through principal institutes, courses, and summer institutes publicized through the initiative, and district-based workshops in which principals met regularly to discuss the implementation of the new standards in their schools.

Universities

Universities approached the task of offering support to their districts in different ways. The following examples show the range of supports provided by university partners:

- providing courses in the district, with direct support to schools that sent participants regularly;
- facilitating principals' study groups on the new standards;
- visiting individual schools regularly to provide support and technical assistance;
- meeting regularly with school teams to continue planning and assessing progress;
- working with individual schools with strong interest in interdisciplinary curriculum development or in a specific curriculum area;
- placing university staff taking sabbaticals in schools, to assist with areas of middle grades improvement; and
- placing student teachers in participating schools.

The role university partners played in their partnership with districts varied in the focus of their change effort, the focus of their services, university staff involved, and sharing of decisionmaking, and can be summarized as (1) facilitator of change, (2) resource provider, and (3) broker of resources. Each is described in table 10.1.

The various characteristics of relationships between the university and district partners developed over time, generally conforming to the unique needs of the districts and the capacity each partner brought to the initiative. The flexibility and variation that emerged was one of the strengths of the partnerships. The partnerships also provided a unique structure on which to build continuing relationships between universities and districts.

MSI as a Department of Education Initiative

The department of education's MSI staff supported the district- and school-level infrastructure through activities that developed awareness

Table 10.1. Roles of Universities in the New York City Middle School Initiative

University role	Focus of change	Focus of services	Staff	Decisionmaking
Facilitator of change, mainly at the district and school levels	District and schools	District teams	Coordinator, plus a person in each school (in some cases a graduate student) All schools in the district work with both individual staff and school teams	Shared with district coordinator and district team
Resource provider, primarily to districts to carry out their agendas	District (works through district coordinator to help promote district change process)	Representatives from schools in large meetings, mainly held at the university	Coordinator, plus occasional additional faculty; other faculty participate through delivery of courses in districts and through workshops or meetings	Joint decisionmaking with district coordinator; district determines the agenda
Broker of resources to and among schools	Not tied to district change agenda; works with individual schools interested in moving forward with middle school reform; puts schools in touch to learn from one another	Individual schools with interest in specific areas of change	Coordinator, plus faculty available for larger meetings and workshops	a. Joint decisionmaking with district coordinator, primarily focused on helping support schools that volunteer change and inform others about their work. b. Primarily with schools; little work on district level because of lack of district team

about middle grades reform and practices, stimulated conversations around the city about what a good middle school looks like, and provided forums to showcase exemplary practices. The department of education MSI activities included

- a staff person hired to support the development of an interdisciplinary curriculum aligned with New York City performance standards;
- district-level work on the new standards, including principal study groups and the development of interdisciplinary units aligned with new standards;
- citywide meetings that provided opportunities to learn about middle grades practices from other districts and schools;
- an annual citywide conference in which more than 600 participants learned about middle grades practices; and
- boroughwide principal leadership institutes and professional development on block scheduling and middle grades practices in literacy development.

The MSI director also monitored the performance of the partnerships through district visits and reviews of district plans. In some cases the MSI leadership intervened to help partners work together more effectively or, in one case, to find a new university partner for a dissatisfied district.

Impact of MSI

As noted earlier, AED conducted a multimethod, five-year external evaluation of MSI. These evaluation data indicated that MSI had an impact in several areas (Academy for Educational Development 2000). First, MSI was clearly successful in increasing awareness of middle grades practices among district and school staff throughout the city. Awareness of the needs of younger adolescents, and how schools could respond to these needs, was also raised. However, high staff turnover at the school and district levels necessitated continuous professional development around effective middle grades practices and the research and theories underlying those practices. Our evaluation data also showed that teachers' agreement with the underlying principles of middle grades reform was strongly correlated with implementation of middle grades practices—further evidence of the importance of raising awareness and knowledge about young adolescents' needs and effective middle grades practices.

In addition to raising awareness, the Academy for Educational Development (2000) found substantial evidence that most schools initiated restructuring efforts as a result of the initiative, especially restructuring into smaller learning communities with the goal of creating more personalized relationships between students and teachers.

We also found evidence that use of effective middle grades practices increased in the majority of participating schools. Survey data showed that the percentage of teachers reporting regular use of interdisciplinary units, portfolio assessment, and other practices increased between 1997 and 1999. Student surveys from the same time also provided evidence that the amount of time students participated in activities such as group work and interdisciplinary projects increased. However, the impact on practices varied widely by schools, and many partners agreed that MSI's impact on teaching and learning was not as great as desired.

AED (2000) also found evidence that implementation of effective middle grades practices, as measured through a scale of teacher and student survey items, was associated with higher levels of mathematics and reading achievement. For example, 50 percent of students in schools with greater implementation of MSI practices scored at or above grade level in mathematics, compared with 41 percent of their peers in schools with a lower level of implementation. Similarly, 37 percent of students in high-implementing schools scored at or above grade level compared with 31 percent of their peers in low-implementing schools (Academy for Educational Development 2000).

Finally, evaluation findings showed that the infrastructure supporting reform was weak in districts and schools without a consistent or knowledgeable district person in charge of the initiative, and with high staff turnover in school and district leadership.

Conclusions about MSI and District-Level Partnerships

AED's findings suggest that district-level infrastructure can provide critical support to school reform efforts, and that district support is a crucial element in comprehensive school reform. Without a district commitment to a change agenda, MSI partners were confined to working with individual schools that wanted to change; however, no district infrastructure to support ongoing middle grades reform was developed.

The university-district partnerships were a unique element that brought a wealth of resources to the schools: providing expertise in effective middle grades practices and school reform, facilitating sharing across schools and universities, and linking schools to other resources. Additionally, the infrastructure provided by the district allowed cross-district sharing and learning that reform partners found invaluable. Indeed, the partners requested more forums and opportunities for such events. Partners also suggested that meetings for those in the same role (e.g., all university partners, all district coordinators) would be valuable, allowing them to participate in a community of practice (Lave and Wenger 1991) and to probe difficult issues arising from the work. Further, there was clear agreement that university partners and districts valued and benefited from a partnership based on trust that addressed the unique needs of each school. Nevertheless, partnerships could be strengthened with a clearer vision for specific goals and benchmarks that would vary according to a partnership's specific resources and needs.

The MSI experience illustrates the benefits of a district-level focus on reform efforts. In districts with strong leadership for reform and policies that supported reform,[4] the initiative had a greater impact, and in a greater proportion of schools. In districts without this level of leadership and support, schools revealed "pockets" of reform rather than deep, sustained change. This case shows how a district-level initiative facilitated reform efforts and where it could have provided more supports to help schools achieve their reform goals.

This case also points to the challenges and complexities of district-level reform. For example, the external evaluation findings provided evidence that to have a substantial impact at the classroom level, the initiative needed to focus on teaching and learning in addition to developing an infrastructure for support. MSI staff and university and district partners agreed universally that the learning phase of the initiative was powerful and involved a substantial number of staff in most districts. However, the implementation phase required more intensive professional development and support if it were to affect the classroom. Even though survey data suggested teachers increased their regular use of middle grades practices, interviews with partners and the MSI coordinator indicated that the classroom-level changes were not deep enough. One university partner said that the initiative was least successful in moving teachers from "chalk and talk" to more active and constructivist approaches to instruction. Resources allocated to the initiative were not sufficient to bring about widespread and sustained change on the classroom level; more needed to be done at the district and school levels to support professional development in the critical areas of middle grades improvement.

Another challenge was related to high staff turnover throughout the city. The learning phase of the initiative was designed as a six-month period during which staff at all levels learned about exemplary middle grades practices. This proved to be a critical precursor to planning and implementing middle grades reform. However, high district and school staff turnover throughout the city diluted the initiative quickly, because new staff were unfamiliar with its philosophy of middle grades reform. The learning phase of the initiative clearly had to be institutionalized at the district level, so that new staff could become familiar with its main goals and central ideas.

Finally, this case illustrated that CSR efforts require cohesion in policy- and decisionmaking at the district and department of education levels. Specifically, MSI was hindered by a lack of voice in the department of education. The initiative was not able to integrate its work with department decisions and policies that affected middle grades education, such as revising the department's external review protocols to include issues critical for the middle grades. As a result, such department policies were viewed as distinct from the work of MSI by district and school staff, and MSI was not always well coordinated with these and other initiatives. Having visibility and impact on department policies would have allowed MSI to be more influential in districts.

A REGIONAL EDUCATIONAL PARTNERSHIP

Experiences such as those at individual schools and within school districts informed the development of the Michigan Middle Start Partnership (MMSP), as shown by the external evaluation of Middle Start (Corbett and Wilson 2005; Corbett, Wilson, and Haring 2004). The MMSP represents a unique approach to building group alliances to reform middle grades education in this country. While it shares with all other reforms a keen interest in promoting better teaching and learning, the initiative's proponents also acted on the belief that sustainable comprehensive reform requires the collaboration and coordinated activity of key actors from institutions of higher education (IHEs), nonprofit social and educational service agencies, school districts, and other interested parties. A partnership of representatives of such organizations augments the intellectual and material resources available to those designing, assisting, and implementing reform and increases the capacity of middle grades advocacy efforts in the state.

Of course, numerous educational improvement efforts create affiliated groups that give those involved opportunities to discuss and plan their actions, but MMSP sees itself as a governing and advocacy body that can promote the maintenance and sustainability of middle grades reform. In its creation, then, MMSP required reform among the variety of agencies that had interests in middle grades education, in addition to those changes sought at the school level. MMSP therefore is a tangible, extraorganizational entity that seeks to act in the best interests of middle grades classrooms while strengthening coalitions across the educational system.

The partnership—consisting of a collection of IHEs, nonprofit social and educational service agencies, and key district-level reformers—coalesced around three simple, albeit not always articulated, ideas:

- Middle grades schools should serve youth well academically, developmentally, and equitably.
- Building schools' capacity to serve students well would require taking action at multiple levels of the educational system, with the involvement of multiple partners.
- The partners should communicate, coordinate, and collaborate in an ongoing relationship that would allow them to seize on opportunities to further middle grades reform whenever they appeared.

Throughout its history, Middle Start partners exemplified shared commitments and the flexibility to act in the present while continuing to plan for the future. But it was the "layering" of the initiative that participants thought would give the reform the strength and longevity to alter the entire fabric of middle grades education in Michigan. Central to the vision of Middle Start has been the recognition that reform is more than improving schools. It also requires a concerted effort to have the various support players contribute. Evaluation data show that MMSP is the mechanism that made that happen in Michigan (Corbett and Wilson 2005). This section traces the numerous benefits partners attributed to a reform with varied associates and discusses how these enhanced the partnership's attempts to address scale and sustainability.

The Benefits of MMSP

In interviews, participants in the Michigan Middle Start Partnership claimed that a host of benefits had accrued from their involvement in a group with multiple associations. These benefits fell into four categories: middle grades reform, the Middle Start approach, the partner organizations, and the participants.

Middle Grades Reform

Middle schools had long been ignored in the Michigan educational system. Despite considerable research that detailed the unique learning needs of early adolescents, educators who worked with that population needed no specific certification, and their training historically had been uncomfortably and ineffectively commingled with elementary and secondary teacher education programs. Partners reported in interviews that they believed MMSP had at a minimum finally put middle grades education on the state's radar, in the same way the New York City Department of Education's MSI increased awareness of middle grades reform.

Data from the external evaluation indicate that awareness increased in a couple of ways (Corbett and Wilson 2005). First, the MMSP brought middle grades improvement into the stated goals and actions of a wide range of organizations. MMSP, for example, involved not only education agencies but also those providing a broader array of social services to children and families. While these latter organizations had always maintained an interest in working on educational matters, the efforts generally were diffused, with a variety of targets, uncoordinated action, and mixed results. MMSP made middle grades improvement a "more central topic of conversation," as one partner put it, and in doing so offered these organizations a clearly defined path into working with educators that had not previously existed. Concrete results ensued, as in the case of one county that started an after-school program directly aimed at young adolescents. In fact, the number of people involved with the program drew the attention of the local United Way chapter that subsequently funded it.

MMSP, in return, had access to a host of resources it could leverage, not the least of which was public relations. Certain social service agencies regularly disseminate information to the public. Once these agencies begun focusing on the middle grades, information on reform entered the pipeline.

Another way that MMSP raised awareness of middle grades reform was in drawing attention to people and institutions that specialized in that arena. As one partner put it, "When Middle Start first started, there weren't many agencies and organizations that middle schools could turn to; those have now broadened and been brought together." Indeed, simply having a publicly acknowledged list of Michigan organizations that advocated for and worked with middle schools created a sense that middle school work was itself deserving, complete with its own knowledge base and priorities.

Middle grades reform received a decided boost somewhat serendipitously as well. When the federal government offered CSR funding to close the achievement gap in low-income schools, the partnership designed the Middle Start comprehensive school model. MMSP seized immediately on this opportunity and emerged as the nation's 10th largest provider to the middle grades and the largest in Michigan— five times larger than the next biggest CSR model provider. While the new source of funding undoubtedly was welcomed and perhaps an essential ingredient to MMSP's continued existence, it gave Michigan's middle schools an avenue to reform that specifically addressed their unique circumstances.

As importantly, schools themselves directly benefited from MMSP's formation. For example, as one partner phrased it:

Schools that have worked with Middle Start concepts began to think differently. They had the right mindset. They began to question old ways of doing things by using data and taking some action. They became less blaming of kids and parents. They started to look internally with their schools and find things they could do to make their schools better. They began to collaborate and had frequent conversations about teaching, curriculum, and kids' performance.

In other words, middle schools began to examine what they could do proactively to change the way adolescents were educated, rather than adopting a victim mindset and hoping for students and parents to change. And, as mentioned above, once schools had determined change was necessary, they also found a cadre of people and organizations ready to help them in that endeavor. Such assistance came from the IHEs, regional educational service agencies, and networks of schools themselves.

Finally, MMSP has formed regional networks of Middle Start schools (three exist to date). These networks are a way of engaging school-based educators in directing their own learning; allowing them to sidestep the limitations of institutional roles, hierarchies, and geographic locations; and encouraging them to work together with many different kinds of people. Participants have opportunities to grow in a professional community that focuses on their development, providing ways of learning that are more in keeping with their professional lives. The network members meet monthly to address the following goals:

- a web of support for professional development and comprehensive school improvement;
- leaders who will move the state and their communities toward a vision of academic excellence, developmental responsiveness, and social equity; and
- better outcomes for all middle grades students in Michigan— especially those who are economically disadvantaged.

The partners outlined the roles and responsibilities for the four key groups that comprise each regional network. *Central office administrators* (superintendents and other key leaders responsible for school improvement) in the participating districts were charged with providing resources and organizational support, policies and community relations on Middle Start principles and practices, and alignment of other district endeavors. *Schools* (building administrators and teachers) in each network were responsible for ensuring the principal and at least one teacher became active members by attending network activities and promoting Middle Start principles and practices in their building. *Regional networks* (coordinated by an employee of each partner organization) provided data to assess the needs of their member schools, created communication systems for their members, promoted and conducted professional development and technical assistance services, engaged the community in improvement efforts, encouraged leadership within the membership and recruited new members, identified policies that promoted the principles and practices, sought out funding opportunities, and built a governance structure for the network. Finally, the *state partnership* (as represented by the members of MMSP) assumed responsibility for quality assurance across network activities, defined the mission and vision for Middle Start, coordinated activities and communications across the networks, set benchmarks for implementation of principles and practices, uncovered funding opportunities, and was the central repository for Middle Start tools and materials.

In interviews, partners pointed to the networks' emergence as important for sustaining middle grades reform in schools whose special funding had run out. A recent external evaluation of the networks suggests that they have not yet become integral in this regard (Gill and Gill 2005). While network participants highly value their professional development offerings and the opportunities to interact with colleagues from other schools, these activities at present seem on the periphery of reform in the schools.

The Middle Start Approach

For a long time, partners used the term *Middle Start approach* without a clear definition. In fact, people tended to speak of Middle Start as being a movement, an idea that highlighted participants' passionate interest in carving out space for middle grades education in the state, rather than a set of principles and practices. The groups' frequent interactions (e.g., quarterly face-to-face meetings with ongoing e-mail dialogue between) eventually clarified their purposes and strategies. People, perhaps, felt that these shared understandings represented more shape and substance than the term "movement" seemed to connote and, thus, the term "approach" became a frequently invoked, holistic reference to the ways MMSP operated.

Putting all of the linguistic nuances of the term aside, we use "approach" here as a way to denote the cumulative impact of MMSP on the partners' collective conceptual and strategic growth. We do this because of the interconnected alliance across the MMSP; partners sought solutions for middle grades reform *and* for structuring a collection of organizations to support that reform. Changing one part of the educational system or another seemed to take precedence during

MMSP meetings, but someone would always reorient the group to the dual nature of their goals. For example:

> We are knee-deep in issues related to structure of the partnership. But we also have to ensure that we focus on content for schools— making sure there is a deep commitment to quality teaching and learning. . . . We don't have to have a prescribed curriculum, but schools do need tools to help them decide if what they are doing meets key learning standards.

Echoing the above statement, partners claimed that the "approach" benefited in two basic ways from MMSP's evolution: (1) engendering commitments as to how partners should work with one another and (2) developing the package of principles, practices, and professional development that Middle Start schools would be expected to implement.

Regular MMSP meetings and other events, as well as numerous phone conversations and e-mails reinforced in partners the idea that collaboration was a powerful intellectual tool. In interviews, nearly all partners referred to how their thinking about middle grades reform had been altered and/or clarified by talking with each other. Had the benefit of interaction ended here, however, MMSP would not have had anything to recommend itself over the plethora of other affiliations the partners enjoyed as part of their professional lives. Instead, MMSP participants also expressed specific and impassioned beliefs about how the partnership itself should operate.

One such aspect was consulting and collaborating with multiple partners on MMSP tasks. For example, the CSR "model" gave a central role to school leadership coaches, who worked with school leaders to help them guide their schools through the reform process. As more and more schools received CSR grants for Middle Start, significant attention inevitably had to be devoted to training coaches, to ensure consistency and quality. Rather than leave this training to the individual preferences of the partner organizations providing technical assistance to each school, the organizations jointly planned and delivered the training. And, over time, this joint planning led to the development of a training manual for all coaches.

Collaboration was more involved than just having representatives from various organizations work together. Within MMSP, roles emerged that gave these representatives distinct places in the partnership's operation, and over time a structure developed for getting work done. The participants formed a steering committee to oversee the long-term sustainability of MMSP and to form four work groups for addressing the partnership's strategic priorities: model development, networks, research and evaluation, and public policy and public engagement. Most importantly, each of the work groups was assigned "constructive" work to do. For example, the participants thought it essential that those seeking to convene regional networks of middle schools have a clear idea about what these networks should do; thus, the network work group established benchmarks for gauging network activities and agreed to responsibilities in writing. Similarly, with the advent of CSR funding, the model development work group clarified and refined the CSR Middle Start model. Evaluation data indicated that in all instances, the work groups were in considerable consultation with each other, always with the understanding that the work would eventually be approved or disapproved by the steering committee (Corbett and Wilson 2005). In this way, the early commitment to collaboration became formalized.

MMSP continues to grapple with what future forms the partnership should take and who should be included as members. Partners are committed to the idea that MMSP will have the capacity to develop, manage, assess, maintain, and continuously improve its structure and will continue to identify priority outcomes for the short and long term. The steering committee will link MMSP with the National Middle Start Center at AED; act as the policy arm of MMSP; and represent partners and their organizations, including leaders for Middle Start CSR coaching, professional development, networks, policy development and pubic engagement, and research and evaluation. The actual structure that will house the enterprise remains under question. Membership is an ongoing debate, with concerns about the recent loss of some Michigan members.

Middle Start, of course, had to become more than a way of working together. It required substance as well. Interestingly, MMSP did not form around a particular and well-specified approach to reforming middle grades education. It originated at the behest of the Kellogg Foundation, as a vehicle for making middle grades reform a distinct priority of Michigan's educational system. Thus, an "approach" for reform evolved hand-in-hand with MMSP's way of working together.

Partners noted a variety of ways in which this aspect of the Middle Start approach had developed:

> The role of data has evolved to a much more meaningful level. When we first started, we just provided a data notebook to the schools and it was not enough. We knew school people were not using the data. . . . We developed training and workshops and modified the notebooks. We came to realize that if schools don't understand the importance of this, then the data are useless.

The work of the coaches has been strengthened—grounded in principles and practices, grounded in shared experiences and a guidebook.

The policy work group has talked about developing community profiles [trend data] and the group has expanded to think of community more broadly than just what happens in schools.

An undeniably significant benefit, then, of putting MMSP into place was that partners' understandings about how to reform the middle grades crystallized into a shared set of ideas about how a partnership should work, supporting a clearly stated and mutually developed approach to school reform. The end result was threefold. According to one person,

The partnership was treated as a true partner by the funding agent rather than a grantee.

Another said,

The development of the principles and practices really helped coaches and schools understand what Middle Start is.

And, more notably perhaps was a third person's observation:

Districts and states that were thoughtful about middle grades reform now have something [a model] to look at.

As another stated,

Michigan Middle Start has a big effect on the National Middle Start model. Michigan is both affected by and affects this work. Most of the trails that Michigan has blazed are going to be adapted and adopted on a national scale.

Thus, the work of MMSP had benefits for not only the Kellogg Foundation, but also Michigan and the nation.

Partner Organizations

MMSP is comprised of representatives from a variety of organizations. One of them, the Academy for Educational Development (AED), which houses the National Middle Start Center, received a grant from the W. K. Kellogg Foundation to administer and oversee the partnership. The oversight responsibilities shifted to the steering committee, whose members were all from Michigan groups. Eventually, some other governing entity for Middle Start will also be created from which the day-to-day activities will be directed, although the steering committee will continue to act as the policymaking body. AED's involvement will continue as the National Center for Middle Start. They will serve five key functions: leadership and management, research and development, quality assurance, financial management, and marketing and communications. But benefits also accrued to the various representatives' home organizations by virtue of being a partner.

Foremost was the establishment of informal and formal alliances with other organizations, which would not have come about were it not for MMSP. For example, one of the IHEs did not have the staff to provide technical assistance directly to schools, nor the capability of training anyone to do so. This greatly hindered the institution's ability to be an active participant in schools receiving CSR grants. One of the other partner IHEs with a sizeable cadre of technical assistance took on the role of training someone to represent the other IHE. Other alliances formed where partner organizations had similar strengths and felt that collaboration would further boost the capacity of each. Less formally, several partners spoke about the comfort they felt in contacting representatives from other organizations, in both partner and other institutions, about substantive matters because of the connections made in the course of MMSP work.

Partner organizations also found that their involvement in MMSP enabled them to extend their work further and attract more resources than if they had remained independent of the partnership. For example, an IHE gained access to more schools to offer professional development, and by virtue of that expansion received additional funds. In another instance, an IHE's involvement with MMSP proved to be the gateway to working with middle schools nationally. Finally, a nonprofit's participation influenced the direction—and scope—of several other programs it undertook.

Participants

An inevitable by-product of the partnership was individual professional growth, according to the interviewees, particularly in understanding of middle grades reform and in broadening their professional networks.

I have grown in my understanding of middle grades reform. I learned a great deal by being exposed to the seminal works. My knowledge also expanded by watching various levels and organizations work with each other. And, finally, I saw the schools change when they worked more together as a team rather than separate departments. It has made me a convert.

Such comments were an often-heard refrain. Partners learned more about how the entire educational system in the state worked; they saw concrete examples of the value of collaboration; they heard different points of view and experienced how productive sustained dialogue could be.

Participants also made connections with other people and groups, both inside and outside MMSP, that they felt were professionally beneficial. Sometimes this involved just having access to a wider audience to whom one's work could be disseminated; in other instances, initial connections led to establishing more permanent involvement with different entities, such as joining advisory groups. But most importantly, people argued that through MMSP they had deepened and extended their involvement with Michigan schools.

Scale and Sustainability

One term often used to define MMSP's essential quality was "organic." MMSP's evolution was partially planned, partially opportunistic, and partially reactive. Problems got resolved as they emerged, because MSP was a new experience—no one could have predicted that those problems would occur. Experience, of course, made people better able to anticipate what would, could, and should happen. And no one disputed that the future success of MMSP hinged on putting new group maintenance ideas into place.

For the moment, MMSP can point to signs that their multiyear, multipartner work generated some gains for middle grades reform. To date, Middle Start has provided comprehensive school improvement to 60 Michigan middle schools;[5] an additional 100 schools have participated in Middle Start professional development, leadership development, and networking activities through Middle Start networks, partnerships, and other programs;[6] and more than 450 schools have taken a comprehensive set of Middle Start self-study surveys administered by the Center for Prevention Research and Development.[7] The MMSP has obviously achieved a considerable presence in the state. Furthermore, in the most recent round of CSR funding in winter 2005, 15 schools prepared applications to become new Middle Start schools. On the network front, the newest regional network (in Detroit) has attracted an enthusiastic group of 25 new schools, whose representatives are meeting regularly and learning about reform options.

Sustainability remains a question. The MMSP steering committee has been wrestling with it for the past few years. The position of the partnership has been this: now that there were viable work groups, a ratified mission and vision, and strong links to like-minded organizations, what was the next step? The short answer was to build sustainability. Initial discussions in 2002 revolved around work with an outside consultant to create a viable organizational structure and an office to support the partners' work. This plan was eventually subsumed by a working relationship with New American Schools, whereby sustainability became synonymous with a viable business plan. The MMSP and the National Center at AED have recently turned their attention to reducing costs and increasing market share. This has led to extended conversations about what is core to the mission and vision (promoting the model and the networks) and where MMSP will turn for additional funding. AED and the partners have begun exploring new CSR options in other states and looking for other funding sources within Michigan. Options have included pooling local education foundation grants and creatively using other federal funding sources for improvement (e.g., Title I, II, III, and V). In addition, to increase Middle Start's visibility, MMSP has successfully applied to coordinate a statewide Schools to Watch program developed by the National Forum to Accelerate Middle Grades Reform ("Schools"). MMSP is also continuing its long-term efforts to promote research and evaluation activities associated with its work and to encourage policy reform.

Conclusions about MMSP and Regional Educational Partnerships

Michigan Middle Start, thus, is an example of a multitiered coalition of reform partners, in which comprehensive school reform is believed to involve both schools and the constellation of organizations that seek to serve schools. Importantly, this kind of collaborative reform expects significant change to occur at multiple levels. This expectation makes MMSP an entirely different entity than the oft-formed affiliations that grow up among schools and/or agencies perceiving to have common interests. MMSP, although extraorganizational (in that it exists outside the boundaries of any particular, existing institution), has taken on organizational characteristics itself—with regular meetings where full attendance, a well-defined agenda of work, and distinct roles related to accomplishing that work are expected.

In interviews, partners were positive about MMSP in general. They all remarked that its shape and the substance of its activities are radically different from—and generally exceed—what they expected (if in fact they had concrete preconceptions of what MMSP would be in the first place). They all also note numerous challenges ahead, most of which have been anticipated in the prior sections of this report. Here, in the participants' own words, are the issues they believe will influence the sustained evolution of MMSP:

Historically it has been an issue with Kellogg funding—you have a project going for three years and then, bang, it is gone. We have program after program that existed and then disappeared. We hope to have an infrastructure that is strong enough that it can go on. The schools have to see value in the activities or connections they have made so they support it themselves.

A couple of areas in the model need more strengthening—equity and literacy. I think we talk a lot about equity but we don't do much about it. We work in low-income schools, but how much accountability is there in the model around equity? We talk a lot about literacy but don't act on it. We always talk about kids not being at the level they should be, but we only have one partner who does anything around reading and writing. Should there be other partners in this area?

I am pessimistic. It is only the money that holds the partnership together. People will go back to their corners and it will be business as usual. They have formed some new personal alliances and they may call on each other now and again.

There is good agreement in the broad strokes about what needs to happen for students and schools, as witnessed by the practices. But we have not articulated how we will get there. The development of the coach's guide is a practical way to hammer away at that, but there is a lack of consensus about the importance of some of the other features, for example, networks, leadership design, self-study, etc.

I don't think people are committed to the networks. If partners stay directive and centralized, the networks will fail.

As the partnership hopefully grows, the partnership will be able to recruit some other groups to provide focused professional development in other areas of the curriculum. Right now, there isn't much [content] to offer schools and so the TAs resort to process things—like teaming. I hope more content will follow. Middle Start looks less appealing as a smattering of process and content.

MMSP is going to be critical in sustaining reform, especially in policy. There will be an extensive amount of work to do and we need an organization to make sense out of that.

With the recent shift in funding away from CSR grants and an acknowledgement of the need for sustainability at its core, most of these issues are being addressed directly by MMSP.

SUMMARY AND CONCLUSIONS

This chapter illustrates the promise and challenge of attempting large-scale reform in the middle grades. Educational partnerships are clearly vital, given the need for reforms to go to scale and to be sustainable in the long run. Schools and districts are focused on improving teaching and learning, and seem to benefit from the support of external educational partners as they bring reforms to scale through schoolwide and districtwide engagement. Schools and districts can also use the assistance of educational partners in formulating policies and budgets that will help institutionalize successful reforms, so that they sustain after the initial implementation. The first example, the Middle Start initiative, shows that sincere efforts on the part of a school and a CSR model resulted in a successful literacy initiative, but gaps remained, especially in the area of social equity. CSR coaches added value through working collaboratively with the school on their reform effort's design and implementation; systematically building the school's leadership and teaching capacity through ongoing and customized professional development; persisting in bringing reforms to scale by engaging the entire staff in key initiatives; supporting the leadership team in raising awareness on equity issues; and garnering the support of the district on issues such as setting up heterogeneously grouped small learning communities. When faced with challenges, coaches responded by building consensus on reforms that could be implemented, while persisting in building support for controversial reforms.

The district-university partnership illustrated in the second case, the New York City Middle School Initiative, showed that district-level support from university partners is critical in integrating policy initiatives with school reform at both the district and city level, and in helping stakeholders at all levels understand and embrace the research and theory behind middle grades education. It also pointed to the need for partnerships that support ongoing professional development to ensure that middle grades reform efforts are not undermined by the high staff turnover endemic to many school- and district-level staff, especially in low-performing schools and districts.

The third example, the Michigan Middle Start Partnership, demonstrated promising results arising from an additional layer of policy, advocacy, and school networking to provide a framework for school- and district-level reform efforts and support long-term partnerships of schools, districts, and external reformers. The partnership positively influenced middle grades educational reform in the state through its collaboration with teacher educators, state and district policymakers, researchers and evaluators, and public engagement organizations.

All three examples in general, and the third in particular, show that educational partnerships can facilitate continued professional development and coaching, mutual quality control, and sustained and coherent implementation of reform in ways that boost academic and social outcomes for middle grades students. However, partnerships cannot guarantee that the goals of scale or sustainability are attained, as their complexity brings attendant problems. Funding for such large-scale, longitudinal reforms is still incipient. Even CSR, a well-designed reform, provided schools with funding and technical assistance for only three years. All three cases showcased the challenges of gaining large-scale buy-in for the goals of reforms and of implementing reforms in a coherent and democratic manner. Assessing the implementation and effectiveness of such a reform can also be difficult, posing the problem of demonstrating the value added by educational partnerships.

The lessons learned from these three examples can be applied to elementary and high schools, as the entire K–12 continuum of public education can improve teaching and learning and reduce gaps in equity. What makes the challenge even more daunting at the middle grades level is the recognition of yet a third, equally important outcome—developmental responsiveness. Students in the middle grades years deserve the added attention to adaptations of instruction (e.g., more active, hands-on activities) and organizational arrangements (e.g., more personalized teams) required for young adolescents. Partnerships can meet these needs by widening the pool of knowledge, skills, and resources available to middle grades educators. They can support schools and districts in taking reforms to scale, whether the focus is a particular school, district, or larger region. Partnerships can play a critical role in boosting the sustainability of educational reform by linking teacher educators, researchers, policymakers, funders, and practitioners in productive relationships that build instructional and leadership capacity within schools and districts, and influence policy in regional and national arenas.

NOTES

1. Adapted from Carnegie Council on Adolescent Development (1989), and as summarized in New York City Board of Education (1998).

2. Throughout this section, *partners* refers to MSI district and university partners.

3. Data are from the Middle School Initiative teacher (n = 688) and principal (n = 50) surveys, administered in 1997 by AED.

4. For example, policies supporting restructuring into small learning communities and organizational structures that would allow staff to meet regularly to plan and improve instructional approaches.

5. Comprehensive school improvement services are provided by locally trained coaches and include the following: aligning instruction with student assessments; guiding and supporting school leadership teams; garnering support for change throughout the school community; creating systems for continuous improvement; establishing small learning communities; establishing teacher teams; facilitating distributed leadership, sustainable partnerships, and broad-based support; and supporting professional learning communities (National Middle Start Center n.d.).

6. The networks were designed to meet the needs of local educators. Thus, specific activities varied depending upon local needs. The first year in one network was characterized by strong emphasis on mentoring new Middle Start teachers, participating in focused professional development for science and technology, and improving teaching of reading and writing. Year two was characterized by creation of leadership teams, reflective practice, support of student-led conferences, and cognitive coaching. Year three was characterized by creation of an integrated curriculum, work on No Child Left Behind and ED Yes! (a Michigan-based school report card) requirements, use of research-based instructional strategies, lesson study, and data-driven decisionmaking.

The second network had only been in existence two years and had a more specific focus. Those schools planned to invest major resources in training school leadership teams to conduct School Self-Assessment (SSA) within their buildings and to serve as reviewers in other schools. The local network coordinator implemented a thorough plan to inform leadership teams about SSA, allowing them to make well-informed decisions about the process. Four schools established a leadership team that held seminars in the first year. These focused on school self-assessment, setting improvement targets, and looking at teacher practice and student work. The leadership teams used the seminars to apply skills and to plan SSA implementation in their schools. In the second year three school teams continued, completing school self-assessments, developing plans for in-school and cross-school learning communities, and establishing three teams that guided their work. Each team had responsibility for one area of focus: use of rubrics as an effective tool for assessment and guiding student learning, looking at student work as a means to improve instruction, and literacy strategies in middle schools (Gill and Gill 2005).

7. The School Improvement Self-Study is a user-friendly research-based data collection system developed and administered by the Center for Prevention Research and Development at the University of Illinois. The Self-Study consists of a set of surveys for middle school students, teachers, and principals. An additional survey is available for parents. These confidential and anonymous surveys ask about middle school classroom practices, integration of instruction and curricula, decisionmaking practices, parent and community involvement, climate and attitudes, professional development needs, educational expectations, school safety, and student well-being. The Self-Study has three objectives: (1) to help schools understand the relationship between the implementation of practices that are part of their school improvement plan and students'

success; (2) to provide schools with specific, reliable data on how the changes and practices targeted in their improvement plan are being implemented at the school, grade, and classroom levels; and (3) to provide schools, local and state agencies, and other policymakers with critical information on the value and impact of bringing the school improvement plan to life (Center for Prevention Research and Development n.d.).

REFERENCES

Academy for Educational Development. 1997. "Preliminary Report on District-University Partnerships in the New York City Middle School Initiative: 1996–1997." New York: Academy for Educational Development.

———. 2000. "New York City Board of Education Middle School Initiative: 1999 Evaluation Report." New York: Academy for Educational Development.

Ames, N. 2004. "Lessons Learned from Comprehensive School Reform Models." In *Reforming Middle Level Education: Considerations for Policymakers*, edited by S. C. Thompson (131–54). Greenwich, CT: Information Age.

Anfara, V. A., Jr. 2001. "Setting the Stage: An Introduction to Middle Level Education." In *The Handbook of Research in Middle Level Education*, edited by V. A. Anfara Jr. (vii–xx). Greenwich, CT: Information Age.

Carnegie Council on Adolescent Development. 1989. "Turning Points: Preparing American Youth for the 21st Century." Report of the Carnegie Task Force on Education of Young Adolescents. New York: Carnegie Corporation of New York.

Center for Comprehensive Reform and Improvement. n.d. "Federal CSR Program Overview." http://www.centerforcsri.org/index.php?option=com_content&task=view&id=29&Itemid=23. (Accessed May 15, 2005.)

Center for Prevention Research and Development. n.d. "School Improvement Self-Study." http://www.cprd.uiuc.edu/self%2Dstudy/ms/index.html. (Accessed January 31, 2006.)

Corbett, H. D., and B. L. Wilson. 2005. "The Evolution of the Michigan Middle Start Partnership." Report. Battle Creek, MI: W. K. Kellogg Foundation.

Corbett, H. D., B. L. Wilson, and C. Haring. 2004. "'Mid-Process' Implementation Variation and Student Benefits in Two Cohorts of Middle Start Comprehensive School Reform Schools." Report. New York: Academy for Educational Development.

Cuban, L. 1990. "Reforming Again, Again, and Again." *Educational Researcher* 19(1): 3–13.

Davis, G. A. 2001. "Point to Point: From *Turning Points* to *Turning Points 2000*." In *The Handbook of Research in Middle Level Education*, edited by V. A. Anfara Jr. (215–40). Greenwich, CT: Information Age Publishing.

Fullan, M. 2002. "Educational Reform as Continuous Improvement." In *The Keys to Effective Schools: Educational Reform as Continuous Improvement*, edited by W. D. Hawley with D. L. Rollie (1–9). Thousand Oaks, CA: Corwin.

Gill, S. J., and N. Gill. 2005. "MMSP Regional Network Evaluation." Final Report. New York: Academy for Educational Development.

Gopalan, P. 2001. "Lake Middle School: A Case Study." Studies of Michigan Middle Start School Improvement. New York: Academy for Educational Development.

Gopalan, P., and P. Jessup. 2001. "Reaching for Goals: Key Areas of Michigan Middle Start Comprehensive School Reform Implementation in 1999–2000." Studies of Middle Start School Improvement. New York: Academy for Educational Development.

Jackson, A. W., and G. A. Davis. 2000. *Turning Points 2000: Educating Adolescents in the 21st Century.* New York: Teachers College Press.

Juvonen, J., V. Le, T. Kaganoff, C. Augustine, and L. Constant. 2004. *Focus on the Wonder Years: Challenges Facing the American Middle School.* Santa Monica: RAND.

Kasak, D. 2004. "What of the Future?" In *Reforming Middle Level Education: Considerations for Policymakers,* edited by S. C. Thompson (231–50). Greenwich, CT: Information Age Publishing.

Lave, J., and E. Wenger. 1991. *Situated Learning: Legitimate Peripheral Participation.* Cambridge: University of Cambridge Press.

Lipsitz, J. 1980. *Growing up Forgotten.* New Brunswick, NJ: Transaction Publishers.

Lipsitz, J., M. H. Mizell, A. W. Jackson, and L. M. Austin. 1997. "Speaking with One Voice: A Manifesto for Middle Grades Reform." *Phi Delta Kappan* 78(7): 533–40.

National Forum to Accelerate Middle Grades Reform. n.d. "Our Vision Statement." http://www.mgforum.org/about/vision.asp. (Accessed May 15, 2005.)

————. n.d. "Schools to Watch Criteria." http://www.mgforum.org/Improvingschools/STW/STWcriteria.asp. (Accessed June 23, 2005.)

National Middle Start Center. n.d. "Middle Start Services." http://www.middlestart.org/services. (Accessed January 31, 2006.)

National Staff Development Council. 2001. "NSDC Standards for Staff Development." http://64.78.6.92/standards/index.cfm. (Accessed January 31, 2006.)

Neufeld, B., and D. Roper. 2003. "Coaching: A Strategy for Developing Instructional Capacity, Promises, and Practicalities." Aspen Urban Superintendents Network Paper. Washington, DC: Aspen Institute Program on Education and Annenberg Institute for School Reform.

New York City Board of Education. 1998. *The New York City Middle School Initiative.* New York: New York City Board of Education.

Newmann, F., B. King, and M. Rigdon. 1997. "Accountability and School Performance: Implications for Restructuring Schools." *Harvard Educational Review* 67(1): 41–69.

Northwest Regional Educational Laboratory. 2006. "The Catalog of School Reform Models." http://www.nwrel.org/scpd/catalog/index.shtml. (Accessed January 31, 2006.)

Tyack, D., and L. Cuban. 1995. *Tinkering toward Utopia: A Century of Public School Reform.* Cambridge, MA: Harvard University Press.

U.S. Department of Education. 2002. "Comprehensive School Reform Program Overview." http://www.ed.gov/programs/compreform/csrdoverview/edlite-index.html. (Accessed January 31, 2006.)

11

COMPREHENSIVE SCHOOL REFORM IN HIGH SCHOOLS

Don E. Dailey, Becky A. Smerdon, and Barbara Means

In the late 1990s, comprehensive school reform (CSR) brought significant attention to the school as a key unit of change in education
reform. Borman and his coauthors (2002, 1) put CSR in the larger
context of educational reform, describing it as a hybrid combining
aspects of top-down standards with bottom-up school change efforts
and decisions by local educators:

> In this case, though, the top-down direction is not in the form of
> distant legislative mandates, but is, in theory, tangible and accessi-
> ble support for school change rooted in research and literally pack-
> aged and delivered to each school.

A defining feature of these efforts is grounding of the reform on
externally developed models focused on the entire school, while implementation of the model is executed by local educators. The emphases

of various approaches to whole-school reform vary greatly (e.g., curriculum as in Success for All; student social and emotional health as in Comer Schools; or adaptive "habits of mind" as espoused by the Coalition of Essential Schools). Despite the many studies on individual reforms, there is no clear research-based consensus on the most effective emphasis for reform initiatives targeting historically underserved students. Moreover, many questions remain about the most effective balance between top-down model specification and latitude for local adaptation.

The landscape for CSR is now expanding from a school-centered strategy designed to strengthen and improve lower-performing schools, to a broader strategy that nestles these reforms in the larger context of system change at the district and state level. In part, this is stimulated by the realization that school change occurs within this larger context, and attempts to improve schools one at a time are potentially impeded by larger system rules, regulations, and reforms that may not fit well with a CSR model. The systemwide changes occurring in public education as a result of No Child Left Behind (NCLB) related to standards, accountability and testing systems, use of scientifically based practices, and support for schools of choice, are increasing attention to system change at the state, district, and school levels; this has possible implications for CSR models being implemented in high schools. Nesting CSR within the larger system provides the basis for a more coherent and sustainable strategy.

In this chapter, we reflect on our experiences evaluating one of the largest privately funded school reform efforts ever attempted in the U.S., and how it fits into the larger world of reform and systems change. First, we describe the essential features of the Bill & Melinda Gates Foundation's high school initiative's first three years. Secondly, we discuss how the initiative fits into the larger reform context and the broader CSR family, drawing out key characteristics that distinguish the initiative from these other reforms. The third section reports emerging evidence of effectiveness and continued challenges being encountered by the schools being developed under this initiative. Finally, the concluding section describes how the Bill & Melinda Gates Foundation itself is changing its education strategy; as a dynamic organization continually revising its strategic thinking and grantmaking, the foundation has embraced the promotion of larger system change to achieve college readiness for all students. In this chapter, we draw most heavily on the foundation's strategies and activities during 2000–2004.

The Foundation's High School Vision

Formally titled the National School District and Network Grants Program, the Bill & Melinda Gates Foundation's education initiative is a highly visible effort to fundamentally reshape America's high schools. The theory of change underlying this initiative begins with the premise that many students—and especially low-income minority students—are poorly served by large, comprehensive high schools. From its beginning, the foundation has believed that the reason fewer than 60 percent of the Hispanic and African American students entering 9th grade earn a high school diploma four years later is the lack of personalization, fragmented focus, and low expectations found in many high schools (Lee et al. 2000). The foundation believes that high school students, particularly underserved students, would enjoy better high school and postsecondary outcomes if they could choose from among high-quality educational alternatives.

Starting with a study of four inner-city elementary schools where students performed above national norms in reading (Weber 1971), a tradition of research studies has articulated school characteristics that correlate with students' achievement: strong principal leadership, a pervasive focus on instruction, an orderly and safe climate, high expectations for students, and continuous assessment of student achievement (Edmonds 1986; Purkey and Smith 1983). Subsequent studies applied a similar lens to high schools, identifying the relative frequency of school practices associated with restructuring, and then measuring the relationship between those features and differences in student achievement (Lee and Smith 1995, 2001). Later studies also gave more attention to the school as a social organization with its own gestalt and expanded the list of effective-school correlates to include constructs such as a rigorous academic program, high-quality staff, and a "bias for action" (Sammons, Hillman, and Mortimore 1995; Wilson and Corcoran 1988).

Drawing on this literature, expert consultation, and their own creative vision, education staff at the Bill & Melinda Gates Foundation developed a conceptual model of high schools that could produce positive outcomes for all students, particularly those in high-need urban areas. In the foundation's vision, effective high schools are characterized by

- a coherent vision and strategy, shared by all stakeholders;
- small size (100 students or fewer per grade);
- powerful teaching and learning, characterized by active inquiry, in-depth learning, and performance-based assessments (see table 11.1); and
- common focus, high expectations, personalization, a climate of respect and responsibility, time for staff to collaborate, performance-based instructional pacing and promotion, and use of technology as a tool.

Table 11.1. The Bill & Melinda Gates Foundation's Seven Attributes of High-Performing Schools

Attribute	Description
Common focus	Staff and students are focused on a few important goals. The school has adopted a consistent research-based instructional approach founded on shared beliefs about teaching and learning. The use of time, tools, materials, and professional development activities are aligned with instruction.
High expectations	Staff members are dedicated to helping students achieve state and local standards; students are engaged in an ambitious and rigorous course of study; and students leave school prepared for success in work, further education, and citizenship.
Personalization	The school is designed to promote sustained student relationships with adults, where every student has an adult advocate and a personal plan for progress. Schools are small: no more than 600 students (less than 400 is strongly recommended).
Respect and responsibility	The environment is authoritative, safe, ethical, and studious. The staff teaches, models, and expects responsible behavior, and relationships are based on mutual respect.
Time for staff collaboration	Staff has time to collaborate and develop skills and plans to meet the needs of all students. Parents are recognized as partners in education. Partnerships are developed with businesses to create work-based opportunities and with institutions of higher education to improve teacher preparation and induction.
Performance-based instruction	Students are promoted to the next instructional level only when they have achieved competency. Students receive additional time and assistance when needed to achieve this competency.
Technology as a tool	Teachers design engaging and imaginative curricula linked to learning standards, analyze results, and have easy access to best practices and learning opportunities. Schools publish their progress to parents and engage the community in dialogue about continuous improvement.

Source: Bill & Melinda Gates Foundation (n.d.).

As the high school initiative was taking shape, foundation staff identified a small set of high schools exemplifying these effective-school attributes and began discussions with the organizations supporting these "model schools," to better understand how to create comparable schools. When the education initiative was launched, a number of these nonprofit organizations received grants to replicate their models. Other

Table 11.2. The Bill & Melinda Gates Foundation's Attributes of Teaching and Learning in High-Performing Schools

Attribute	Description
Active inquiry	Students are engaged in active participation, exploration, and research; activities draw out perceptions and develop understanding; students are encouraged to make decisions about their learning; and teachers utilize students' diverse experiences to build effective learning.
In-depth learning	The focus is competence, not coverage. Students struggle with complex problems, explore core concepts to develop deep understanding, and apply knowledge in real-word contexts.
Performance assessment	Clear expectations define what students should know and be able to do; students produce quality work products and present to real audiences; student work shows evidence of understanding, not just recall; assessment tasks allow students to exhibit higher-order thinking; and teachers and students set learning goals and monitor progress.

Source: Bill & Melinda Gates Foundation (n.d.).

intermediary organizations received grants to create new schools exemplifying the high-performing school attributes or to work with large high schools seeking to convert into smaller units. For the most part, the grantee organizations have viewed their job as supporting the creation of schools with a *structure* conducive to the foundation's seven effective-school attributes.

The foundation thinks about its funding in terms of two different high school reform strategies. Under the "start-up" strategy, nonprofit intermediary organizations receive grants to catalyze the creation of new small schools "from scratch." The alternative, "conversion" strategy, has grantee organizations working with large, comprehensive high schools to divide themselves into smaller autonomous schools, academies, or learning communities, typically sharing the same school building or campus but each having a distinct program and its own set of teachers and students.

From the beginning, the foundation has tried to learn from the experiences of its grantee organizations and the schools they work with to assess the viability and likely impacts of the two approaches, as well as to understand how they can complement each other when they are both executed within a given jurisdiction. Through either strategy, the resulting small schools are expected to exhibit the seven effective-school attributes and to feature classrooms in which teachers use student-centered, performance-oriented pedagogy. In the foundation's theory of change, desired outcomes for students include the demonstration of deep learning, college preparedness, high school graduation, college matriculation, labor market participation, and involved citizenship. The foundation believes that if a sizable number of small schools demonstrate their effectiveness and if innovation is systemically implemented and supported through advocacy efforts, demand for more such schools will increase until education systems start implementing them without direct financial support from private philanthropy.

THE FOUNDATION'S INITIATIVE IN CONTEXT

The larger education policy context for the foundation's initiative has been largely shaped by systemic, standards-based reform (Smith and O'Day 1991). Standards-based reform efforts have employed three critical policy levers: (1) content and performance standards (e.g., the National Science Foundation's Statewide Systemic Initiatives), (2) assessments (the New Standards Project), and (3) accountability systems that hold schools, districts, and states responsible for producing better student achievement (illustrated most prominently by the latest federal education legislation, No Child Left Behind).

Starting in the 1980s, subject-area professional associations (such as the National Council of Teachers of Mathematics) and state and district education agencies have produced specific recommendations or requirements for the content knowledge and skills students should acquire in specific grades and subject areas. In California, for example, 8th graders are expected to know that the velocity of an object will change when the forces on the object are unbalanced. Illinois 9th graders are expected to be able to explain the importance and impact of a country's balance of trade. These recommendations and requirements for teaching specific content and competencies have had a heavy influence on the content of textbooks and testing systems. Standards-based reform is often allied with accountability strategies in which state assessment systems are geared to the specific grade-by-grade content standards the state has adopted for its students.

Although the National School District and Network Grants Program promotes "rigorous" content for all students as one of its desired school characteristics, it does not specify the particular content or skill areas that would qualify as rigorous. Conspicuously missing from the foundation's change strategy is a specific curriculum or pedagogy. The foundation began with an emphasis on inquiry approaches to instruction, but nothing about curriculum. As a result, the organizations receiving foundation grants vary widely on fundamental issues such as basic skills versus constructivist curricula and instruction. In fact, some grantee organizations have a philosophy on curriculum and instruction, while others do not. Schools receiving support through the initiative are also diverse. Some can be characterized as traditionally academic, others as theme based, and still others as extremely student centered, with each student pursuing an individual course of study designed to fit his or her interests and capabilities.

Thus, the foundation's initiative was not based on a particular curriculum or testing system structured around specific content standards as the primary catalyst for improving high schools. Rather, the foundation's reform parallels the logic of the effective-schools education literature (Edmonds 1986; Wilson and Corcoran 1988)—looking for features of schools that appear to have had good success with diverse student bodies, and then encouraging other schools to put those features in place.

FEATURES DISTINGUISHING THE FOUNDATION'S INITIATIVE

There are some fundamental similarities between the foundation's education initiative and the majority of CSR models and other whole-school reform efforts covered in this volume. Like most of the other reforms, the foundation's initiative considers urban schools serving low-income, minority students as its highest priority. Also similar to the other school reform efforts, the foundation's initiative promotes reform of all aspects of a school, rather than focusing on just curriculum, or governance, or a particular teaching method.

On the other hand, a number of important features distinguish the foundation's initiative from most CSR models. Most obviously, the focus on secondary schools sets the initiative apart from most of the early CSR models, with their focus on elementary school. In addition, the foundation's initiative is distinguished by its focus on

- starting new high schools, in addition to converting existing high schools into multiple smaller units;
- emphasizing small size in creating a positive school climate and reaching all students in a personalized environment;
- supporting and implementing diverse school models; and
- primarily funding nonprofit organizations (as opposed to school districts) to create or convert large high schools, either in partnership with local school districts or as independent charters.

Perhaps the biggest difference between the foundation's strategy and that of the other reform efforts described in this volume is the *emphasis on starting new schools*, in addition to trying to change existing institutions. This strategy is a dramatic reaction to the infamous resistance of the education system to fundamental change. The foundation believed that they had to create more good secondary schools that could serve as "existence proofs," demonstrating that students from racial/ethnic minority and economically disadvantaged backgrounds could do rigorous secondary work and go on to successful college experiences. They judged that creating an organization with the right set of values, structures, and processes from scratch would be easier and faster than turning around a dysfunctional organization. Accordingly, much of their early grantmaking provided support for creating new (start-up) schools or a combination of school start-ups and conversions, rather than for working exclusively with existing schools.

A second major distinguishing feature is the foundation's *emphasis on small size* to help create a positive school climate and reach all students. The unusually small size that the foundation has recommended for high schools (100 or fewer students per grade) receives the most attention from external audiences, but the foundation does not regard making schools small as an end in itself. The foundation considers small size a necessary but not sufficient condition for high schools to provide a high-quality education for students who have not been well served by large, comprehensive high schools. Small size is expected to enable a climate where students and teachers know each other well and where teachers have strong ties to each other based on collective responsibility for the same students (e.g., where a math teacher participating in a team responsible for a group of 9th graders works more closely with other teachers on that team than with other math teachers in the same building).

A third distinguishing feature, at least with respect to the other reforms discussed in this volume, is the *absence of a single school model*. The foundation has laid out a set of effective-school attributes at a level of generality comparable to the U.S. Department of Education's CSR components.[1] The foundation believes that different schools can possess these attributes—ranging from those stressing traditional college preparatory academics, to those organized around a vocational or philosophical theme, to those providing completely individualized education based largely on internships and other authentic workplace experiences. Thus, the foundation's initiative is much less specific and prescriptive than many of the CSR models. However, the foundation has begun funding and emphasizing school transformation and development efforts that are much more specific and prescriptive than those they had advocated in the past.

Finally, the Bill & Melinda Gates Foundation has chosen (for the most part) not to make grants to local education agencies, but rather to *fund nonprofit organizations* to create or convert high schools, either in partnership with school districts or as independent charters. Given the politics of urban school districts, the foundation did not believe that districts could be expected to have the sustained will to make fundamental changes in their own secondary schools, and thus turned to outside organizations as the agents of change. The natures of the organizations receiving foundation funding and the scope of their grants have varied widely. For example, among the first 12 grantee organizations charged with creating small high schools outside of Washington state, the number of high schools they proposed to create ranged from 5 to 60. The organizations varied markedly in their histories and missions. Among the original 12, the oldest had been in existence since 1989. Several were created expressly to act as the fiscal agent for a foundation grant. Three were associated with an existing small high school the foundation viewed as a model and funded the organization to replicate. Most had strong connections to national reform networks, and many had close ties to leading educational reformer Ted Sizer and his Coalition of Essential Schools. Three-quarters of the first organizations receiving grants had experience helping start new schools. Two-thirds had prior experience coaching schools on educational improvement, though only one had coached a school conversion process prior to receiving its grant.

ABOUT THE EVALUATION

In March 2001, the Bill & Melinda Gates Foundation contracted with the American Institutes for Research (AIR) and SRI International to evaluate their National School District and Network Grants Program. The evaluation has primarily been focused on exploring and testing the basic assumptions underlying the foundation's initiative, and is designed around three overarching research questions:

- To what extent do the projects funded by the foundation initiative lead to secondary schools and classrooms with desired attributes and to better outcomes?
- What factors influence the success of the foundation-supported schools?
- To what extent have grantees developed mechanisms to scale up and sustain their efforts when foundation support ends?

The findings reported in this chapter primarily relate to the first two questions, drawing on data collected over the past three years. The schools receiving funding and technical support that serve as the basis for targeted change around these two questions come in many shapes and sizes. The evaluation has focused on studying three types of schools that make up this variety: model schools, pre-conversion and conversion schools, and start-ups. These school types are briefly described below.

- **Model schools:** Foundation officials visited these and other innovative schools in 1999 and 2000, gaining inspiration concerning high school restructuring and the seven attributes of effective high schools. The model schools are small (enrollments range from 104 to 335) and most are located in urban districts and enroll historically underserved students.

- **Pre-conversion/conversion schools:** Most of the converting schools are in urban districts. All of them are public schools serving the common secondary grade levels (i.e., 9–12). These are large high schools with enrollments ranging from approximately 900 to more than 2,000 students, and staff ranges from 50 to more than 100 teachers. Most of the schools enroll relatively high proportions of historically underserved (minority and low-income) students, drawing most of their students from the surrounding neighborhood attendance areas. Conversion occurs as the school is broken into smaller units, or "learning communities."

- **Start-up schools:** Looking at start-up schools' characteristics during their first year of operation, we see that, like converting and model schools, a majority in this initiative are in urban settings and serve traditionally underserved students. Like model schools, start-up schools are small—in fact sometimes very small in their initial year (e.g., 30 to 60 students) in part because they often open with only a single grade. Many begin operation serving only 9th or 9th and 10th grades, and then add a grade level each year until they are enrolling students in grades 9–12. The sample of start-up schools in our study includes charters, public magnets, and regular public schools. Most are "schools of choice."[2] Looking at school enrollments in start-up schools' first and second years of operation, it is clear that a number of schools increased their student body size dramatically from their first year to their second. In most cases, this enrollment growth resulted from the planned addition of another grade level. Even so, all of these schools remain small by public school standards (i.e., ranging from 153 to 360 students).

In measuring comparative change across these varying schools, the evaluation design collected data through four basic activities:

- interviews with staff of grantee organizations and any closely affiliated school districts;

- site visits to schools associated with the grantee organizations;
- teacher, student, and principal surveys in schools associated with the grantee organizations; and
- extant data on student body demographics, teaching staff, school attendance, progression rates, and student outcomes.

New schools were surveyed and visited during each of their first three years of operation. The data collected allow us to track change over time in individual schools. Schools undergoing conversion were surveyed in their planning year and again two years later. The data gathered support pre- and post-reform comparisons, as these schools were also visited for three consecutive years (in their planning year, and in the first and second years of implementing the conversion). We also collected survey and site visit data from established schools that served as models for the new schools, to provide benchmark data for the new schools. Additionally, we collected the assignments given in class by teachers, and the work students produced in response to those assignments. To examine student outcomes, we also collected extant data from foundation-supported schools and other schools within their jurisdictions (in four districts). Focusing on surveys and site visits as the primary source of data supporting the evaluation, table 11.4 provides an

Table 11.3. Data Collection Activities by School Type

School type	Data available
Model schools	Districts supplied demographic and student outcome data from 2001–2002, 2002–2003, and 2003–2004.
Pre-conversion/ Conversion schools[a]	Data were drawn from site visits in each of the three funded years. Schools were surveyed in the planning year and again two years later (in the second year of redesign). Teacher assignments and student work were collected during the planning year for one group in 2002–2003 and for another group in 2003–2004. Districts supplied demographic and student outcome data from 2001–2002, 2002–2003, and 2003–2004.
Start-up schools[b]	Data were gathered from surveys and site visits in each of the school's first three years, beginning in 2001–2002. Teacher assignments and student work were collected in 2003–2004 and 2004–2005. Districts supplied demographic and student outcome data from 2001–2002, 2002–2003, and 2003–2004.

[a] Rolling sample of schools (i.e., new schools are added each year, and each stays in the sample for three years), beginning with those that began to receive foundation funding in 2001–2002 (typically their planning year).
[b] Rolling sample of schools.

Table 11.4. Number of Surveys and Site Visits

Year	Student surveys (N = students)	Teacher surveys (N = teachers)	Principal surveys (N = principals)	Demographic surveys (N = schools)	Site visits (N = schools)
2001–2002	8,863	742	26	21	8
2002–2003	3,778	316	23	24	14
2003–2004	14,016	1,138	67	71	21

overview of the number of surveys and site visits conducted over the first three years of the evaluation.

In analyzing survey data we developed a school attribute index that was especially useful. The index measured the extent to which foundation-supported small high schools exhibited the targeted school attributes and improvement in these attributes over time. To provide context for interpreting the attribute index values for these small schools, we added data for model and pre-conversion high schools to the dataset and used hierarchical linear values by school type, taking into account differences in the characteristics of enrolled students and teacher backgrounds. Qualitative data were used to illustrate the strength of start-up schools on each dimension.

Comparison of school demographic and non-assessment-based outcomes relied on school-level data. Comparison of assessment information was done at the student level. Since the small number of high schools serving each district's students limited the statistical power of comparison, we relied primarily on the substantive difference in values across school types, rather than statistical significance in school-level analyses. Conversely, the large number of students in the achievement analyses made statistical significance relatively easy to achieve, so we focused on the magnitude of differences rather than statistical significance at the student level as well.

EVALUATION FINDINGS

Small Schools

We find a positive school climate can be put in place quickly in a new, small school. When compared with large high schools, small start-up schools are able to create an environment characterized by greater levels of personalization, common focus and high expectations, and teacher collaboration (AIR/SRI 2003; 2004). Staff and student comments suggest that small size fosters this positive climate.

In start-up schools, measures of implementation of the foundation's effective-school attributes are generally above those of the large schools in our evaluation, and the schools have many of the qualities found in more mature model schools. While conversions are seeing slower progress as they work to change existing structures, cultures, and beliefs, they too are showing gains over their pre-conversion state, most notably in the personalization of school culture—students feel known by their teachers and supported by them both academically and personally.

After three years, however, many of the small high schools are far from stable. In students' and teachers' reports concerning school climate, the second year typically sees some slippage from the highly positive views held in the first year. This "sophomore slump" appears to be related to rapid growth, as start-up schools grow by an average of 50 percent in their second year of operation. By their third year, start-up schools typically achieve more stability, though growing pains and change are still occurring (AIR/SRI 2005a). For the small learning communities created through school conversions, some of the initial logistical issues are likely to be resolved and some general progress is evident, but many staff are still grappling with the difficult challenges of raising expectations for all students, or developing truly collaborative teacher communities. Most of our respondents agree that reform is an exciting process that is already transforming students' lives, but there are many challenges and the burdens placed on teachers are quite large (AIR/SRI 2005a).

Smallness also creates instructional difficulties in trying to ensure that all students get appropriate exposure to the full range of content needed for college and that they get taught by highly qualified teachers. This challenge is especially problematic for math and science. A related issue is the small school's heightened vulnerability to staff turnover. Especially when a staff member leaves in the middle of an academic year, students feel a personal loss because of the close relationships they have with their teachers. Further, there often is no other teacher qualified to teach in the departed teacher's field; the result can be a desperation hire or a principal offering stopgap instruction. Leadership turnover is also especially damaging to small schools as they are launching during the first years. When staff are trying to do something new and challenging, they greatly depend on a strong leader to give them direction and encouragement. Finally, operating within a funding system based on average daily attendance puts small schools at a disadvantage due to much smaller enrollments (and hence much smaller budgets) at these schools.

Teaching and Learning

Despite the foundation's lack of prescription with respect to curriculum and instructional techniques, its schoolwide structures and principles appear to, indeed, support a different kind of teaching and learning in the classroom. Our findings indicate that teaching and learning tend to lag behind structural change in these schools—both for start-ups and for conversion efforts. Initially, the nuts and bolts of designing and putting the small school structures in place tend to take precedence over curriculum and teaching. It takes time to develop a curriculum and to have new teaching approaches widely adopted by a school's staff. Nevertheless, teachers' reports suggest that there is more student-centered instruction in start-up schools than in large high schools, and that when large high schools convert into smaller learning communities, student-centered instruction becomes more prevalent.

When survey responses from teachers in small start-up and large high schools are compared, the former reported more frequent use of student-centered instructional approaches while the latter reported more use of teacher-directed instruction. The model schools' teachers reported more student-centered practices than either of these two groups.

Teachers at schools that have converted into smaller learning communities report doing both more student-centered instruction and more teacher-directed instruction than before conversion two years earlier. Teachers described ways in which smaller classes, professional development, and closer relationships with students enable them to do more teaching (AIR/SRI 2005b).

That small start-up schools created under this initiative are doing more inquiry-oriented instruction than large schools on average may be a function of the types of leaders, teachers, and families these schools attract. It is harder to form such alternative explanations for the greater emphasis on student-centered, inquiry-oriented instruction after learning communities are created through conversion of large, comprehensive high schools.

A particularly exciting aspect of our evaluation is the collection of teacher assignments and student work. Using independent judgments of the quality of teacher assignments (teacher ratings of rigor and relevance), we are able to corroborate the conclusion that teaching is more reform-oriented in small high schools.[3] We found that in start-up schools, teachers' language arts and mathematics assignments are more likely to have relevance, in terms of real-world connections and student choice, than those given in large high schools. English/language arts assignments in small start-up schools are also more rigorous than the assignments teachers give in large high schools. Mathematics assignments in start-up schools also tend to be more rigorous than those in large schools, but this difference was not statistically significant (AIR/SRI 2005b).

Despite these positive findings, we also have indications that reform-oriented student-centered instruction may be difficult to maintain over time, especially when teachers are inexperienced in these methods and students have basic skills deficiencies or behavioral issues. Both quantitative and qualitative data suggest that start-up schools find it hard to continue reform-like instruction as new teachers and students enter the school, bringing greater variability among teachers and students. We see a small decline in the use of student-centered instruction among second-year start-ups, echoing the decline in implementation of the foundation's effective-school features described above. Furthermore, we have found wide variation among start-up schools in the rigor and relevance of the assignments they give—especially in mathematics. This suggests that while progress is occurring, challenges are evident in maintaining this progress for all teachers and students in all schools. These challenges undermine the foundation's goal of having all students graduate well prepared for college.

There are indications that many foundation-supported small schools are struggling with curriculum and instruction, particularly in the areas of math and science. In some cases the school model or principles promoted by the grantee organization and district and state standards for math and science do not appear to match. Some schools have stressed relevance and student engagement with less attention to curriculum coverage and rigor. The early data suggest that small schools engage students to a greater extent than do large high schools, but many are concerned about how well they prepare students for future academic work.

Indicators of Success

In terms of traditional education indicator variables, analyses in five districts where the Bill & Melinda Gates Foundation has made a significant investment suggest some promising patterns in achievement data. In three districts, we found some evidence to suggest that students in foundation-supported schools may be narrowing the achievement gap between minority and majority students that existed prior to the foundation initiative (AIR/SRI 2005c). In most of these districts, the small high schools appear to have better attendance and disciplinary records than other schools when the entering characteristics of their students are taken into account. However, our achievement results are preliminary due to the timing of the interventions and delay that comes in the release of extant data.

COLLEGE READINESS AND THE THREE R'S

Building on these findings and on growing insight into the nature of the education system, the Bill & Melinda Gates Foundation is embarking on a new strategy for helping all students graduate from high school well prepared for college. The foundation is moving toward explaining its high school vision in terms of what it calls "the new three R's"—rigor, relevance, and relationships.

Calling for coherent, academically rigorous, standards-based curricula, the foundation is looking to reformers to create curricula that combine rigor with a strong connection to students' lives and aspirations. The foundation is calling for high schools that focus on student success and provide organizational structures that support multiyear relationships between faculty and students. These changes are in the same spirit as the effective school attributes displayed earlier, but they are presented in a new light. Increasingly, foundation staff emphasize that these school qualities must be aimed at increasing students' graduation rates, college readiness, and college attendance.

National data indicate that only one-third of U.S. students graduate from high school with the skill levels and academic preparation needed for college (National Commission 2001). While some students do college-preparatory work in high school, others languish in remedial courses. Fully two-thirds of students, many of them low-income and minority students, either drop out or are tracked into courses that leave them critically unprepared. The foundation had committed to changing these dismal numbers within the next decade. But coupled with the foundation's appreciation of the slow progress and continuing struggles of the first high schools created under its original education strategy, this commitment to significant large-scale change in outcomes has been rethought. Even in a city where the foundation is making a large investment and helping catalyze the creation of more than 100 small schools, only a small fraction of students will be served. The foundation wants to see a high proportion of students who enter 9th grade in urban districts attain their high school diplomas, and that means changing not just one school at a time but the education system itself. Accordingly, the foundation has turned its attention to the larger policy context surrounding schools and to the state and district demands and supports that can help schools implement the three R's and achieve college readiness for all of their students.

WHOLE-SYSTEM CHANGE

Tyack and Cuban (1995) contend that education reform initiatives over the past century have primarily attempted to "tinker toward utopia," focusing on relatively small changes in the system, schools, and classrooms. They argue that few efforts at reform produce lasting change because these small targets quickly get absorbed or smothered by the larger system. Cuban (1993) expounds on how the deeply ingrained assumptions about schooling, and long-standing structures, routines, and processes around which schools are organized and operate are powerful stalwarts of stability and resistance to change. He further elaborates how federal, state, and district policies and activity reinforce these structures at the school level. Working from this premise, attempts to change a small part of a school will eventually be discarded and old patterns will reemerge. Attempts to restructure whole schools, or even to create new schools, will also face challenges stemming from policies and pressures from the larger system that promote conventional values and structures.

The foundation's evaluation has found a number of instances in which district and state policies have constrained grantee organizations' efforts to create and sustain new ways of schooling. Higher education institutions' requirements for traditional transcripts based on seat time and grades in conventional courses can stymie schools offering interdisciplinary courses with strong internship components. District hiring and layoff policies based on seniority can mean constant staff turnover for new schools with untenured teachers, and forced hiring of teachers who neither understand nor agree with the school's instructional approach. In other cases, the foundation has seen opportunities for states and districts to serve as powerful organizing resources for supporting high school reform. Clearly, the foundation appreciates more than ever that schools exist within larger state and district systems that affect the conditions under which schooling and teaching unfold.

Another important dimension is the potential impact sweeping federal and state policies may have on the context in which school-based reform occurs. NCLB calls for changes in state standards, accountability, and assessment systems, and how instruction will occur through scientifically-based practices. There is also more attention to raising test scores for students with disabilities and other special needs. This mandate may support or constrain implementation of CSR models, depending on the alignment that exists with their own unique purposes, goals, organizing structures, curricula, and methods of instruction.

The foundation has decided to address these issues of district and state contexts for new models of secondary education head-on. The foundation is developing a multilayered vision of the policy changes, resources, and actions needed to ensure that all students attain the knowledge and skills needed to be ready for college. Districts and states are integral parts of this vision of whole-system change, with college readiness for all students functioning as the rallying point for their efforts.

State and District Policy Platform

The foundation seeks to support this vision for schools by promoting state and district polices and practices that will strengthen the capacity of secondary schools to help all students achieve college-ready standards. At both the state and district levels, the foundation has identified a set of policies they believe will provide the conditions necessary to elevate college-ready graduation rates for all students. This includes policies and structures that consistently articulate high demands to achieve college-ready standards for all students, and a variety of supports designed to strengthen school capacity to achieve these standards. The foundation is working with experts in the field, and with state and district leaders to articulate the essentials of a policy system that will support high-performing schools. While the major themes for state and district policy are still evolving, some include the following.

- *College-ready standards.* This concept links to standards-based reform, which promoted the goal of all students achieving world-class standards. This goal has not been achieved, and the standards enacted in most states fall short of world-class or college-ready standards. The foundation has challenged states to require their schools to set the same standards for high school graduation that are used for admission to the states' four-year universities. Essential to this strategy is the commitment of state and district education systems to develop a shared mission and focus around helping all students achieve these standards. Additionally, a key part of college readiness is promoting students' awareness of what is required to reach the goal of college attendance.
- *Accountability and support systems.* Using college-ready standards as the core goal of the secondary education system, a strong accountability system is needed to provide incentives and supports to help high schools achieve these standards. State and local policy-makers are expected to create an integrated, coordinated system that rewards schools, staff, and students who reach expectations, and to provide resources and supports for those failing to meet standards. The accountability system should be primarily focused on student outcomes, and make effective use of data to support decisions about schools.
- *Assessments.* Assessments play a key role in articulating standards to schools and teachers, and in validly capturing the degree to which students are achieving standards. Consistent with the foundation's objectives, therefore, it is especially important that state and district assessments be aligned with college-ready standards. Furthermore, the foundation embraces the notion of using varying

types of assessments that will capture more aspects of student performance and be appropriate for students coming from diverse backgrounds.

- *Diverse school options and choice.* The Gates Foundation promotes the notion that districts should create a range of quality school options for all students, and should ensure equitable access to all of these options through some system of public school choice. They believe all students, not just the affluent, should have the opportunity to attend an excellent high school suited to their interests and preferred approach to learning. Districts are encouraged to create a portfolio of schools designed to meet varying student needs and preferences. This will involve states and districts removing barriers to the creation of new schools. Examples include charter school–friendly legislation and regulations. This also involves public oversight and support systems designed to ensure that access and equity are achieved and protected.

- *Finance.* The foundation believes that the financial systems supporting schools must be redesigned to increase equity and better support student learning. In addition, funding should be efficiently allocated and utilized to meet standards, following students to the schools they choose to attend. To the degree possible, schools should be granted autonomy and flexibility in how they use resources and make critical decisions about curriculum, teaching, and professional development. School budgets should reflect real costs, rather than average teacher salaries.[4] Clearly, funding should be linked to the costs of meeting college-ready standards, and financial incentives developed for rewarding improved performance.

- *System of supports.* Embedded throughout many of these policy levers is the concept of supports—that is, a healthy system of assistance designed to strengthen the capacity of schools to help all students attain college-ready standards. In addition to the articulated standards, assessments, and financial supports described above, the support system should include technical assistance, various forms of professional development, and policies designed to bolster the supply of well-qualified educators as well as policies supporting greater autonomy and creativity at the school level.

- *Community engagement.* The foundation is developing plans to engage communities around these issues, to build demand for college-ready standards and other components of its policy platform. In the foundation's view, the community includes parents, students, and teachers, as well as leaders from businesses, civic organizations, and institutions of higher education. The foundation realizes that its leadership alone won't be sufficient to mobilize the needed changes. State and local system leaders will need to make a compelling case for change and consistently and frequently articulate the the education system's goals.

Having described the foundation's aspirations for state and district change, we must now return to the issue of how schools fit into these policy themes. States and districts depend on schools and teachers to implement college-ready standards, and often the curriculum intended by the state or district and the curriculum enacted by the school is different (Porter 1994). By folding the school into this picture, we can start to suggest an initial conceptual framework for understanding and studying the evolution of the foundation initiative.

This model essentially builds around four critical levels of the system: states, districts, grantees, and schools and classrooms. These different levels operate as part of an interdependent system. First, states are enacting policies and developing structures that place both consistent demands and supports on districts and schools to achieve college-ready standards. Districts interpret state policy, and align with state policy in the ways that make most sense to their unique circumstances and needs. They also enact their own policies to create a portfolio of diverse, high-performing high schools. Community engagement becomes especially critical at the local level, both as a way to build support for college-ready standards and as an additional source of demand on schools. The intermediary organizations receiving grants from the foundation play a critical role in placing demands on the district, engaging the community, and both managing and supporting their network of schools.

Finally, these policy demands are interpreted, implemented, and manifested in the school through the three R's. Drawing on the portfolio concept, schools will not just function as empty vessels designed purely to adopt state and district standards, but will be lively, highly creative organizations that actively engage with college-ready standards and think about ways to meet them. Some schools will experiment, practice, and develop innovative, student-centered approaches that work effectively for their students. Others may have a highly structured whole-school model or teacher-directed instructional approach through which college-ready standards will be attained; while their instruction may be traditional, however, they will engage students through strong student-teacher relationships, just as schools with more innovative approaches do. Though the foundation envisions that the three R's will be necessary to achieve these standards, they can be implemented through a wide diversity of approaches.

While at first glance this may appear to be a top-down model, note how each level of the system plays varying roles as part of an interdependent system of demands, supports, and practice. States and districts depend on schools to implement standards and embrace the goal of readying all students for college. This will occur through incentives, supports, and some degree of negotiation. Systems also need schools to function as highly dynamic and innovative organizations characterized by strong capability and motivation to reach all students. This will not likely happen on its own in all schools. Many schools currently lacking the capacity and motivation to attain college readiness for all of their students will benefit from strong relationships with external organizations that can provide assistance. They will also be strengthened by operating in a state with clearly defined expectations and a groundswell of public support. On the other hand, systems should not be so inflexible that schools with strong, innovative models are unable to implement them.

What we are describing is a highly interdependent system, and one that brings together a number of streams of reform: a standards-based approach centered on college readiness for all students, a market-based reform focused on encouraging diversity and creativity, and a school-based reform strengthening the rigor, relevance, and relationships that make up the life of a school.

CONCLUSION

Comprehensive school reform as initially launched focused attention on restructuring and improving schools, with special attention to the whole school. CSR models emerging since this initial period have continued to share this focus on the whole school, though varying models have emerged with distinguishing characteristics. The Bill & Melinda Gates Foundation's work in this field has been distinguished by its openness to supporting a variety of school models and nonprofit organizations as school developers and intermediary organizations. This approach has always encouraged the creation of schools that represent diverse educational options for students and parents, though developing small high schools with more personalized learning environments has been a common theme in most cases. For example, over time, the foundation has increasingly focused attention on working harder to help grantees develop good business plans and reorganization plans to support systemic change.

The AIR-SRI evaluation has documented that foundation-supported schools are able to quickly create a positive school climate, and they are more likely to assume the key attributes desired of effective schools. Though the foundation has not emphasized a particular instructional model, we find teachers in foundation-supported schools more likely to engage in reform-like, student-centered instructional practices. The foundation has also provided growing attention to larger issues related to grantees supporting systemic change.

Building on its growing experience and knowledge, the foundation is focusing its attention on achieving the three R's in all its schools, and eventually in all schools across the nation. This vision is manifested in its goal to help students be prepared for college, work, and citizenship. College readiness is a critical root around which the three R's will be nourished and grow.

To achieve this vision, the foundation is developing a larger policy platform designed to facilitate the growth of model states and districts that can effectively build and support a system of high-performing high schools embodying the three R's. This resonates with recent attention in the field to the role of districts and larger systems in bringing about needed change. The foundation and the field in general appear to be moving beyond merely whole-*school* change to whole-*system* change.

In particular, as this vision unfolds over the coming years, we would expect to learn more about the extent to which the foundation and other CSR models help build

- schools, districts, and states that better prepare students for college, with an emphasis on student outcomes for historically under-served populations;
- systems of support, at the district and state levels, for more high-performing schools;
- factors at the school, district, and state levels associated with the creation and maintenance of more high-performing schools;
- a seamless, integrated, coherent whole system where state, district, and school goals and strategies intersect; and
- teaching and learning environments with the capacity to impact student outcomes related to college readiness.

The education field is rediscovering that schools, districts, and states do not function as isolated, highly bounded entities, but as part of an interdependent system being energized with new ideas for whole-system change that are tied to achieving college readiness for all students.

NOTES

1. See chapter 4 for a discussion of the 11 federally mandated CSR components.

2. That is, schools that parents and students have chosen to attend.

3. *Rigor* refers to the extent to which an assignment asks students to move beyond reproduction of information to the construction of knowledge, demon-

strate conceptual understanding of important content, and communicate clearly and well. *Relevance* refers to the extent to which an assignment asks students to take on plausible writing roles and submit their work to real audiences, address questions or problems with real-world applications, and make choices about what they will study and how they will learn. For more information, see AIR/SRI (2005b).

4. The use of average teacher salaries across the district in school budgets contributes to inequality because the schools serving the neediest students typically have the least experienced teachers (with salaries below the district average) while those serving the most affluent students tend to have the most senior teachers (with salaries above the district average). The use of district averages in school budgets masks differences in the real costs of running schools with teachers of varying qualifications and seniority levels.

REFERENCES

AIR/SRI. See American Institutes for Research and SRI International.

American Institutes for Research and SRI International. 2003. "High Time for High School Reform: Early Findings from the Evaluation of the National School District and Network Grants Program." Report to the Bill & Melinda Gates Foundation. Washington, DC: American Institutes for Research.

———. 2004. "The National School District and Network Grants Program: Year 2 Evaluation Report." Report to the Bill & Melinda Gates Foundation. Washington, DC: American Institutes for Research.

———. 2005a. "Creating Cultures for Learning: Supportive Relationships in Small High Schools." Report to the Bill & Melinda Gates Foundation. Washington, DC: American Institutes for Research.

———. 2005b. "Rigor and Relevance in Small High Schools." Report to the Bill & Melinda Gates Foundation. Washington, DC: American Institutes for Research.

———. 2005c. "Getting to Results: Early Student Outcomes in Reforming High Schools." Report to the Bill & Melinda Gates Foundation. Washington, DC: American Institutes for Research.

Bill & Melinda Gates Foundation. n.d. "Helping All Students Achieve." Pamphlet. Seattle: Bill & Melinda Gates Foundation.

Borman, G. D., G. M. Hewes, L. T. Overman, and S. Brown. 2002. "Comprehensive School Reform and Student Achievement: A Meta-Analysis." Technical Report No. 59. Baltimore: Center for Research on the Education of Students Placed at Risk, Johns Hopkins University.

Cuban, L. 1993. *How Teachers Taught: Constancy and Change in American Classrooms, 1890–1990*. New York: Teachers College Press.

Edmonds, R. 1986. "Characteristics of Effective Schools." In *The School Achievement of Minority Children*, edited by E. Neisser (93–104). Hillsdale, NJ: Erlbaum.

Lee, V. E., and J. B. Smith. 1995. "Effects of High School Restructuring and Size on Early Gains in Achievement and Engagement." *Sociology of Education* 68(4): 241–70.

———. 2001. *Restructuring High Schools for Equity and Excellence: What Works*. New York: Teachers College Press.

Lee, V. E., B. A. Smerdon, C. Alfeld-Liro, and S. L. Brown. 2000. "Inside Large and Small High Schools: Curriculum and Social Relations." *Educational Evaluation and Policy Analysis* 22(2): 147–71.

National Commission on the High School. 2001. *The Lost Opportunity of the Senior Year: Finding a Better Way.* Washington, DC: U.S. Department of Education.

Porter, A. 1994. "National Standards and School Improvement in the 1990s: Issues and Promise." *American Journal of Education* 102(4): 421–49.

Purkey, S., and M. Smith. 1983. "Effective Schools: A Review." *Elementary School Journal* 83(4): 427–52.

Sammons, P., J. Hillman, and P. Mortimore. 1995. "Key Characteristics of Effective Schools: A Review of School Effectiveness Research." Report to the Office for Standards in Education. London: University Institute of Education.

Smith, M. S., and J. A. O'Day. 1991. "Systemic School Reform." In *The Politics of Curriculum and Testing: The 1990 Yearbook of the Politics of Education Association*, edited by S. H. Fuhrman and B. Malen (233–67). New York: Falmer.

Tyack, D., and L. Cuban. 1995. *Tinkering toward Utopia: A Century of Public School Reform.* Cambridge, MA: Harvard University Press.

Weber, G. 1971. "Inner-City Children Can Be Taught to Read: Four Successful Schools." Monograph. Washington, DC: Council for Basic Education.

Wilson, B. L., and T. B. Corcoran. 1988. *Successful Secondary Schools: Visions of Excellence in American Public Education.* New York: Falmer.

12

COMPREHENSIVE SCHOOL REFORM MODELS VS. INSTRUCTIONAL PRACTICES

*Bridget A. Cotner, Ted Boydston,
Kathryn M. Borman, and
Suzannah Herrmann*

The process of implementing comprehensive school reform (CSR) at the school level can be understood by taking into account both the perceptions of school-level stakeholders and their classroom instructional practices. The qualitative, comparative case study described here (Borman et al. 2006) examines how CSR implementation—in particular the instructional practices component of CSR—is understood and enacted by school stakeholders. We investigated teachers' and school leaders' understanding of CSR components and how this understanding influenced the process of implementation.

We also examined the interrelationship between CSR understanding and classroom instructional practices. First, we determined school stakeholders' perceptions of the comprehensiveness and schoolwide use of the CSR model in question. *Comprehensiveness* reflects stakeholders' perceptions of the multiple components constituting each CSR model. *Schoolwide use* refers to school stakeholders' realization that their CSR model reform extends to all grade levels and classrooms in the school. Next, we uncovered school-level factors including the perceived quality of the principal's instructional leadership, technical assistance provided by the model developer, and related indicators of support at the district and school level identified by stakeholders as influencing CSR model implementation. Finally, we examined observers' accounts of classroom instructional strategies in line with best practices indices, to determine how these are related to teachers' understanding of CSR.

Guiding research questions include the following:

- How does stakeholders' understanding of model comprehensiveness and schoolwide use relate to teachers' observed instructional practice?
- What factors do stakeholders report as influencing their understanding of model components?
- What factors do stakeholders report as influencing their instructional strategies?

To answer these questions, qualitative data were collected during semistructured, in-depth interviews with school administrators and teachers in 24 schools that had adopted CSR models. In addition, classroom observations were undertaken in a subset of classrooms in these schools. We organized and analyzed interview data using a rubric that rated data from each interview along two constructs—comprehensiveness of model component understanding and schoolwide use of components. To analyze classroom observational data, we constructed a measure that indicated quality of instruction in line with the principles of authentic instruction (Newmann and Associates 1996) and standards-based practices, reasoning that all models are designed to incorporate such approaches to instruction. Our intent was to employ an omnibus measure of instructional quality that would tap the research-based nature of observed classroom instruction and not favor the components of one model over another.

After a brief review of related literature, we first discuss school stakeholders' perceptions of CSR in relation to comprehensiveness and schoolwide use. Then, two qualitative school cases are presented to illustrate how stakeholders negotiate school factors and how their actions and activities influence implementation of the model. We conclude by showing the patterns of interrelationships among comprehensiveness, schoolwide use, and classroom instructional practices.

A REVIEW OF THE LITERATURE

After successfully adopting a CSR model, school stakeholders must undertake the next phase of the CSR life cycle: implementing change. To implement change through school reform, we argue that accounting for school, model, and district factors that support or hinder reform processes is essential. Research studies investigating the implementation process suggest that implementation varies not only within but also across schools (Desimone 2000), in large part because of variations in school culture as well as other contextual influences. Guided by theory related to the "street-level bureaucrat," we argue that school stakeholders respond to unique factors in school contexts that affect their understanding of CSR and ultimately, their decisions to use model practices.

The role of the street-level bureaucrat is critical in the process of implementing services in general and reforms in particular. Understanding the actions and perspectives of street-level bureaucrats can assist in analyzing the variance, noted above, in CSR implementation. Michael Lipsky (1980) was among the first to use the term *street-level bureaucrat* to refer to individuals employed by large, multilayered organizations to render public services. The theoretical framework of Lipsky and others emphasizes roles taken by individuals working in public organizations as they make policy decisions, taking into account constraining conditions and other limiting factors inherent in the organization. Lipsky (1980, xii) argued that "decisions of street-level bureaucrats, the routines they establish, and the devices they invent to cope with uncertainties and work pressures effectively *become* the public policies they carry out." This is a useful characterization of how teachers and principals engage in CSR implementation, because individuals interpret the meaning of specific aspects of the reform as it is implemented. In addition, teachers and principals are caught up in an organizational environment that may either support or undermine reform.

The conceptual framework guiding this study depicts the organizational contexts of the school, model design, and district influences on school stakeholders' (principals and teachers) understanding of CSR and ultimately, their decisions to use model practices (see figure 12.1).

Figure 12.1. Factors Influencing Understanding of Comprehensive School Reform and Classroom Instruction

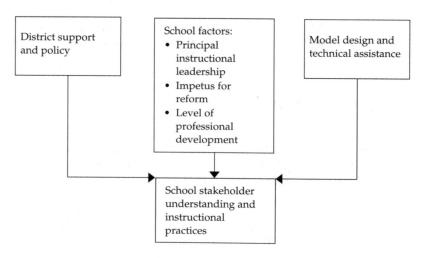

Our qualitative study builds on street-level bureaucrat theory by investigating school stakeholders' understanding of CSR and the influence of contextual factors on the stakeholders' understanding and decisions to implement CSR.

FACTORS THAT INFLUENCE UNDERSTANDING AND IMPLEMENTATION OF CSR INSTRUCTIONAL STRATEGIES

Research on the social organization of the school has identified numerous factors that are critically important in either impeding or supporting educational change, including implementation of instructional change as implied by CSR. These factors, associated with the school, the model, and the district, may either undermine or support key actors' activities in conducting reform. School factors include faculty commitment/buy-in and school leadership activities. Model factors encompass the type of support offered by the developer as well as the model's design features, including efficacy and perceived "goodness of fit" between the school's needs and programs and the characteristics of the reform (Berends, Chun, et al. 2002). District factors include policies and programs that are mandated and may conflict with CSR implementation efforts. These three sets of factors—school, model, and district—are discussed below.

School Factors

Faculty Commitment/Buy-In

Teachers' understanding of curricular reform centers on their own ideologies and experiences in the classroom (Datnow, Borman, and Stringfield 2000). In other words, teachers interpret a reform on the basis of their pedagogical beliefs and adapt the reform accordingly. Therefore, variation in implementation is inevitable as teachers (like street-level bureaucrats anywhere) adjust policies and programs to match their views. The process of reforming classroom instruction is facilitated by teachers' understanding and accepting the changes they are being asked to make (Hawkins, Stancavage, and Dossey 1998). Supovitz and Turner (2000, 974) found that "teachers with more sympathetic attitudes toward reform used inquiry-based practices significantly more frequently and had more investigative classroom cultures than did more skeptical teachers." To lessen the teachers' skepticism about a reform program that aims to change their practices, teachers need to be reassured that the reform can be implemented in their classrooms. Cohen and Ball (1999, 1) explain,

> When school improvement interventions introduce new curricular materials or provide teacher "training," they rarely create adequate conditions for teachers to learn about or develop the knowledge, skills, and beliefs needed to enact these interventions successfully in the classroom.

Without support for understanding a new program and the skills needed to implement it, teachers are left to their own devices when putting instructional reforms aimed at improving teaching and learning in place. Moreover, teachers adapt policies and curricular reform to meet what they perceive as student needs (Datnow et al. 2000). When teachers do not believe that the changes required in their instruction are necessary for improving student outcomes, resistance to implementation results (Desimone 2000). Therefore, teacher buy-in to the need for reform as well as to the suggested practices is essential for successful implementation.

School Leadership

Consistency of implementation across classrooms is an important consideration in implementing CSR designs. Teachers play a crucial role in implementing reform, and it is critical that both the school principal and teacher leaders emphasize collaboration, communication, and responsibility among teachers in achieving coherent model implementation (Supovitz and Poglinco 2001).

Teacher leadership is the process by which teachers influence their colleagues, administrators, and other members of the school community in improving teaching and learning to enhance student achievement (York-Barr and Duke 2004). The school principal also plays an essential role during the CSR implementation by providing teachers with opportunities to select a CSR model and by monitoring its implementation. CSR may require new or expanded leadership activities. Researchers have described such an expansion among street-level bureaucrats or school stakeholders as *distributed leadership* (Camburn, Rowan, and Taylor 2003; Spillane 2005; Spillane, Halverson, and Diamond 2004; Supovitz and Poglinco 2001). Spillane (2005) describes distributed leadership as the interactions among leaders and followers that create reciprocal interdependency.

Leadership practices can be stretched over leaders through time; be coordinated among leaders; be seen as situational; and be dependent on relationships that can enable, constrain, or transform. Research has indicated that increasing teachers' roles in leadership activities is an important aspect of successful school reform (Camburn et al. 2003). During implementation, teacher leaders primarily influence their colleagues through developing and sustaining collaborative relationships; thus, all the teachers can focus on improving student achievement. Wider distribution of leadership activities also can build collaborative relationships that in turn change teachers' instructional practices and beliefs.

Model Factors

Developer Support

Previous research underscores the importance of the developer's support during the implementation process. This support is especially important in providing ongoing professional development for teachers. Desimone (2000, 20) states that "a critical source of support for implementation of CSR models is the presence of developers or design teams working within the school with teachers as they implement reforms in the classroom."

Although developers support school stakeholders in a number of ways, such as providing information and monitoring implementation, the primary support activity is providing professional development.

Desimone (2000, 22) states that professional development is a "critical component of restructuring efforts." Other researchers have also found links between successful implementation and professional development. For example, Berends, Chun, and their coauthors (2002, 15) find that levels of implementation were higher in schools that received design team support through whole-school training, the involvement of facilitators, and extensive professional development than in schools that did not receive such support. Professional development opportunities provided by the developer enable teachers to renew their knowledge and understanding of a model's reform strategies. In addition, professional development can assist implementation by addressing resistance among teachers through informational and training sessions (Haynes 1998).

Model Design Alignment

As the street-level bureaucrats of educational reform, teachers must be able to negotiate the demands placed on them. According to Berends, Chun, and colleagues (2002, 12), "[Teachers'] ability to cope with these demands and their commitment to changes are crucial to coherent and sustained implementation." Policies and reform programs aligned in their goals and activities facilitate teachers' managing the pressures of multiple demands. Because schools in high-poverty areas are the focus of Title I and Comprehensive School Reform Demonstration funds, these schools are more likely to have fragmented and conflicting environments (Berends, Chun, et al. 2002, 135). The degree to which the model fits or aligns with a school's goals, pedagogical philosophy, and other school programs is termed *model appropriateness*. How appropriate a model is for a particular school depends on the perspective of the school's stakeholders and their ability to see links between various school programs.

District Factors

Honig and Hatch (2004) argue that achieving policy coherence at the district level and across district schools is a goal often cited but seldom achieved. When the goal is not achieved, a gap is created between policy and practice. Addressing this gap requires that coherence be reconceptualized as a dynamic process, rather than the simple alignment of external requirements. Honig and Hatch (2004, 18) see policy coherence "as a continual process of negotiating the relationship between schools' internal circumstances and their external demands that involves both schools and organizations external to schools."

Activities that schools use to build coherence include (1) setting school-wide goals and strategies that allow them to cast new demands into tried-and-true forms of handling them, then (2) using schoolwide goals and strategies to decide whether to align with the new policies or buffer themselves from the associated external demands. These bridging and buffering activities include "pulling the environment in" by placing district personnel within schools to support change; "shaping the terms of compliance" by placing school personnel on district-level committees; "adding peripheral structures," such as school-level facilitators; "symbolically adopting external demands" by using the vocabulary of reform but not the activities; and "suspending ties" by not participating or ignoring feedback. School district central offices can enable or restrain these school-level processes in a variety of ways, ranging from policy mandates to continually searching for and using information about schools' goals and experiences to inform their policymaking operations.

Summary

While implementing instructional reform, school stakeholders can be influenced by school, model, and district factors that affect their understanding of school reforms and ultimately their decisions to use model practices. As street-level bureaucrats, school stakeholders may internalize and interpret school reforms in idiosyncratic ways depending on these factors.

METHODOLOGY

Data Collection Activities and Participants

Qualitative data were used to answer the research questions in this chapter. Semistructured interviews with administrators and teachers, as well as observations of 123 teachers across grades 3–8 in 223 mathematics and/or reading classrooms, were the core data collection activities. Over the course of two school years, the research team conducted 57 interviews of administrators (principals, assistant principals, and facilitators) and 192 interviews of teachers. In-depth interviewing with multiple school stakeholders provided an opportunity to discuss school processes and perceptions of CSR implementation (Spradley 1979). Individual interviews of administrators lasted approximately 60 minutes. Individual interviews of teachers ranged from 15 to 30 minutes. During the interviews, the participants were asked questions about their implementation of CSR model components (i.e., school culture, organization and governance, curriculum and instruction, assessment, and professional development). Participants were also asked to discuss, among other topics, challenges and supports they received for implementation. Data collection occurred in 24 schools, with CSR models representing 10 different reform models, during fall 2002 and spring 2003. A subset of eight schools, representing five reform models, was visited in spring 2004. The schools were matched as closely as possible based on a number of variables including achievement, student demographics, model type, and number of years of implementation.

Analytic Approaches

To examine our research questions, this qualitative study collected and analyzed an array of data from schools that had implemented a given CSR model.[1] Four methods or approaches were used to analyze the qualitative data. The first approach was to construct an analytical rubric (the NLECSR analytic rubric, as this research was conducted under the auspices of the National Longitudinal Evaluation of Comprehensive School Reform) to examine school-level stakeholders' perceptions of a given CSR model, as indicated by their understanding of model comprehensiveness and schoolwide use. From this analytic rubric, ratings were assigned to the schools to identify high and low levels of understanding and schoolwide use. To partial out explanations for differences in stakeholder understanding and schoolwide use, we used a second approach: a thematic analysis to generate themes across all 24 model schools, to help us uncover factors influencing school stakeholders' understanding of CSR. The third approach involved using classroom observation data to understand the relationship between instruction and understanding of CSR. Finally, a qualitative case study approach was used for an in-depth focus on two schools. The presentation of two school cases depicts the relationship between school and model factors and street-level bureaucrats' understanding of CSR. We used these analytic approaches with the qualitative data collectively to develop a fuller understanding of stakeholders' perceptions of CSR and their instructional practices.

NLECSR Analytic Rubric

We developed a rubric to facilitate the systematic analysis of school-level support for CSR and related constructs. The NLECSR analytic rubric contains four primary sections: *constructs related to understanding of CSR, perceptions of the CSR model, school-level processes related to the model*, and *professional resources*. In this chapter, we present findings from the constructs related to the component *understanding of CSR*. This aspect of the rubric comprises two constructs: comprehensiveness and schoolwide use. To accomplish this analysis, we delineated five distinct levels identified by a 0–4 rating scale and defined each carefully for both constructs (see tables 12.1 and 12.2). To complete a rubric for each school, a researcher read all principal, facilitator, and teacher interview and focus group transcripts, identified text that informed the constructs related to understanding of CSR, and rated each respondent's comments for both constructs.

With all data coded, an aggregate score for each CSR school was generated for each construct. These scores were used to identify schools that had either high or low levels of CSR model understanding. Two schools were selected as case studies on the basis of this information, to represent each end of the continuum of CSR understanding. The thematic analysis described below enabled us to provide explanations for the variations in levels of understanding based on stakeholder comments about model components and implementation.

Thematic Analysis

Interview and focus group transcripts were coded by using a construct key based on the components of CSR models. Throughout the coding process, researchers discussed the codes and defined them based on

Table 12.1. Comprehensiveness Rating Descriptions

Construct description	Rating descriptor
The construct reflects the degree to which stakeholders perceive the breadth of CSR or, in contrast, focus on a narrow range of components	**4:** The interviewee clearly describes a range of CSR activities, including professional development, parent involvement, and instruction, as appropriate.
	3: The interviewee describes two components in detail and demonstrates awareness of other components.
	2: The interviewee describes one component in detail and demonstrates awareness of other components.
	1: The interviewee describes one or two components, but with thin detail. The interviewee is aware of some terminology associated with the model but is unable to provide any additional information.
	0: The interviewee exhibits no awareness of the CSR model or associated activities.

CSR = comprehensive school reform

Table 12.2. Schoolwide Use Rating Descriptions

Construct description	Rating descriptor
"Schoolwide use of components" is related to the degree to which stakeholders perceive the reform to be implemented across the entire school (or across the relevant grades, if applicable) rather than in isolated classrooms.	**4:** The interviewee clearly expresses an understanding that the reform is intended to be a schoolwide effort and provides details that substantiate this.
	3: The interviewee's comments indicate an understanding that the reform should span more than one grade, but the commentary lacks substantive detail or the interviewee describes a process that falls somewhat short of a true schoolwide effort.
	2: The interviewee describes an implementation process that focuses on a few classrooms, engages a subset of teachers, or has resulted in divisions among faculty.
	1: The interviewee makes only the vaguest suggestion that the reform extends beyond his or her personal activities.
	0: The interviewee describes his or her implementation activities in isolation, without reference to other stakeholders.

the data. Once all transcripts were coded, coded text was organized by using NUD*IST v.6, a qualitative software program. Using these coded data, we wrote case reports for each school and developed within- and cross-case data displays (Miles and Huberman 1994).

Emergent themes were identified from the cross-case displays of the 24 CSR model schools in the study. Themes were explored, to capture stakeholders' perceptions of the conditions associated with understanding and making decisions about CSR model practices. Four main themes or conditions arose from this analysis: the importance of developer support, principals' support activities for understanding and implementation, the challenges to obtaining teacher buy-in created by high teacher turnover, and the CSR model's fit with ongoing school and district programs and policies. While other possible conditions associated with understanding may exist, such as school size or cost of model implementation, the four main themes or conditions that emerged from the data are presented in this chapter.

Instructional Analyses

A classroom checklist was used to summarize classroom observational data. After each observation, a researcher completed the checklist for the observation. This checklist provided a qualitative measure of the quality of instructional practices in six areas: (1) the cognitive levels emphasized during instruction, composed of the six levels of Bloom's taxonomy of the cognitive domain (1956, 2); (2) the degree to which the lesson connects to student experiences; (3) the kind of substantive conversation that occurred; (4) the type of social support provided by the teacher during the course of the classroom observation; (5) the level of student engagement; and (6) lesson depth and coherence. This checklist enabled researchers to rate the degree to which instruction emphasized each of these six areas. The checklist also included ratings for the use of technology, the use of instructional materials, and the use of student grouping during the observation. Although each of the models found in our sample of schools used a variety of instructional strategies and curricula, the classroom checklist allowed us to view the major instructional components of each model with a common lens. The models represented in our sample of schools utilized one or more of the following: some aspects of authentic instruction,[2] gifted and talented strategies for all students, standards, and extended projects. Also, those models that used aspects of direct instruction also emphasized cross-age grouping, pair work, small groups, or cooperative learning, all highly rated by the checklist.

A set of analyses were undertaken to determine the relationship between instructional practices, measured by the classroom checklist, and understanding, indicated by the NLECSR analytic rubric. These analyses involved the conversion of school-level ratings to standardized z-scores (with a mean of 0 and a standard deviation of 1) for the variables of interest: comprehensiveness, schoolwide use, and instructional practices.

Case Study

To develop a more nuanced, in-depth depiction of those factors identified by school stakeholders as influencing their understanding of model components and the process of implementation, two schools were selected as cases. Selection began with the NLECSR analytic rubric ratings for understanding. Any schools in the sample that had either high or low ratings for these two constructs were considered potential cases to examine. Another criterion for selection was that schools be visited in both waves of data collection. The final criterion was that models be well represented in the study. On the basis of all these criteria, we selected two schools as case studies: Chamberland and Ivyton.

Findings

Successful CSR implementation requires that school-level stakeholders use the practices endorsed by their CSR models, because they are the primary implementers of reform (Cohen and Ball 1999; Darling-Hammond 1990; Davidson and St. John 1996; Smith et al. 1997; Spillane, Reiser, and Reimer 2002; Woodbury and Gess-Newsome 2002). However, as street-level bureaucrats, school stakeholders' understanding of reform and their decisions to implement it are influenced by contextual factors.

We first examine the perceptions of school stakeholders' understanding of CSR through rubric scores and themes generated to uncover contextual factors that may influence understanding of CSR. We also weave our findings from the instructional analyses throughout. Then, we present two school cases to highlight (1) the conditions identified by school-level stakeholders that affect their understanding of CSR, (2) the decisions that school-level stakeholders make about using model practices, and (3) the instructional practices observed at each school, and how that relates to model understanding.

SCHOOL STAKEHOLDERS' UNDERSTANDING OF CSR

NLECSR Analytic Rubric

We analyzed the model schools in this study by using a rubric that rated individual school stakeholders' level of comprehensiveness and schoolwide use of the CSR model. All individual ratings from stakeholders in a school were computed to create a school score for comprehensiveness and schoolwide use of CSR components. Based on the school scores, five categories of understanding were created. The five categories were labeled

- **Unfamiliar (0.00–0.20):** school-level stakeholders have no awareness of CSR components or their use across classrooms and grades.
- **Acquainted (0.21–0.40):** school-level stakeholders hold awareness of terminology associated with the model and limited understanding that CSR extends beyond personal activities.
- **Informed (0.41–0.60):** school-level stakeholders hold in-depth awareness of one CSR component, and implementation is perceived across a few classrooms or a subset of teachers.
- **Knowledgeable (0.61–0.80):** school-level stakeholders hold in-depth awareness of at least two components and know that CSR

at least spans more than one grade, but they fall short of expressing CSR as a schoolwide initiative.

- **Fully Articulate (0.81–1.00):** school-level stakeholders hold detailed awareness of more than two components of the CSR model, and that CSR is implemented across all grades and classrooms.

As a first step, we depicted in a graphic format the model schools' ratings for comprehensiveness and schoolwide use. Figure 12.2 shows the comprehensiveness ratings for 22 model schools, and Figure 12.3 displays the schoolwide use ratings for 20 model schools.[3] For both comprehensiveness and schoolwide use, school scores were in only four categories: Acquainted, Informed, Knowledgeable, and Fully Articulate. None of the model schools in this study had a school rating below 0.21; therefore, no model schools were assigned to the Unfamiliar category. School ratings for comprehensiveness ranged from 0.25 to 1.00 (see figure 12.2). The ratings for schoolwide use ranged from 0.38 to 1.00 (see figure 12.3).

When comparing ratings for comprehensiveness and schoolwide use, comprehensiveness shows more variation among schools. When we looked at comprehensiveness scores of 22 schools in groups, 91 percent were in the Informed, Knowledgeable, and Fully Articulate categories. Two schools were in the Acquainted category, and no schools were in the Unfamiliar category. When we examined the ratings of schoolwide use across 20 model schools, 85 percent were in the Knowledgeable

Figure 12.2. Comprehensiveness, School Scores by Category

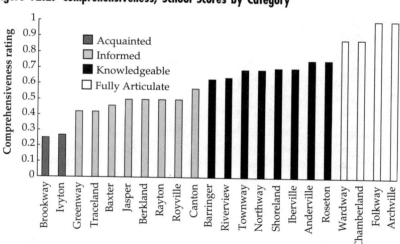

Source: Authors' calculations.

Note: Names are pseudonyms; those with the same suffix are in the same district.

Figure 12.3. Schoolwide Use, School Scores by Category

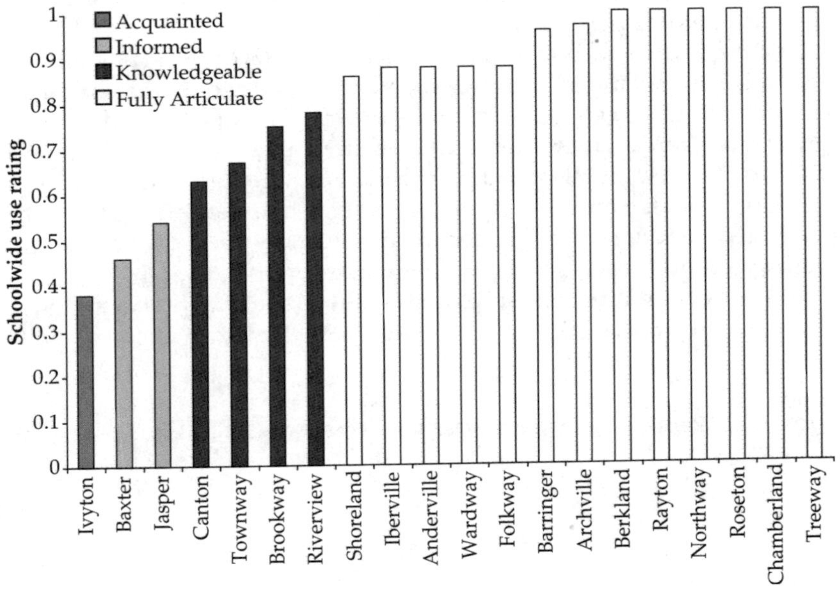

Source: Authors' calculations.
Note: Names are pseudonyms; those with the same suffix are in the same district.

and Fully Articulate categories. Two schools were in the Informed category. Only one school was in the Acquainted category, and no schools were in the Unfamiliar category (see table 12.3).

Across model schools, school-level stakeholders understand that the CSR model is to be implemented schoolwide. However, their understanding of model comprehensiveness varied considerably. Clearly, stakeholders had different levels of understanding of the CSR model

Table 12.3. Percentage of Schools in Each Category

	Comprehensiveness		Schoolwide use	
	n	%	n	%
Category (range of scores)				
Unfamiliar (0.00–0.20)	0	0.0	0	0.0
Acquainted (0.21–0.40)	2	9.1	1	5.0
Informed (0.41–0.60)	8	36.4	2	10.0
Knowledgeable (0.61–0.80)	8	36.4	4	20.0
Fully Articulate (0.81–1.00)	4	18.2	13	65.0

Source: Authors' calculations.

components. The conditions or explanations that emerged from the thematic analysis provide a context for exploring the different levels of understanding.

Next, we address our research question: how does stakeholders' understanding of model comprehensiveness and schoolwide use relate to teachers' observed instructional practice? Because we know that street-level bureaucrats must consider more than the policy at hand (CSR in this case) while carrying out their day-to-day responsibilities (including classroom instruction), we sought to determine how teachers' understanding of model comprehensiveness and schoolwide use aligns with our observations of their classroom practice.

When we look at relationships among the model comprehensiveness scores and instructional practices scores from the observation checklist

Figure 12.4. Relationship between Comprehensiveness and Instruction

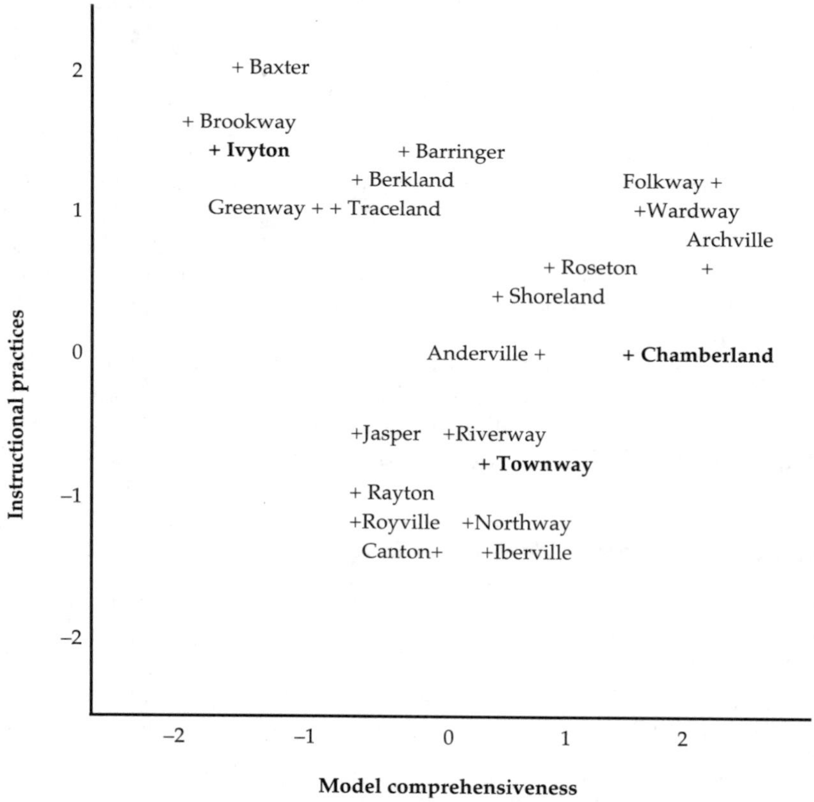

Source: Authors' calculations.
Note: Names are pseudonyms; those with the same suffix are in the same district.

(converted to z scores with a mean of 0 and a standard deviation of 1), the schools fall into two groups (see figure 12.4). One grouping of schools contains seven schools that have higher instructional practices and lower comprehensiveness scores (upper left quadrant of figure 12.4). The other grouping of schools contains 15 schools that show a positive, linear relationship between comprehensiveness and instruction. In other words, some of the schools have lower comprehensiveness and lower instruction ratings and others have higher comprehensiveness and higher instruction ratings.

When we look at the relationship between instruction and schoolwide use ratings, the two groupings of schools remain. However, the grouping in the upper left quadrant of the figure is smaller, that is, it contains fewer schools. In addition, the large grouping of schools has

Figure 12.5. Relationship between Schoolwide Use and Instruction

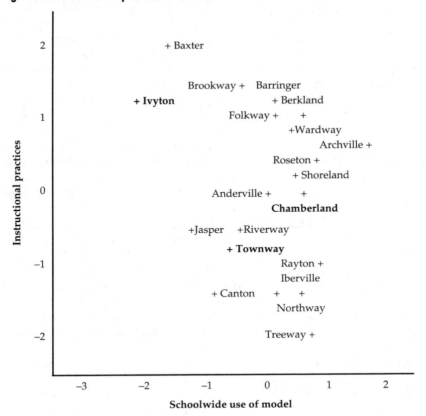

Source: Authors' calculations.
Note: Names are pseudonyms; those with the same suffix are in the same district.

a less clear positive relationship between instruction and schoolwide use compared with instruction and comprehensiveness. Because understanding of the schoolwide nature of CSR varied less among schools, it is surprising to see three schools (Ivyton, Baxter, Brookway) as outliers from the remaining schools.

To offer insight into why the schools formed these two groupings when comprehensiveness and schoolwide use scores are compared with instruction, we look at the contextual themes next. Our guiding research questions are these: What factors do stakeholders report as influencing their understanding of model components? In particular, what factors do stakeholders report as influencing their instructional strategies?

Factors that Challenge or Enhance CSR

A number of factors at the school level challenge or enhance CSR implementation, such as the complexity of the model and cost for implementation. Research on CSR implementation has shown great variability: implementation of the same CSR model may vary across school districts and schools, as well as by teachers within a school (Berends, Bodilly, et al. 2002; Rowan, Barnes, and Camburn 2004). However, to answer our research questions, we turned to the findings from our thematic analysis as well as our analyses of instructional variables.

First, interview and focus group data were analyzed using cross-case data displays (Miles and Huberman 1994) to identify school-level factors that may explain the variations in school-level stakeholders' perceptions of their challenges and of the supports available to assist in CSR. Five themes arose from this analysis. First, school stakeholders described the challenge of getting buy-in from new teachers. This was especially problematic in schools with high levels of teacher turnover. The activities the school stakeholders undertook to meet these challenges are referred to as "new teacher induction." Second, principals' leadership (such as monitoring) emerged as a theme, because school stakeholders described these activities as supporting implementation. Third, model design features, such as whether school stakeholders perceived the model as aligning with ongoing school programs, were identified as affecting decisions to implement. Fourth, developer support was perceived by school stakeholders as an important influence in helping them understand the intricacies of a CSR model. Stakeholders described developer support as the type and frequency of developer support activities, such as professional development opportunities. Fifth, district and federal policy, as well as state assessments, were found to influence stakeholders' decisions to implement model components. If school stakeholders cannot align their model implementation activities with the goals of outside policy and assessments, model implementation may suffer.

As we analyzed the five themes that school stakeholders described as affecting their understanding of CSR and ultimately their decision to implement the model, we classified them in terms of the factors listed in figure 12.1: district support and policy, school factors, and model design and technical assistance features.

School Contextual Factors

New Teacher Induction

When high numbers of faculty leave CSR model schools, school stakeholders must provide new teachers with information about the model and encourage buy-in.

Model Learning. School stakeholders perceived that CSR models required extensive learning for new teachers, and that a lack of knowledge could compromise the implementation process. Because of high rates of teacher turnover in general, school stakeholders stressed the importance of providing new teachers with adequate information. One principal pointed out that new teachers must learn the model in a crash course that becomes "sink or swim, which is not very productive." Stakeholders emphasized that practice and time are required to master instructional strategies associated with a particular CSR program. One principal stated, "It takes a good deal of time to really learn this reading program, get entrenched in it, maneuver it, and make it exciting. First, you have to teach the new teachers how to teach the program before you can get into the deeper things with them."

Model Buy-in. Not only do new teachers need to learn about the model, but they also must buy into its philosophy and processes. A stakeholder pointed out that in her school, teachers buy into the model at different times and for different reasons. Stakeholders explained that teachers who had participated in the adoption process were more committed to the model than new teachers. One explained, "Someone who has been here since the start of the process sees it differently than someone [who] came in September." A reform model facilitator noted that after new teachers at the school began to see positive results from model practices, their opinion began to change.

Principal Leadership

The principal plays an active role in ensuring that implementation occurs at the school. Two activities that supported implementation were making organizational changes and monitoring the implementation process.

Making Organizational Changes. Principals prepared their schools for implementation in several ways. Some reorganized the school day to allow the appropriate amount of instructional time for a subject area, as required by some models. Others ensured that teachers had common planning or preparation times to meet and discuss model-related activities. A principal pointed out that common planning time "has been very helpful for new teachers coming in because they have that opportunity to share and grow."

Another organizational change that facilitated implementation was altering governance structures to encourage decisionmaking for teachers. One teacher's description of how decisionmaking is conducted at her school exemplified this organizational change. She stated, "Everyone is given their wings when they walk in the door and [is] allowed to fly. We vote on things, we talk about things, we make our decision." Shared decisionmaking was done through leadership teams, such as committees and/or team meetings. A teacher in a focus group said, "We all make decisions together," and explained the process the leadership team followed. "Even though there is a leadership team, those of us in mathematics and language arts, those that teach those particular subjects, we all get together, and we talk about what we need and what we'd like to have [happen]." These types of decisionmaking opportunities facilitated communication among teachers and enabled them to become invested in model implementation.

Monitoring Implementation. Visiting classrooms was the primary way for principals to monitor implementation. It is important to note that some school district's teacher contracts may specify guidelines for scheduled classroom observations by the principal. In our sample, none of the principals or teachers described any regulations related to their contracts. Instead, the principals in our study described the various methods they used for conducting observations. Some followed a schedule, others visited every classroom for some amount of time each week, and others "popped in" classrooms daily. One principal said, "It doesn't take you 50 minutes to observe a classroom to see if teaching is going on." This principal described stopping in classrooms throughout the day to observe instruction.

Reviewing lesson plans was another method principals used to monitor implementation. One facilitator commented, "[The principal] wants to know how [the teachers] tie model practices and philosophy into their lesson plans throughout the week." One teacher explained, "We submit our lesson plans so our administration can see what we're teaching." Reviewing lesson plans enabled principals to monitor instructional activities and how lesson plans reflected model activities.

Regardless of the method they used to monitor classroom instructional practices, principals had clear expectations for instruction. That is, principals expected teachers to integrate model practice into their instruction.

Model Design Features

Developer Support

School stakeholders described the types of developer support activities they received at their schools. Based on their descriptions, two types of activities emerged: ongoing support and on-site technical assistance.

Ongoing Support. School stakeholders emphasized the value and importance of ongoing developer support and viewed it as critical to the implementation process. Throughout model implementation, developers offered on-site and off-site workshops that focused on model components and strategies for instruction, and also provided information on the model through videos or national conferences. One principal described the value of ongoing developer support by saying, "We've had numerous in-services, and they've been wonderful and we've gained a lot of insight into various facets of the curriculum." When school stakeholders did not receive the necessary type or level of ongoing support, they became frustrated. One principal's remarks captured this well: "I think they [model developers] can do more. I think that [for] the amount of money that we are paying them, we are not getting the services that we should have. I think there should be more technical assistance at the school, at least monthly."

On-Site Technical Assistance. School-level stakeholders also emphasized the importance of on-site technical assistance. Generally, developers offered on-site support by conducting site visits that included observations of classroom instruction and feedback to observed teachers. Furthermore, model developers worked with teachers either individually or during grade-level and team meetings. One principal suggested that on-site support and feedback were useful in sustaining implementation, particularly when developers met with teachers to monitor and address their needs. Model developers also provided on-site technical assistance to address problems. One teacher explained, "If there was a problem that came out, if we needed professional development, [the developers] were here." When on-site support was *not* present, stakeholders expressed the need for more frequent contact with the developer. One principal stated, "When we took on the model, they [the developer] promised more than what they produced. They promised us that there would be on-site consultants for our needs. That did not materialize." When on-site support *was* received, it allowed stakeholders to have their questions answered and needs met by the developer.

Model Efficacy

Model efficacy refers to results that school-level stakeholders attributed to the reform model. If school-level stakeholders perceived the model as useful, they continued to employ practices associated with the model. School-level stakeholders valued seeing model results especially as evidenced in positive student outcomes, the growth of professional community, and improvement in instructional practice.

Student Outcomes. School-level stakeholders judged the model to be useful if student outcomes improved. Seeing positive results confirmed that model implementation was worth the effort. One teacher explained,

> The number of students on grade level just keeps increasing and increasing every year. Now that we are in the fourth year, we are really starting to see results. The first year was frustrating because you don't see any movement. This is the first year that I've been here where I can see the reading program really working with our students.

Other stakeholders identified the model as providing necessary support for their school's particular student population. A principal stated, "I recommend the model for any group of students who are very transient, who are second-language learners, for students whose homes are not print rich and no one is reading." With the model in place, teachers were capable of addressing students' weak reading skills, a major issue in most of the schools.

Professional Community. School-level stakeholders valued how CSR models addressed the maintenance and enhancement of professional community. Teachers felt supported by their colleagues during model implementation. Describing how the professional community changed through the implementation, one teacher stated, "Teachers have expanded on working with each other. The communication has brought us closer together as a family." Communicating about student work and instructional practices enabled the teachers to develop collaborative relationships. One principal suggested that the model gave the teachers the feeling that "We are in this thing together; you are not alone."

Instructional Practices. School-level stakeholders saw particular value in implementing CSR with respect to instruction. Teachers began seeing their classroom instruction improve throughout the implementation. One teacher stated, "[The model] helped us as a faculty to improve our skills to help our children prepare academically for the world." The reform models offered schools opportunities to engage faculty in professional development and to improve their instructional practices. A principal explained that the model provided a way to show teachers how to teach reading "without the district spending millions of dollars to send everyone back to school."

School Programmatic Fit

When stakeholders perceived that the goals among ongoing school programs and philosophies and their CSR model aligned, they were likely to see the model fitting well with the school's priorities. School-level stakeholders valued this alignment. A principal stated, "We thought we had good programs here. We didn't need to change our whole program." This principal thought the model fit the instructional style of the teachers by emphasizing authentic student-centered learning. Another principal remarked that one program could not possibly have everything; therefore, school programs should supplement each other. Thus, models that supplemented other school programs were frequently viewed as fitting a particular school. Models that matched the school's philosophy were also deemed appropriate. For example, one stakeholder stated, "The [model's] philosophy was a fit for the school's gifted and talented program."

District Factors

Other Initiatives

Other initiatives refers to programs, including school district and state assessments, and federal policies. Because federal policy and state assessments are filtered through a school district, we interpret the term *district factors* as also incorporating these additional features. Both implementing district programs and accountability issues influenced school stakeholders' assessments of their model's appropriateness.

District-Mandated Programs. When the model appeared to compete with district-mandated programs or initiatives, school stakeholders saw the model as inappropriate for their school. As teachers in one focus group explained,

> The demands that are administered to us from the board of education in terms of our curriculum and how it should be laid out—those demands far exceed the demands for the [model] this year.

How can we incorporate [the model] and also incorporate what is mandated [by the district]?

District-mandated programs took precedence over other school programs. When stakeholders were not able to align their model with district programs, model implementation suffered. Teachers in one school remarked, "The district says, no, I'm sorry, you can't do that [use model-related curricula]. We have our own scope and sequence, and we have our own themes." When a program was mandated by the district, school stakeholders uniformly believed that district policy took precedence over all else, including CSR.

Required Testing. How well a model prepared students for mandated assessments was an important factor in its appropriateness. One teacher explained, "We have so much pressure on us to get these scores up that sometimes you get away from the model." Other stakeholders agreed that, when it came to testing, preparing the students took priority over model implementation. Teachers in a focus group stated, "When you have to deviate from your instructional program to bring in things that they need to know for this or that test, that takes two or three weeks out of the program ... it's just interruptive." Being unable to align a model's activities with preparation for state accountability measures challenged implementation for most models.

Two School Cases

The section above focused on five conditions identified by school stakeholders that directly or indirectly affected their decisions to use model practices. Using findings from the rubric, we identified two schools that highlighted the extremes of CSR for comprehensiveness and schoolwide use. Chamberland fell into the Fully Articulate category of comprehensiveness and schoolwide use (comprehensiveness, 0.88, and schoolwide use, 1.0). Ivyton fell into the Acquainted category of comprehensiveness and schoolwide use (comprehensiveness, 0.27, and schoolwide use, 0.38). The relationship between comprehensiveness and instruction and similarly, schoolwide use and instruction, show that these two schools fall into separate groups (see figures 12.4 and 12.5). These two cases and conditions are described in more detail below.

A Case of Fully Articulated Understanding: Chamberland

General School Information

Chamberland (a pseudonym) is an elementary school, grades K–8, with 771 students and 33 teachers comprising its faculty. The school is located in a high-poverty area of a large urban district. In 2002, public housing around the school was being demolished, causing families to move farther away and often out of the school's attendance zone. Nevertheless, parents—some of whom attended Chamberland as children—were finding ways to make sure their children continued to attend Chamberland. The principal and teachers as well as the parents expressed their commitment to the school. The principal had spent her entire career at Chamberland, beginning as a substitute teacher in the 1960s and becoming principal 30 years later. However, the principal was retiring at the end of the 2002–2003 school year. The new principal (for the 2003–2004 school year) served as an assistant principal at the school prior to her promotion. Many teachers stayed at Chamberland until retirement or promotion, resulting in minimal teacher turnover. Because the school has had a history of a dedicated administrators, faculty, and parents, school stakeholders were able to create a supportive, family-like environment.

In 2001, during our first site visit, we learned that Chamberland had adopted the Accelerated Schools Project model eight years earlier. The principal said that, for the school to be eligible for CSR model adoption, she had to beg the district for approval. She declared, "The only way you are going to get something for the school is to beg." The main reason the stakeholders wanted a CSR model was to bring in additional funds to "support what we were already doing." The school was resource poor; that fact influenced which model was chosen. The principal explained that the school's teachers and administrators alike wished to implement a model that did not require many resources, believing that Accelerated Schools' $50,000 award did not stretch very far. Teachers voted for Accelerated Schools Project because, of the three choices they were given, "We thought it would best fit with what we were already doing."

Although funding for the model ended five years before our site visit in 2001, school-level stakeholders still provided detailed accounts of the model's components. In particular, they identified model practices associated with school governance. School-level stakeholders at Chamberland fully articulated the use of committees as central to their decisionmaking efforts. Committees focused on what the teachers deemed to be the four important areas at Chamberland: academic performance, community involvement, school spirit, and discipline. The committees' purpose was to work out problems and give suggestions to the principal. All teachers participated in at least one committee that met once a month. Chamberland's dedicated faculty, administration, and parents supported communication among stakeholder groups and facilitated a conjoint understanding of activities and programs implemented in the school, including the CSR model.

School Factors

New Teacher Induction. Chamberland had a low rate of teacher turnover. Teachers expressed commitment to the school, and many stayed at Chamberland until retirement or promotion. The principal commented, "Once they get here, they don't want to leave." When teacher turnover did occur, school staff at Chamberland ensured that new teachers were trained properly. Teachers attended workshops and national conferences on Accelerated Schools Project during the three years of its implementation to "hear what was going on." Teachers tried to get newer teachers to attend so "they will learn what the rest of us already know." The combination of low teacher turnover and support for new teachers encouraged a deeper understanding of model components.

Principal Leadership. Chamberland's principal during the implementation phase supported teachers in implementing the model, by allowing them to form committees for consensus decisionmaking on school-related activities and issues. Teachers in the focus group explained,

> [Chamberland] has for the last four years been affiliated with [the model], so in keeping with that process, we have formed committees that focus on what the teachers have deemed to be the important areas at [Chamberland]. And so all decisions are made—those areas are academic performance, community involvement, school spirit, and discipline. Any problems that come about in that way, those problems are sent to that committee. Then the committee tries to work them out, and they send a report in turn to the principal with the suggestions that we have made. Everyone is on at least one committee. We meet once a month.

Teacher committees regularly assisted with school governance. During the 2002–2003 school year, one teacher stated, "The principal has an open door. Anything that you want to bring to the table is up for discussion." The committees, formed during the early phase of model implementation, gave teachers an opportunity to communicate and become invested in school activities.

The principal also monitored model implementation by visiting classrooms and encouraging the use of model-specific instructional activities. The principal explained that she noticed these activities in the classroom "when kids are actively engaged in a lesson. So that's what we are trying to do." By supporting teachers in their instructional activities and providing opportunities to participate in school decisions, the principal's activities encouraged discourse and understanding about the model.

Model Design Features

Developer Support. Implementation of the model was supported for three years by ongoing training at the state capital. (The principal explained that the money for the program came from state dollars, so the teachers had to go to the capital for training.) In addition to that training, model trainers came to the school to instruct the teachers. According to the principal, "Then we had a coach who was also trained and was in the building every week, assisting and training the teachers." This training over the first three years consisted of two-day in-service sessions on every phase of the program. The principal described the type of training:

> Like [model specific instructional activities]—we had an in-service on that, introducing the model, how the model was to be introduced, we had an in-service on that. So we had an in-service on everything, every phase of the program. They did a great job in acclimating us to the program.

The training provided by the developer assisted the faculty and administration in understanding every phase of the program. In addition, the model design required one of the school's teachers to be a coach for model implementation, thus assuring on-site technical assistance.

Model Efficacy. At Chamberland, teachers perceived that the model had been helpful. When asked if the model helped to achieve their goals, a teacher reported, "Yes, because we are still using it now. Every teacher is on a team or is committed to working and everything. We've all had that training." Teachers have seen results for their students. One teacher stated that she noticed the students enjoying mathematics more since the model began. This teacher noted improvement, "By doing those investigations and seeing things and saying, 'Oh, I knew this but now I know why.'" Teachers thought students enjoyed the lessons more when they were able to make connections between their everyday experiences and observations with the instructional material. Teachers also noticed improvement in their instruction because they became more focused on reading.

District Context. Chamberland had programs other than reading, and initially selected a model that would support all school priorities. However, the district's reading initiative had a major effect on the school. "That is the main thing," the principal explained. "You gotta do that first." Professional development opportunities for teachers during the 2003–2004 school year centered on the reading initiative, and class schedules were altered to allow more instructional time for the initiative's areas of emphasis.

Although the implementation of the model has concluded, funding has stopped, the principal associated with the implementation process has retired, *and* the district's reading initiative has become the focus, school stakeholders continue to implement Accelerated Schools. The current principal explained, "We provide lots of professional development here and utilize the same theories of shared decisionmaking [through the committees], so the structure of our school enables us to continue that implementation very easily."

Summary

Chamberland is an example of a school where stakeholders have a well-developed understanding of their model and have continued to use its components schoolwide, years after implementation ended. School-level factors in addition to model features encouraged school stakeholders to continue implementation. Developer support throughout the implementation process enabled teachers to receive appropriate training, optimized by low levels of teacher turnover. Therefore, teachers had an opportunity to develop a deeper understanding of the model as a stable community of learners.

The former principal, who retired at the end of the 2002–2003 school year, also played an important role in supporting implementation. Through the creation of committees, she encouraged teachers' involvement in decisionmaking. In addition, the principal regularly monitored instructional practices to ensure the use of model-specific instructional activities and sought alignment with ongoing programs. The principal who took her place continued to support the committees and model-specific instructional activities. These conditions helped school stakeholders develop a deeper understanding of the model.

In our analyses between instructional practices and the analytic rubric scores for comprehensiveness and schoolwide use, Chamberland consistently fell in the middle of the second large group of schools, with average classroom observation scores (see figures 12.4 and 12.5). We would expect schools with greater understanding of the components of their CSR model to exhibit higher quality instruction.

Street-level bureaucrats at Chamberland have made decisions that support implementation. The principal and teachers have opted to align their model activities with other school goals and programs, to continue to use committees as a decisionmaking structure for the teachers, and to embed model-specific activities in their instructional practices. Sustained implementation of the model may be in jeopardy because of the district's current reading initiative, but school-level stakeholders' positive opinions of the model and continued use of "the process" may curb further decline.

A Case of Acquainted Understanding: Ivyton

General School Information

Ivyton (a pseudonym) is an elementary school that includes grades K–8, with 487 students and 28 teachers on staff. The school is located in a high-poverty area of a large urban school district. The principal referred to the school's location as an "urban blight area" with few community resources. Ivyton had adopted the Atlas Communities model six years before our site visit in 2003. The principal described model implementation at Ivyton as intense during the first three years. However, only the principal of the school was knowledgeable about the model. She commented that teachers would not recognize the model's name but would recognize many of its aspects. Teachers who participated in the study during the 2003 and 2004 site visits lacked awareness of the model. One of the few teachers familiar with the model noted that, "There is a trickle here and a trickle there, but it's not the model that was modeled at one of the site schools." This "trickle" of implementation was described as team meetings where teachers reviewed student work to assess and make decisions about how to meet student needs. "That's the extent of [the model] at the school," said one teacher.

School Factors

New Teacher Induction. Ivyton Elementary experienced high levels of teacher turnover. The school hired 10 new teachers and a new principal in the 2001–2002 school year. The principal's description of teachers' experience at the school was, "[We have] seasoned veteran people on this hand and then a whole [batch] of new folks [on the other hand]. So with that mix, it's working well . . . for the most part they are very willing. . . . Most of the young teachers are in school and meet requirements."

High teacher turnover continued the following year, 2004,[4] creating a school environment unsupportive of reform. That year, the principal noted that 85 percent of her staff were new and that 80 percent were younger than 27. As one teacher pointed out, "The school is new, as far as teachers. So everybody's learning." Furthermore, five different principals had served during the previous six years. The current principal explained, "The staff had a reputation for being resistant and for driving people out." When the principal began at the school in 2001, she asked the staff to "consider transferring" if they couldn't buy into the model.

The principal also conceded that, because 85 percent of the teachers were new during the 2003–2004 school year, they would not recognize Atlas Communities or articulate its components, although "15 percent could still say, from A to Z, that this is [the model]." Concurring that Ivyton lacked teachers who understood the model, one teacher stated, "People haven't been educated as to what [the model] is. And our school has a very high turnover rate for teachers." The one teacher in the focus group who had heard of the model said, "Now, [the model] was brought up this year, in the beginning of the year. But I don't remember anything happening from there." Teachers did not appear to be aware of the model primarily because so many were new and also because no process seemed to be in place to support its implementation.

Principal Leadership. The principal at Ivyton described model implementation at the school as having progressed from an Atlas Communities site to "teaching for understanding." One way the principal supported the continued implementation of the model was through team meetings with a main focus of reviewing student work: "Looking at student work is definitely [part of the model]. So that is a major part." The principal stated that the main component of the model still in use was the team meetings, during which teachers have the opportunity to meet weekly for one hour.

The principal did not describe any method for monitoring model implementation still in place at Ivyton. However, she was concerned with ensuring that instruction was taking place and that students were actively involved in lessons. The principal described making daily visits to classrooms to assess teachers' awareness of instructional objectives.

> In the morning I'll try to do a quick round to see if the first period is being used as an instructional period, because sometimes people use it just as advisory. . . . Kids are waiting for things to do . . . so we will run around and make sure that children are engaged first thing in the morning with some type of activity.

The principal was concerned with ensuring that teachers were instructing during the first period, not on the quality of instruction or whether or not the instruction matched the goals of the model.

Model Design Features

Developer Support. School stakeholders at Ivyton did not describe any developer activities at the school. One teacher knowledgeable about

Atlas Communities remarked, "I don't think enough people actually understand the model. It hasn't been emphasized in professional development." Training by the developer may have occurred during the model implementation phase, but teachers were not receiving any model-related support at the time of site visits in 2003 and 2004.

Model Efficacy. The principal found teacher team meetings to be effective.

> The tone of conversation changed . . . not that little Johnny is dumb, but actually having documentation that shows what little Johnny's challenges are and how can we as a team come up with a plan so that we can address those changes so that they can turn into success.

A positive outcome attributed to the model is teachers' commitment to reviewing student work and discussing it among themselves regularly. In addition, the principal pointed out that the team meetings encouraged teachers to work together. Overall, team meetings were the model component found by the principal to be most helpful in increasing collaboration and helping students succeed.

District Context. School-level stakeholders identified several established priorities at Ivyton. Teachers mentioned an emphasis on standards; one teacher commented on No Child Left Behind, stating that Ivyton was "standards driven." Additional district mandates also drove other priorities, such as the curriculum in grades K–8. Ivyton began implementing the district's curriculum in 2003.

Summary

Ivyton is an example of a school whose stakeholders have a limited understanding of the model and only the vaguest familiarity with model-related terminology and practices. However, Ivyton faced a number of challenges that influenced model understanding and implementation. Most dramatic was the high level of teacher turnover. At the time of the site visit in 2004, the rate was 85 percent. High turnover was problematic in relation to reform, because few teachers initially trained in the model remained, and the school no longer received developer-supported training. Furthermore, no structure appeared to be in place to inform new teachers about model activities.

From our analyses between instructional practices and the analytic rubric scores for both comprehensiveness and schoolwide use, we found Ivyton to be consistently in the small outlier group of schools (see figures 12.4 and 12.5). These schools had low scores for comprehensiveness and schoolwide use, but high ratings for instruction. We would expect schools with little understanding of their model to exhibit lower instructional practices. One possible explanation for Ivyton's better instructional practices is that this school was "restructured" by its district due to persistent low achievement scores; restructuring brought a variety of consultants, specialists, and facilitators into classrooms. As a result of the extensive professional development by the school district (unrelated to the model) and the intense oversight of classroom practices by outside evaluators, our classroom observation scores for this school were higher than for other schools.

As street-level bureaucrats, Ivyton teachers were in the position of not having enough information—in many cases, no information—about Atlas Communities. Without basic information and understanding of model activities, teachers were unable to make "bureaucratic" decisions related to model implementation. Although few school stakeholders were aware of the model, the principal and some teachers mentioned team meetings, one of the model's emphases. Teachers continued weekly team meetings to discuss student work; however, few teachers linked the weekly meeting to the model. From the principal's perspective, teachers continued to implement the model: "We still use the philosophy, and we still use the protocols." These meetings were viewed positively by the principal because they encouraged collaboration among teachers at the school; however, without higher levels of teacher understanding, implementation will continue to be unsuccessful.

CONCLUSION

Research on CSR processes suggests that implementation varies within and across schools (Berends 2000; Desimone 2000). Despite model developers' best intentions to make school stakeholders adhere strictly to the implementation of model components, they have inevitably made adaptations (Datnow and Castellano 2000). There are multiple ways to explore why variance in implementation occurs. One is to probe school stakeholders' perceptions of CSR.

Guided by theory related to the "street-level bureaucrat," we argue that school stakeholders respond to factors in the school context in ways that affect their understanding of CSR and ultimately, their decisions to use model practices. In this study, we analyzed school stakeholders' perceptions of CSR and linked these perceptions to our observations of classroom instruction. We suggest that school stakeholders implement changes based on their understanding of the reform. Although our study shows that stakeholders generally understand that the reform model is to be implemented schoolwide, their understanding of implementing reform components varies by school. School stakeholders' decisions about CSR have the potential to be strongly influenced by their understanding of CSR, given particular contextual factors; the school site, the model design, and the district all play roles in influencing understanding and ultimately, stakeholders' practices associated with the CSR model.

School stakeholders' perceptions of different school factors influence their understanding of their model and the reform effort. School contextual factors most importantly include teacher induction and principal leadership. Teacher turnover was identified as a major challenge to implementation, because new teachers have to buy in to the model as well as learn the basics of implementation. Schools with high teacher turnover that compensated with a system to provide training in model-appropriate activities, philosophy, and components were more likely to continue implementation. Similarly, schools in which the principal monitored or made organizational changes to enable implementation were perceived as supporting understanding and implementation.

Model design features, such as the perception of model efficacy and developer support, were described by school stakeholders as supporting understanding and implementation. As street-level bureaucrats, school stakeholders decide, on the basis of their perceptions of these features, which components to implement and how. Therefore, school stakeholders who viewed their model as effectively increasing student outcomes, enhancing professional community, and improving instructional practices were more likely to implement the model than stakeholders who did not view the model as resulting in positive outcomes. School stakeholders perceiving that they did not receive adequate assistance from the developer was discussed as another challenge. On the other hand, school stakeholders who received ongoing and/or on-site technical assistance from developers were more likely to feel supported in their implementation.

Another factor stakeholders considered critical was how well the model aligned with other initiatives at the school, district, state, and federal levels. When stakeholders were able to match the model's activities or goals with ongoing school programs, they were more likely to continue implementation. However, when stakeholders did not perceive alignment in relation to state assessments or mandates from the district or federal government, model implementation suffered. The conditions related to alignment were important considerations for stakeholders.

School stakeholders' understanding of model components and the schoolwide nature of CSR is related to their instructional practices. That is, schools with a fuller understanding of their model exhibited a positive relationship to instruction. However, some schools whose stakeholders were only acquainted with their model had higher instructional practices scores; contextual factors in these school, models, and districts offer insight into this phenomenon.

We have addressed the importance of analyzing school stakeholders' perceptions to uncover their understanding of CSR models. Our study implies that CSR is a complicated process of school stakeholder understanding and context. Specific factors associated with the school, model, and district settings that affect school-level stakeholder perceptions of CSR need to be investigated. With in-depth consideration of school stakeholders' perceptions of CSR, we can start to uncover the pathways in which practitioners decide to use model practices that ultimately lead to CSR model implementation.

NOTES

1. At the time of our data collection in 2002, the number of years schools had been implementing their reform model ranged from 2 to 11, with most (71 percent) having had their model for 2 to 6 years. For a description of the NLECSR study, please refer to chapter 1.

2. The term "authentic instructional practices" was adapted from the research of Newmann and associates (1996). Aspects of authentic instruction include the degree to which students are participating as active learners or using higher-order thinking skills, whether the instruction is connected to real-world examples, the type of communication and social support used during instruction, how engaged the students are during the class, and how coherently the material was presented.

3. The number of model schools included in the rubric analysis varies because some schools did not have enough data available to enable a rating to be assigned.

4. Turnover was primarily due to retirement, promotion to district-level positions, and lack of certification.

REFERENCES

Berends, M. 2000. "Teacher-Reported Effects of New American School Designs: Exploring Relationships to Teacher Background and School Context." *Educational Evaluation and Policy Analysis* 22(1): 65–82.

Berends, M., S. J. Bodilly, and S. N. Kirby. 2002. "Facing the Challenges of Whole School Reform: New American Schools after a Decade." Monograph/Report MR-1498-EDU. Santa Monica: RAND.

Berends, M., J. Chun, G. Schuyler, S. Stockly, and R. J. Briggs. 2002. "Challenges of Conflicting School Reforms: Effects of New American Schools in a High-Poverty District." Monograph/Report MR-1483-EDU. Santa Monica: RAND.

Bloom, B. S., M. Englehart, E. Furst, W. Hill, and D. R. Krathwohl. 1956. *Taxonomy of Educational Objectives: The Classification of Educational Goals, Handbook I: Cognitive Domain.* New York: Longmans / Toronto: Green.

Borman, K. M., C. Clarke, B. Cotner, and R. Lee. 2006. "Cross-Case Analysis." In *Handbook of Complementary Methods in Education Research*, 3rd ed., edited by J. L. Green, G. Camilli, and P. B. Elmore. Washington, DC: American Educational Research Association.

Camburn, E., B. Rowan, and J. E. Taylor. 2003. "Distributed Leadership in Schools: The Case of Elementary Schools Adopting Comprehensive School Reform Models." *Educational Evaluation and Policy Analysis* 25: 347–73.

Cohen, D. K., and D. L. Ball. 1999. "Instruction, Capacity, and Improvement." Research Report Series RR-43. Philadelphia: Consortium for Policy Research in Education, University of Pennsylvania.

Darling-Hammond, L. 1990. "Teaching and Knowledge: Policy Issues Posed by Alternate Certification for Teachers." *Peabody Journal of Education* 67(3): 123–54.

Datnow, A., and M. Castellano. 2000. "Teachers' Responses to Success for All: How Beliefs, Experiences, and Adaptations Shape Implementation." *American Educational Research Journal* 37(3): 775–99.

Datnow, A., G. Borman, and S. Stringfield. 2000. "School Reform through a Highly Specified Curriculum: Implementation and Effects of the Core Knowledge Sequence." *Elementary School Journal* 101(2): 167–96.

Davidson, B., and E. St. John. 1996. "Principals' Changing Roles: Analysis of Selected Case Studies." In *Accelerated Schools in Action: Lessons from the Field*, edited by C. Finnan, E. St. John, J. McCarthy, and S. P. Slovacek (169–84). Thousand Oaks, CA: Corwin.

Desimone, L. 2000. "Making Comprehensive School Reform Work." Urban Diversity Series No. 112. East Lansing, MI: Clearinghouse on Urban Education, Institute for Urban and Minority Education.

Hawkins, E. F., F. B. Stancavage, and J. A. Dossey. 1998. *School Policies and Practices Affecting Instruction in Mathematics: Findings from the National Assessment of Educational Progress.* National Center for Education Statistics Publication No. 98-495. Washington, DC: U.S. Department of Education.

Haynes, N. M. 1998. "Summary and Conclusions: Lessons Learned." *Journal of Education for Students Placed at Risk* 3(1): 87–99.

Honig, M. I., and T. C. Hatch. 2004. "Crafting Coherence: How Schools Strategically Manage Multiple, External Demands." *Educational Researcher* 33(8): 16–30.

Lipsky, M. 1980. *Street-Level Bureaucracy: The Dilemmas of the Individual in Public Services.* New York: Russell Sage.

Miles, M. B., and A. M. Huberman. 1994. *Qualitative Data Analysis: An Expanded Sourcebook*, 2nd ed. Newbury Park, CA: Sage.

Newmann, F. M., and Associates. 1996. *Authentic Achievement: Restructuring Schools for Intellectual Quality.* San Francisco: Jossey-Bass.

Rowan, B., C. Barnes, and E. Camburn. 2004. "Benefiting from Comprehensive School Reform: A Review of Research on CSR Implementation." In *Putting the Pieces Together: Lessons from Comprehensive School Reform Research*, edited by C. T. Cross (1–52). Washington, DC: National Clearinghouse for Comprehensive School Reform.

Smith, J., S. Maxwell, D. Lowther, D. Hacker, L. Bol, and J. Nunnery. 1997. "Activities in Schools and Programs Experiencing the Most, and Least,

Early Implementation Success." *School Effectiveness and School Improvement* 8(1): 125–50.

Spillane, J. P. 2005. "Distributed Leadership." *Educational Forum* 69: 143–50.

Spillane, J., B. Reiser, and T. Reimer. 2002. "Policy Implementation and Cognition: Reframing and Refocusing Policy Implementation Research." *Review of Educational Research* 72(3): 387–431.

Spillane, J. P., R. Halverson, and J. B. Diamond. 2004. "Towards a Theory of Leadership Practice: A Distributed Perspective." *Journal of Curriculum Studies* 36(1): 3–34.

Spradley, J. P. 1979. *The Ethnographic Interview.* Orlando, FL: Holt, Rinehart & Winston.

Supovitz, J. A., and S. M. Poglinco. 2001. *Instructional Leadership in a Standards-Based Reform.* Consortium for Policy Research in Education Report. Philadelphia: University of Pennsylvania.

Supovitz, J. A., and H. M. Turner. 2000. "The Effects of Professional Development on Science Teaching Practices and Classroom Culture." *Journal of Research in Science Teaching* 37(9): 963–80.

Woodbury, S., and J. Gess-Newsome. 2002. "Overcoming the Paradox of Change without Difference: A Model of Change in the Arena of Fundamental School Reform." *Educational Policy* 16: 764–83.

York-Barr, J., and K. Duke. 2004. "What Do We Know about Teacher Leadership? Findings from Two Decades of Scholarship." *Review of Educational Research* 74(3): 255–316.

ABOUT THE EDITORS

Daniel K. Aladjem is a principal research scientist at the American Institutes for Research. He is project director for the National Longitudinal Evaluation of Comprehensive School Reform, the largest federally funded study of CSR. In addition to his work on CSR, he has studied several other school reform initiatives, including small schools, school choice and vouchers, and Title I. Dr. Aladjem holds an A.B. (history) and A.M. (education, secondary teaching) from Stanford University. He earned his Ph.D. (public policy) from the University of Southern California.

Kathryn M. Borman is a professor of anthropology and associate director of the David C. Anchin Center at the University of South Florida. She received her doctorate in the Sociology of Education from the University of Minnesota in 1976. Currently, Dr. Borman is working with the American Institutes of Research and National Opinion Research Center on the National Longitudinal Evaluation of Comprehensive School Reform, directing the focus study of 40 schools in five districts. She served as the editor of the *Review of Educational Research* and currently is the editor of the *International Journal of Educational Policy, Research and Practice*.

ABOUT THE CONTRIBUTORS

Geoffrey D. Borman is associate professor of educational leadership and policy analysis, educational policy studies, and educational psychology at the University of Wisconsin–Madison; the deputy director of the Interdisciplinary Training Program for Predoctoral Research in Education Sciences; a senior researcher with the Consortium for Policy Research in Education; and the lead analyst for the Center for Data-Driven Reform in Education at Johns Hopkins University. He has recently coedited with Samuel C. Stringfield and Robert E. Slavin *Title I: Compensatory Education at the Crossroads* (Erlbaum).

Ted Boydston taught high school science in Miami-Dade County Public Schools for 18 years and was science department chairperson for 12 years. After retiring from the Miami-Dade school system, he earned a Ph.D. in science education at Florida State University. His research interests include developing strategies to improve teacher practice and helping teachers implement these strategies in the classroom.

Andrea Boyle is a research associate at the American Institutes for Research, where her research focuses on school reform, state education policy, and district support issues. In addition to her work on the National Longitudinal Evaluation of Comprehensive School Reform, she currently contributes to a qualitative examination of systems change in three school districts as part of the GE Foundation's College Bound Initiative. She received her B.A. from Cornell University.

Kerstin Carlson Le Floch is a senior research analyst the American Institutes for Research. She currently directs the Study of State Implementation of Accountability and Teacher Quality under the No Child Left Behind Act, and contributes to the National Longitudinal Evaluation of Comprehensive School Reform. She received her Ph.D. (education policy) and M.A. (political science) from the University of North Carolina–Chapel Hill, and completed her B.A. at Middlebury College.

Anne M. Chamberlain is a research scientist at the Success for All Foundation. Her areas of interest include program evaluation, mixed methodology, and participatory evaluation.

Bette Chambers is vice president of Development at the Success for All Foundation. Her areas of interest include early childhood education, early reading, and the use of technology in education.

Alan C. K. Cheung is an associate professor at the Hong Kong Institute of Education in the Department of Educational Policy and Administration. His areas of specialization include large-scale assessment, research reviews, research methods, and private education.

H. Dickson Corbett is an independent educational researcher. He and Dr. Bruce L. Wilson collaborate on studies of comprehensive school reform, having investigated the implementation and impact of numerous national reform models. He earned both his B.A. (religion) and Ph.D. (social foundations of education) from the University of North Carolina–Chapel Hill.

Bridget A. Cotner is a research associate with the David C. Anchin Center at the University of South Florida. She has conducted research with several evaluation projects, including the assessment of the National Science Foundation's Urban Systemic Initiative and the National Longitudinal Evaluation of Comprehensive School Reform. She received her M.A. in applied anthropology from the University of South Florida in 2001 and is currently in the College of Education's doctoral program at the University of South Florida.

Don E. Dailey is a principal research analyst at the American Institutes for Research. He has directed a number of studies and projects focused on school restructuring and system change, most recently for the Bill & Melinda Gates Foundation. He holds a Ph.D. in policy development and program evaluation from Vanderbilt University and an M.A. in education studies and a B.A. in history and political science from the University of Alabama.

C heri Fancsali is a senior program officer at the Academy for Educational Development, where she currently directs the multiyear evaluations of the National Writing Project Reading Initiative and the National Science Foundation–funded Teacher Leaders for Mathematics Success. Dr. Fancsali earned a B.S. (special education) from the University of Wisconsin and a Ph.D. (sociology and education) from Columbia University.

D an Goldhaber is a research associate professor at the University of Washington's Evans School of Public Affairs and an affiliated scholar with the Urban Institute's Education Policy Center. Dr. Goldhaber holds degrees from the University of Vermont (B.A., economics) and Cornell University (M.S. and Ph.D., labor economics).

P ritha Gopalan is an independent researcher focused on school reform and community education. Until recently, she worked as an educational researcher at the Academy for Educational Development in New York as the lead internal researcher for Middle Start. Dr. Gopalan holds a doctorate in anthropology and education and an M.A. in communications, both from the University of Pennsylvania.

D onna M. Harris is a Mellon Postdoctoral Fellow at Wellesley College. Prior to her position at Wellesley, Dr. Harris was a researcher at the Consortium for Policy Research in Education at the University of Pennsylvania. She worked on an evaluation of America's Choice, a comprehensive school reform model. Dr. Harris holds her Ph.D. (education) from the University of Wisconsin–Madison.

S uzannah Herrmann is a research analyst with the American Institutes for Research. She currently works on the National Longitudinal Evaluation of Comprehensive School Reform as well as on the Enhanced Reading Opportunities Project that evaluates the impact of adolescent literacy programs in freshman academies. Dr. Herrmann has served as a project coordinator of the Carolina Family Literacy Studies for the Frank Porter Graham Child Development Center and of the state evaluation for the North Carolina Even Start Family Literacy Programs.

S ally B. Kilgore is the president and CEO of the Modern Red School-House Institute and president of the Coalition for Comprehensive School Improvement. In the 1980s, she coauthored *High School Achievement* (Basic Books) with Thomas Hoffer and James S. Coleman. She has also served on the editorial boards of the *Review of Research in Education*, the *American Education Research Journal*, and *Sociology of Education*. Dr. Kilgore received her Ph.D. in sociology from the University of Chicago.

E lgin L. Klugh graduated from Morehouse College with a B.A. in international studies, and from the University of South Florida with an M.A. and a Ph.D. in applied anthropology. He is currently an assistant professor of anthropology at Montclair State University. Most recently, Dr. Klugh's participatory research has aided community organizations in Bealsville, Florida, and Silver Spring, Maryland, in preserving segregation-era schoolhouses and establishing educational museums.

A nja Kurki is a research scientist at the American Institutes for Research, specializing in educational program evaluation, quantitative analysis, and design and methods of program evaluation. She currently serves as a task leader for the National Longitudinal Evaluation of Comprehensive School Reform and on the Professional Development Impact Study, developing data analysis plans and data collection instruments and analyzing data from experimental field study. Dr. Kurki holds a Ph.D. in political science from the University of Maryland–College Park.

N ancy A. Madden is the president and CEO of the Success for All Foundation. Her areas of interest include cooperative learning, comprehensive school reform, evidence-based policy, English-language learners, and research methods.

B arbara Means directs SRI's Center for Technology in Learning and is co-principal investigator for the national evaluation of the Bill & Melinda Gates Foundation National School District and Network Grants Program. Dr. Means is editor of *Teaching Advanced Skills to At-Risk Students* and *Evaluating Educational Technology*, as well as coauthor of *The Connected School* and *Comparative Studies of How People Think*. Dr. Means earned her Ph.D. in education and intellectual development at the University of California–Berkeley.

R obert E. Slavin is a principal research scientist and director of the Center for Data-Driven Reform in Education, Johns Hopkins University. His areas of interest include cooperative learning, comprehensive school reform, evidence-based policy, English-language learners, and research methods.

Becky A. Smerdon is a principal research scientist at the American Institutes for Research and principal investigator for the evaluation studies of the Bill & Melinda Gates Foundation's secondary school reform initiative. Her research has focused primarily on equity in education and high school organization and reform. She holds a Ph.D. and an M.A. in education studies and a B.A. in political science and history from the University of Michigan.

Brenda J. Turnbull, a founder and principal of Policy Studies Associates, has been studying school change and improvement for 30 years. Her published research has addressed academic challenge in high-poverty schools; federal program implementation at the school, district, and state levels; and knowledge transfer and innovation in education. She holds an Ed.D. in social policy analysis from the Harvard Graduate School of Education and an A.B. from Harvard College.

Naida Tushnet directs WestEd's Evaluation Research Program, which conducts evaluations of mathematics and science programs at the elementary, secondary, collegiate, and graduate levels; studies of school reform; and evaluations of community- and school-based projects for children placed at risk. A member of WestEd's staff since 1989, Dr. Tushnet also serves as an organizational advisor on evaluation and is responsible for internal evaluation and quality assurance.

Georges Vernez is a senior social scientist and director of the Center for Research on Immigration Policy at RAND. He has published several books, including *Closing the Educational Gap: Benefits and Costs*, *How Immigrants Fare in U.S. Education*, and *Immigration in a Changing Economy: California's Experience*. Dr. Vernez currently directs a national longitudinal survey of No Child Left Behind and a longitudinal evaluation of comprehensive school reform models. He holds a Ph.D. in urban and regional planning from the University of California–Berkeley.

Alexandra Weinbaum is coexecutive director of the Center for School and Community Services at the Academy for Educational Development. Dr. Weinbaum is coauthor of *Teaching as Inquiry: Asking Hard Questions to Improve Practice and Student Achievement*, which includes guidelines for teacher inquiry into student work and case studies of four national projects.

Bruce L. Wilson is an independent educational researcher. He and Dr. H. Dickson Corbett collaborate on studies of comprehensive school reform, having investigated the implementation and impact of numerous national reform models. Dr. Wilson received his A.B. (sociology) and Ph.D. (sociology of education) from Stanford University.

INDEX

professional development
  availability in districts using
    CSR, 87–89, 98, 125, 128,
    137
  importance for success of CSR,
    119–20, 134–35, 315
  limitations on, 77, 79n6, 101,
    155–56
  student-centered instruction tech-
    niques and, 298
  training for CSR. *See* training of
    school staff on CSR
  turnover, effect of, 7, 138n3
  district support of CSR and,
    167–69
  elementary schools, 326, 327,
    334, 337–38, 342n4
  high schools, 297, 301
  middle schools, 266–67
  No Child Left Behind and, 172,
    173
  sustainability and, 154–55
technical assistance
  for CSR implementation, 50–51,
    119–20, 125, 128, 134–35,
    137, 155–56, 170–71, 172,
    173, 195
  developer support, 211–12, 215,
    314–15, 326, 329–30,
    335–36, 338–39
  recommendations for, 212,
    214–15
  for grant writing, 49–50, 64–65
Tennessee
  CSRD model and targeting of
    improvement funding, 58
  Student/Achievement Ration
    class-size reduction study,
    240
test preparation focus
  CSR approach versus, 102, 332
  temporary suspension of Ameri-
    ca's Choice program in
    favor of, 72
Texas study of implementation of
  CSR, 182, 216n3
time pressure as issue for CSR implementation, 103, 212–13
Title I schools, 3, 24–25
  accountability systems of, 43
  IASA funding for improvement
    of, 35, 58
  jumble of programs used at, 13

NCLB requirements and, 147–48
state system of support for, 44–46
improvement plans as part of,
  48
targeting of CSR funds to Title
  I–eligible but not Title
  I–served schools, 47
training of school staff on CSR
  during federal expansion, 25
  initial training for implementa-
    tion, 2, 191
  middle grade coaches, 272
  in pilot programs, 18–19
  recommendations for model devel-
    opers on, 211–12, 215
  shortcomings of, 7, 208–9, 215
Turnbull, B. J., 5
"Turning Points: Preparing American Youth for the 21st Century" (Carnegie Council on
  Adolescent Development),
  247, 257–58
turnover of school professionals. *See*
  changes in CSR leadership,
  effect of; teachers
tutoring as part of Success for All,
  220, 223, 245–46
21st Century Community Learning
  Centers programs, 240
Tyack, D., 300–301

underserved students. *See* minority
  students
union contracts and teacher professional development, 77
universities' role in New York City
  Middle School Initiative, 258,
  262, 263, 265, 266
University of Pennsylvania's Consortium for Policy Research in
  Education. *See* Consortium
  for Policy Research in Education (CPRE)
University of Washington assessment of CSR models, 186–87,
  216n2
urban systems. *See also specific cities*
  design scale-up and, 20, 24
  high school reform
    Gates Foundation and. *See* high
     school reform, Gates
     Foundation's vision of